KATHRYN SHEEHAN AND MARY WAIDNER, PH.D.

EARTH CHILD

Games, Stories, Activities, Experiments & Ideas About Living Lightly on Planet Earth

Illustrated with original drawings by Angela Lowry

Edited and designed by Carol Haralson

COUNCIL OAK BOOKS ☘ TULSA

Printed in the United States of America
on sixty-pound Cross Pointe Torchglow Opaque
made from 50% recycled fiber,
including 10% postconsumer waste.
Electronically composed in Adobe Garamond
and OPTI Amway.
Printed in the United States of America.

ISBN 0-933031-42-4, clothbound
ISBN 0-933031-39-4, paperbound
Library of Congress Catalog Number 91-70225

ORIGINAL PENCIL AND INK DRAWINGS BY ANGELA LOWRY.
ADDITIONAL ILLUSTRATIONS FROM VARIOUS SOURCES.
EDITING, DESIGN, AND ELECTRONIC COMPOSITION BY CAROL HARALSON.

PUBLISHED AND DISTRIBUTED BY
COUNCIL OAK BOOKS
1428 South St. Louis
Tulsa, Oklahoma 74120
1 800 247.8850
In Oklahoma, 918 587.6454
FAX 918 583.4995

The Iroquois tribal council began each meeting with this invocation: "Let us remember in our deliberations the effect our decisions may have on the next seven generations." Any vote taken was not only for those present, but also for those who would live two hundred years in the future.

In this spirit we dedicate this book to Maralee, Andrea, Ryan, Kevin, Eric, Casey, Raivan, Stephen, and Desirée – on and on to the seventh generation.

CONTENTS

Prologue: KEEPING THE WONDER ALIVE 9

O N E
THE CIRCLE OF DAY AND NIGHT 17

T W O
EARTH CELEBRATIONS THROUGHOUT THE YEAR 55

T H R E E
WONDERS IN A GARDEN 97

F O U R
TREES ARE TERRIFIC! 133

F I V E
WET AND WONDERFUL! 159

S I X
HOME, SWEET HOME 197

S E V E N
GOING, GOING, GONE...? 235

E I G H T
HURT NO LIVING THING 263

Epilogue: LET THERE BE PEACE ON EARTH 297

Afterword: EARTH EDUCATOR'S BOOKSHELF 317

Index

Introduction
Keeping the Wonder Alive

Many educators believe that a small child possesses inherent attitudes of care and compassion for fellow creatures, both human and non-human. But the quality of our children's environmental awareness and their sense of wonder in the natural world must be supported, channeled, and encouraged in order for them to fully develop a respect for the beauty and complexity of their planetary home.

The development of environmental awareness in young children is definitely a joint project. As Rachel Carson has pointed out, shared experiences with trusted adults are essential in fostering a deep and lasting compassion for the Earth and its creatures in children. Children in preschool and early elementary-school years are indelibly marked by the attitudes of the grownups in their lives. If their parents, other family members, and teachers surround them with an evident attitude of compassion and concern for the planet we all share, they will grow up with a deep-rooted connectedness with the natural world.

This guide is designed to help adults and children share the wonder that a deep awareness of their environment can bring. Through activities, musings, and wondrous children's books, chosen especially for their unique way of looking at our world, adults and children can share stories and activities that softly and subtly make the point that the planet is in our hands and that it is up to us to take care of it. There isn't much a preschooler can do about global warming, pollutants in our waters, or the chopping

If a child is to keep alive his inborn sense of wonder . . . he needs the companionship of at least one adult who can share it, rediscovering with him the joy, excitement and mystery of the world we live in."

RACHEL CARSON
THE SENSE OF WONDER

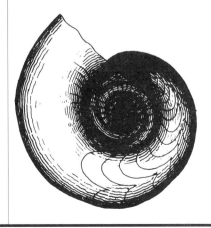

There was a child went forth every day,
And the first object he looked upon, that object he became,
And that object became part of him for the day or a certain part of the day,
Or for many years or stretching cycles of years.
The early lilacs became part of this child,
And grass and white and red morning glories, and white and red clover, and
the song of the phoebe-bird,
And the third-month lambs and the sow's pink-faint litter, and the mare's
foal, and the cow's calf.

WALT WHITMAN

down of the world's rainforests. But even very young children can be aware of the freshness of the air on a spring day, the sight and sound of a mountain stream, the majesty of a great tree. And this is where it all begins: with awareness, with love of the Earth – which, when ingrained in our children, will grow with them into adulthood. This guide acknowledges that we are part of the ecological systems of the Earth and that the world and its resources are not a horn of plenty whose riches we may consume, but a finite vessel harboring delicate resources that must be protected and conserved. A belief in the interconnectedness of all things informs the holistic approach reflected in the choice of books, activities, and suggestions presented here.

This guide also fosters a love and appreciation for books and learning, another awareness seed that needs to be planted at a very early age. The natural curiosity of children about the world and their place in it can be no better served than by combining the worlds offered on the pages of books with the reinforcement offered by activities which actually put a child in contact with the cycles of life. What better way for a young child to experience the world than to be a baby panda living in an endangered forest, to be a caterpillar waiting to become a beautiful butterfly, or to be in a drop of rain landing on the petal of a flower? After all, children teach us that the most encompassing experiences of nature include the dreams and myths that reside in our own minds. One of the concepts fostered by "deep ecology" thinkers is that we pick a place on the planet, learn its rhythms, live within its rhythms, even imagine ourselves as a species other than our own in this place. If we learn to do this as young children, we will develop a natural connection with Earth and our place in it.

We parents and teachers and friends or relatives of young children can learn so much from listening. Children know, for example, that all the animals within the natural world, human and non-human, are part of a big, extended family. They have heard it in their stories and felt it in their hearts. So those of us who have the humility of a child, who see through the eyes of a child, may find again a reverence and respect for our planet and a kinship with all living things.

The Ecology of Imagination in Childhood

One of the most important ideas in deep ecology, the alteration of one's basic attitudes and lifestyle towards living in harmony with the Earth, is that of empathy – putting oneself into the situation of another living thing, be it plant or animal. Because this concept runs through all the chapters of *Earth Child*, and because it is essential for developing a real understanding of nature in young children, we feel that it is important to immerse children immediately in the art of role playing.

This process can be accomplished by reading imaginative books that place your children in the worlds of other living creatures. By reading the special books described at the end of this section, your child can "become" a snail, a Canadian goose, an ant, a spider, a turtle, or a butterfly. As Judith and Herbert Kohl point out in *The View from the Oak*, exercises in imagining new worlds "help provide the openness that must inform any serious and respectful study of animal life." Some activities that enhance the experience of empathy through role playing can be used with all of the suggested stories.

⁓ Observe the creature in its natural habitat. By watching a spider spinning its intricate web, a child can better relate to the creature and its fragile environment.

⁓ Learn about the animal and how it uses its senses to move about, find food, etc. For instance, a mole has very poor eyesight, but is familiar with its underground world through its sense of hearing, touch, and smell.

⁓ Write a diary entry for a day in the life of another creature.

⁓ Create simple props or costumes to enrich the role playing experience, such as tying a pair of silky scarves to your child's wrists and collar to simulate a pair of butterfly wings.

This concept of "being and becoming" will be interspersed throughout all of the chapters of *Earth Child*, but has been highlighted in this introductory section, and accompanied by a list of books that very effectively demonstrate the idea of empathy with many of the Earth's creatures.

Ethology Studies

For an investigation of ethology, the study of precisely how an animal experiences the world and organizes its environment, see the books *View from the Oak* (Little, Brown and Co., Boston, 1977) or *What Do Animals See, Hear, Smell, and Feel* , published by the National Wildlife Federation. They are appropriate for ages six through twelve.

Children have never been very good at listening to their elders, but they have never failed to imitate them..

JAMES BALDWIN

Explaining the "Whats" and "Whys" to Your Child

In the area of environmental education today, a problem with the supplementary approach has been the failure to integrate philosophy with the suggested activities. Teachers and parents have had no environmental awareness courses to guide them in teaching children. Many of the workshops available today fill a participant's hands with an array of activities to do with children, but do not supply the background information or philosophy necessary to teach a child true love and respect for nature. Without this integration, the task is incomplete. It's one thing to probe and dissect a plant in order to learn about its parts, but without a love for its beauty and complexity, an adult or child will never respect it as a living thing worthy of our care.

Throughout the following chapters, we have attempted to explain the necessary facts and feelings of empathy in a simple language that will help you talk to your child about the cycles of life on our planet and the very great need to care for the people, animals, plants, and resources that make up our world. Each chapter is set up in a way that will guide you through the process from beginning to end. The activities alone offer wonderful and fulfilling experiences to share with your child, but we feel it is the combination of shared stories and the related activities that will achieve the most satisfying and complete understanding.

What Are Dream Starters?

A special feature of each chapter is the Dream Starter, a quiet and simple story to guide your child, through his or her imagination, into the life and feelings of another animal, insect, or plant. These tales use guided imagery and verbal cues to help your child become another creature fluttering from flower to flower, roaming through a mountain forest searching for food, or swimming through the dark and mysterious underwater world.

To prepare your child for these bedtime fantasies, you will need to create a comfortable atmosphere to help your little one relax. At home, most likely your child will be in his or her own bed. At school, the napping mats will be equally appropriate, or you can allow children to rest their heads and arms on their desks. Eliminate all outside interference, such as televisions or people talking. Ask your children to close their eyes before telling the story. Here are some suggested ways to help your child relax and enjoy sweet dreams:

Deep Breathing: To relax and purify the body, ask your child to breath deeply and steadily. Speak to your child in a soft and rhythmic tone. Tell your child to pretend that with each inhalation the waves of the ocean splash upon the shore and fill the beach and that with each exhalation the waves pull away . . . coming . . . and going . . . coming . . . and going. (Watch your child's breathing and match your words to the intake or exhale of air.) If this imagery is too difficult for your child to understand, choose an image from his or her experience or simply count from one to four repeatedly. Speak softly, and even more softly, until your voice is a whisper.

Massage: You might want to have your children rest on their tummies while you rub their backs using circular motions. When the children's breathing has settled into a pattern and they appear to be relaxed, slowly read the Dream Starter in a soft voice. Keep your voice at a steady level and include dramatic pauses often to give time for formulation of ideas in your listeners' minds. The Dream Starters can be modified for very young children by eliminating all adjectives and substituting any difficult language with words known to the child. Just imagine the fun your children will have going to sleep at naptime or at night!

Setting Up a Recycle Craft Box

You will find many craft activities to share with your children in the pages of this book. The authors believe that the best kind of materials to use in these projects are discarded scraps. It is very easy to set up a large box in the garage, basement, or closet to be filled with treasures that would otherwise end up in the trash. Some things to collect are empty cardboard and plastic containers, paper and poster board scraps, used ribbons and wrapping paper, yarn, rick-rack, discarded silk flowers, etc. Once you get into the habit of collecting these goodies, you will never look at trash the same way again!

"Enter My World" Books for Children

The following books will help your child "become," in imagination, some of the Earth's inhabitants for a time. Helping children experience the worlds of other creatures gives them a better understanding of their rightful place on the planet.

Where Butterflies Grow by **Joanne Ryder.** Illustrations by Lynne Cherry. Lodestar Books, E. P. Dutton, NY, 1989. This book takes the child on an imaginative journey where he can experience one of nature's wondrous processes - the transformation from caterpillar to black swallowtail butterfly. (ages 4 - 8)

White Bear, Ice Bear by **Joanne Ryder.** Illustrations by Michael Rothman. Just For a Day Series, Morrow, NY, 1989. What is it like to live in a place where the moon is the only light because it is night all winter long? This book will provide that experience. (ages 4 - 9)

Catching the Wind by **Joanne Ryder.** Illustrations by Michael Rothman. Just For a Day Series, Morro, NY, 1989. Imagine that you wake up one crisp, autumn morning and you feel the wind calling to you, changing you into a magnificent Canada goose. (ages 4 - 9)

Lizard in the Sun by **Joanne Ryder.** Illustrations by Michael Rothman. Just For a Day Series, Morrw, NY, 1990. What would it be like to grow smaller and smaller, changing your shape, until you have four brown feet and a long brown tail? You have become an "American" chameleon! (ages 4 - 9)

The Snail's Spell by **Joanne Ryder.** Illustrations by Lynne Cherry. F. Warne, NY, 1982. Even a lettuce leaf is an enormous obstacle as a little boy becomes as small as a snail. An excellent choice to establish a feeling of empathy for the natural world in your child. (ages 3 - 7)

Simon Underground by **Joanne Ryder.** Illustrations by John Schoenherr. Harper & Row, Pub., NY, 1976. Simon the mole digs deep into the ground until he makes a secret place for himself and you can join him in your imagination. (ages 4 - 8)

Two Bad Ants by **Chris Van Allsburg.** Houghton Mifflin Co., Boston, 1988. When two ants desert their colony, they experience a dangerous adventure. The reader will share firsthand their fall into a cup of coffee, climb over huge sugar crystals, and many other exciting adventures. (ages 3 - 7)

Pretend You're a Cat by **Jean Marzallo and Jerry Pinkney.** Dial Books for Young Readers, NY, 1990. A delightful book of verse which urges young readers to stretch their minds along with their bodies, thinking and acting like a fish, a bird, a chick, a cow, or any animal they can imagine. Fresh, sparkling illustrations. (ages 3 - 5)

Just Me by **Marie Hall Ets.** Viking Press, NY, 1965. A little boy spends his day visiting all the animals in his world and each time he meets one, he imitates its characteristic movements. He copies a cat, a rooster, a pig, a rabbit, a snake, a horse, a turtle, and several other animal friends. At the end of the day, running towards his father, he "ran like nobody else at all. Just me!" This is a perfect book for assisting a child in role-playing. (ages 3 - 5)

My Father Doesn't Know About the Woods and Me by **Dennis Haseley.** Illustrations by Michael Hays. Atheneum, NY, 1988. As a child walks through the woods with his father, he is transformed into animals enjoying the freedom of nature. The father doesn't realize that the wolf he sees, and the hawk, and the fish leaping from the stream are his son. But when the boy encounters a great stag in a thicket, the look in the stag's eyes, and in his father's eyes later, tell the boy that he and his father share more than he ever thought. A beautiful and thought-provoking book. (age 5 and up)

If You Were an Ant . . . **by Barbara Brenner.** Illustrations by Fred Brenner. Harper and Row, NY, 1973. This unique book not only covers the basic facts of ant anatomy and life, but brings them dramatically alive. (ages 4 - 9)

If You Were an Ant **by S. J. Calder.** Illustrations by Cornelius Van Wright, Silver Press, Englewood Cliffs, NJ, 1989. Narrated and illustrated from the ant's perspective, this book offers the fascinating opportunity to explore an ant's environment, physical attributes, diet, and way of life. Also in the "First Facts Series": a bird, cat, and fish. (ages 3 - 7)

The Spider Web **by Julie Brinckloe.** Doubleday & Co., Inc., Garden City, NY, 1974. This wordless book makes a powerful statement about the creation of natural beauty and human recklessness. (ages 4 - 8)

Imagine **by Alison Lester.** Houghton Mifflin, Boston, 1990. "Imagine if you were deep in the jungle, where butterflies drift and jaguars prowl, where parakeets squawk and wild monkeys howl." In intricately detailed pictures that children will explore again and again, animals are portrayed living in their specialized environments. (ages 4 - 8)

Box Turtle at Long Pond **by William T. George.** Illustrations by Lindsay Barnett George. Greenwillow Books, NY, 1989. Imagine what it would be like to be a box turtle for a day. Superbly detailed illustrations. (ages 4 - 8)

Beaver at Long Pond **by William T. George.** Illustrations by Lindsay Barrett George. Greenwillow Books, NY, 1988. Dusk at Long Pond means that most of the animals have settled down for the night. But not so for beaver because night is his day, and his adventures are just beginning. (ages 4 - 8)

Before I Go to Sleep **by Thomas Hood.** Illustrations by Maryjane Begin-Callanan. G. P. Putnam's Sons, NY, 1990. A perfect bedtime book that effectively reinforces the idea of empathy with the animal world. A child drifting off to sleep imagines all the exotic and wonderful animals he would like to be. (ages 3 - 6)

Cloudy **by Deborah King.** Philomel Books, NY, 1989. "I am a little gray cat called Cloudy. I am the color of thunder and rain. It's difficult to see me on dull days." Thus begins the young reader's journey through the day of Cloudy's secret life among the trees, fields, and meadows of the countryside, away from human eyes. (ages 4 - 8)

If I Were a Penguin **by Heidi Goennel.** Little, Brown & Co., Boston, 1989. Who hasn't imagined the joy of soaring like an eagle or the delight of hiding in a tiny mouse hole? Children imagine all of these things and more in this colorfully illustrated book that looks through the eyes of animals and birds. (ages 4 - 8)

Today I am a Cat **by Jane Bottomley.** Ideals Children's Books, Nashville, TN, 1989. For a child, the line between fantasy and reality is often blurred. This book crosses the line with these trips into a fantastic world. Also in this series are *Today I am an Alligator.* (ages 3 - 6)

Could You Be a Mouse? and *Could You Be a Frog?* . Text and photographs by John Norris. Illustrations by Derick Brown. The Survival Series, Ideals Children's Books, Nashville, TN, 1990. (For ordering information, call 1-800-327-5113) These books are designed to be played like a game. Within each story, the reader is given choices to make as the animal. So depending on the choices, the ending can be different every time. Other titles in this series: *Could You Be a Squirrel?* and *Could You Be a Deer?* Text by Roger Tabor, photographs by Fiona Pragoff, and illustrations by Derick Brown. (ages 6 - 11)

The Circle of Day and Night

The adventure of the sun is the great natural drama by which we live, and not to have joy in it and awe of it, not to share in it, is to close a dull door on nature's sustaining and poetic spirit.

With our lights, and ever more lights, we drive the holiness and beauty of night back into the forests and the sea.
HENRY BESTON
The Outermost House

L*ight and dark. Day and night. Awake and asleep.* These are among the first conditions a child distinguishes. Children still within the womb turn their heads away from bright lights, shielding their eyes with their hands like children fixed in the spotlights of early home movies. Within a few weeks of birth, children fall into the pattern of daytime wakefulness and nighttime sleep.

At this time they develop a very basic awareness of the Earth cycle of day and night and begin to respond to its rhythm.

The stories and activities in this chapter are intended to show children that the sun we take for granted is much more than a big lightbulb in the sky.

The Way to Start a Day, by Byrd Baylor. Illustrations by Peter Parnall. Charles Scribner's Sons, NY, 1978.

"A morning needs to be sung to. A new day needs to be honored," writes Byrd Baylor in this beautiful book about how people all over the world have paid their respects to the wonder of each new sunrise throughout history. "You have to make a good day— you have to make a good world for the sun to spend its one-day life in." This book explores insights about how others have stayed in touch with the fundamentals of life and how we can, too. (age 6 and up)

The sun supplies the Earth with many forms of energy that warm the land and the seas, nourish plants, create clouds, and provide light. Periods of light and dark are the basic units of the calendar we humans use. In this chapter, you and your children will celebrate the joy of living each day, explore the rudiments of solar energy, and discover the movement of the Earth that causes day and night.

This chapter will also look at the other half of a day, when the sun is invisible to us – but when over half of the creatures on the planet wake up and become active. Together, you and your children can wonder about the many other stars like "our" sun and examine how other animals thrive in the deep, dark night.

Greet the New Day

Share a Sunrise

Think about the times you have been up so early that the world is still asleep. The pre-dawn hour is a special time to think and plan your day. You can really feel the magic of the waking world in those wee hours. Plan to share a special morning with your children: pack a steaming thermos of cocoa and a blanket, and visit a special place to witness the beginning of the day. Listen to the music of the awakening world. What are the sounds you hear? How do the colors change around you as the sun comes closer and closer to the horizon? Find a tree limb or flowering shrub that was only barely visible and watch as it grows clearer and more detailed to your eyes. What a beautiful backdrop to share your dreams and plans!

Greet the Day Celebration

For children, each day begins with special anticipation and excitement. They burst out of slumber, bounce on the foot of your bed already full of energy, and wonder what the day will bring. The following activities may sound too cheerful and idealistic first thing in the morning, but they are great ways to start a happy day. Here are some suggestions for planning morning celebrations to make you and your children aware of each other and the gifts each day can bring.

• Sing a "good morning" song together upon awakening.

• Watch a sunrise and make a wish for the day.

• Take an early morning walk around the neighborhood and greet each person and animal you see.

• Do you ever hear songbirds in the morning? Share an embrace as you listen together to their beautiful music.

• Make a light breakfast of toast, fruit, and juice. Have a morning picnic outside in your backyard, or at a park or other special place.

• Make a point of going outside every morning to feed the birds, smell the flowers, feel the morning dew on the grass, or take a walk. Choose any morning ritual that is meaningful to you and will make you and your children aware of the new day.

Feel The Sun's Warmth

Certainly the simplest way to begin learning about the sun is to experience its light and warmth. Ask your children to sit facing the sun with their eyes closed (they should never look directly into the bright sun), and feel the heat on their faces. Even in midwinter, the sun's warmth can make a freezing day comfortable. Experience the temperature difference by moving from the sunlight into the shade. Ask your children to describe the change. Talk with them about the warm sensation of sunlight on their skin and explain that they are experiencing the heat from our flaming star, the sun. Children who live in a desert or semi-desert environment will probably already have noticed the difference between daytime and nighttime temperatures. For others, the phenomenon may be less dramatic, but it is still an important part of the rhythm of day and night. Talk with your children about this daily cycle.

Good Morning Song

Tune: Jack and Jill

The sun comes up to wake us up
"Good Morning, Mister Sunshine!"
We'll start today and be on our way
To share the day together.

The sunbeams have filled me like a honeycomb. It is the moment of fulness, and the top of the morning.

D. H. LAWRENCE

A Day In the Life of Laura

Age 9½

7:30 When I woke up, Sandy was sitting on my chest and purring.

8:00 Mom made French toast for breakfast. We talked about how the bees make honey and how they live all together in round houses.

10:00 Annalee and I played outside in the corner of the yard. We built kitchens with cement blocks and made soup with grass and pans of water. We pretended that we were the Boxcar Children who lived in the pine forest.

12:00 Mom and Annalee and Brian and I made sandwiches with brown and white bread and peanut butter. We cut them into long, thin stripes. We had bananas and cookies. We put the lunch in a basket and carried it into the back yard under the tree. It was hot and wasps were buzzing in the bushes.

3:30 Today in my piano lesson, I learned a song called "Indian Drum Song."

6:30 I helped Mom make dinner. She cooked my favorite soup. No grass! After dinner, we wrote the last parts in my book of this day and we are going to tie the edges with string.

Plants Need Sunlight

Most young children know that plants need sunlight to thrive. But do they realize that a plant will seek out the light and turn toward it? Observe a houseplant and notice how the leaves are facing the brightest source of light (usually a sunny window). Turn the plant around so its leaves are away from the sun. Check the plant later. Within hours its leaves will reach toward the light again.

Many flowers open each morning and close in the evening. Examples are dandelions, morning glories, and African marigolds. Test a dandelion's response to darkness and light. Find one in the bright sun and cover it with a bucket. Check it after about an hour to see that it has closed its bud. Remove the bucket and the bud will reopen. (For information and activities about how plants use energy from the sun to make food, see the "Wonders in a Garden" chapter.)

Create a Day Diary

After a day is spent, it can be difficult to recall its many events. This activity will help your children become aware of time and what fills the hours in their day. It will also result in a keepsake to be tucked away for later or to be sent to a distant grandparent.

1. Put together a booklet by folding several pieces of drawing paper and one piece of construction paper in half. Slip the drawing paper inside the construction paper cover and staple the folded edge.

2. Write the title, "A Day In the Life of *(child's name)*" on the cover and allow your child to decorate it as he or she wishes. If you like, take a photo of your child and paste it on the title page.

3. Throughout the day, have your child dictate an account of events to you; then let him illustrate each page with crayons, markers, or paint. You may wish to quote the time and make an entry every couple of hours or just write an entry when something special occurs.

4. At the end of the day, read the book together and talk about the special happenings.

5. As an extension, look over the book again the next morning. Ask your child, "Will this day be the same?" and "How will it be different?" Make plans to share another special day.

Playing With the Sun

Light from the sun can create rainbows, shadows, and reflections on the wall. Discover a new playmate in the sun!

Colors of the Sun: Sunlight, which we tend to represent as yellowish, is actually made up of many colors: red, orange, yellow, green, blue, indigo, and violet. After a rainstorm, drops of water act like tiny prisms, breaking up the sunlight into its colors to make a rainbow. Your children can make their own private rainbow without rain. Set a garden hose nozzle to a fine, misty spray. Have your children stand with their backs to the sun, hold the hose high, and look at the spray. The rainbow they will see is created in the same fashion as one after a rain shower.

Shadows Throughout the Day: When children first discover their shadows, they view them as separate from themselves. As they become more mature and realize that their interaction with the sunlight is causing their shadows to move, they will deliberately make movements and observe their changing "pictures." Have fun with the light, play shadow charades, or create animal pictures. Observe your shadows at different times of day. Explain that they are short and squatty when the sun is directly overhead and tall and thin when the sun is near the horizon. Use a flashlight and a small doll to demonstrate how shadows change throughout the day.

Sun Reflectors: It's easy to see that sunlight reflects off shiny objects or water. Make sun reflectors to hang near a window. Cut bits of aluminum foil and glue them to construction paper or scrap cardboard. Press them very flat. Hold your reflectors in the sun and see how the light sparkles. Move them around until your design shines on the wall and watch the light wiggle and jump! Attach pieces of string to your reflectors and hang them near a window; as they move, designs will shine on the walls in the room.

Vibrant Visors: Help your children make paper visors to wear on sunny days. Cut two ten-inch circles out of scrap cardboard and lay one circle partly over the other to make a crescent shape on the lower circle. Draw around the curved edge, then cut out the crescent shape. Staple a piece of elastic on one end and adjust to fit before stapling the other end. Allow your children to decorate their visors with paint, crayons, markers, or glitter.

Using the Sun's Energy

The sun gives us much more than light: it also provides power that can be harnessed and used in many ways. Do your children know that all sources of fuel (coal, oil and gas) are a result of the sun's power? Under the ground, considerable pressure and heat transform the decayed plant and animal matter (sun energy guzzlers) from our ancient past into the fossil fuels that we are rapidly consuming today. When we burn these sources of fuel, they release pollution into our air and waterways. Solar energy systems, however, concentrate rays from the sun to heat water or generate electricity. You may have noticed solar panels on houses or windmills (which are turned by currents of heated air) dotting the countryside. These systems utilize the sun as a safe and clean source of energy. The book *Sunlight* by Sally Cartwright and the activities that follow focus on the fundamental principles of solar energy and suggest some ways that your children can put the sun to work for them.

Heat from the Sun

The following activities are suggested to show that the sun delivers significant amounts of energy; and energy from the sun is quite accessible as an alternative to fossil fuels.

• The heat emitted from the sun is powerful enough to cause serious skin burns. Explain to your child that when you spend a lot of time in the sun without sunscreen protection, at the swimming pool, for example, your skin will begin to redden and burn.

• The difference in air temperature can be quite dramatic from sunlight to shade. Let your child experiment with a thermometer in the sun and shade. Notice how much warmer the air in direct sunlight registers. Prepare two pails of water and place a thermometer in each. Set one in the sun and the other in the shade. Let the sun heat up the water for about an hour and compare the temperature differences. (Just putting your hand in each pail will tell you that one is warmer than the other). After this experiment, ask the children, "Where would be the best place to set your pet's water bowl? Why?"

Sunlight, by Sally Cartwright. Illustrations by Marylin Hafner. Coward, McCann and Geoghegan, Inc., NY, 1974.

This book begins: "Do you ever wake early when the day is starting? Sunlight comes over the towns and hills, to your street, to your house, to your room. Days are filled with the light and warmth of the sun." The book poses many questions. Can sunlight shine through a pane of glass? Can it shine through a tree? Through water? Look and see. *Sunlight* encourages the reader to "find out" through his or her own action, exploration, and discovery. (ages 5 - 9)

• There is a reason for wearing light-colored clothing in the summer and dark-colored clothing in winter; colors absorb solar heat differently. To see which colors absorb more heat, try this simple experiment called "The Ice Cube Race." Place pieces of construction paper of various colors in direct sunlight, being sure to include black and white. Place ice cubes in clear plastic sandwich bags. Place a cube on each piece of paper and watch. Which ice cubes begin to melt first? Which ice cube is winning the melting race? After about 15-20 minutes, measure the water from each bag into a measuring cup, one at a time. Chart which bags had the most water and which ones the least. Line up the colored paper in order according to melting rate. (The cubes placed on darker colors should have melted faster than the ones on lighter colors because dark colors absorb more solar heat than lighter colors. The ice cube on the white piece of paper should have melted the least because white reflects the most heat.) Now pose the question, "On a hot summer day, what colors should you wear to stay cool?"

• Another interesting fact, vital to the use of solar energy systems, is that different materials absorb and release heat at different rates. To make this observation clear, place three identical cups in a box and fill one with cool water, one with soil, and one with shredded newspaper. Make sure your children test each cup by putting their fingers in it. Place the box in direct sunlight for about an hour. Then have everyone do a second "finger test" in each cup. Which one is the warmest? (The soil.) Now, take the box inside and place it in a cool, shaded area. Every five minutes, run another "finger test" in the cups. Which material released its heat the quickest? (The newspaper.) Which material held its heat the longest? (The water.) From this experiment, which material would you say is best for "storing" solar heat?

Solar Snacks

While children should be taught that solar energy can be used for heating homes and water or running electric appliances, toasting a snack with the help of the sun will give a tasty hands-on example of another use of solar energy. Just say, "Let's eat!"

T his grand show is eternal. It is always sunrise somewhere.

JOHN MUIR

To Make a Solar Toaster:

1. Take an empty oatmeal box and cut out half of the box from its side to make it look like a doll's cradle. Tape the lid onto the box.

2. Line the box entirely with aluminum foil until all the cardboard is covered. Punch a hole in each of the round ends to insert a wire.

3. *Adult:* Straighten a wire coat hanger and cut a length of it at least three inches longer than the cooker.

4. To roast a precooked hot dog, slide the wire through one end, pass it through the wiener, then through the other hole. Place the solar cooker in direct sunlight with the open and lined side towards the sun. Occasionally turn the hot dog to heat all sides. While it is toasting, talk about how the sun is used to cook the wiener. Why is the foil used? Taste the "solar dog." Did the sun add flavor to the hot dog?

5. Try making a fruit and vegetable kabob. Slide cherry tomatoes and pineapple, apple, and sweet bell pepper chunks onto the wire (you may wish to add cooked ham chunks) and place the toaster in the sun. Turn the kabob occasionally. When the kabob is thoroughly heated, enjoy this tasty treat!

Sun Tea

Let the sun do the work for you! Fill a clear glass jar with cold water. Add one or two tea bags for a small jar or several for a larger jar. Cover the jar with a lid and place it in the sun. In about an hour, remove the bags and pour the tea over ice; you may also wish to add honey, sugar, or lemon to taste. Enjoy a refreshing drink from the sun!

What Does the Sun Have to Do With Wind?

Answer: The heat from the sun makes the wind blow.

Energy from the sun is not distributed evenly on the Earth; it is warmer at the equator than at the poles. As the air is warmed at the equator, it rises into the atmosphere and flows towards the north and south poles. The heavier cold air from the poles rushes in to take its place, flowing toward the equator. This moving air is wind. Once it reaches the equator, the air is heated and the cycle starts again. This process may be too difficult to be understood by young children, but they can harness the wind to power some simple "machines."

Make a Mini-Windmill: A common pinwheel is a miniature version of a windmill. Windmills can use the power from the wind to generate electricity. Wind is a clean and inexpensive alternative power source.

1. Take a six-inch square piece of stiff paper. Fold the paper diagonally both ways and cut on the folded lines to within one inch of the center point.

2. Roll a small strip of paper into a tube. Tape or glue the end so that it won't unroll. Trim the tube so that it is about one-fourth inch long.

3. Take each corner of the paper and bring it to the center, letting the ends overlap slightly.

4. Push a ball-headed straight pin through all four layers. Place the paper tube on the pin, then push it into an eraser of a pencil.

5. Blow on the pinwheel and watch it spin freely. Take it outside on a windy day and see how it catches the wind in its "sails" to make it spin.

Wind-Powered Music: Wind chimes are fun to make and they show children that music doesn't need to come strictly from radios or television.

1. The chimes can be made from a wide variety of materials: wooden spools, shells, bamboo, or small metal objects. Experiment with different materials by tapping them together. Choose materials that will result in a sound pleasing to your ear.

2. Cut several pieces of string, each about one foot long. Take a dowel rod or sturdy length of wood and tie the pieces of string to it an inch or so apart. Attach the chimes to the end of the strings.

3. Hold the wind chime delicately between your thumb and middle finger to find its balancing point. Attach another string at that point and hang it in a spot that will receive a breeze.

4. Sit back with your children and listen to the tinkling of the chimes. Their soft music can be quite enjoyable and relaxing. What does the sound from the chimes remind you of? What do they tell you about the wind and weather?

Oatmeal Raisin Cookies

Here is a delicious way to use the raisins your children and the sun make "magically" from bunches of grapes.

¾ cups butter

• 1 cup brown sugar

2 eggs

2 cups flour

1 cup old-fashioned oatmeal

1 teaspoon baking soda

1 teaspoon ground nutmeg

1 teaspoon ground allspice

2 teaspoons ground cinnamon

¼ teaspoon salt

¾ cup raisins

½ cup coarsely chopped pecans

Cream the butter and sugar and beat in the eggs. In a separate bowl, combine the flour, oatmeal, soda, spices, and salt. Stir the egg mixture and flour mixture together, blending well. Fold in the raisins and nuts. Place on a buttered cookie sheet by rounded teaspoonfuls. Bake in a preheated 350° oven 12 to 15 minutes. Makes about four dozen cookies.

The Sun Makes Rain

Young children may ask, "How does the sun make rain? The sun is hidden behind the clouds on a rainy day!" To explain, you need to take your child a step back in the process. The sun shines on the Earth, heating the land and water. The heat from the sun evaporates water from all parts of the Earth and the water vapor rises in the atmosphere. This water vapor forms clouds. Under the right conditions, the vapor condenses into water droplets that fall to the Earth and the water cycle starts over. (For more information about the water cycle, see the "Wet and Wonderful" chapter.) Here are some suggested ways to teach your children to recognize the sun's role in the evaporation of water around them:

• Have your children jump into a swimming pool or play in the water sprinkler. Instead of drying off with towels, let the sun evaporate the water from their skin.

• After a rainstorm, visit the puddles that have formed around your yard. In the next hour or so, check back on them and notice their shrinking size. The heat energy from the sun (shining from the sky or stored in the concrete) causes the pooled water to evaporate into the air.

• Instead of using the electric dryer, pin your wash on a clothesline. It won't take long before the wind and heat from the sun have them ready to be folded and tucked into drawers.

• Together, prepare a tasty treat of dried fruit and raisins. Cut an apple, pear, peach, or apricot into thin slices or pick and wash a bunch of grapes. Pat the fruit with paper towels and place it in a clear glass pan. Arrange pieces so they are not touching. Cover the pan with several layers of cheesecloth to prevent birds or insects from sampling your snack while still allowing the water vapor to be released into the air. Place the pan in direct sunlight, but not on the ground, and check it periodically. Your fruit will need a drying time of about eight hours (grapes can take longer to turn into raisins, so it may be necessary take the pan indoors at night). When the fruit is dried, taste it. Does it look and taste different from the fresh slices? How is dried fruit different from fresh? As you share this snack, talk to your children about how the heat energy from the sun evaporated the water in the fruit. Where is the water from the fruit now?

• Take your children on an imaginary journey through the water cycle. For example, if you have just dried apple slices, have your children close their eyes as you tell them this or a similar story about the water in the fruit.

Imagine you are a tiny droplet of water in an apple slice. The heat from the sun touches you, and you float out of the fruit and into the air. Because you are lighter than air, you drift higher and higher into the atmosphere where you meet other droplets of water. Together you form a cloud and sail across the sky. One by one, you begin to join other droplets until you become a bigger and heavier drop. Soon you become heavier than the air and you begin to fall out of the sky in the form of a rain drop. Down you go, . . . SPLASH! Lots of rain drops land near the same spot and you pool together to form a puddle. After the storm, the heat from the sun touches you and there you go again!

Sun Pictures

The light from the sun can fade colors. Unfortunately, you may have noticed this on curtains or furniture near a sunny window. Your children can experiment with the bleaching power of the sun by making sun pictures or signs.

1. On a calm, sunny day, collect pieces of colored construction paper. Blue, red, purple, and green work best. (Instead you may wish to use light-sensitive paper from an educational supply store. It's not necessary, but using it brings quicker results.) Find a variety of flat objects, such as keys, leaves, feathers, small blocks, pressed flowers, puzzle pieces, etc. You can also cut letters from scrap paper to create words.

2. Place the construction paper in direct sunlight and arrange the objects in a decorative fashion on top of the paper. Light objects and paper letters may need to be weighted with small pebbles or dried beans to keep them from blowing away.

3. Let the picture sit in the sun for about three or four hours without being disturbed. The longer your picture is left in the sun, the greater the bleaching effect.

4. Remove the objects or letters and admire your sun picture. Ask your children, "How did the sun print your picture?" Listen to them as they tell you how the sun faded the paper that was not covered, leaving the paper under the objects darker and more vivid.

"What Time Is It, Mr. Sun?"

The sun is our oldest clock. For centuries, people have measured time by watching the movement of the sun in the sky and their changing shadows throughout the day. The principle of a sundial is based on the relationship between the sun and an upright object that casts a shadow. You and your children can create a simple sundial using ordinary materials.

1. Cut a ten- or twelve-inch circle from a piece of scrap cardboard and gather together a straight stick, dowel rod, or pencil about eight inches long. Mark the center point on the circle with a small hole.

2. Find a place in your yard that receives sun all day. Place the cardboard circle on the ground. Poke the stick, dowel rod, or pencil into the center hole and push it straight into the ground. This will keep the circle in place. Also, you will notice the stick makes a shadow on the circle.

3. Every hour, use a pencil to draw a line along the shadow created by the stick and mark it with the time of day. When you are finished, your sundial will be marked with lines of varying sizes. You will notice that the shortest line is at the noon shadow; mark this line "N" for noon and north.

4. Each time you would like to use your sundial, point the line for the noon shadow to the north. Observe the shadow of the stick. What time is it?

What Is a Clock?

Talk with your children about time and how it is measured. A clock is just a device used to divide up the days and nights in a way that a certain group of people have agreed upon. All people have not always divided up time in the same way. The calendar was invented by human beings. But the sun follows its own cycle, no matter what calendar we decide to use. Can the sun itself be a clock? Can the moon be a clock? Is the change in the seasons a sort of clock?

> **D**ost thou love life, then do not squander time, for that's the stuff life is made of.
>
> BENJAMIN FRANKLIN, 1757

The Food Chain

We Are Sun-Powered!

Take a ride on a bicycle. What power source makes you go? It is the sun! This system, in which all creatures are linked to the sun, is known as the food chain. (For the purpose of simplicity, the last members of the food chain, the decomposers, are not discussed here. Information on that subject can be found in the "Wonders in a Garden" and "Trees are Terrific" chapters.) Read this seemingly simple paragraph to your children and let them act out each part of the chain, following the particles of sunlight from their original source through each link.

Cricket in the Grass, by Philip Van Saelen. Sierra Club Books/ Charles Scribner's Sons, NY, 1979.

In this unusual, almost totally visual book, five interconnected stories are told through pictures alone. The careful drawings reveal the drama of everyday life and sudden death in five neighboring ecosystems. Because the child actively "sees" what happens when the food chain is at work, he is more able to understand his place in it. (ages 5 - 9)

Curl into a ball and imagine that you are a tiny seed buried in the rich soil. The energy from the sun is stored inside your seed lobes and nourishes you as you begin to grow. Soon you burst open and your roots grow downward, sucking in particles of sunlight energy and water that have waited for hundreds of years for you. Your grasses grow tall as they use the sun's energy to make food out of water and air. A bug crawls through your grassy top, nibbling on the green blades. Now the bug has absorbed the particles of sunlight. *(Pretend to be the bug because the particles of sunlight are now part of him.)* The bug crawls high on a blade of grass. A sudden burst of wind shakes the grass, the bug loses his grip. . . and splash! The bug has fallen into a stream. Under the water a fish notices the rippling surface. . . and snap! The fish has eaten the bug. *(Become the fish because the particles of sunlight are now part of him.)* Wading along the edge of the stream is a bear. He slaps his great paw into the water and the fish lands on the ground. Then, gulp! The bear has swallowed the fish. *(Pretend to be the bear.)* Quietly creeping through the woods is an Indian brave. He silently sets an arrow in his bow and lets it fly. The Indian has killed the bear. The bear meat is made into a stew and served at dinner. *(Pretend to be the Indian.)* Now the particles of sunlight are part of you. Where will they go from here?

T hrough digestion, living things break down the organization of other living things.

The Food Chain Pyramid

Young children can better visualize a concept after experiencing it with all of their senses. When trying to teach them about the simple food chain, just eating a variety of foods and discussing their origin isn't enough. These milk carton blocks are easy to assemble and your child can manipulate them to experiment with the pyramid that is created in an actual food chain.

1. Take ten clean, empty milk cartons (quart or half-gallon size is best) and measure one edge (from point to point) of the bottom of a carton. Measure that same distance up the side of the carton from the bottom and mark it. Measure the same distance again from the mark and mark that. Cut a carton all the way around at each mark, until you have two square-shaped boxes (one will be open at both ends).

2. Take the box that is opened at both ends, turn it sideways and stuff it into the other box to make a cube. Tape the edges closed.

3. Repeat with the other cartons until you have ten cubes or "blocks." If desired, and for easier decorating, wrap each block with scrap drawing paper (like a gift).

4. Take four of the blocks and decorate with pictures of the sun on all sides.

5. Take three blocks and decorate with pictures of grass, plants, and seeds cut from magazines or drawn with markers.

6. Take two blocks and decorate with pictures of plant-eating animals, such as people, rabbits, mice, squirrels, cows, chickens, etc.

7. Take the last block and decorate with pictures of meat-eating animals, such as people, owls, hawks, foxes, etc.

8. After completing the set of blocks, let your children build a food chain pyramid: the four sun blocks act as the base, three plant blocks on top of those, two plant-eater blocks next, and finally the meat-eater block on top. Explain to your child why the blocks are arranged in this way.

9. Manipulate the pyramid by asking these questions: What happens if you take away a plant block from the pyramid? (The pyramid, or at least part of it, will collapse.) What happens when

you take a sun block away? Does the pyramid collapse if you take away the meat-eaters? (Blocks do not fall, but it is no longer a pyramid.) Why are the meat-eaters important to the food chain? (To keep the plant-eaters from overpopulating an area and eating all the plants.) Explain to your children that this pyramid of many plants, fewer plant-eaters and even fewer meat-eaters is how nature maintains population in a given area.

Nature Detective

You can find evidence of the food chain in progress in your own backyard, at a park, or in the woods. Tell your children that Scotland Yard has just assigned them to the detective branch and needs them to prove that, indeed, the food chain is real. Divide them into three groups and give each child a badge labeled either the plants, the plant-eaters, or the meat-eaters. Give each detective a magnifying lens and ask them to search the area for signs of the food chain at work. Here are some suggestions:

Plants: That's easy! Collect fallen leaves, twigs, grass, seeds and nuts, berries, etc.

Plant-eaters: That gets a bit tougher. Gather chewed leaves, half-eaten seeds and nuts, fruit, berries, etc.

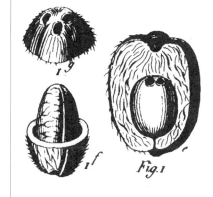

The Sun Powers All

Tune: Farmer in the Dell

The sun shines on the Earth,
The sun shines on the Earth,
The sun shines down and
powers all,
The sun shines on the Earth.

A plant munches the sun,
A plant munches the sun,
One-by-one they're linked to
the sun,
A plant munches the sun.

An insect chews a leaf,
An insect chews a leaf,
One-by-one they're linked to
the sun,
An insect chews a leaf.

An animal eats a bug,
An animal eats a bug
One-by-one they're linked to
the sun,
An animal eats a bug.

A meat-eater hunts for food,
A meat-eater hunts for food,
One-by-one they're linked to
the sun,
A meat-eater hunts for food.

The food chain is complete,
The food chain is complete.
One-by-one they're linked to
the sun,
The food chain is complete.

Meat-eaters: You'll need a really good eye for these! Scour around for signs of eaten animals, such as feathers, insect wings, bones, or broken egg shells. (If this group finds a dead animal, ask them not to pick it up! They can tell everyone about it.)

After they have hunted and collected the actual proof, come together as a group and share what has been found. You can either slash-count or lay the items in a food chain pyramid, with the plants on the bottom, plant-eater items in the middle and the meat-eater items on the top. After it has all been counted, ask these questions: Which group has the most items? (The plants.) Which has the least? (The meat-eaters.) Do you notice any pattern? (A triangle or pyramid.) Why are there more plants than plant-eaters or meat-eaters?

At home or school, take these collected items and glue them onto a yellow, triangle-shaped paper. Tell your children that the yellow paper represents the sun's energy. Through this exercise, children will realize that the power they receive from their food always begins with particles of sunlight energy stored in the plants and animals they eat.

The Sun Powers All

Act out the food chain set to music. Instruct your children to hold hands and form a circle; choose one child to be the sun and ask him or her to stand in the middle. Sing the first verse as the children move in a circle around the "sun." During the second verse, let the "sun" choose two players to be "plants," one for each hand, which will begin two food chains. During successive verses, allow each child on the end of the "food chains" to choose another child from the circle. When you have finished the game, begin with the sun and take a roll call of each food chain, letting each child identify what plant, insect, or animal he or she is pretending to be.

"It's Lonely At the Top" Mobile

Creating a food chain mobile will help you further explain to your children how humans are dependent on other animals, the plants, and the sun. When the mobile is completed, follow one of the lines from a sun to a plant, then to a plant-eater, and finally to the meat-eater. As you move from one level to the next, less and less of the sun's energy is being transferred. That is why more plants are needed to sustain fewer plant-eaters; and that number of plant-eaters are necessary to sustain even fewer meat-eaters. This project demands a balancing act, but the results are worth it!

1. Start by cutting eight sun figures. Cut seven circular disks from poster board or cardboard.

2. On four disks, paste or draw pictures of plants on both sides. On two disks, put pictures of plant-eaters (remember to include man). And on the last disk, put a picture of a human on one side and another meat-eating animal on the other.

3. Cut twenty-two pieces of yarn or string (each about six inches long) and attach one to the top of each sun cut-out and picture disk.

4. *Adult:* With a wire cutter, cut wire hangers into straight rods (each about five inches long).

5. Help your children assemble the mobile. Tie two sun cut-outs to a rod to create four sun rods. Tie two plant disks to a rod to create two plant rods. Tie two plant-eater disks to a rod to create one plant-eater rod.

6. Finally, attach one sun rod to the bottom of each plant disk. Attach one plant rod to the bottom of each plant-eater disk. And attach the plant-eater rod to the meat-eater disk.

7. Tie the last yarn or string to the top of the mobile and make a loop for hanging. Gently slide the yarn knots, if necessary, to balance the mobile. Once everything is balanced, place a drop of glue on each knot to keep it in place.

A Food Chain Story Circle

Prepare some super sun-charged snacks, such as fresh vegetables, fruit, pretzels, or crackers. Bring your children together in a circle and share a food chain story as you nibble. Begin telling the story (always starting with the sun) and then, one by one, let the children add to it. Here are some story starters:

• The bright, summer sun shone on a calm, blue lake. The sun touched a small bit of algae floating in that lake and it began to use its energy to make food for itself. Along came a tiny minnow and nibbled some of it away. . . .

• The soft light from the rising sun touched a morning glory and

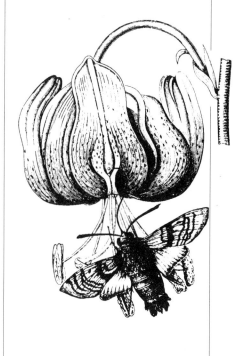

grass rabbit fox vulture
flower nectar butterfly nighthawk
water potato beetle opposum

it opened its beautiful petals. Its fragrance spread over the whole garden, inviting a visitor to come and taste the sweet nectar. . . .

• A ripening acorn hanging from a mighty oak tree stored the energy from the setting sun in its plump nut. Soon the soft darkness of night spread over the woods. A small mouse very cautiously peeked out of his nest hidden in the roots of the tree. . . .

Create a Food Chain Canopy

Do you remember making paper chains as a child? Your children can use paper to make a food chain in order to learn how all Earth's creatures and plants are linked to each other and to the sun.

1. Cut half-inch strips of colored construction paper, one color for each category: plants, insects, plant-eaters, and meat-eaters (do not use yellow). Help your children draw or paste cutout pictures on the strips of plants, animals, birds, insects.

2. Let the children link the strips together into food chains. Some examples are: grass > a rabbit > a fox; corn > a chicken > man; seeds > a quail > a bobcat; algae > a minnow > a bass > man; grass > a grasshopper > a mouse > an owl; leaves > caterpillar > a bird > a snake > a hawk.

3. When these are completed, make a larger ring out of yellow construction paper to represent the sun. Ask everyone to look carefully at their food chains and decide if the sun needs to be added to them. (Yes.) Let the children link their food chains to your large ring with yellow strips. When you are finished, display the chains by hanging them (with the sun in the middle) to create a food chain canopy.

4. Older children may lay the chains on the floor (with the sun in the middle and the food chains projecting like rays). Look carefully to see if any of the independent food chains can be linked together to create a food web. For instance, the "grass > rabbit > fox" chain can be linked from the rabbit to the owl, because owls also eat rabbits. "Man" can be linked to the rabbit, corn, chicken, quail and bass; since he also eats those things. (To link chains together, use longer strips or run string from one to another so that the web will hang nicely when completed.) When you are finished, display the food web from the ceiling with the sun in the middle.

As the World Turns

Each day slowly turns to night as our part of the world spins away from the sun. It is difficult to convince young children that the Earth is spinning all the time. They can't feel it, but they can observe it by watching the movement of the sun, moon, and stars across the sky. The book selections and related activities in this section will help you explain the cycle of day and night.

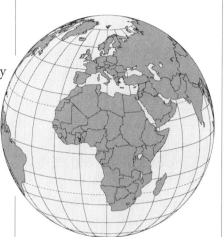

The Spinning Earth

"What? We are spinning? Right now?! I don't feel dizzy." That might be the response you'd get if you told an uninformed child that the Earth is constantly spinning like a top. There is a way to observe our revolving planet without having to go to the moon to watch it. Just note the changing position of the sun or moon in the course of a day. They may appear to be moving across the sky, but in fact it is the Earth that is moving. Here is an experiment that will demonstrate to your children how day and night occur:

1. Take an apple (to represent the Earth) and a flashlight. Stick a toothpick into one side of the apple (to represent your child) and tie a string from its stem.

2. Darken the room and shine the flashlight to represent the sun. Let your child dangle the apple in the path of light. The "sun" is shining on the "Earth."

3. Have your child slowly let the apple spin, watching carefully to see how his toothpick figure moves in and out of the light. Tell him that when his figure is in the light, it is daytime. When it is in darkness, it is night. Ask him to stop the apple from spinning when his figure is having day. Let it slowly spin again. Ask him to stop it when his figure is having night.

Plan a Sunset Picnic

Take the time to enjoy the beauty of a golden sunset with your family. Pack an easy dinner and eat outdoors, or roast hot dogs or vegetables over a fire. Watch the colors from the setting sun spread over the horizon, until finally they disappear. It's better than TV! Then sit around the campfire and enjoy each other's company.

The Day We Saw the Sun Come Up, by Alice Goudey. Illustrations by Adrienne Adams. Charles Scribner's Sons, NY, 1961.

Follow Christopher and Sue as they explore their world from the early hours of dawn to dusk. At night, with their parents, they share storytime, questioning time, and talking time before going to bed. Their mother reveals the mysteries of the Earth and sun. She answers their basic questions such as, "How big is the Earth?" and "Why is there day and night?" The children conclude that they are glad the Earth rotates to bring them the light from the sun during the day and the soft darkness of night. (ages 4 - 8)

Where Does the Day Go? by Walter M. Myers. Illustrations by Leo Carty. Parents' Magazine Press, NY, 1969.

A group of children and one Daddy are walking through Central Park when one child asks, "Where does the day go?" All the children try to answer and offer some ingenious ideas. But it is Michael, the youngest of the group, who comes closest to the truth. Before the stroll has ended, Daddy has explained the scientific facts in a simple, unforgettable way to everyone's satisfaction. (ages 6 - 9)

The Goodnight Circle, by Carolyn Lesser. Illustrations by Lorinda Bryan Cauley. Harcourt Brace Jovanovich, NY, 1984.

As the sun sets and the goodnight circle begins, a mother deer nudges her fawns into a bed of soft, fragrant pine needles. The noisy squirrels and the mother fox settle their babies for the night. Now it is time for the luna moths, the owl, the opossum, and beavers to wake up and hunt for food. As dawn streaks the sky, mother raccoon takes her young to fish in the pond. The circle is completed as the mother deer nuzzles her sleepy fawns awake. (ages 4 - 8)

A Special Time of Day

A fascinating transformation takes place at that special moment when daytime ends and nighttime begins. Take a walk or sit with your children at dusk. Watch the changing scenery and listen to the sounds of early night. As the sun sets and its last golden rays illuminate the sky, an ordinary tree will change into a gilt-edged silhouette. What do you hear? Listen for that time when the buzzing of insects replaces the chirping of birds. Night has begun. The change even takes place in your mind. When you hear a nearby animal crunching leaves under its feet in the daylight, you think, "It's probably just a squirrel or bird." But at night, that same crunching sound creates images of mice, skunks, or even coyotes in your mind. Share this time of evening with your children. It's a time to relax, review the events of the day, share stories, and enjoy each other's love.

Experience the Night

"Time to wake up!" That is the last thing your children expect to hear as darkness settles over your part of the world and night has begun. But that is exactly what is happening outside. Many creatures do their living, hunting, and eating in the concealing darkness of night. They are equipped with unique ways for coping with the darkness. For instance, owls have large eyes and can see as well as we can during the day. Also, many animals use a keen sense of smell or hearing to locate food. Bats are especially interesting, since they use radar (echolocation) to map out their surroundings, and to find and catch insects in the air. Humans are not so well-equipped for making their way in darkness since our eyes take time to adjust for better night vision, but we can use our other senses, such as hearing and sense of touch to help guide us. Observe the nighttime around you: can you hear the scurrying of a mouse? The chirping of a cricket? The fluttering wings of a bat? Feel ordinary things like tree bark, leaves, and grass. Do they feel the same as they do in the daylight? (Maybe their temperature is cooler or they feel damp.) Other than darkness, what makes night different than day?

Night Blooming Flowers

Just as there are morning bloomers, there are also flowers that open their petals only at night. These tend to be quite fragrant, since that is how they attract the insects necessary for pollination. Some examples are the evening primrose, moonflower, and nicotiana. Plant some of these and when you are out in the garden at night, these sweet-smelling flowers will add a special touch to your nighttime discoveries.

Pitch a Tent

You don't have to drive far away to enjoy a campout! You and your children can experience the pleasure of sleeping under the stars in your own backyard. Pitch a tent or bundle up in sleeping bags and share a memorable night of talking, giggling, counting shooting stars, and listening to the noises of the night.

Fireflies

Can you remember when you were young, armed with an empty jelly jar, creeping through the grass looking for lightning bugs? It was so much fun! Fireflies (or lightning bugs) are a species of beetle that produce chemicals within their bodies to produce light. In the daylight you will find them an ordinary brown color, but at night, when they are flashing their special light, they become quite beautiful. Fireflies begin their illuminated mating ritual soon after dusk and continue until about midnight during the months of July through September. Read the story *Fireflies* by Julie Brinckloe, grab a clean jar, poke some holes in the lid, and join your children for a firefly hunt. Just be sure to let the insects go free after the hunt is over.

Nocturnal Animals

What would it be like to live and hunt in total darkness? Many animals are especially adapted to their dark environment and use alternative methods, other than vision, to move about. To experience some of these ways, you and your children can pretend to be some common nighttime animals.

Step Into the Night, by Joanne Ryder. Illustrations by Dennis Nolan. Macmillan Publishing Co., NY, 1988.

When the sun hides behind the rooftop, a child steps outside to see the night begin. She imagines that she becomes many of the night creatures as they move silently in the unseen, half-sensed world of the darkness. A young mouse creeps under the vines, finding tasty berries; a firefly flashes, searching for a mate; a spider builds a sticky web and waits for his next meal and more. Exquisitely illustrated with soft moonlight illuminating the nighttime scenes, this is a beautiful book to be shared at bedtime or anytime. (ages 4 - 8)

Noises of the Night

Tune: Brahm's Lullaby

Oh, little one, listen with care

To the noises of the night;

Cricket chirping, locust buzzing,

See fireflies light the sky.

Although the day is almost through

And you'll soon need to sleep,

A little mouse begins his search

For breakfast to eat.

A Bat: Bats use echolocation to locate their food and avoid bumping into each other or objects when they are in flight. Pretend to be a bat by blindfolding your eyes. Have another person pretend to be an insect flying about in another part of the room. To locate your dinner, send out "beeps" into the room. The insect must answer each time with a "beep." Continue this exchange until you locate and capture the insect. This game, similar to "Marco Polo," will simulate the radar system that bats use to "see" in the dark. They send out sound waves, the waves bounce off the objects around them, and the bats listen for the wave to return to their ears. From this, they can tell how big and how far away the object is.

A Firefly: To locate a mate in total darkness, fireflies rely totally on their sense of sight, since they cannot hear or smell. The males fly around, sending out flashes of light, and search the ground for their signals to be returned by a female. In a given area there can be many species of fireflies, each with a different signal. Choose several pairs of children to play. Divide the children into partners and assign each pair a flashing signal but do not tell the children who their partners are, only what signals to look for; for instance, one short flash or a short flash followed by a long flash, etc. Designate one in each pair to be stationary during the game. Give each player a flashlight and darken the room. Allow the fireflies to begin signaling with their lights. They will soon discover, that in the midst of all the flashing, it can be quite difficult to find their partners.

A Mole: This weak-eyed creature lives mostly underground in a series of tunnels that it has created. Although it relies heavily on its senses of touch and hearing to move about in the tunnels, to locate food it uses an astonishing sense of smell. (You may have also noticed that your dog has a keen sense of smell. Try playing ball with him in total darkness; he uses his nose to locate the ball, not his eyes.) To let your children experience being dependent on the sense of smell, pop a bag of popcorn in a microwave. Do not open the bag immediately. Hide it somewhere in the house, in a closet or under a bed. When it is situated, open the bag and let your children locate the aromatic snack with their noses.

Bedtime Rituals

There is something about a predictable routine that comforts a young child. Plan a bedtime ritual for your children, such as a bath, brushing teeth, prayers, a story, talking time, a lullaby, then lights out. If you are able to go through the same nightly routine with your children, bedtime will be easier for them and you.

D R E A M S T A R T E R

*D*eep within a dark cave is a nursery roost for baby bats and their mothers. Imagine that you are a newly born bat. Your mother cradles you in her tail flap until you are able to crawl upon her belly and cling safely to her warm chest. You have no fur of your own and your eyes have not opened yet, so you rely on your sense of touch, smell, and hearing to become acquainted with your mother and your new surroundings. Your wings are not strong enough to fly just yet, so you must grasp tightly to your mother's fur for protection and warmth. For now, she is your world. She gives you warm, nutritious milk to drink that helps you grow stronger every day. Within days, your eyes open and you view the world for the first time. You immediately look up into your mother's furry face. She has big, rounded ears and small, dark eyes, and you think she is beautiful. After not eating for many days, your mother has become hungry and she must fly from the cave in search of tasty mosquitoes, moths, and beetles. But you are too small and defenseless to be left alone, so she tells you to hold on tight and away she flies.

Through the cave and into the dark night sky she soars as you cling even more tightly to her furry body. You can hear the flapping of her wings as she dips to the ground and snaps up an insect. She perches on a tree branch and you watch as she devours the crunchy

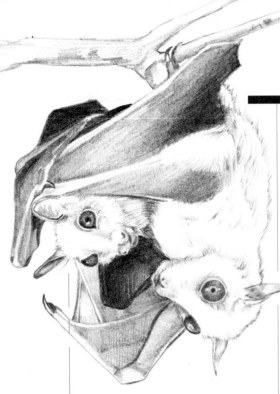

bug. "Hold on," she warns and off you both go again for more hunting. After many successful catches, she returns to the nursery roost where she holds you protectively in her folded wings. You snuggle closer to rest after the exciting flight.

"Is it wonderful to fly?," you whisper to your mother. "Soon you will know," she answers tenderly.

Weeks pass by quickly. The milk from your mother has made you stronger. Fur has begun to cover your body and you exercise your wings every day to strengthen them as you dream of the night when you will fly alone through the warm, dark sky. Each night is full of adventure as you continue to accompany your mother for insect hunting. You sense that it is getting late in the day and your mother is becoming restless. You know that it will not be long before she needs to search again for food. You anxiously await this night's fantastic journey, but just as she prepares for takeoff, she pushes you to one side. "You are getting big and are too heavy to carry," she says. "Tonight you must stay in the nursery. I will return to feed you later."

Off she flies, leaving you alone with the other babies in the cave. You share the warmth of the other baby bats, dreaming the whole time about the night sky and missing the feeling of wind in your fur. It is tricky to hold on to the rock and you grope for a jagged perch. The other bats crawl around and over you searching for their mothers. Like you, many of them have never been alone before. When the mother bats return at dawn, they scramble through the babies sniffing and calling for their own. Soon you hear a familiar and comforting voice. You answer as she approaches and you both smell each other to be sure. Yes, your mother is back! You crawl onto her warm chest. After filling your stomach with her delicious milk, you nestle into her folded wings and coo softly.

You grow quickly and soon you begin practicing short flights within the safety of the cave. Your mother has prompted you to taste the zesty flavor of a few small insects, but you wonder if you are ready for the vast and open sky. "The night has come," she announces one evening. "This night we will fly together." You follow your mother to the opening and away she goes. Without hesitating you take off behind her. You instinctively send out chirps and clicks, and you listen carefully as the sound bounces back into your ears. Something small is just ahead, and you swoop down and capture a fluttering moth in your tail flap. While in flight, you bend your body to grab the insect. You crunch and swallow: it is very different from your mother's milk, but it tastes good! All night, you fly through the sky, chirping and clicking and catching bugs. Finally full and exhausted, you head for the warmth and comfort of the cave.

Once there, you listen for your mother's call. There she is! She lets you climb on her belly, her furry body is comforting after the active night. "It was wonderful," you tell her. She gently wraps her wings around you as you snuggle closer to her beating heart, ready to share a good day's rest.

The Night Sky

Discover the Moon

As the moon hovers over the horizon, it seems bigger and more beautiful than at any other time. In reality, it is not larger, but, set against trees and houses, it seems larger. Take a moonlit walk on the evening of a full or crescent moon. Talk about how it is not the moon that is glowing, but its reflection of the sun that we see. You can demonstrate this. In a darkened room, place a small ball atop a candlestick in the center of a small table and shine a flashlight beam on it from a little distance away. The ball will reflect the light from the flashlight just as the moon reflects light from the sun. Have your child pretend to be the earth and position himself in each of the four cardinal directions around the "moon." From each of the four positions, he will see the ball take on the shape of one of the moon's four phases – new moon, quarter moon, half-moon, and full moon. As the moon orbits around the Earth, and the Earth orbits around the sun, it's the angle from which we view the moon that determines its shape. During the course of a moon's cycle, it may look as if the moon is shrinking or growing, but in fact it is the relationship between the earth, moon, and sun that is changing from day to day.

Sky All Around, by Anna Grossnickle Hines. Clarion Books, NY, 1989.

A father and daughter share a special time when they go out on a clear night to watch the stars. They settle down in their spot on the hill and look for pictures in the sky. They find the Big Dipper, the planet Jupiter, and other familiar constellations. When they see the Northern Crown, the little girl decides to wear it. She's Daddy's star princess now! This book will be a delightful experience to share with a young star discoverer. (ages 4 - 8)

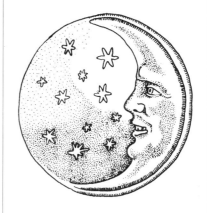

Twinkle, Twinkle, Little Star

by Jane Taylor

Twinkle, twinkle, little star,
How I wonder what you are!
Up above the world so high,
Like a diamond in the sky.

When the blazing sun is gone,
When he nothing shines upon,
Then you show your little light,
Twinkle, twinkle, all the night.

Then the traveler in the dark
Thanks you for your tiny spark;
He could not see which way to go,
If you did not twinkle so.

In the dark blue sky you keep
And often through my curtains peep,
For you never shut your eye
Till the sun is in the sky.

As your bright and tiny spark
Lights the traveler in the dark,
Though I know not what you are,
Twinkle, twinkle, little star.

The moon is like a large rock, covered with craters and dust. For humans it is an inhospitable place. When astronauts visit the moon for even a short time, they need to bring a lot of special equipment to survive. Imagine what life would be like on the moon. Let your child design a moon city, taking into account all the special features it would require to accommodate our needs for air, water, food, and shelter. Most likely, it would be a complicated structure. If we ran out of room on our planet, would it be an easy thing to just move to the moon? What do we need to do to assure that there will always be enough space, air, food, and water on Earth for the creatures that live here? Listen and talk with your child as together you make some suggestions for caring for the Earth and its resources.

Starlight, Starbright

Many adults still know this childhood rhyme by heart: "Starlight, starbright, the first star I've seen tonight. I wish I may, I wish I might, have the wish I wish tonight." Refusing to abandon our hopes and dreams, we still look into the evening sky waiting for that first magical star. Another star rhyme, "Twinkle, Twinkle Little Star," has been a continuous favorite since its first publication in 1806. The spread of twinkling light across the night sky holds much mystery and fascination and the act of searching the starlit sky is often an occasion for expressing our innermost thoughts.

Children of all ages need this quiet time for meditation and interaction with the heavens. Encourage your children to wonder and dream as together you silently watch the night sky appear. Let each child choose a private and personal star to call his or her very own; a star for wishing on, for reflecting on, and for companionship when the night is dark and still. There are no rules for selecting a personal star; your children can tell you about their stars or keep them a secret. To make it "official," you can issue certificates made from construction paper with the wishful rhyme printed on it. Let your children decorate their certificates with gold and silver adhesive stars, then sing a song, such as "Twinkle, Twinkle Little Star" to their newly chosen friends.

Like Diamonds in the Sky

From the Earth, stars look like small points of light. Do your children realize that each one is a sun, just like our sun? It is their great distance from Earth that makes them appear small. Stargazing is best done away from city lights and on a dark, moonless night. Take a blanket or sleeping bag or some folding chairs to recline in and gaze skyward. If you take a flashlight along for reading star charts, cover the lens with red cellophane so your eyes will stay adjusted to the darkness. If you plan to stay the night, don't be surprised if you get very little sleeping done! The night sky is full of wonderful and mysterious things to see and think about. It's much better than renting a popular video! Enjoy this peaceful time with your children, talk about the universe, shooting stars, animals of the night, or look for pictures in the sky. Nights like these will not be quickly forgotten.

Pictures in the Sky

Throughout human history, certain stars or arrangements of stars have served as symbols for many powerful or heroic legends. These stories have been passed from generation to generation and today can be found in many anthologies, such as *The Heavenly Zoo* by Alison Lurie. Read some of these stories to your children, then go out to locate those particular constellations.

If this is your first time out to stargaze at the constellations, take the book, *The Stars* by H. A. Rey and a red cellophane-covered flashlight. Probably the easiest and most famous constellations are the Big and Little Dippers, which are visible year round. Another interesting and well-defined constellation is Orion, the hunter, with his belt of three bright stars and his companion, the Dog Star Sirius.

Visit a Planetarium

There's a place you can go, day or evening, to see the night sky. It's a planetarium! Some science museums (and some universities) have dome-shaped rooms especially designed for presenting shows about the solar system and stars. The shows vary throughout the year. Many presenters provide their guests with a basic stargazing lesson or a question and answer session after the main feature.

An Invitation to a Cosmic Celebration

Your child can invite her friends to an intergalactic party with an invitation that locates the "address" of Planet Earth.

Come to a Cosmic Celebration!

Date: January 1

Time: 4:00 p.m.

Street: Your Address

City: Your City

State: Your State

Country: The United States

Continent: North America

Hemisphere: The Northern

Planet: The Earth

Galaxy: The Milky Way

Directions to Earth: We are the third planet in a solar system containing nine planets. (Look for the blue and green one.) We circle a medium-sized star that we call the sun. Our sun is located in the arm of a spiral-shaped galaxy known as "The Milky Way." See you there!

Children (over three years of age) are welcome, provided they can sit quietly through the 30-60 minute presentation. Check your area to see if there is a planetarium near you, and plan a trip to the stars.

Constellation Cans

If you can't visit a planetarium, you can make a miniature one at home! Just take clean fruit and vegetable cans and tap holes into the bottom of each to create real (or imagined) constellation patterns. Darken the room, place a flashlight inside a can, and shine the light through the holes onto a bare wall. Change constellation cans periodically to present your own, private planetarium show!

Is Anyone Out There?

Have you ever wondered if we are alone in the universe? When you look into the vastness of the night sky, knowing that each star you see (and the many you can't see) is a sun and that each sun could have planets revolving around it, you have to ask yourself, "Is there other life out there?" Humankind has launched unmanned probes to venture into the cosmos and send pictures and information back to Earth. These machines will leave our solar system and eventually our galaxy to journey to other parts of the universe. Each of these probes is equipped with a message for any intelligent life form that might find it. The information tells in picture form about Earth and the people who live there. In 1977, the Voyager space probes also included special recordings containing music, a spoken message, songs, animal calls, and a greeting in sixty languages. If your children could tell a being from a faraway planet about Earth, what would they say? What are some things about our planet that they feel are unique? Let them design individual plaques and make a tape recording of the sights and sounds of Earth.

Have an Intergalactic Celebration

After reading *My Place in Space* by Robin and Sally Hirst, plan a cosmic celebration! Ask your guests to dress up like "beings" from other planets. Invite them to come prepared to share with the group some of the special qualities of their home planets. Play "Pin the Sun in the Solar System" and serve Intergalactic Punch!

Get Involved!

Although it may not be possible for your family to install a solar energy system in your house, you can set a good example for your children by conserving the energy you use in many easy ways. To begin, teach them about the fuel that is used to heat your house, run your electrical appliances, and motor your car. Explain that our society is lucky to be able to turn a dial or key to make things happen. But, where does the energy come from? Being aware of its origin, any resulting by-products, and the way in which they are disposed of is the first step to making environmentally-wise energy choices.

Energy Officers At Work!

What do we take for granted, believing it will always be there at the flip of a switch? Energy. Young children are not directly involved in creating an energy efficient home and may not even be aware of the items they use everyday that are electrically powered. This activity is not only a great lesson in energy awareness; it will help remind you and your children to conserve precious fuel. (You might even lower your monthly utility bill!)

1. Supply yellow construction paper and scissors. Have your children cut out sun-shaped labels.

2. Tell them that they have been promoted to the rank of "Energy Officer." Armed with tape and sun cutouts, ask them to go around your house or school and place a paper sun on each item that uses energy. Make sure to label appliances that are used every day, such as light switches in every room, lamps, the refrigerator, television, stove (away from burners), thermostat, microwave, ceiling fans, telephone, radio, record player, powered toys, etc.

3. Make hats and badges out of scrap construction paper from your Recycle Craft Box. Tell your children that their daily duty will be to make certain that these labeled items are turned off when not in use. Every morning assign a different "Chief Detective," whose job will be to report the status of the energy saving operation. Reward your energy conscious officers often for a job well done!

To Save Energy . . .

* **1.** Use small pots and pans for cooking when possible.

* **2.** Use cold water for rinsing dishes, cleaning fruits and vegetables, and other small jobs. Using less hot water will help to save the energy necessary to run your hot water heater. During the day, turn your hot water heater dial to "pilot," and in ordinary circumstances, the heated water will last most of the day.

* **3.** Decide what to choose from the refrigerator before you open it.

* **4.** When refrigerating leftovers, allow them to cool at room temperature first.

* **5.** Recycle paper, glass, plastic, and aluminum. Purchase items in recycled containers.

* **6.** Put your leftovers or lunch in reusable containers.

* **7.** Choose reusable cloth kitchen towels and napkins in place of paper, especially for hand drying. Not only are many trees cut down to make paper towels and napkins, but energy is consumed and pollution is added to our waterways as a result of the manufacturing process.

* **8.** Whenever possible, choose a manual appliance over an electrical one. Some examples

include can openers, toothbrushes, knives, food processors,
mixers, remote controls, blankets
or heating pads.

* **9.** Turn off all lights when you
leave a room for more than five
minutes. Check the wattages of
your light bulbs, never using
more than is recommended. Use
energy efficient bulbs.

* **10.** Keep the thermostat at an
energy saving level. In winter,
wear warm clothing in the day
and use two blankets at night.
Utilize sunny windows on cold
afternoons and let the sun shine
in! In summer, turn off the air
conditioner at night and use fans
instead. Draw curtains or blinds
when in direct sunlight.

* **11.** Carpool and use mass
transit whenever possible.
Rediscover bicycles and walking,
especially for short trips.

* **12.** Use a clothesline instead of
an electric dryer when practical.

The Bat: Friend or Foe?

Bats are fascinating creatures and are unjustly feared by many
people. There are a lot of rumors going around about bats, most of
which are exaggerated or false! Here are some common misconcep-
tions about bats and the true facts. Using scrap cardboard, your
children can make and illustrate a set of "Bat Fact" cards to share
with their friends. Help spread the good word about bats!

• MYTH: *A lot of people think bats are flying rodents – a kind of
mouse.*

FACT: Bats are more closely related to humans than they are to
mice. They are the only true flying mammal in the world. Unlike
mice, they reproduce quite slowly, usually giving birth to only one
baby per year.

• MYTH: *When you are out at night, bats will fly into your hair.*

FACT: Bats have no interest at all in getting into your hair. If a
bat can detect a brown moth in the dark, he certainly isn't going to
blunder into your head!

• MYTH: *Bats can't see. You've heard the saying, "Blind as a bat."*

FACT: Bats are not blind, and, as a matter of fact, they can see
quite well. It's just that when you make your living by catching
mosquitoes and small insects in the dark, good eyesight isn't
enough. Echolocation is a much more efficient way of detecting
objects in the darkness of night.

• MYTH: *Bats are dirty creatures that carry strange diseases.*

FACT: Bats are actually very clean little animals. An unfounded
study done about 50 years ago said that bats carry rabies. More
recent studies have concluded that healthy bats do not carry any
diseases that are harmful to humans or animals. Some bats, just as
some dogs and cats, can get rabies. But they are rarely aggressive,
even when infected. If you ever find a bat, the best rule is to leave it
alone.

• MYTH: *Bats will suck your blood.*

FACT: Bats generally fall into three categories: fruit, nectar, or
insect eating. Mostly found in the tropics, fruit and nectar bats do
not use sonar. They eat fruit and drink nectar from flowers, and
help pollinate many tropical delights, such as bananas, guavas, figs,
cashews, and avocados. Most of the bats found in the United States

dine on insects (three species are nectar-eating). There is a species of bat found in Latin America called the vampire bat. It can inflict wounds on animals and livestock and will drink the resulting blood. This species of bat constitutes only about one-third of one percent of the bat population. Unfortunately, many people think that all bats are out for blood, but this is not true.

• MYTH: *Bats are everywhere. They are not at risk of extinction.*

FACT: Bats can be found all over the world, excluding the arctic regions. They have no natural enemies to speak of, except man. There are many species of bats that are listed as endangered and are currently at risk of extinction, partly because people kill them out of unjustified fear. To help save bats from extinction, you and your family need to learn all you can about bats, especially the ones found in your area. If natural roosting sites are limited in your region due to urban development, you can aid bats by building and hanging bat boxes.

For more information about bats and how you can help save them, and for a free catalog offering bat boxes and plans, contact :
Bat Conservation International
P.O. Box 162603
Austin, TX 78716

More Books To Share With Children

Wake Up, Jeremiah by **Ronald Himler.** Harper & Row, NY, 1979. This beautifully illustrated book captures a young boy's exuberant greeting of the sun and a new day. (ages 3 - 6)

An Ordinary Day by **Sally Mitchell Motyka.** Illustrations by Donna Ayers. Simon & Schuster Books for Young Readers, NY, 1989. The delights of a little boy's ordinary day, filled with things to touch, taste, see, and enjoy. (ages 3 - 7)

When the Sun Rose by **Barbara Helen Berger.** Philomel Books, NY, 1986. The sun visits a little girl in her playhouse and takes on many beautiful shapes. The little girl and the sun girl play all day long, making rainbows, until her friend has to say goodbye at sunset. The clear, though unspoken, reference is to the reliability of the natural order of the cycle of day and night. A magical book with radiant illustrations that extend the dream-like quality of the story. (ages 3 - 7)

High in the Mountains by **Ruth Yaffe Radin.** Illustrations by Ed Young. Macmillan Co., NY, 1989. This lyrical story traces the adventures of a little girl for one day "high in the mountains far away." In the sunlight, the girl runs through the wildflowers in an alpine meadow, sees deer at play, and hears the song of a stream as it rushes to the river far below. (ages 4 - 8)

Dawn by **Uri Shulevitz.** Farrar, Straus & Giroux, NY, 1974. Winner of the Caldecott award, this lovely tale is based on the text of an ancient Chinese poem that unforgettably portrays the drama of a pastoral dawn shared by an old man and his grandson. (ages 4 - 8)

The Sun's Day by **Mordicai Gerstein.** Harper and Row, NY, 1989. Children will find joy and harmony in the sun's magnificent journey through a day, as well as a warm sense of security and belonging in the rituals of every day life in this enchanting book. (ages 3 - 7)

Under the Sun by **Ellen Kandoian.** Dodd, Mead & Co., NY, 1987. Molly's mother answers her question about where the sun goes each night by taking her on a visual journey around the world. (ages 4 - 8)

Legends of the Sun and Moon by **Eric and Tessa Hadley.** Illustrations by Jan Nesbitt. Cambridge Univ. Press, NY, 1983. This book collects legends from around the world which attempt to explain the mysteries of the sun's journeying across the sky and the moon's waxing and waning. (ages 8 - 12)

Our Friend the Sun by **Janet Palazzo.** Illustrations by Susan Hall. Troll Assoc., Mahwah, NJ, 1982. This is a bright, cheery book for the very young child that explains why the sun is our friend. (ages 3 - 5)

Play With the Sun by **Howard E. Smith, Jr.** Illustrations by Frank Bozzo. McGraw Hill Book Co., NY, 1975. This is an excellent book to show children how to play with the sun, to make discoveries, and to have sun-filled adventures. All of the suggested experiments are simple enough for a young child and are made with household equipment. (ages 7 - 12)

Done in the Sun: Solar Projects for Children by **Anne Hillerman.** Illustrations by Mina Yamashita. Sunstone Press, Santa Fe, NM, 1983. This book demonstrates through simple experiments and craft projects how the sun's light and heat can be used to help us in our everyday lives. (ages 6 - 10)

Sun Fun by **Caroline Arnold.** Franklin Watts, NY, 1981. *Sun Fun* presents ten projects that use energy from the sun, including the making of a sun clock, sun prints, and cooking with the sun. (ages 6 - 9)

Sun Calendar by **Una Jacobs.** Silver Burdett Co., Morristown, NJ, 1983. In simple language with superb color illustrations, this book describes how life on Earth changes as our planet moves around the sun. It explains the seasons and temperatures, and shows how plants and animals depend on the sun for light, warmth, and energy and how they adapt to the sun's changing year. (ages 5 - 9)

Dining on a Sunbeam: Food Chains and Food Webs **by Phyllis S. Busch.** Photographs by Les Line. Four Winds Press, NY, 1973. "Where does food get its magic power? From the sun." This marvelous book goes on to explain in a clear text sprinkled with excellent photographs just how the sun's energy gives us the food we eat, and keeps us and all other animals, as well as plants, alive. (read-aloud, ages 7 - 11)

Mousekin's Close Call **by Edna Miller.** Prentice-Hall, Inc., Englewood Cliffs, NJ, 1978. The reader can experience what it is like to be on the lower end of the food chain in a forest of hungry predators. (ages 5 - 8)

Night in the Country **by Cynthia Rylant.** Illustrations by Mary Szilagyi. Bradbury Press, NY, 1986. Through the night a river flows, an owl swoops down for prey, a rabbit scampers. The author and illustrator give readers a night full of sounds and mystery, alive and vibrant, at each end framed by the dim colors of day. (ages 4 - 9)

North Country Night **by Daniel San Souci.** Doubleday, NY, 1990. This beautiful book takes young readers through the woods on a winter night to visit the great horned owl, the long-tailed weasel, the graceful mule deer, and other creatures that come alive when the sun goes down. (ages 5 - 9)

Out in the Night **by Karen Liptak.** Illustrations by Sandy Ferguson Fuller. Harbinger House, Inc., Tucson, AZ, 1989. From the Arctic to the Amazon, from Malaysia to Minnesota, a marvelous array of mammals, birds, reptiles, and amphibians are introduced here in fourteen nighttime environments. (ages 7 - 10)

Sleepy Book **by Charlotte Zolotow.** Illustrations by Ilse Plume. Harper & Row, NY, 1988. In this beautifully illustrated book, animals, birds, insects, and children sleep in their own special places, in their own special ways. This is a perfect choice for a bedtime story for very young children. (ages 3 - 5)

Night Owls **by Sharon Phillips Denslow.** Illustrations by Jill Kastner. Bradbury Press, NY, 1990. This is the story of an aunt and her nephew sharing a midsummer visit and enjoying everything wonderful that goes on late at night. (ages 5 - 8)

Moonsong Lullaby **by Jamake Highwater.** Photographs by Marcia Keegan. Lothrop, Lee & Shepard, NY, 1981. The Moon watching over the night is an important theme in Native American lore. This original lullaby is inspired by the ancient stories and Jamake Highwater's own deep feelings for the natural world as he learned it from his ancestors. (all ages)

Still as a Star: A Book of Nighttime Poems **selected by Lee Bennett Hopkins.** Illustrations by Karen Milone. Little Brown, Boston, 1989. This collection of poems and lullabies perfectly captures that dreamy nighttime mood - as rabbits dance on new fallen snow and a child leans out of the window to gaze at the moon. Among the well-known poets whose works appear are Nikki Giovanni, Carl Sandburg, and Eleanor Farjeon. (read-aloud, ages 4 - 8)

The Midnight Farm **by Reeve Lindbergh.** Illustrations by Susan Jeffers. Dial Books for Young Readers, NY, 1989. In this lovely story, a mother takes her child for a walk outside at night, giving him a chance to meet his familiar animal friends in the darkness of the summer night. He sees raccoons, cows, chicks, field mice, and many other animals. The delicately colored illustrations lend a perfect touch to the soft beauty of this book. (ages 2 - 6)

Animals of the Night **by Merry Banks.** Illustrations by

Ronald Himler. Charles Scribner, NY, 1990. What happens when the sun sets and the stars appear and sleepy children go to bed? It is time for the night animals to come out from the cool, dark places where they have been sleeping during the day. (ages 3 - 6)

Grandfather Twilight by **Barbara Berger.** Philomel Books, NY, 1984. When day is done and the shadows begin to deepen, Grandfather Twilight closes his book, puts on his jacket and goes for a walk in the forest. Each night he takes one pearl that grows in his hand as he walks. When he reaches the shoreline, he gently gives the pearl to the silence above the sea and the moon appears. This is a companion book to *When the Sun Rose* also by Barbara Berger. (ages 3 - 7)

The Sun's Asleep Behind the Hill by **Mirra Ginsburg.** Illustrations by Paul O. Zelinsky. Greenwillow Books, NY, 1982. The sun, the breeze, the leaves, the bird, the squirrel, and the child all grow tired after a long day and fall asleep as night falls. (ages 3 - 6)

The Night Book by **Mark Strand.** Illustrations by William Pene DuBois. Clarkson N. Potter, Inc., NY, 1985. A rising moon sees a little girl who is afraid of the night and sends down a magic moonbeam to show her the many wondrous things to see during the dark hours. (ages 3 - 7)

Fireflies by **Julie Brinckloe.** Macmillan Pub. Co., NY, 1985. A young boy is proud of having caught a jar full of fireflies, which seems to him like owning a piece of moonlight. As the light begins to dim, he realizes he must set the insects free or they will die. (ages 4 - 8)

Fireflies by **Joanne Ryder.** Illustrations by Don Bolognese. Harper and Row, NY, 1977. This book has an easy-to-read text that describes the physical characteristics and life cycle of a firefly from the time it is a glowworm until it reaches adulthood. (ages 5 - 9)

Owl at Night by **Ann Whitford Paul.** Illustrations by Catherine Stock. G. P. Putnam's Sons, NY, 1985.

This story follows the nighttime activities of an owl, at his busiest while other animals and people are asleep. (ages 4 - 8)

Owls by **Lynn M. Stone.** Rourke Enterprises, Inc., Vero Beach, FL, 1989. The stunning close up photographs in this book will help young readers see the detail of an owl's appearance which they might not see in the wild. The easy to understand text describes the appearance, habits, daily life, nesting, and hunting ability of this unique nocturnal bird. (ages 6 - 10)

Owl Moon by **Jane Yolen.** Illustrations by John Schoenherr. Philomel Books, NY, 1987. On a cold, winter's night under a full moon, father and daughter trek into the woods to seek out the Great Horned Owl. Distinguished author Jane Yolen has created a gentle, poetic story that lovingly depicts the special companionship of humans and the natural world. (ages 4 - 9)

Wufu: The Story of a Little Brown Bat by **Berniece Freschet.** Illustrations by Albert Michini. Putnam, NY, 1975. A bat is born in a deserted barn, grows up, learns to fly, deals with enemies, and finally takes his place among his family. The spring and summer activities of Wufu are captured in every small, intimate detail in this fascinating story. It also points out that the farmer that owns the barn in which the bat family lives is grateful for their presence. He says that the bats catch many of the harmful insects that otherwise would ruin his apple orchard and vegetable garden. "He hoped they would stay a long time in the old barn." (ages 6 - 10)

Little Bat's Secret by **Kathy Darling.** Illustrations by Cyndy Szekeres. Garrard Pub. Co., Champaign, IL, 1974. A little brown bat experiences her first night flight. She becomes separated from her mother soon after their departure and, not having discovered her powers of echolocation, becomes disoriented and lost. The little bat befriends a lightning bug who helps lead her through the darkness. (ages 3 - 7)

The Magic School Bus Lost in the Solar System by **Joanna Cole.** Illustrations by Bruce Degen. Scholastic Inc., NY, 1990. Here we have another outrageous adventure for the students in Ms. Fizzle's science class. This time, the magic school bus transforms into a spaceship and the class is blasted off to explore the stars and planets. (ages 7 - 12)

The Glow in the Dark Night Sky Book by **Clint Hatchett.** Random House, NY, 1988. This unusual book contains wonderful "star maps" that glow in the dark after being exposed to bright light. Take them outside and look up to find the constellations. (all ages)

The Stars: A New Way To See Them by **H. A. Rey.** Houghton Mifflin Co., Boston, 1952. A beginning guide for the young star enthusiast. Although it is written for older children, the available star charts and basic facts about constellations will aid parents and children out in the field. (with help, ages 7 - 14)

The Heavenly Zoo: Legends and Tales of the Stars retold by **Alison Lurie.** Illustrations by Monika Beisner. Farrar Straus and Giroux, NY, 1979. The illuminated creatures of the sky formed the basis for fantastic stories that were passed down from one generation to another. This book is a collection of such tales from all over the world. (read-aloud, ages 6 - 10)

My Place in Space by **Robin and Sally Hirst.** Orchard Books, NY, 1988. When two children are asked if they know where they live, they respond each time by stepping away from their address, into their city, country, hemisphere, planet and on. . .to the universe! (ages 5 - 9)

My First Space Book by **Graham Brown.** Simon and Schuster, NY, 1990. This is a beginning book for children interested in exploring the solar system. Three dimensional planets and an easy-to-read text show children the Earth and its place among the other planets. (ages 4 - 7)

Resources for Parents and Teachers

The National Geographic Society has educational filmstrips, films, kits, and videos. They offer filmstrip sets with cassettes entitled *Earth, Moon, Sun, and Space* (primary grades) and *Today and Tomorrow in Space* (upper grades). *Reflecting on the Moon* is for intermediate and advanced students and is available on film or video. Write to National Geographic Society, Educational Services, Dept 89, Washington, D.C. 20036. To preview or rent these materials write to Karol Media, 22 Riverview Dr., Wayne, NJ 07470.

The Astronomical Society of the Pacific offers slides, audio cassettes, and astronomy maps and charts. The Society also offers a newsletter on teaching astronomy entitled *The Universe in the Classroom.* The newsletter is free if ordered on school letterhead. Order their catalogue from the Society, Dept. L89, 390 Ashton Ave., San Francisco, CA 94122.

The Rocky Mountain Institute offers a bibliography of information and product sources for alternative energy ideas called *Resource-Efficient Housing Guide.* (RMI Publication #E89-25, $15 postpaid.) RMI is a non-profit resource policy center founded in 1982 by energy analysts Hunter and Amory Lovins. Its mission is to foster the efficient and sustainable use of resources as a path to global security. It offers many books, articles, and brochures on efficient uses of energy. Write to 1739 Snowmass Creek Road, Snowmass, CO 81654-9199.

Catch a Sunbeam: A Book of Solar Study and Experiments by Florence Adams. Harcourt Brace Jovanovich, Pub., NY, 1978.

Energy: 101 Practical Tips for Home and Work by Susan Hassol and Beth Richman. The Windstar Foundation, Snowmass, CO, 1989.

Information on conserving energy can be obtained from the Conservation and Renewable Energy Inquiry and Referral Service, US DOE, Box 8900, Silver Spring, MD 20907.

Seventh Generation is a company that offers an incredible array of energy-conserving products. Send for their catalogue at 10 Farrell Street, South Burlington, VT 05403.

Jade Mountain offers a catalogue of energy saving items from boats and cars to solar cooling devices and solar electric panels. They also carry the *Alternative Energy Sourcebook* which lists over 1,200 items for only $4. Write to Jade Mountain, P.O. Box 4616, Boulder, CO 80306.

The Green Lifestyle Handbook: 1001 Ways You Can Heal the Earth by Jeremy Rifkin. Henry Holt & Co., NY, 1990. See especially "Home ECOnomics" by Kirk B. Smith, pp. 1-10. This article is an excellent resource for all sorts of information about saving energy in the home.

Astronomy Adventures, Naturescope Vol. 2, No. 2, The National Wildlife Federation, 1400 16th St., NW, Washington, D.C. 20036-2266. Provides a general look at the universe and solar system, especially from the viewpoint of how we see things from Earth. Offers many activities and ideas for young minds (and parents and teachers).

Odyssey is a magazine of space exploration and astronomy for young people. It contains interesting, factual stories about outer space, colorful star charts, and many other projects and games. Write to Box 1612, Waukesha, WI 53187-9950.

National Geographic Picture Atlas of Our Universe by Roy A Gallant. National Geographic Society, Washington, D.C., 1986.

A Spotter's Guide to the Night Sky by Nigel Henbest. Mayflower Books, NY, 1979.

Solar System (from the Planet Earth Series) by Kendrick Frazier and the Editors of Time-Life Books. Time-Life Books, NY, 1985.

Whitney's Star Finder by Charles A. Whitney. Knopf, NY, 1981.

Astronomy Education Materials Resource Guide offers activity sources for elementary and secondary teachers. Order the guide from Astronomy Education Materials Network, Dept. of Curriculum and Instruction, West Virginia University, Morgantown, WV 26506.

National Air and Space Museum's Education Resource Center offers an activity guide entitled "Exploring the Planets Tour." Order the guide from the Office of Education, P-700, National Air and Space Museum, Washington, D.C. 20560.

The National Science Teachers Association has available an activity guide containing reprints from the journal, *The Science Teacher* entitled "Astronomy on a Shoestring." To order write to the Association at 1742 Connecticut Ave., NW, Washington, D.C. 20009. This guide is for upper-level students.

NASA has booklets, fact sheets, and a newsletter for teachers containing activities for the classroom entitled *Educational Briefs.* It has also set up regional teacher resource centers that provide materials for education in the field of astronomy. For information about both the materials offered and a list of the centers, contact NASA, Educational Publications Services, XEP, Washington, D.C. 20546.

On Silent Wings. Beacon Films, P.O. Box 575, Norwood, MA, 1984. (On VHS video or film - 16 minutes, color). An exploration of the world of the owl, its general appearance, feeding habits, behavior patterns, and adaptability. Although the text is suited for an older audience, young children will enjoy seeing these common owls in their natural habitat. (age 7 and up)

Energy, Resources, and Environment by John W. Christensen. Kendall/Hunt, Dubuque, Iowa, 1981. This is an excellent overview of the field of energy use and its effects on the environment.

Power Station Sun: The Story of Energy by John Mason. Facts on File, NY, 1987.

Man, Energy, Society by Earl Cook. W.H. Freeman, San Francisco, 1976. This is an excellent introduction to energy concepts, problems, and alternatives.

Soft Energy Paths by Amory Lovins. Ballinger, Cambridge, MA, 1977. A superb analysis of energy alternatives.

Energy Unbound: A Fable for America's Future by L. Hunter and Amory B. Lovins, and Seth Zuckerman. Random House, NY.

Energy Source, Use, and Role in Human Affairs by Carol E. Steinhart and John S. Steinhart. Duxbury Press, North Scituate, Mass, 1974. This book offers an excellent treatment of energy principles and options.

Energy and Ecology by David M. Gates. Sinauer, Sunderland, Mass, 1985. A detailed analysis of all major energy alternatives.

Environment, Energy, and Society by Craig. R. Humphrey and Frederick R. Buttell. Wadsworth, Belmont, CA, 1982. An excellent overview of energy problems and possible alternatives.

99 Ways to a Simple Lifestyle. Center for Science in the Public Interest, Doubleday, NY, 1977. Presents a summary of how you can conserve matter and energy.

Energy Productivity: Key to Environmental Protection and Economic Progress by William U. Chandler. Worldwatch Institute, Washington, D.C., 1985. Offers a thorough discussion of ways to save energy.

Energy Today and Tomorrow - Living with Uncertainty by Joel Darmstadter, et al. Prentice-Hall, Englewood Cliffs, NJ, 1983. Analysis of energy problems and solutions.

Energy and Architecture: The Solar and Conservation Potential by Christopher Flavin. Worldwatch Institute, Washington, D.C., 1980.

The Energy Saver's Handbook: For Town and City People, Massachusetts Audubon Society, Rodale Press, Emmaus, PA, 1982.

Audubon Energy Plan by Jan Beyea. National Audubon Society, 950 Third Ave., New York, NY, 10022.

The Solar Home Book by Bruce Anderson. Cheshire Books, Harrisville, NY, 1976.

Energy Efficiency: A New Agenda by William Chandler, Howard Geller, and Mark Ledbetter. American Council for an Energy Efficient Economy, 1001 Connecticut Ave, NW, Suite 535, Washington, D.C. 20036.

A journal that will keep you in touch with developments in the field of home energy conservation is *Home Energy: The Magazine of Residential Energy Conservation.* Write to Home Energy, 2124 Kittredge, Suite 95, Berkeley, CA 94704.

A free mail-order catalogue listing pamphlets and books in the field of appropriate technology is offered by the Environmental Action Resource Service. Write P.O. Box 8, Laveta, CO 81055.

The Green Consumer by John Elkington, Julia Hailes, and Joel Makower. Penguin Books, NY, 1988. See especially pp. 276-277 for bibliography on energy conservation.

CHAPTER TWO

Earth Celebrations Throughout the Year

Sing a song of seasons!
Something bright in all!
Flowers in the Summer.
Fires in the Fall.
Robert Louis Stevenson
"Autumn Fires," 1885

I n ancient times, celebrations and festivals were firmly rooted in seasonal cycles because the lives of human beings were affected by the changing relationship between the sun and the Earth. For instance, Candlemas Day, celebrated February 2 (midway between the winter solstice and the spring equinox), was a day for rejoicing in the return of the sun's warmth and the eventual coming of spring.

Many traditional holidays of today have their origins in the changing of the seasons. Although a few remnants of the original focus remain, they are often lost in today's commercialism. By returning to the Earth as a basis for our festivals, we can make the natural world and its cycles a more intimate part of our

I'm in Charge of Celebrations, by Byrd Baylor. Illustrations by Peter Parnall. Charles Scribner's Sons, NY, 1986.

This book is a celebration itself! The author shares with us many of the hundred and eight celebrations she gave herself one year. March 11 was Dust Devil Day, a time to celebrate tumbleweeds "dancing in time to their own windy music." Or how about August 9? Rainbow Celebration Day was the day she saw a triple rainbow that ended in a canyon where she had just been the day before. Then came Coyote Day and the Time of Falling Stars. This book makes us realize that the Earth and its seasons give us endless reasons to celebrate almost any day of the year. (age 5 and up)

lives. This chapter offers many ideas for special celebrations: when the most spectacular natural event of your particular place happens, or at the points of the year when the Earth manifests itself in dramatic change, celebrate!

In the not so distant past, seasonal changes were indicated by routine yearly tasks that, in themselves, bound people more closely to the Earth. In the days before supermarkets, the planting, tending, and harvesting of the family garden were essential for survival. The "putting by" of the autumn harvest guaranteed food for the harsh and isolating cold of winter. While the snow was still thick on the ground, maple sugaring time was cause for great excitement. Although the world was still frozen, the running of the sap indicated that spring was indeed on its way. With the greening of the land, the Earth promised that the cycle of renewal was beginning once again. The celebrations and activities of this chapter have been developed to reacquaint you and your children, in a very real sense, with the seasonal wonders of the Earth.

Celebrate!

Celebrations for Every Day!

Just as the book, *I'm in Charge of Celebrations* suggests, every day can be a cause for celebration! Sit down with your children and look around. Undoubtedly, you will see something unusual or beautiful that fills you with awe or makes your heart sing. You and your children can respond to the phenomenal events in nature by spontaneously creating a ceremony of singing or dancing, writing a poem, or painting a picture to express your feelings. By searching outdoors for objects or events to commemorate, you and your children will become more aware of the seasonal changes in the natural world and better appreciate the many extraordinary gifts our planet has to offer. Some occasions to celebrate include the coming of rain after a long dry spell, the sighting of a rainbow, the shower of golden leaves on an autumn afternoon, moon phases, wildlife encounters, and so on. You'll need to be watchful, letting no detail pass unnoticed! And be spontaneous, choosing whatever event strikes you and your children as special and worth a celebration. The following suggestions are but a small sampling of ways to express the excitement and joy generated by these natural happenings.

Forms of Expression

Often a child's imagination can be best expressed through painting and sculpture, or by writing a poem, story, or song. Allow your children's hands, through different mediums, to communicate some of the magical feelings that nature can evoke by providing the materials and opportunity. You will find that the items collected in your Recycle Craft Box are excellent for sculpture and collage. By praising your children and their efforts toward expression, you will help foster a sensitivity towards the natural world.

A Celebrations Diary

Sometimes, after the memory of an encounter with nature fades, it is difficult to recall one's emotional response to it. This is especially true for young children, who often forget the details of childhood as they grow older. One way to keep their experiences and feelings alive is to create a diary to record these everyday celebrations of life and nature. Have your children fill the pages with drawings, photographs, written expressions, and also mementoes from nature, such as a leaf, the shell of a bird's egg, or pressed flowers, to remind them of these special occasions as they grow into adulthood.

An Offering of Friendship

If you and your children are celebrating a wildlife encounter, such as observing a rabbit in your yard or discovering a nest of birds, you might like to offer your friendship in the form of food. Your offering might be as simple as scattering some birdseed, but the resulting feeling of connectedness with the animal world will be worthwhile for you and your children. Here are some common food offerings:

Sunflower Seeds: *cardinals, goldfinches, chickadees, nuthatches, bluejays, squirrels, mice, chipmunks*

Cut-up Fruit or Wild Fruit (Wild Currants, Bayberries, etc.): *Robins, woodpeckers, bluebirds, flickers*

Mixed Seeds: *Sparrows, brown thrashers, cowbirds*

Breadcrumbs, Old Doughnuts, Cold Cereal: *Downy woodpeckers, bluejays, cardinals, wrens, chickadees, brown thrashers*

Nuts and Grains: *Squirrels, mice, chipmunks*

Corn (especially fresh on the cob): *Raccoons*

Crushed Peanuts or Peanut Butter: *Woodpeckers, sparrows, bluejays, catbirds, chickadees*

On the Day You Were Born, by Debra Frasier. Harcourt Brace Jovanovich, NY, 1991.

Join in a celebration of our natural world as it extends a loving welcome to each arriving member of the human family. (ages 3 - 7)

Happy Birthday to You!

Walking the Globe

Think, quick! How many times have you been around the sun? Your children might not even understand the question! Help them to understand by reenacting this yearly journey with a special ritual.

1. Have all of the family and party members sit in a circle (representing the sun) on the floor. Give the birthday child a globe (or ball) to represent the Earth and ask him or her to walk around the outside of the circle.

2. For each time the child travels around, the party members count out loud. Continue until the child has gone around the circle as many years as he is old. If you would like, for each completed circle you can hold up pictures of the birthday child taken that year. For example, after the child has walked around one time, hold up a picture of that child as a one-year-old for the group to admire.

Remember When?

Using old photographs and mementoes, help your children create scrapbooks of their lives since birth. Beside the photographs, attach "dialogue balloons" and write quotes that correspond with the facial expressions. On special occasions or rainy days, your children will find it entertaining to sit with you, thumbing through the pages, sharing stories, and recalling the events of each year.

Birthday Time Capsules

Think for a moment about the past year. What were its most memorable events? Recalling past experiences brings us joy and helps us to grow emotionally. What better way to remember the details of a passing year than to encapsulate them? Have your child create a "time capsule" using a shoebox. Fill it with memorabilia that represent the outstanding happenings of the past year and tuck it away in a safe place. On his next birthday, allow your child to open the time capsule like a gift. He will be surprised and delighted to remember what was important to him just the year before. Afterwards, place new items in the capsule for another year.

Spring

After a long sleep, the Earth wakes up. The falling rain refreshes and nourishes the soil, and the plants and trees begin to blossom in the warm sunshine. It even feels as if we are awakening and seeing the world anew; after being indoors for much of the winter, we long to be a part of the natural world and to witness its rebirth. The stories, celebrations, and activities of this section spotlight some of the natural events that occur in this season of renewal.

Signs of Spring Scavenger Hunt

This scavenger hunt can be played with teams or be a cooperative effort for a family or group. The object is to go out and search for signs of spring, such as a robin, a bee, a flower, green buds or leaves on tree branches, sprouting grass, a bird's nest, ants or other insects moving about, and other animal life (a bird, squirrel, rabbit, etc.). After your group has successfully located every item on the list, reward yourselves with a banana split party to celebrate the arrival of spring.

The Feast of the First Flower

For most people today, it is the blooming of flowers that truly signifies the arrival of spring. Many adults don't let this happening go unnoticed: they tend their gardens, enjoy the warming breezes of the new season, and adorn their tables with fresh flowers. Most young children are in school, and although they are allowed to play outdoors for longer periods, they may not take much notice of sprouting trees and grass and blooming flowers. The purpose of this brief ritual is to create an opportunity for your children to develop an awareness of the most lovely indicators of spring and to come to anticipate their appearance each year. It is a perfect way to celebrate the spring equinox (when both day and night are of equal length) which occurs on or around March 21.

Before the Ceremony: Choose a child to be the sun, another to be the rain, and another to be the bee. Prepare them before the ceremony by telling them what their parts will be. Have the group form a circle around a blooming flower or gather around a bed of flowers.

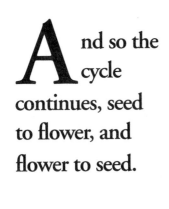

And so the cycle continues, seed to flower, and flower to seed.

Reader: The dark, cold soil was touched by the penetrating warmth of the sun. The gentle rains seeped into the Earth and awakened the sleeping bulbs (or seeds). The green stalks reached for the sunshine and right before our eyes the colorful buds opened to wave their beautiful petals in the spring breeze.

All: Thank you, Earth, for all of the pretty flowers.

Reader: Curl up, my little seeds, and live the life of a flower.

(Have the children curl into balls on the ground and act out the following story as it is told.)

Reader: It is dark and cold in the ground. As the days grow longer, the warmth of the sun enters the soil and gently awakens you. Feel the heat from the sun touching you. It is the energy of life.

(Have the sun child gently tickle each child's back.)

The rains begin to fall and seep into the ground. You are thirsty, so you take it in eagerly. Drink in the liquid of life.

(Have the rain child go to each child and pretend to sprinkle water on him or her. Ask the children to pretend to drink.)

(read slowly) Soon you begin to grow, reaching towards the sunlight. Each day you become stronger and taller. Your leaves grab the rays of sunshine and use their energy to make food for your growing body. After many days you are ready to blossom.

(Ask the children to slowly uncurl and to pretend to be growing flowers. As they reach upward, ask them to cup their hands overhead to represent their flower buds.)

One bright and sunny morning you slowly open your delicate petals. Your delicious perfume travels with the breeze and calls to the honeybee to come and drink and spread your golden pollen to the other flowers in the garden.

(Have the honeybee child pretend to fly to each child and tickle the palm of his or her open hands.)

After you have been pollinated, you close your petals and slowly wither to the ground. There you will become part of the soil again. Your body will break down and enrich the soil for the grass and other flowers that will bloom later.

(Ask the children to slowly sink back to the Earth, until they are curled up in a ball once again.)

Reader: Arise, my little flower children and all join hands. Let's sing and be happy because spring is here!

(Play the traditional game "Ring O' Ring a Roses" several times, then all applaud the flowers and the new season.)

Mud Madness

For people of the north and mountain regions, spring can be known as "mud season." The melting snow saturates the ground, creating puddles of slush and mud. Instead of being exasperated by the mess, bundle up your children in their boots and rain slickers and celebrate the return of warmer weather! Stir up the "goo" with sticks, fingerpaint with mud, create that classical favorite, mud pie, and when you're finished just jump in the shower (clothes and all, if necessary), and then share a mug of cocoa. A great way to end a day of mud madness is to whip together a real Chocolate Cream Pie for dessert.

Kite Day

In many places in China, a day which is traditionally celebrated in the fall is given over to kite flying. Thousands of kite flyers and observers gather on the surrounding hills to watch the spectacular kites zig-zagging and chasing each other in the sky. These kite festivals are huge affairs. In our country, most children consider the windy days of March perfect for kite flying. Why not organize a "kite flying festival" of your own? Challenge your children and their friends to create their own kites; then have a picnic and enjoy an afternoon of kite flying.

Maypoles and Baskets

In the latter part of our century, the observance of May Day had all but disappeared in the United States. It is currently making a comeback! There are more and more families and school children making May baskets and dancing around Maypoles. This festival has its roots in ancient times, when peasants would bring trees from the woods to be used as Maypoles. They would dance around the Maypole to celebrate the changing of seasons and the coming of summer. May baskets are another early tradition in which lovers

The Boy Who Didn't Believe in Spring, by Lucille Clifton. Illustrations by Brinton Turkle. Dutton Pub., NY, 1973.

A little boy named King Shabozz lives in the inner city and he doesn't believe in spring. No way! He and a friend set out to find what his teacher, his mother, and everyone around him are talking about. Just what is spring? It's not as easy to find in the crowded urban setting, but it's still there if you look. Young readers, especially young city readers, will relate to this story. (ages 6 - 10)

How Does a Kite Fly?

Have you ever wondered how a kite flies?

It is not a powered vehicle, like a plane. It is not lighter than air, like a helium balloon. While you have to "tow" it to get it started, the kite stays in the air because the age-old designs (and some exciting new ones) combine the sizes and angles of the kite's surfaces to make the air pressure under the kite (lift) greater than the drag forces (wind, gravity, weight of string, etc.) that try to drop your beautiful kite unceremoniously to the ground. Or, as usual, into a very tall tree.

"We do not inherit the Earth from our ancestors, we borrow it from our children."

RALPH WALDO EMERSON

Life Story, by Virginia Lee Burton. Houghton Mifflin and Co., NY, 1962.

In this classic book, a sequence of thirty-five colorful paintings shows the Earth from its beginning, through its various ages of sea creatures, the appearance of plants, the magnificent dinosaurs, the mammals, and finally the works of man. Although the text is appropriate for older children, very young children can "read" the pictures and see the dramatic changes and growth of our planet from the beginning of time. (ages 7 - 12)

hung baskets of flowers on their beloved's doorknob. People today are beginning to revive these old customs because they are slowly coming to see that life and love (represented by the renewal of spring) have power over the cold grip of winter.

Making a Maypole: A Maypole can be any height. Even a tree with a long, bare trunk can be used. The streamers should be made of different colored fabric (crepe paper is usually too delicate) that is about double the length of the pole. Tie all of the streamers together if desired and attach them to the top of the pole with heavy-duty string or rope.

The Maypole Dance: Assign each streamer to represent the sun, rain, or a different plant, bird, animal, or insect. Choose species of plants or animals that live in your particular area of the world. Have each child choose which "part" they will play in the dance by grabbing on to its corresponding streamer. Have the children form a circle of pairs around the pole, the outer child facing right and the inner child facing left. When the music is started, the outer circle skips to the right while the inner circle skips to the left. As they skip around, the children weave back and forth through the other dancers. When the dance is complete, the resulting braided pole will represent how the elements and every species are connected to each other on the Earth.

May Baskets: May baskets are easily made from items in your Recycle Craft Box: cardboard containers, strawberry baskets, scrap paper, etc. Fill them with homemade treats and flowers. On the morning of May 1, go around the neighborhood and hang them on people's doorknobs as a spring greeting and a sign of friendship. The traditional custom is to ring their doorbell and run, but instead you may wish to knock on their door and wish them a Happy May Day.

Here are some treats for May Baskets: Popcorn balls wrapped in waxed paper and tied with pretty ribbons; nosegays of flowers from your garden; colorful bird feathers; poems about spring written on paper, rolled up, and tied with streamers.

Summer

The Gaia Earth Festival Honoring Mother Earth

The name "Gaia" refers to the Greek goddess of Earth. As the story goes, Gaia, the Earth, came out of darkness so long ago that no one really remembers or knows when or how. She was young, and since nothing lived on her yet to keep her company, she was also very lonely. One solitary night Uranus, the Sky, rose above her. He was beautiful to behold, strewn with sparkling stars against his dark blue sky. Gaia looked up at him and immediately fell in love. They gazed upon each other and smiled, and soon they were joined in love. Young Earth then became Mother Earth, the mother of all living things. (It is from this and other creation myths that our term "Mother Earth" is derived.) The ancient Greeks loved and respected their mother, the Earth. They were thankful for all of the wonderful gifts she gave to them and in return, they praised her and made offerings to her, so that she would always care for them.

Although this is an ancient story, it still has a message for us and the children of today. We need to be aware that it is from the Earth that we receive our essential needs to continue living: air to breathe, water to drink, food to eat, and the materials to build our homes. These should not be taken for granted and we need to be thankful for these gifts. In return, we should love and respect our Earth, make offerings (such as keeping our planet and its air clean), and understand the Earth cycles that sustain our lives. Just as we celebrate the anniversary of our birth each year, it is only right that we should set aside a day to be thankful and honor our Mother, the Earth. The following activities will help you and your children to create a meaningful Gaia Earth Festival. But keep in mind that Earth Day shouldn't be a one-day, yearly event, because we live and depend on our Earth every day. Instead, we need to continue doing what we can every single day to live harmoniously with our planet and its many inhabitants.

When the Root Children Wake Up (Originally published in 1906 by Lippincott, NY.) Text by Helen Dean Fish. Illustrations by Sibylle von Olfers. Green Tiger Press, San Marcos, CA, 1988.

This enchanting picture book tells the story of the Root Children who spend the winter underground under the care of their wise Earth Mother. In the spring, she gently awakens them, and they set to work sewing new colorful gowns and painting the insects with bright spring colors. Then they scatter far and wide to spend the summer dancing through the meadow and forest as a poppy, bluebell, daisy, or cornflower. When the chill of autumn comes, they return once again to their Earth Mother who welcomes them back into their dark underground home. This is a story of nature and seasons. Young children cannot help but feel a part of these cycles and will imagine themselves as part of the story. (ages 2 - 8)

DREAM STARTER

*I*magine that you are the Earth. Your body is round like a globe. It is spinning in the cold darkness of space. Not far away there is a star. This star shines brightly on you and its heat warms your body. Your insides become hot, so hot that the rock melts and you can feel it sloshing and flowing under your skin. The melted rock bubbles and boils and occasionally pushes its way to the surface and spills out. You know that this is a volcano and you enjoy watching the hot lava spew like a fountain. The molten rock oozes over your land and cools to form mountains and ridges.

Above you float puffy clouds that are made of tiny droplets of water. These clouds become so heavy with water that they can't hold it any longer. The raindrops fall, and you can feel them thump and pat as they splash upon your land. Some of the rain seeps down through the dirt and rock, but it rains so much that the ground can't hold it all. The water tickles as it flows across the land forming rivers and streams. The deep valleys become filled until the land is dotted with lakes and surrounded by blue oceans. In these great bodies of water, many fish and other sea creatures live. Feel the rippling of the water as they swoosh their tails and swim about.

All over the rich soil of your land sprout many plants and trees. Feel the roots of these plants reaching downward into you. Their thirsty roots creep and grow as they drink the water. Many insects, birds, and animals live together among the trees and plants. One of these animals is known as a human being. These humans are very smart and there are a lot of them. They make you tingle all over as they walk, run, ride their bicycles, and drive their cars all over your land.

There are some humans that are careless and forget to put out their campfires, so some of your beautiful forests burn and the animals no longer have a place to live. Some humans dump garbage into your rivers and oceans, making the fish and other creatures sick and the water too dirty to drink. And then there are some humans who allow their smoke and pollution to poison the fresh air, making it hard to breathe. These people and their thoughtlessness make you very sad.

But then you look around and notice other human beings that love you. They know that you are sad and they are doing their best to help you. They take care of your oceans and rivers and try to clean up after the careless ones. These good people take care of your forests, so that the animals and birds will always have a place to live. As you feel these caring people walk upon your land, and tickle you with their rakes as they plant their gardens, you are happy again. You know that as long as these humans and others like them are around and continue their good work, you will always be a healthy and beautiful Earth.

Make a Globe Cake

When you think of a cake, you probably think of a flat sheet or multi-layered one. Well, this one is unique because it is globe-shaped! This cake is fun to make and will make a spectacular dessert to serve at your Mother Earth celebration.

To make a globe cake, make the cake using the recipe at right. After the two layers of the cake are cooled, sandwich together their flat sufaces with butter icing and you will have the round shape of a globe. Divide the remaining frosting into two batches and make one green and the other blue, using food coloring. Decorate the outside of the globe cake to represent Planet Earth.

To make the Butter Frosting: Blend together ⅓ cup butter and 3 cups powdered sugar. Stir in 1½ teaspoons vanilla and 2 tablespoons milk. Beat until the frosting is smooth and of spreading consistency.

If you like, you can make little flags (using toothpicks or wooden skewers and construction paper) to insert in the globe cake showing the place where you live or other places of special interest to you.

Globe Cake

4 eggs, separated
1½ cups sugar
½ cup boiling water or hot milk
1 teaspoon vanilla
1 tablespoon grated orange rind or
  2 teaspoons grated lemon rind
1½ cups sifted cake flour
¼ teaspoon salt
1½ teaspoons baking powder

Separate the eggs and beat the yolks until very thick. Add ½ cup of the sugar and beat until light. Slowly add the hot water or milk and flavoring and beat well. Sift the flour with the salt and baking powder and fold in. Beat the egg whites until foamy and slowly add the remaining sugar (1 cup). Beat until soft peaks are formed. Fold the egg whites into the egg/flour mixture just until well combined. Grease and flour two round-bottomed glass bowls. Divide the batter between them. Bake at 325° for about one hour. When the cake springs back when lightly touched and pulls from the sides, it is done. Cool on racks.

Mother Earth Pageant

Cast of Characters:

Mother Earth	Water Child
Animal Child	Cotton Child
Tree Child	Thirsty Child
Food Child	Hungry Child
Grain Child	Sick Child
	Lonely Child

Stage Setting: The stage is empty, except for a large sun affixed to the back wall with long rays radiating outward.

Costumes: Mother Earth is draped in a green and blue flowing robe. Attached to the robe are bountiful earth ornaments, such as vines, fruits, vegetables, a fish, sheaf of wheat, cotton balls, and a crown of leaves and twigs. She is holding a stuffed animal in her arms. The other players are dressed in ordinary clothing.

Curtain Opens
(For the first 15 seconds the stage is empty; then Mother Earth walks out to the middle of the stage and stands under the sun.)

Mother Earth: I am Mother Earth. Look around to see that my oceans are full of fish and many wondrous sea creatures and my lakes and streams are filled with cool water to drink. In this season of warmth and sunshine, my land is covered with green pastures, fruit-filled trees, and row after row of vegetables. My air is pure so you can see for miles from a mountaintop. In my forests, many kinds of birds and animals live in harmony. It is a wonderful world, but something is lacking. I need children to make this beautiful world complete.

(Children come in and skip around Mother Earth before settling in a semicircle at her feet.)

Mother Earth: Welcome, children, to Planet Earth. I love you and want to care and provide for you while you are here. I have many gifts to give you that will make you live happily with each other and in harmony with me.

(Mother Earth approaches each child and presents a gift.)

(to Animal Child): To you I pass along all of the animals to share the world with you and be your companions.

(To Tree Child): To you I pass along the trees to give you pure air to breath, fruit and nuts to eat, and to provide homes for you, the animals, and the birds.

(To Food Child): To you I pass along the fields and gardens full of delicious vegetables and fruits for you to eat and the rich soil in which to grow them.

(To Grain Child): To you I pass along the rolling fields of grain to feed the animals, insects and birds, and to be harvested for your bread.

(To Water Child): To you I pass along the water of the Earth to provide you with fish to eat and admire, pure water to drink, and to grow your crops.

(To Cotton Child): To you I pass along cotton to be spun into thread and made into clothing.

(To all): Remember always to help one another and to share all of these gifts that I have given to you.

(Mother Earth backs up to stand quietly under the sun. For about two minutes, all of the children, even the four with no gifts, mingle about sharing the food and water, and petting the animal. Then, on cue, one child refuses to share and turns away from the group, which starts a chain reaction. One by one, each child says "no" and turns away greedily clutching his gift until all six "gift" children are sitting in a line with their backs to the audience. Finally, only the four empty-handed children remain.)

Animal Child: No! It's mine.

Tree Child: No! It's all mine.

Food Child: Go away! You can't have any!

Grain Child: No! It's mine.

Water Child: Go away! It's mine.

Cotton Child: No! It's all mine.

(The four empty-handed children walk from child to child pleading for help, but they just shake their heads while clutching their gifts even tighter. Finally one speaks out to them.)

"The Earth is at the same time mother. She is mother of all that is natural, mother of all that is human. She is the mother of all, for contained in her are the seeds of all."

HILDEGARD OF BINGEN, 12TH CENTURY

Thirsty Child: Please listen! Mother Earth said these gifts were not for us to keep; they were given to us to share with each other.

Cotton Child: There is plenty where this came from. Just go and ask Mother Earth for more.

(So Thirsty Child walks over to Mother Earth and looks into her eyes.)

Thirsty Child: Mother Earth, I'm thirsty. Is there more clean water to drink?

Mother Earth *(shaking her head):* I'm sorry, my child. My lakes and streams have become too dirty to drink because some people are filling them with trash and chemicals. They are using water unwisely.

(Hungry Child walks over to Mother Earth.)

Hungry Child: Mother Earth, I am so hungry. In my part of the world there is not enough food to eat.

Mother Earth *(shaking her head):* I'm sorry, my child. In your part of the world there is not enough rain or rich soil to grow food because some people have used the land carelessly.

(Sick Child approaches Mother Earth.)

Sick Child: Mother Earth, I'm sick. It hurts my lungs to breathe. Please make the air clean again.

Mother Earth *(shaking her head):* I'm sorry, my child. In some places the air has become unbreathable because some people are filling it with poisons.

(Lonely Child approaches Mother Earth.)

Lonely Child: Mother Earth, in my part of the world many of the beautiful animals are gone. Please bring them back.

Mother Earth *(shaking her head):* I'm sorry, my child. In your part of the world the beautiful animals are dying out because some people are thoughtlessly destroying the animals' homes, so that they have no place to live.

(Animal Child leans over to the greedy child next to him.)

Animal Child *(spoken loudly while pointing):* Man, I am sure glad I'm not one of them.

Mother Earth: Children, everything on this Earth is connected. Whatever happens to one of you will happen to all of you. So, what will happen to the Earth now depends on you.

(Mother Earth bows her head and stands quietly. All of the children stand up and gather together in a loose semicircle, facing the audience.)

Food Child: Our Earth is in trouble and so are we. But, what can we do? *(He reaches out to the Hungry Child.)* Here, would you like something to eat?

All of the other greedy children *(opening their arms):* Yes! Here, have some!

(All of the children begin to share with one another. After a brief interaction, dialogue begins again.)

Grain Child: So what will you do to help Mother Earth?

Water Child: We don't use our water carefully. From now on I'm not going to just stand there and let the water run down the drain.

(Everyone agrees heartily, nodding their heads, and saying things like: "Yes!", "Same here!", "Me too!", or "Good idea!")

Tree Child: Our air is getting dirty. Tomorrow I'm going to ride my bike to school instead of having my mom drive me in the car. That way the exhaust from the car won't pollute the air.

Animal Child: The animals and birds are losing their homes. I'm going to plant some trees.

(Children begin to cheer and Mother Earth comes forward and gathers them in her arms.)

Mother Earth *(to the children):* I knew I could count on you. *(Now, to the audience.)* Now, I invite all of you to join with these children. Would any of you like to tell us what you will do to help Mother Earth?

(Allow members from the audience to share their commitments with the group. Or if your audience is small enough, form a commitment circle. After sharing time, close the performance by all joining hands and reciting the following chant.)

The Earth is like my Mother, *(form hands into globe shape)*
She gives me all I need. *(hold out hands as if receiving)*
I will love and care for her *(hug yourself)*
Just you wait and see! *(pretend to hold binoculars to eyes)*
Close curtain and applause.

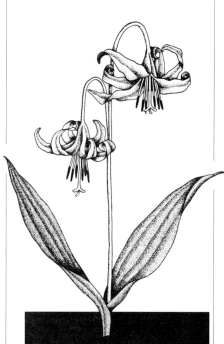

I n the end, we will conserve only what we love, we will love only what we understand, we will understand only what we teach.
BABA DIOUM

Celebrate the Full Moon

On the night of the full moon, gather your family together to watch the moon rise over the trees. Later that night, sit in a circle outdoors in the moonlight or around a picture of a full moon. Read the story *Moon Song* by Byrd Baylor to your children, recite a poem, sing a song together, and all howl at the moon before feasting on delicious moon cakes – puffy moon-shaped sugar cookies – and milk.

What Is a Blue Moon?

A full moon happens once about every 28 days. When there are two full moons in one month, the second one is called a "blue moon." This happens very rarely, hence the saying "once in a blue moon."

Take an Imagination Journey

As part of your Mother Earth Celebration, invite your children and adult guests (a group of mixed ages works best) to take a voyage away from the planet in order to "see" it better. Ask everyone to come together in a circle and in the middle of the group place a globe. (A ball can be substituted to represent the Earth.) Before you begin, explain that to prepare properly for their trip, everyone should take some time for relaxation or deep-breathing. You also might suggest that eyes be closed so that the journey inward can begin. Once the group is quiet and peaceful, the passengers are ready for departure.

Guide: Imagine that you have been chosen to become the first astronaut to make a "secret" solo flight. On the morning of lift-off, you gather together your equipment and provisions and board your spacecraft. The countdown begins: 5 - 4 - 3 - 2 - 1 - we have lift-off! You travel at an incredibly high speed through the Earth's atmosphere and beyond. Through the window of your spaceship you look back at the Earth, and as you travel farther away, it looks like a beautiful blue, green, and white marble floating in the darkness of space. All is silent as your capsule races towards the sun. After a time, you finally reach your destination, which is halfway between the Earth and sun. You slowly turn your spaceship around until you feel a glowing warmth on your back. You gaze down at the tiny blue-green Earth as it is viewed by the sun. Imagine in your mind what you see on the planet below. Think of anything you might wish to say to the Earth or the people that live on it.

(Allow about 3 - 5 minutes for the travelers to make their imaginary journey; then ask everyone to head home in their spaceships and get ready to make a report on their discoveries.)

After a minute or so, when everyone appears to have returned from their inner journeys, take the globe and pass it to each person in the circle as he or she relates a story. *(Although it is encouraged that all participants give a report, each person also has the privilege to pass, if desired. There are times, especially with adults, when some thoughts are so personal that they are not easily shared with a large group.)*

Take a Mother Earth Awareness Walk

As you and your children walk through your neighborhood, say this chant and play this "I Spy" game to discover ways to keep our planet healthy, clean, and energy efficient. And when you arrive home, be sure to put your own house through the same scrutiny.

Chant: *Who cares? Earth cares. Who cares? I care!*

As you and your children walk, chant the rhyme, count to ten or twenty, then repeat the rhyme again. When you are finished, stop. Look around and identify something nearby that aids Mother Earth or something that can be done, altered, or added to conserve precious energy or stop harmful pollution. Things you might see are: clothes hanging on a clothesline, a fruit tree, a garden, someone riding a bicycle, or trash cans that need to be put away, litter, windows that could be shielded with awnings, etc. Repeat the game often throughout the walk.

Mother Earth, May I?

This game is played like the traditional "Mother, May I?" you may remember from your childhood. But in this version there is a new twist – the players think of ways to make Mother Earth happy.

1. Choose one child to be Mother Earth and ask him or her to stand on one side of the playing area. Ask the other players to stand in a line opposite Mother Earth on the other side.

2. Starting on one end, Mother Earth calls out the names of the children one by one. When a child's name is called, he must tell Mother Earth what he will do to make her happy, such as plant a tree, ride his bicycle or walk somewhere, pick up litter in his neighborhood, turn off the faucet while brushing his teeth, take a shower instead of bath, etc.

3. After hearing his plan, Mother Earth rewards him with steps to take towards her. For example: "You may take two giant steps." The child then must be polite and ask, "Mother Earth, May I?" And he or she responds, "Yes, you may." After that, the child takes the allotted steps.

4. Continue playing in this manner until one child has reached Mother Earth. That child then becomes Mother Earth for the next game.

Coyote's Song

Tune: Twinkle, Twinkle Little Star

Young coyote in the night
Wanders alone in the moonlight.
He lifts his head and howls to
the moon,
We hear his sad and lonely tune.
And then to keep him company
Others join in harmony.
Woof, woof, woof, woooooooo!

Moon Song, by Byrd Baylor. Illustrations by Ronald Himler. Charles Scribner's Sons, NY, 1982.

In this Pima Indian legend, the mother of Coyote was the moon. But she couldn't stay with her child because she had to do the important work of pulling the tides. As she left him, Coyote ran across the hills trying to catch her, but she was always out of his reach. Now all coyotes, descendants of the first, sing the same moon song. It is a song of love and separation that haunts the darkness of night. (ages 5 - 9)

Autumn

In many parts of our beautiful country, autumn brings with it a shower of earth colors. The red, orange, and golden yellow leaves mingle with the dark brown of Earth and the rich green of the evergreens to create a spectacular scene that no artist can truly duplicate. In this season of cooler weather, the Earth seems to call to us on a whispering wind to prepare for the winter ahead. In this section, you and your children are asked to discover and celebrate whatever seasonal happenings occur in your particular area of the world. It could be a dazzling show of turning leaves, the harvesting of fruits and vegetables, incomparable autumn sunsets, or the arrival of much needed rain. Whatever the event, experience it and celebrate its coming. Although apple harvesting does not happen in all places, apples do become available in abundance in most areas so that the following story and activities can be enjoyed by almost all children.

Fall is Apple Picking Time!

There is nothing as stimulating to the senses as walking through an apple orchard where every gnarled branch and most of the dew-covered ground are covered with ripe, fragrant apples! Bite into one. You can hear the snap at the same instant you taste the tart and juicy fruit. It is a fact that apples taste best right off the branch. So, if you have a pick-your-own orchard nearby, or if there are roadside stands that offer freshly harvested apples, pack up the family for an Apple Picking Day!

Dried Apple Slices

The history of the apple in America is interesting. Before the settlers came to this country, the only type of apple in North America was the crabapple. It was very sour, so the native people didn't eat it. But the settlers brought sweet apples, seeds, or even seedlings with them from Europe. When Native Americans tasted the delicious flavor of sweet apples, they also began planting apple orchards. To the pioneers, the apple was essential for survival.

There wasn't a part of the tree they didn't use! They used the apples for eating (fresh, dried, or cooked), as food for livestock, and for making juice, cider, and vinegar to preserve certain foods. They also used the wood for making furniture, machine parts, and toys. Finally, if a tree died, they dug up the roots to burn in the cold winter. So it was no surprise that, when they moved from place to place, they took apple seeds with them. Try this recipe to make a sweet and crunchy "pioneer" snack.

1. Core and peel several apples. Cut them into rings about one-fourth inch thick. Take a long piece of string and put it through the center of the apple rings, as if you were stringing beads.

2. Hang the string of apple rings in a warm and dry place. Make certain that none of the rings touch each other so that air can flow around each one. (Good air circulation is the key to success here.)

3. Leave them hanging for about a week. Then take them down and taste a snack that your ancestors would have enjoyed. To store them, place them in a paper bag or a glass jar.

Mmmm, Applesauce!

Applesauce is a favorite of many children and is extremely easy to prepare from fresh apples. Most applesauce is a blend of two or more varieties of apples, but this is not necessary. Experiment with the ones you and your children may have harvested or chosen from a roadside stand or supermarket. Good tasting apples usually don't need additional sweetening, but sometimes a dash of cinnamon or a few drops of lemon juice adds a special touch.

1. Core, peel, and slice at least six apples. Place them in a heavy saucepan that has a tight-fitting lid. Add about one-fourth cup of water to the apples to keep them from sticking to the pan.

2. Cook over low heat until they are soft. (*Note:* An adult should supervise any cooking activity, especially one requiring the use of a stove.)

3. Let the apples cool. Then, using a potato masher or fork, mash them to the desired consistency. It usually isn't necessary, but if needed, the apples can be run through a food mill or processor to obtain a finely ground sauce.

The Seasons of Arnold's Apple Tree, by Gail Gibbons. Harcourt Brace Jovanovich, NY, 1984.

Arnold's apple tree is his own secret place and this bright and cheerfully illustrated book allows the reader to share the fragrance of its blossoms, the taste of its lovely red fruit, the gold of its leaves in autumn, and its winter-time snow-covered boughs. Throughout the year, the tree changes with the seasons, and Arnold changes the tree in his own special ways. The book also describes how a cider press works and includes a recipe for Arnold's apple pie. (ages 3 - 7)

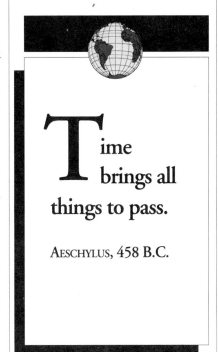

Time brings all things to pass.

Aeschylus, 458 B.C.

Apple Butter

4 pounds cooking apples (peeled, cored and sliced)

4 tablespoons butter

¾ cup sugar

2 teaspoons cinnamon

4 whole cloves

1 cup water

Place all the ingredients in a heavy saucepan. Cover and simmer over medium heat until the apples are quite soft. Remove the whole cloves. Beat the mixture until creamy. Pour into a Dutch oven or heavy ovenproof pan. Place in a 300°oven. Bake until thick, which may require several hours, stirring every 30 minutes. Cool only slightly, then pour into sterilized jars and seal.

To sterilize jars, immerse them completely in rapidly boiling water for 10 minutes. Keep hot until they are used. *To seal filled jars,* have ready enough new two-part lids for the number of jars you are filling. Follow the jar and lid manufacturer's instructions for sealing jars. Most suggest immersing the clean flat lids in boiling hot water before using. Some recommend making doubly sure of seal and sterilization by immersing the filled, sealed jars in the boiling water bath for an additional 10-15 minutes.

Apple Leather

Today there is a popular commercially prepared version of this classic treat available, but it doesn't compare with this sweet home-made fruit "leather." That there are no added sweeteners, dyes, or preservatives is another bonus. In pioneer times, this candy was prepared in the fall, set out in the sun to evaporate, then cut and hung from the kitchen ceiling. Later, during the cold winter months when sugar and honey were difficult to obtain, it was a welcome treat. It was also a favorite sweet for school lunches. Today your children can enjoy the same old-fashioned candy in their modern-day lunch boxes .

1. Preheat the oven to 400°. Pour your homemade applesauce into a greased shallow pan. Spread evenly with a spatula.

2. Place the pan in the hot oven and immediately reduce the temperature to 180°. Cook for approximately three hours until the fruit "leather" can be peeled from the pan. Cut with scissors to serve.

Thanksgiving for the Birds

When we think of Thanksgiving Day, what usually comes to our minds are family and friends, seated around a bountiful feast, commemorating the first abundant harvest of our Pilgrim fathers. There is another old "thanksgiving" custom that was observed by American Indians. It was an expressive tradition that still has meaning for all people today.

To thank the Great Spirit for a plentiful harvest in the fall, it was customary for Native Americans to hang three ears of corn and a hollowed gourd containing a few morsels and seeds outside the teepee for the birds. The corn would be hung facing the west, but the gourd (representing the fourth season) would be hung facing the south. The gourd needed the sun of summer, and by the time of the fourth season, the gourd or seeds would be all that remained to live on. When the birds came to eat the seeds, they represented Him from the heavens accepting the people's gift.

You and your children can revive this old custom by offering a "gift" to the birds in your own backyard. Make natural bird feeders (see the "Hurt No Living Thing" chapter for suggestions) and hang them in the branches of the trees as a way of saying "thank you" for the autumn harvest, because it is from this yield that your family receives food to eat during the many months before the next crops can be harvested.

Ancestor Day

In this season of thanksgiving, it is important to be appreciative of the people that came before us. They are in our blood, making us who we are today. You might not like being named after "Cousin Egbert" or be proud to have inherited a nose "just like Aunt Sue," but there is no denying the fact that we are all descended from ancestors. Have you ever looked through a pile of fading photographs, wondering who those people were and how they lived? Children have this same curiosity about the past, making their most repeated request "tell me about when you were little." These anecdotes are entertaining, but they also help to mold our spirit and develop our sense of family. As adults, we are responsible for keeping the past alive and passing this heritage to our children. When we draw our family tree, the many leaves represent our ancestors; and it is the nourishment these leaves produced that gave life to our family tree. Autumn is an excellent time for an Ancestor Celebration, one that we hope will take you and your children back to your roots and will become a tradition in your family.

Thumbing Through the Past

There really is no better way to introduce your children to their myriad of ancestors than by just sitting down with old scrapbooks, boxes of photographs, or other treasured memorabilia and talking! But instead of just rattling off a bunch of names they may have never heard, try telling a brief story about each person to make them come alive for your children. You and your family will discover that taking the lid off an old photo box can be like opening a buried treasure; it is full of old, wonderful, and priceless relics to gaze upon, touch, talk about, and enjoy!

Penny in the Road, by Katharine Wilson Precek. Illustrations by Patricia Cullen-Clark. Macmillan Pub. Co., NY, 1989.

A long time ago, in the year 1913, a boy walking down a country road in Pennsylvania spotted a penny at the bottom of a muddy puddle. It was stamped with the date 1793. Who might have dropped it? What would life have been like for that boy growing up in such a different world? What did he eat? How did he get to school? The young boy in 1913 is a grandfather in 1989 and his grandchildren wonder what life would have been like for both of these boys from long ago. Thus, this evocative story comes full circle over a span of nearly two hundred years. After reading this book, you will never be able to pick up a coin on the street again without thinking of its history and past owners. (ages 6 - 10)

To Make a Family Map

1. Adhere a United States map to cardboard. With a marker, trace your family's journey from their arrival in the United States (or earliest known location) to their present residence.

2. At key places, jot a few words to describe who lived there and what they did. For instance, "Great-grandparents arrived in New York from Germany in 1893" or "1830s - our people were forced to relocate to Oklahoma and many died along the way. The path is now known as the Trail of Tears."

3. Finally, pin small photographs of your relatives to their places of residence on the map.

Your Family Map

Think about the family get-togethers when you were a child; sometimes the house was so full of aunts, uncles, and cousins that it appeared to be bursting at the seams! It wasn't so much that families were larger then (although some were), but because people didn't move so much. If you currently live near a lot of family, you are lucky. Today, employment opportunities often scatter families across the globe. This is not a bad thing, but it can be difficult to develop a deep sense of "family" when seeing relatives only once or twice a year. If this describes your situation, give your children some background information with which to understand why they may live in California, for example, while Grandma and Grandpa live in New Mexico. Learning about your family's migration can help your child become acquainted with extended family members. You can use your family map to stay up-to-date and connected with faraway relatives by replacing older snapshots with newer ones. You might even post recently-received letters or cards on the map.

Note: Classroom groups can make "family maps" using colored tacks to show where the grandparents or parents of each child originated.

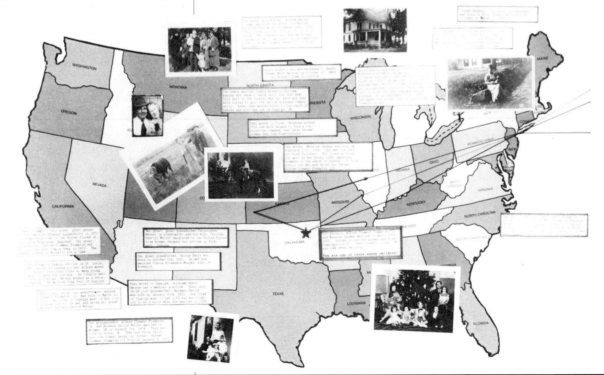

Grandma's Secret Recipes

Create a family cookbook or recipe calendar. This is a wonderful project for older children and it results in a treasured gift for family members. Help children dig through old recipe files, call older relatives for their "secret" concoctions, and record these delectable memories before they are lost. Then prepare some of the delightful morsels for your Ancestor Day party. Classroom groups can create collective cookbooks celebrating beloved family dishes contributed by all the students in the classroom.

The Hall of Inheritance

A hallway or wall clustered with old photographs lends itself to conversation. Even in the home of an acquaintance, you will stand in front of such a display and ask questions! Set aside a hallway, wall, or bulletin board in your home or classroom to display interesting old photos of past and living family members. Don't be surprised if, one day, you discover your youngster wandering down the hall, his eyes searching every photograph, before running to you with a list of questions about who was who on his family tree.

Recreating the Past

Sometimes a picture turns up of a relative whom no one recalls. Or a piece of jewelry, furniture, or other memento passed through many generations loses its "story" along the way. The memory of these people doesn't have to die away forever; you and your children can use your imaginations to recreate it. Pretend to be a modern Sherlock Holmes and deduce from what little evidence is available what kind of people they might have been: record their likes and dislikes, what they might have thought, their personalities, etc. Here is an entertaining game to get everyone involved: Sit together in a circle and examine the photographs or memorabilia. When someone has formed the beginning of a story about the forgotten relative, let that person tell it to the group. At regular intervals, pass the item to the next person in the circle. That next person must continue the story where it left off, adding his or her own interesting details to the thickening plot. When the photo or item has gone around the entire circle, the past relative will have "life" again.

The Ox-Cart Man, by Donald Hall. Illustrations by Barbara Cooney. Viking Press, NY, 1979.

This story of the ox-cart man comes originally from the oral tradition of New England. It is a perfect book to illustrate to young readers the household tasks that went along with the seasons in the early years of America. The ox-cart man packs his goods - the wool from his sheep, the shawl his wife made from the wool, the linen she had woven, the candles they made, the birch brooms his son carved, and even the goose feathers the children gathered from the barnyard geese. At Portsmouth Market he sells all of his goods (including the ox and cart), buys provisions, and carries them home on foot, so that the whole cycle can begin once again to carry the family through another year. (ages 6 - 10)

Winter

It's easy to envision how many Americans grew their own food when most people lived on farms. We can have that experience today by planting, tending, and eating the produce from a family vegetable garden. It's much harder for us to imagine what life would be like if we had to make most of the common items that we use every day around the house. Our ancestors purchased tools and the raw materials to make what they needed from peddlers, general stores, other farmers, or through catalogues. The task of making household articles was often performed in the winter months, when the families stayed inside to keep warm. Winter was often a time to repair tools and to make clothes, furniture, candles, and other necessary items that would serve throughout the year. Even though nearly everything we use today is purchased easily at supermarkets and shopping centers, children can better appreciate that we still live from the land by realizing how everyday items and favorite foods are made and by participating in the process. This harkening back to the "old ways" bonds us more closely with the Earth and what it gives to us.

100 Years Ago Today

How would it be if a time machine were actually invented? Present this idea to your children and share fantastic stories about how it could be used. If they could go back in time, what would they change about how the Earth has been cared for? Then tell them that they have been selected to travel in such a "machine" and to have the experience of living, for one day, 100 years in the past. Ask how their homes or classrooms would be different on that day 100 years ago. Ask them to list all the items that their ancestors would not have owned, such as televisions, cars, electric appliances, air conditioners or heaters, etc., many of which are causing pollution and degradation of our planet. Plan ahead and live through an entire day without any of these conveniences. Afterward, sit together and share thoughts about life, then and now.

Bread Baking

Nothing smells or tastes as delicious as a loaf of freshly baked bread. Most people opt to purchase their bread from the supermarket shelf, cold and wrapped in plastic. They miss out on the feelings of pleasure and pride that come from creating a warm, toasty loaf from scratch. It's certainly not as easy as removing a plastic wrapper, but it is only by becoming involved in the baking process that our children will learn how bread is made and begin to understand their dependence on the land.

1 package active dry yeast

1½ to 2 cups warm water (approximately 100°)

2 teaspoons granulated sugar

3¾ to 4 cups all-purpose flour

1 tablespoon salt

softened butter

First, proof the yeast, which means checking to see if it is still active. Simply pour the yeast into ½ cup warm water, add the sugar and stir well. After a few minutes, the yeast should begin to ferment. You will notice that the mixture swells slightly and small bubbles will appear on the surface.

While the yeast is proofing, measure 3¾ cups of unsifted flour into a large mixing bowl. Add the salt and blend well. Pour about ¾ cup of warm water into the flour and stir with a wooden spoon or with your hands. Add the yeast mixture and continue stirring until all of the ingredients are well blended and have formed a ball. (If the dough is stiff, add a very small amount of water and blend.) Transfer the dough to a floured surface.

It is necessary to knead the dough so that the yeast is evenly distributed throughout. Sprinkle the dough lightly with flour and dust your hands with a little more flour. Push the heel of your hand down into the dough away from you. Fold the dough over, give it a quarter turn, and push again with the heel of your hand. Continue this process of pushing, folding and turning, adding more flour if necessary, until the dough is no longer sticky and has a smooth and elastic texture. This usually takes from five to ten minutes.

Now the dough is ready for its first rising. The dough rises because the yeast produces tiny bubbles of carbon dioxide which

A Time to Keep: The Tasha Tudor Book of Holidays, by Tasha Tudor. Rand McNally and Co., NY, 1977.

In this exquisitely illustrated book, the author translates her joy in a flower, her happiness and pride in a task well done, her pleasure in the turning of the seasons, her appreciation of the traditional values of her own childhood, into a form that speaks eloquently to readers of all ages. The beautiful watercolor paintings and simple text describe the traditional holiday celebrations throughout the year in a New England household. Readers can join in the New Year's bonfire, the sugaring-off party in March, tending the new farm animals in spring, May Day, planting the garden, Midsummer's Eve in June, the Doll's Fair on Labor Day, cider making time, candle making in November, and the special events of the Christmas season. This book is full of suggestions that will help you and your children rediscover "old ways" to enhance your own traditional family celebrations. (all ages)

stretches the gluten in the flour. First, let the dough rest on the counter for a few minutes while you wash and dry the mixing bowl. Rub the bowl with softened butter, place the ball of dough inside, and turn it over so that it is completely coated with butter. Cover the bowl with a towel and place it in a warm, draft-free place. Allow the dough to rise undisturbed for 1 to 2 hours, until it is doubled in bulk. Test the dough by making an indentation with two fingers, and if the dough does not spring back, it is ready. Meanwhile, prepare your bread tin (one 9 x 5 x 3-inch or two 8 x 4 x 2-inch) by thoroughly spreading with softened butter.

Deflate the dough by pushing your fist down into the center. Transfer to a floured surface and knead for three minutes. Form the dough into a loaf shape. Let it rest for about five minutes, then place it in the prepared pan. Cover the pan and let it rise in a warm place for about 1 to 1½ hours, until doubled in size.

Set the oven for 400°. Brush the top of the dough with cold water, which will help give it a textured crust, and to prevent cracking make three diagonal slashes about one-half inch deep across the top of the loaf. Place in the center of the oven and bake for 35 minutes. After that time, test it by rapping your knuckles on the top of the loaf. It will sound hollow when it is done. Total baking time can be as long as 50 minutes. Remove the pan from the oven and invert the loaf into a towel held in one hand and test the bottom as well. If your test shows that the bottom of the loaf is still soft, return it to the pan and continue baking for five minutes, then retest. When the bread is completely baked, remove it from the pan and cool it on a wire rack for at least two hours before slicing.

Sweet Homemade Butter

You don't have to build a butter churn to enjoy the sweet taste of homemade butter. All you need is a clean container with a lid (preferably a clear glass jar so that your children can witness the transformation) and whipping cream. Take a half or full pint of whipping cream and let it warm to room temperature. Pour it into the container and secure the lid. Allow your children to take turns shaking the jar vigorously. Within a few minutes the cream will separate into two parts: butter and whey. After this happens, simply

pour off the liquid (whey). Rinse the ball of butter in very cold water to harden it slightly. Then you can immediately spread it on bread or crackers and enjoy its creamy texture. Refrigerate the rest to eat later as a spread or to use in cooking.

Creamy Cottage Cheese

Cheese-making has been known since the ancient times. Until about 100 years ago, every farm household had its own secret cheese-making recipe, so flavors and textures varied even within a small community. After processing, hard cheeses must be left to mature from one to sixteen months. On the contrary, cottage cheese can be made in a day; so even young children can experience the basic elements of cheese-making and be eating the result by the next afternoon. It is delicious served with fruit, heaped upon a baked potato, or seasoned with pepper and chives.

You will need: *1 pint milk (2% milk-fat or higher) and 1 tablespoon vinegar or lemon juice*

Heat the milk in a saucepan until it bubbles and begins to rise. Remove from heat and stir in the vinegar or lemon juice. Pour the milk into a bowl, cover with a cloth and allow to stand undisturbed for 4-12 hours (or overnight). Ladle the curds into a muslin bag or several layers of cheesecloth placed over a colander. Tie up the bag with string and hang it somewhere so that the whey can drain into a bowl for 4 hours or overnight. Resist the temptation to squeeze out all of the whey, because this will result in a dry cheese. (If desired, whey can be added to soups, stews, or cakes to aid digestion.) Remove the cottage cheese from the cloth, place it a bowl and season to taste. Store in a refrigerator for up to three days. Makes about 4 ounces.

Candy Kitchen!

It is unfortunate that candy making is not the delightful pasttime it once was, but with our busy schedules and the convenience of ready-made candies, candy made from scratch is foreign to most households. It used to be common entertainment at parties or family gatherings to pull taffy, or to make fudge or other luscious sweets. Since almost all children love candy, making it is an excel-

How Old Is Cheese?

Cheese has probably existed since about 9000 B.C., when milk-yielding animals were domesticated in the Middle East and Europe. Archaeologists have traced it back to 4000 B.C. in the records of the Sumerians, Egyptians, and Chaldeans. This almost perfect food was thought in early times to have special curative powers.

Snowball Cupcakes

2¼ cups all-purpose flour
1½ cups sugar
3½ teaspoons baking powder
1 teaspoon salt
½ cup shortening
1 cup milk
1 teaspoon vanilla
4 egg whites (½ cup)

Preheat the oven to 350°.
Prepare muffin tins by gener-
ously greasing each cup. Measure all of the ingredients, except
the egg whites, into a large
mixing bowl. Blend for ½
minute at low speed, scraping the
bowl constantly. Then beat for 2
minutes on high speed, scraping
the bowl occasionally. Add the
egg whites and beat for 2 minutes on high speed. Fill each
muffin cup one-half full and
bake for 20 minutes. Remove
from oven and let stand for five
minutes; then remove cupcakes
from pan and allow to cool
completely on a wire rack.

After the cupcakes have cooled,
spread the sides and top of each
with frosting. Then, gently roll
and dip in shredded coconut
until the frosting is completely
covered.

Frosting: Blend together ⅓ cup
softened butter and 3 cups of
powdered sugar. Stir in 1½
teaspoons vanilla and 2 tablespoons milk. Beat smooth.

lent way to show them how assorted ingredients are put together to
create a delectable end result. In the past, making candy used to be
tricky, but today, with the aid of a candy thermometer, most of the
guesswork is taken out. (Before cooking, test your thermometer by
placing it in rapidly boiling water; it should read 212° F. If it
doesn't, compensate for the difference when cooking. For instance,
if it reads 208°, subtract 4° from the temperature in the recipe.)
The following recipes make wonderful rainy day projects or special
holiday gifts for friends and family.

Have an Old-Fashioned Taffy Pull

"Taffy pulls" were a favorite form of party entertainment for
young people from the late eighteenth to the mid-twentieth centuries. This is a special winter memory-maker that's fun for the entire
family.

1½ cups light molasses
1½ cups sugar
½ cup water
1 tablespoon vinegar
¼ teaspoon salt
3 tablespoons butter
1 teaspoon vanilla

Combine the molasses, sugar, water, vinegar, and salt in a 4-quart
saucepan. Cook and stir over low heat until the sugar dissolves.
Add the butter and cook, without stirring, until the mixture boils
and reaches between 260° to 268° on the candy thermometer (hard
ball stage). Pour out onto a greased large shallow pan and after a
few minutes sprinkle with vanilla. Allow the taffy to cool for about
15 minutes or until it can be handled safely. The edges will cool
more quickly, so turn them in towards the center to form a mass.
Butter your hands. Cut off pieces of candy, then pull and twist
them until they change to a bronze color. Twist into shapes or cut
into one-inch pieces with a pair of greased scissors. Store taffy in an
air-tight container or wrap each piece in a square of waxed paper.

Popcorn Balls

You might remember seeing these in your Halloween trick-or-treat bag as a child. They taste just as good now as they did back then! Pop a large batch of popcorn and give your children the experience of molding it into chewy delicious balls. Popcorn balls also add a nice homemade touch to any Christmas tree: just wrap them in cellophane tied up with a colorful ribbon.

3 to 4 quarts of lightly salted popcorn

2 cups sugar

½ cup light corn syrup

½ cup water

2 teaspoons vanilla

butter or oil for hands

Place the popped corn in a large buttered mixing bowl. Measure the sugar, corn syrup and water into a 3-quart saucepan. Bring to a boil over medium heat, brushing down the sides of the pan with a pastry brush dipped in water to avoid sugar granules. Cook until the mixture reaches 264° to 270° on the candy thermometer (hard ball stage). Remove from heat and stir in the vanilla. Carefully pour the hot syrup over the popcorn while stirring with a long-handled spoon. Butter your hands very well. As soon as the mixture cools enough to be handled comfortably, gather some popcorn into your hands, press it into a ball, and place the ball on a greased cookie sheet. Continue with the rest of the popcorn, working as quickly as possible so that the syrup will not harden before you are finished. Makes about 12 balls. Store in an air-tight container.

Stitching Memories Together

Out of fashion or worn-out clothing doesn't need to be discarded; it is the perfect fabric for making a family (or classroom) quilt. Each article of clothing carries with it powerful memories of pleasant or sometimes sad events that are part of your family history. The piles of old baby clothes represent the passage of time and the growth of your children. So, instead of giving them away or packing them in a box and tucking them away in the attic, create a family "keeping" quilt that can be enjoyed by your own children and the generations of children to come.

The Patchwork Quilt, by Valerie Flournoy. Illustrations by Jerry Pinkley. Dial Books for Young Readers, NY, 1985.

Using scraps from the family's old clothing, Tanya helps her grandmother make a beautiful quilt that actually tells the story of her family's life - a family history alive with shared memories. The trust and sharing between a young girl and her grandmother, as well as the passing down of family memories and traditions, are rendered in this lovely story. (ages 6 - 10)

The Keeping Quilt, by Patricia Polacco. Simon and Schuster Books for Young Readers, Simon and Schuster, Inc., NY, 1988.

In this true story, a homemade quilt ties together the lives of four generations of an immigrant Jewish family. The keeping quilt is passed from mother to daughter for almost a century and is used as a Sabbath tablecloth, a wedding canopy, and a warm blanket to welcome new babies into the world. The author, who is the present caretaker of the quilt, tells the story of her own family and the quilt that remains a symbol of their enduring love and faith. (ages 4 - 9)

What If the Fudge Doesn't?

Fudge is an assured success if you use a candy thermometer, but if it doesn't "fudge," you can always add a touch of milk, melt it down, and try again!

It's Fudge Night!

On some wintry evening when it's too cold to do anything outdoors, instead of huddling around the television, pull out the saucepan and make a luscious batch of creamy fudge.

3 cups sugar

⅔ cup cocoa powder

⅛ teaspoon salt

1½ cups milk

¼ cup butter

1 teaspoon vanilla

First, butter the inside of the saucepan, especially the sides. Measure the sugar, cocoa, salt, and milk in a heavy 4-quart saucepan. Cook over medium heat, stirring gently, until the mixture comes to a boil. Then cook, without stirring, until the thermometer reaches 234° (soft ball stage). Remove from heat and add the butter and vanilla. Do not stir! Cool at room temperature to lukewarm (110°); then beat with a wooden spoon until the fudge thickens and loses its gloss. (Watch carefully at this stage because from the time it loses its gloss to hardening is rapid; too much beating will result in a crumbly texture.) Quickly spread in a buttered 8 or 9-inch square pan and cool completely, then cut.

Butterscotch Pennies

You may remember these old-fashioned butterscotch caramels that your grandmother used to make. They are one of the easiest candies to make and their chewy texture melts in your mouth.

¾ cup sugar

½ cup corn syrup (dark or light)

4 tablespoons butter (½ stick)

1 teaspoon vanilla

Measure all of the ingredients into a heavy saucepan. Cook over medium heat, stirring occasionally, until the butter melts, sugar dissolves, and the mixture boils. Then cook, without stirring, until the thermometer reaches 236° (medium/soft ball stage). Immediately remove from heat. Drop from a teaspoon into small disks onto a buttered cookie sheet. Let cool and then wrap each piece in a square of wax paper for storage.

Making Sand Candles

What child doesn't enjoy digging in the sand? Because damp sand is so easily molded, sand candles are one of the easiest types of candles to make and are especially fun for children. Since each child's mold will be different, you and your children will enjoy the variety of results. These candles make excellent gifts, too.

Caution: Since wax is a fuel and can ignite at very high temperatures, an adult should be present at every step of the candle making process.

Preparing the Sand Mold: Pour slightly damp sand into a large, deep, heat-proof mixing bowl until it is three-fourths full. Have your child use a spoon or his hands to dig a hole about the size of his fist. Help your child level the bottom of his mold so the candle will be able to stand upright. This can be done by pushing the bottom of a drinking glass into the hole. If desired, the sides (not the bottom) of the mold can be lined with small shells to add decoration to the finished candle.

Melting Wax: Take an empty one-pound coffee can and bend it on one side to form a spout. Fill the can only half full of commercially purchased paraffin or old candle stubs and set the can into a pan one-fourth filled with water. (Never place the can directly on the source of heat). Melt the wax over *very low heat.* When the wax chunks have melted completely, it is ready for an adult to pour. Do not heat the wax any further. Turn off the stove and always remember to use a potholder when handling the hot can of wax.

Making a Wick: Cut a piece of cotton twine (36-ply works well) about four to six inches longer than the depth of your mold. Dip the twine into the melted wax and lay it straight on a flat surface to harden. Or, if you prefer, wicking may be purchased at a craft store.

Pouring the Candle: When the wax is melted, an adult should very carefully fill the sand mold to one inch from the top. Let the wax cool until it is thick but still soft. Then make a hole with a pipe cleaner down the center of the candle to the bottom. Insert the wick. When the candle has cooled completely, remove it from the mold, brush off any excess sand, and trim the wick. Place the candle on a small plate and burn it only when an adult is present.

Candlemaking

Before electricity, it was essential that people make candles to light their homes after dark. Candlemaking is one of the oldest home crafts and most family members were involved in this important yearly task.

Is It True That No Two Snow-flakes Are Ever Alike?

Yes.

Probably one of the most fascinating things about snow-flakes is that each crystal forms in a slightly different way from any other, so that no two flakes look exactly alike. To encourage closeup examination of snow-flakes, take along a magnifying lens. Let your children experi-ence the feeling of melting snowflakes upon their faces and taste the delicate flavor as they land on their outstretched tongues. Under every mound is a treasure to be discovered, so allow your child the freedom to run, roll, and dig.

Make a Snowflake Mobile

After reveling in the snow, expand your child's experience by creating a snowflake mobile. Children enjoy cutting snowflakes from paper and this project will provide a unique way of displaying their handiwork. Also, it can easily be made from materials found in your Recycle Craft Box.

1. First, find a stick about one to two feet long. Holding the stick in one hand, dab white paint along the top edge to represent accumulated snow. Allow to dry completely.

2. Meanwhile, take a piece of white scrap paper and fold in half. Fold it in half again. Then, keeping the inner, folded corner as the center, fold again and possibly a fourth time. If desired, round off the corners. Cut designs in the paper, making sure that you leave some paper between each cut. Unfold, carefully press flat and you have a beautiful paper snowflake.

3. Create as many snowflakes as desired, trying to make each different from the others. With different lengths of thread, tie them to the twig or stick. Hang from the ceiling or use as a window decoration.

Have a Snow Carnival!

After a substantial snowfall, have an outdoor snow carnival. Set up target games, build snow forts, and allow your children to participate in other snow activities, such as snowman building, making snow angels, sledding, or skiing. Make a grand day of it! Afterward, dry off and share in the warmth of a freshly-made pot of hot cocoa or spiced cider.

Make a Snowbird Man

People usually experience a few setbacks or inconveniences in snowy weather, but snow has a great impact on nature. Even a couple of inches of snow can make finding food a very difficult task for many animals. One way you can assist them is to scatter some food in convenient places. Did you realize that your newly-built snowman can double as a birdfeeder? Dress him handsomely in all sorts of goodies for your feathered friends! Instead of coal, try using dates or prunes for eyes and a nose, and raisins or cranberries for a smile. Apple rings make good ears and pine cones spread with peanut butter and dipped in birdseed make tasty buttons. Have your children string popcorn, cranberries, raisins, and cereal to be hung as a belt or draped on his hat. And finally, the birds will need a place to perch, so install sturdy branches for his arms.

Old-Fashioned Maple Snowcream

Snow ice cream is one of the earliest forms of confection and was standard fare at sugaring-off parties during the maple sugaring season in pioneer days.

1. Pour about ½ cup real maple syrup into a saucepan and cook over low heat until it just begins to boil. Meanwhile, collect a large bowl full of freshly-fallen clean snow.

2. Spoon a generous amount of snow into a mixing bowl. Very gradually add the syrup, stirring constantly. As the snow melts, add more snow and stir. After all of the syrup has been added, continue adding spoonfuls of snow and toss until the syrup is evenly distributed and has frozen. The snowcream should have the consistency of shaved ice or sherbet. (If it gets too slushy, simply add more snow until it reaches your favorite consistency.) Spoon into individual serving bowls and enjoy!

Winter Solstice Celebration

The first official day of winter falls on or around the twenty-first of December. In our northern hemisphere, it is the shortest day of the year, also known as the winter solstice. This is a very important time when the sun reaches its winter house, turns around, and begins its journey back towards summer. Throughout history and across many cultures, it is one of the most important festival days of the year. It was once believed that humans needed to contribute their energy in order to coax the sun to turn. If they were not successful in pleasing the sun, it would not return and its time of light would become shorter and shorter until darkness befell the Earth. Although we now know that it is the relationship between the sun and the tilting of our planet that creates the seasonal changes, you and your children can still join the many people around the globe who continue to honor the sun and celebrate this special day with meaningful rituals and ceremonies..

First Snowflake Chant

A snowflake falls this wintry day,

I welcome you and shout, "Hooray!"

Midnight Snowman, by Caroline F. Bauer. Illustrations by Catherine Stock. Atheneum, NY, 1987.

In a town where it hardly ever snows, one neighborhood's children and parents take advantage of a late night snow by building a gigantic snowman before the snow turns to rain and melts away. Young readers will share in the excitement and fun as the whole neighborhood gets involved in the project. This charming story is an excellent example of how people can spontaneously celebrate a special natural happening by just going outside and joyfully experiencing the moment before it is gone forever. (ages 4 - 8)

Rainbow Crow, retold by Nancy Van Laan. Illustrations by Beatriz Videl. Alfred A. Knopf, NY, 1989.

This wonderful Lenape Indian tale tells of a time before man when the first snowfall threatens to engulf all of the animals. Someone must go and tell the Great Sky Spirit of their plight. Finally, Rainbow Crow, the most beautiful bird on Earth, says he will be the messenger. The Great Spirit says it cannot stop the snow, but gives the bird the gift of fire to warm the Earth and melt the snow. As he flies with the fire, Rainbow Crow's feathers are blackened with soot and the blowing ashes cause his voice to become cracked and hoarse. By the time he returns to Earth, he is no longer beautiful. But, he saves his animal friends and is well rewarded for his bravery by the Great Spirit in surprising ways. (ages 6 - 10)

Fire Ceremony in Honor of the Sun

In ancient times, some people lit huge bonfires to encourage the sun to continue shining on the Earth through the winter. Although the next few months were still very cold, the winter solstice was a celebration of hope that the return of the sun would eventually bring the warmer weather of spring. During this dark time of the year, you and your children can take part in your own Fire Ceremony to acknowledge the importance of the sun in your lives.

Preparation for the Ceremony:

1. Prepare your children by dressing each one in a simple white vestment (a long rectangular piece of cloth with a hole in the middle for the head). Using face make-up, paint a yellow circle on each child's forehead and two yellow rays on each cheek to represent the sun. Give each child a small candle, stuck into a cardboard drip-catcher, to hold during the ceremony. *(Note: The children should never be left unattended with their candles.)* Teach the children their part of the ceremony. When they hear a bell or bong, they say, "We are children of the sun."

2. The reader (an adult) should be dressed similarly, but instead of face make-up, might wear a yellow circle glued to a headband to represent the sun. Rays of sunshine can be painted on cheeks. A larger lighted candle, in a drip-catcher, is held throughout the ceremony.

3. Just before beginning, prepare a plate of apple slices (any fruit or vegetable can be substituted) and place it conveniently nearby. A bell, triangle or gong will be needed to cue the children.

(Have the children quietly file into a dimly lit room and stand in a semicircle around the reader. Children should stand a small distance from each other with their candles held out in front of their bodies.)

Reader: Tonight, the longest night of the year, we join with people all over the world to speak to the sun as it makes a turn back towards its summer house. *(ring the bell)*

All: We are children of the sun.

Reader: The sun is the basis of all life on Earth. The plants capture rays of sunshine to live and grow. *(Offer a section of apple to each person.)* Within this food the sun lives. Taste the goodness of the sun. *(eat apple slice)*

We thank you, sun, for the life and warmth you bring to the Earth. We wish you a good journey back to your summer home. *(ring the bell)*

All: We are children of the sun.

Reader: I will ask each of you to come forward and name one thing the sun has done for you. As a symbol of thanks, you may light your candle and take a piece of the sun with you.

(Call each person forward. Each names something about the sun he or she is thankful for, then lights his or her candle from the reader's candle.)

Reader: *(repeating as each participant lights a candle)*: You are a child of the sun.

(Sing "The Winter Solstice Song" or play a recording of "Here Comes the Sun" by the Beatles [ABBEY ROAD album] and then have everyone blow out their candles.)

Before you light a fire in your fireplace (or outdoor bonfire), hold up a log and say, "Energy from the sun has been stored in the fibers of this wood for hundreds of years. We are going to set it free. Watch as the flames reach toward the sky, asking the sun to stay with us a bit longer each day until it reaches its summer house."

Fire-Baked Apples

To conclude your evening's celebration, cook apples in the glowing embers of the fireplace. Using an apple corer or paring knife, cut out the core without going all the way through the apple. Fill the opening with a small amount of butter, sugar and cinnamon. Wrap each apple securely in foil and place it in the embers of the fire. After about 20-30 minutes, carefully remove the apples and unwrap them. Be careful – the filling will be very hot! If desired, serve with vanilla ice cream. The combination of hot apple and cold ice cream represents the warmth of the sun that will eventually melt the snows of winter.

The Winter Solstice Song

Tune: Mary Had a Little Lamb

We are thankful for the sun,

Its golden rays touch everyone.

We are thankful for the sun,

On this longest night.

Without it there would not be,

Grass and trees, or you and me.

We are children of the sun,

Each and every one.

More Books To Share With Children

Around the Year by Tasha Tudor. Oxford University Press, NY, 1957. Discover the seasonal joys and holidays of yesterday. This exquisitely illustrated book depicts children engaged in all kinds of seasonal activities and celebrations. (all ages)

The Wisewoman's Sacred Wheel of the Year by Naomi Strichartz. Illustrations by Ella Moore. Printed by The Grapevine Press Inc., Ithaca, NY. Available in a paperback edition through Cranehill Press, 708 Comfort Road, Spencer, NY, 14883. This delightful book contains stories about a special woman who shares her fascination of nature with two young children that live on a nearby farm. Together they celebrate the Earth's seasonal changes and some not-so-traditional holidays. (age 4 and up)

Children of the Forest by Elsa Beskow. Floris Books, 21 Napier Road, Edinburgh EH10 5A2, 1982. Deep in the roots of an old pine tree live the children of the forest. Playing hide-and-seek with the squirrels, snowballing in the winter, each season brings its own adventures. This book provides a look at how all of nature can work together in a spirit of cooperation. (ages 4 - 8)

January Brings the Snow: A Seasonal Hide and Seek by Elizabeth Falconer and Sara Coleridge. Franklin Watts, NY, 1989. Two stories are interwoven in one ingeniously designed book based on Sara Coleridge's beloved classic poem. In the first, a little girl and boy discover the joys of each month. Then, when the flaps are lifted, there appears a second picture story of a fieldmouse family enjoying the seasons in their own way. (ages 3 - 7)

Winter and *Spring* by Ron Hirschi. Color photos by Thomas D. Mangelsen. Cobblehill Books, NY, 1990.

These beautiful books are designed to open the youngest eyes to nature's wonders. (ages 3 - 7)

Seasons by Warabé Aska. With poetry selected by Alberto Manguel. Doubleday, NY, 1990. In a stunning book with universal appeal, Warabé Aska has captured the joy and magic of the four seasons. His vivid, playful and often fantastic paintings will delight both children and adults. (all ages)

The Big Snow by Berta and Elmer Hader. Macmillan Pub. Co., NY, 1948. (New edition, 1976) This lovely book tells what happens to the forest animals and birds when the geese begin to fly south. Each creature knows this is a sign to get ready for winter, and each does so in its own particular way. (ages 5 - 8)

A Child's Book of Seasons by Satomi Ichikawa. Parents' Magazine Press, NY, 1975. With enchantingly delicate illustrations, the author shows children engaged in the activities of every season, from one winter to the next. (ages 3 - 6)

Suzette and Nicholas and the Seasons Clock by Satomi Ichikawa. Philomel Books, NY, 1978. (Translated from the French by Joan Chevalier) Suzette makes a "seasons clock" in school. When she turns the hand around, the seasons change one into the other. The clock moves around the year with wonderful nature activities for the children to enjoy in each season. (ages 5 - 8)

The First Snowfall by Anne and Harlow Rockwell. Macmillan Pub. Co., NY, 1987. The very young reader will enjoy sharing the special sights and activities that go with the first snowfall of the year in this brightly illustrated book. (ages 3 - 5)

Seasons by Melvin Berger. Illustrations by Ron Jones. Doubleday, NY, 1990. This beautifully illustrated book describes in simple text the changing of the seasons and the effect these changes have on the Earth and all its creatures. (ages 8 - 12)

Autumn Harvest **by Alvin Tresselt.** Illustrations by Roger Duvoisin. Lothrop, Lee, and Shepard, NY, 1951. This book captures all the wonderful sights and sounds of autumn in the country, from the first song of the katydid to a family's big Thanksgiving feast. (ages 6 - 9)

Earth Circles **by Sandra Ure Griffin.** Walker and Co., NY, 1989. One bright spring morning a mother and daughter walk to the top of a hill near their home. Along the way they discover a never-ending world of rising sun, falling seeds, and tugging ocean tides. They listen to the "circle songs" of the Earth, songs that reveal the wonder of nature's life cycles. (all ages)

Sing a Song of Seasons **compiled by Linda Jennings.** Illustrations by Sally Gregory. Hodder and Stoughton, London, 1985. This is a collection of classic poems that expresses feelings of joy and curiosity through the works of poets such as Stevenson, Wordsworth, Blake, and Browning. (ages 5 - 9)

The Year at Maple Hill Farm **by Alice and Martin Provensen.** Atheneum, NY, 1984. Animals don't know about years but they do know about seasons. People, animals, and plants are shown in this delightful book as they all change throughout a year on the farm. (ages 4 - 7)

Seasons on the Farm, **by Jane Miller.** Prentice-Hall Books for Young Readers, NY, 1986. In beautiful color photographs, this book portrays activities on the farm and the farm animals throughout the four seasons. (ages 3 - 6)

Magical Hands **by Marjorie Barker.** Illustrations by Yoshi. Picture Book Studio, Saxonville, MA, 1989. This is an unusual book about the real meaning of birthdays and friendship. This story runs through the course of a year and the birthdays of four friends. It is rich in detail and focuses on the wholesome values of small town life in the years gone by. (ages 8 - 12)

Happy Birthday! A Book of Birthday Celebrations **by Satomi Ichikawa.** Text by Elizabeth Laird. Philomel Books, NY, 1987. This beautifully illustrated book follows a year of different birthday celebrations in a little girl's life and describes how birthdays are celebrated around the world. (ages 5 - 8)

The Day I Was Born **by Marjorie and Mitchell Sharmat.** Illustrations by Diane Dawson. E. P. Dutton, NY, 1980. Although lighthearted, this book focuses on what a birthday is really about - the day a child was born. (ages 4 - 8)

Indian Festivals **by Paul Showers.** Illustrations by Lorence Bjorklund. Thomas Y. Crowell Co., NY, 1969. In the United States today there are many Indian tribes, each with its own ancient customs and celebrations, most of which reflect the Native American's reverence for the Earth. This little book explains these celebrations in a simple text that children can understand. (ages 6 - 9)

Festivals **by Beverley Birch.** Silver Burdett Co., Morristown, NJ, 1986. People all over the world look forward to the coming of spring, a good harvest, or the traditions of their religious beliefs. This book is a good introduction to festivals throughout the world and it may give you some ideas about celebrating within your own family. (ages 8 - 12)

Festivals Around the World **by Philip Steele.** Dillon Press, Minneapolis, MN, 1986. Simple text and colorful full-spread photographs describe festivals from all over the world: Africa, Asia, Europe, Russia, and the United States. (ages 6 - 10)

Yonder **by Tony Johnston.** Illustrations by Lloyd Bloom. Dial Books for Young Readers, NY, 1988. Come and visit a time and place, somewhere in the nineteenth century, where one family's life began — yonder. The story begins with a young farmer putting down roots, building a cabin, and planting a plum tree.

The farmer grows old, as does the plum tree, but along the way the reader can take part in a time when life was much more simple and more connected to the Earth. (ages 5 - 9)

Home Place by **Crescent Dragonwagon.** Illustrations by Jerry Pinkney. Macmillan Pub. Co., NY, 1990. A family out on a hike comes upon the site of an old ruined house. After searching for clues, they find a piece of china plate, a doll's arm, a round blue marble, a horseshoe, and a small yellow bottle. From these artifacts the timeless place and long ago family who lived there leap to life. (age 7 and up)

People of the Breaking Day by **Marcia Sewell.** Atheneum, NY, 1990. This lovely book recreates the world of the Wampanoag Indians as they lived on Cape Cod before the Europeans arrived. It tells of the people's oneness with the natural world, their ceremonies, and their sense of community. (age 8 and up)

Sarah Morton's Day: A Day in the Life of a Pilgrim Girl by **Kate Waters.** Photographs by Russ Kendall. Scholastic, NY, 1989. The text and photographs of Plymouth Plantation follow a pilgrim girl through a typical day as she milks the goats, cooks and serves meals, and learns her letters. (ages 6 - 9)

My Prairie Year by **Brett Harvey.** Illustrations by Deborah Kogan Ray. Holiday House, NY, 1986. This story is based on the diary of the author's grandmother who was nine years old in 1889 when her family moved from Maine to a homestead in the Dakota Territory. Young readers will be fascinated with the very different way of life this book portrays, a way closely aligned to the changes of the seasons. (ages 6 - 10)

Family Farm text and paintings by **Thomas Locker.** Dial Books, NY, 1988. This is an appealing story of one year on a farm in the heartland of America. Thomas Locker's remarkable paintings render the beauty of the changing seasons and the expressive text effectively tells of one American family's year. (ages 6 - 10)

Snow Toward Evening: A Year in a River Valley **paintings by Thomas Locker.** Poems selected by Josette Frank. Dial Books, NY, 1990. This book features a well-loved poem and a museum-quality painting for each month of the year. (age 5 and up)

Hannah's Farm: The Seasons on an Early American Homestead **written and illustrated with wood engravings by Michael McCurdy.** Holiday House, NY, 1988. As the seasons roll by, all the members of Hannah's family engage in activities on their farm in the Berkshire Hills of Massachusetts. (ages 6 - 10)

Linnea's Almanac by **Christina Bjork.** Illustrations by Lena Anderson. R & S Books, distributed by Farrar, Straus & Giroux, NY, 1989. Linnea is a girl named after the linnaea - a little pink woodland flower. But she doesn't live in the woods; she lives right in the middle of the city. Linnea has written her own almanac where she keeps track of her indoor and outdoor activities through the seasons. (ages 6 - 10)

Bread, Bread, Bread by **Ann Morris.** Photographs by Ken Heyman. Lothrop, Lee and Shepard Books, NY, 1989. Through stunning photographs and simple text, this book celebrates the many different kinds of breads that can be found around the world and how they can be enjoyed. (ages 3 - 7)

Sugaring Time by **Kathryn Lasky.** Aladdin Books, Macmillan Pub. Co., NY, 1986. Go with the Lacey family to the sugarbush and tap the sap from the maple trees. Then follow the step by step process as it is boiled into delicious maple syrup and enjoy one of the lovely gifts of the Earth. (ages 8 - 12)

The Quilt Story by **Tony Johnston.** Illustrations by Tomie de Paola. G. P. Putnam's Sons, NY, 1985. A pioneer mother lovingly stitches a beautiful quilt decorated with falling stars. She gives it to her daughter to warm and comfort her through many years. Many generations later, another little girl finds the old quilt tucked away in the attic. (ages 4 - 7)

Patchwork Tales by Susan L. Roth and Ruth Phang. Atheneum, NY, 1984. It's bedtime and a little girl asks her grandmother to tell her the patchwork quilt stories. So grandma tells how one patch reminds her of her wedding, another of the things the little girl's mother did as a child, and so on. For those that want to create their own memory quilt, there are instructions at the end of the book for a beginner's quilt. (ages 5 - 8)

Ring of Earth by Jane Yolen. Illustrations by John Wallner. Harcourt Brace Jovanovich Pub., NY, 1986. The four seasons are viewed in poetry and illustrated in rich, watercolor paintings. (read aloud - age 8 and up)

Under Your Feet by Joanne Ryder. Illustrations by Dennis Nolan. Macmillan Pub. Co., Four Winds Press, NY, 1990. This is a collection of poems about nature and wildlife, spanning all the seasons of the year. (ages 5 - 9)

Turtle in July by Marilyn Singer. Illustrations by Jerry Pinkney. Macmillan Pub. Co., 1989. This book of poetry relates, from the animals' point of view, what they are doing in a particular season. These evocative verses bring the natural world vividly to life. (all ages)

Voices on the Wind—Poems for All Seasons selected by David Booth. Illustrations by Michelle Lemieux. Morrow, NY, 1990. Readers will sail through the seasons on winds of poetry in this delightful anthology. Some of the poets included are William Blake, Beatrix Potter, John Ciardi, and Jack Prelutsky. (ages 5 - 9)

Resources for Parents and Teachers

Earth Festivals: Seasonal Celebrations for Everyone Young and Old by Dolores LaChapelle and Janet Bourque. Illustrations by Randy LaChapelle. Finn Hill Arts,

Publishers. P.O. Box 542, Silverton, CO 81433, 1973. (Although this book is out of print, a xeroxed copy can be ordered from the publisher.) *Earth Festivals* suggests many celebrations and rituals dealing with the spring and autumn equinox, the web of life, the energy cycle, the vegetation cycle, and festivals for the celebration of the solstices.

Earth Wisdom by Dolores LaChapelle. Finn Hill Arts, Silverton, Colorado, 1978. This fascinating book touches many aspects of seasonal ritual and bioregionalism. Her book, *Sacred Land* (Finn Hill, 1988), offers one of the most complete studies of these topics.

Seasonal Stories for Family Festivals by Armandine Kelly. Resource Publication, Inc., San Jose, CA, 1987. This collection tells the original stories behind well known holidays and feasts as well as some not-so-famous ones, such as a Spring Equinox Festival or the Spring Festival of Venus.

The Book of Festivals and Holidays the World Over by Marguerite Ickis. Illustrations by Richard E. Howard. Dodd, Mead & Company, New York, 1970.

The Long Ago Lake: A Book of Nature Lore and Crafts by Marne Wilkins. Illustrations by Martha Weston. Chronicle Books, San Francisco, 1989. The joys of childhood summers are lovingly recollected in this rich volume of nature lore and crafts, many borrowed from the author's Chippewa Indian neighbors.

Children's Experience of Place by Roger Hart. Irvington Pub. Inc., NY, 1979. (Distributed by John Wiley and Sons.)

The Ecology of Imagination in Childhood by Edith Cobb. Columbia University Press, 1977. This classic book deals with the idea that a truly cosmic relationship with the Earth lies at the root of all human development.

The Magical Child by Joseph Chilton Pearce. E. P. Dutton, NY, 1977.

Festivals is a bimonthly journal focused on personal and communal transformation through ritual, celebration, and festivity. Write: 160 E. Virginia Street, Suite 290, San Jose, CA 95112.

In Tune With the World: a Theory of Festivity by Josef Pieper. Harcourt, Brace and World, NY, 1965.

Ceremony by Leslie Mormon Silko. Viking Press, NY, 1977. (Also Penguin, NY, 1987). This is an extraordinary novel, a "telling" in the Native American tradition of the healing that is possible through ritual.

Seasonal Feasts and Festivals by E. O. James. Barnes and Noble Publishers, London, 1961.

Seven Arrows by Hyemeyohsts Storm. Harper and Row, NY, 1972. An essential book for those desiring a deeper insight into Native American ritual and inner vision.

The Old Ways by Gary Snyder. City Lights Books, San Francisco, 1977.

Black Elk Speaks by John Neihardt. University of Nebraska Press, Lincoln, 1961. This book provides an important source for beginning to understand the spiritual values of the Native American.

A Sand County Almanac by Aldo Leopold. Oxford University Press, NY, 1966. These essays offer excellent insights into the interrelationship of all things on the Earth.

A Sense of the Earth by David Leveson. Natural History Press, NY, 1972. A combination of poetic and scientific writing about the relationship of man to the forms of the Earth.

Pilgrim at Tinker Creek by Annie Dillard. Harper Magazine Press, 1974. The author writes movingly of her deep relationship to her place on the planet.

The Secret Life of Plants by Peter Tomkins and Christopher Bryd. Harper & Row, 1973. This entertaining book provides a study of the relationship of man and plants in the vegetation cycle.

The Sacred Pipe: Black Elk's Account of the Seven Rites of the Oglala Sioux by Joseph Epes Brown. University of Oklahoma Press, Norman, 1953.

Festivals, Family, and Food by Diana Carey and Judy Large. Illustrations by Cornelie Morris and Sylvia Mehta. Hawthorne Press, Gloucestershire, England, 1982. The underlying theme of this excellent book is that if celebrating festivals was formerly the focus of community life, then rediscovered in the modern context, such seasonal festivals should greatly enhance our lives.

Let's Make a Memory by Gloria Gaither and Shirley Dobson. Illustrations by Russ Flint. Word Publishing, Dallas, 1983. This book offers many ideas for keeping memories alive through activities for holidays and special family occasions.

Festivals With Children by Brigitte Borg. Floris Books, Edinburgh, Scotland, 1984. The author describes the nature and character of the years' festivals, their symbols and customs, and offers practical suggestions for celebrating these in the family.

Follow the Year: A Celebration of Family Holidays by Mala Powers. Illustrations by Frances E. Livens. Harper & Row, Publisher, San Francisco, 1985.

For ideas about how to give to the Earth this holiday season read *The First Green Christmas: How to Make This Holiday an Ecological Celebration.* Available from the Evergreen Alliance, Halo Books, P. O. Box 2529, San Francisco, CA 94126.

The Amazing Apple Book by Paulette Bourgeois. Illustrations by Linda Hendry. Addison-Wesley Publishing Co., Inc., NY, 1987. This book describes, in simple text and illustrations, the history, cultivation, and many uses and activities to do with apples. Perfect if you plan a fall apple festival!

James Beard's American Cookery by James Beard. Illustrations by Earl Thollander. Little, Brown and Company, Boston, 1972. This is the perfect cookbook to use when looking for recipes from earlier times along with some of the lore that goes along with them.

Candles for Beginners To Make by Alice Gilbreath. Illustrations by Jenni Oliver. William Morrow and Co., NY, 1975. Provides detailed safety precautions and instructions for making a variety of candles in designs that will appeal to young children.

Foxfire is a quarterly publication concerned with researching, recording, and preserving Appalachian traditions. A typical issue contains articles on quilting, soap making, home remedies, regional poetry and book reviews. *Foxfire* also publishes *Hands On: a Journal for Teachers,* and produces tapes of folk music. All from The Foxfire Fund, Inc., P.O. Box B, Rabun Gap, GA 30568. Of special interest in the series is *A Foxfire Christmas,* ed. by Eliot Wigginton, Doubleday, NY, 1989.

Voluntary Simplicity: Toward a Way of Life that is Outwardly Simple, Inwardly Rich by Duane Elgin. William Morrow & Co., NY, 1981. This book points out that as we live more simply, we find it easier to bring our undivided attention to our passage through life, and thereby are enabled to live more consciously.

Wonders in a Garden

Does your child need an invitation to dig in the dirt? Most likely, the answer is no. Young children are fascinated by the natural world and take every opportunity to dig right in! Sit back and watch your children interact with the growing things around them. Their curiosity is so strong that they will observe, poke, pull, and dissect in order to satisfy their need to know. You can harness this inquisitiveness about how things grow and encourage a kinship between your children and plant life by engaging in some hands-on activities with soil, seeds, and plants. Teaching your children to respect the Earth through growing things is one of the greatest treasures you can give them. And as their gardening mentor, you will find it exciting to witness their growth in understanding.

There are many ways to garden, from planting a window box to cultivating a vegetable plot in

The Tiny Seed, by Eric Carle. Picture Book Studio, Saxonville, MA, 1987.

Dazzling, colorful, collage illustrations and simple, but dramatic text tell the story of the life cycle of a flower in terms of the adventures of a tiny seed. The life journey is perilous and the little seed has many close calls but keeps going all the while as the reader cheers it on. They will long remember the message of the tiny seed's perseverance in the face of many obstacles until its final joyful success. This story puts the child directly into the cycle of plant life in an extremely imaginative way. (ages 3 - 8)

the backyard. So whether you live in a city or in the country, you can discover a gardening arrangement to fit your lifestyle. If you were not born with two green thumbs – don't panic! The point of gardening with children is not an abundant, award-winning harvest, but the privilege of witnessing and taking part in the miracle of growth. It is a family activity that you can share in the fresh air and warm sunshine. It will provide fun, healthy exercise for everyone, and it will teach your children about the seasons, the cycles of plants, and food production. So, roll up your sleeves, pull on your gardening gloves, and dig in!

Seeds

What Is a Seed?

Take a moment and think about seeds. Seeds are everywhere! They are there when you bite into a juicy apple, they float through the air on a windy day, and they stick to your dog's fur when he frolics through tall grass. They come in different shapes, sizes, and packaging. Here are some enjoyable suggestions for seed gathering, so you and your child can take a closer look.

1. A Seed Collector: Take an old tube sock or nylon stocking and fill it with crumpled newspaper. Tie a long string to one end. Drag your collector through a field or across a forest floor. The seeds will stick to the surface of the sock which can be examined more closely with a magnifying lens.

2. Sprouting Your Socks: Let your child pull an old pair of tube socks over his shoes, then run through tall grass and brush to collect seeds. The socks can be carefully removed and their ends placed in a pan of water. Put the pan and socks in a warm place. The water will creep up the socks to moisten them and after a week or two the socks will sprout!

3. A Sheet Harvester. To gather seeds from a tree, spread an old sheet under its branches when the seeds are ripe and ready to fall. Shake the branches of the tree gently and a shower of nuts or seed pods should fill your harvester.

4. Pod Gathering. In autumn, milkweed pods open and send their seeds flying in the wind. In late fall, cattails bordering ponds and marshes burst and puff, sending out their seeds. Collect some samples of these before they burst and examine them. Guess how many seeds are in a milkweed pod, then have your child help you count them out into piles of ten. How close is your estimate to the actual number?

"From Here to There" Matching Game

Many seeds are designed to MOVE! Some hitch a ride on a passerby, some twirl or glide, some are eaten by birds and are deposited miles from the parent plant, and some are carried away by animals. This game will help your children become more aware of "seeds on the go."

Prepare a Seed Grab Bag from the plants in your backyard or playground, with at least one example from each category (if possible). Allow each child to choose a seed from the bag and determine its "method of moving," then ask him to go hunting for the parent plant. (Older children may be asked to find another seed that moves in the same fashion.)

Hitchhikers: cockleburs, sand burrs, and burdocks

Twirlers: ash, elm, and maple

Gliders (or Parachutists): dandelion, milkweed, and thistle

Edibles: apples, cherries, berries, figs, pears, nuts, etc.

After reading *The Tiny Seed* by Eric Carle and playing this matching game, have your children write and illustrate an adventure story about their seeds and how they travel from the parent plant to an eventual "home." (If your child is too young to write an elaborate story, have him dictate the story as you write the words under his picture.)

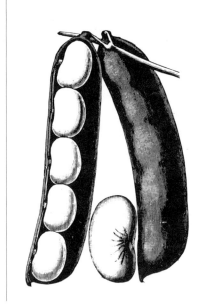

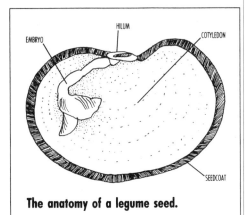

The anatomy of a legume seed.

Sprout a Nest

The building materials that birds use to construct their nests are varied and quite ingenious. Children are intrigued by animal homes and will enjoy having a closer look. Try this interesting experiment, as the results may surprise you!

After the leaves have fallen from the trees in late fall, bird nests are easily spotted in the branches. Since most birds build new nests every year, you are welcome to take any you find. When approaching an abandoned nest, however, check first for signs of a new occupant (such as a mouse or insects) and leave the nest undisturbed if it is someone's home. Using a magnifying glass, look closely at the items used for building. You might see bits of yarn, string, or paper, grass, twigs, feathers, leaves, and mud. Notice how the nest is intricately woven together. Do you see any seeds the birds may have used in building or eaten while nesting?

After examining the nest, try this experiment: place the nest in a shallow container lined with plastic, such as a bowl or baking pan. Water the nest and place it in a warm spot. It will be necessary to keep the nest moist and, within a week or two, any seeds will sprout and begin to grow!

The Plant Within the Seed

If your child has never had any experience with growing plants, their appearance from a planted seed may seem like "magic" to him. This is a very basic experiment that will help explain the germination process to even the youngest observer.

1. Dry Beans: Look closely at lima or other dried beans. What do you see? How do they feel? (They will be hard and flat with an oval-like shape. They have a pale coating or skin than sometimes can be seen flaking off.) Take five of your beans and lay them side by side on a small piece of paper. Trace around them with a pencil.

2. Soak Your Beans: Place your five beans in a cup and cover them with ½ cup water. Leave them to soak overnight. Arrange the soaked beans on your paper in the same fashion as when they were dried. How are they different from the day before? (They are bigger.) Measure the remaining water in a measuring cup. How much water was absorbed by the beans?

3. What's Inside?: Very gently, peel the seed coat from one of your beans. Open the bean into two halves; these lobes are the food for the plant until it grows green leaves and can make food for itself. Look closely for the tiny plant, called an embryo, that is resting inside the bean waiting to grow. With a magnifying lens, you can see the tiny root, stem, and two leaves. Take two of your remaining beans and place them in a seed viewer (see next activity) and plant the other two in a cup or pot of potting soil. Watch them over the next week to see what happens.

Make a Seed Viewer

Help your children make this simple seed viewer so that they can observe the process of germination day by day. While two seeds are germinating in the seed viewer, plant the remaining two seeds in a cup or pot of potting soil. Water both cups and place them in a warm spot. The seed viewer will allow your child to actually see what is happening to the seeds under the soil!

1. Take a glass jar or clear plastic cup and line the inside with construction paper.

2. Place two of your bean seeds between the glass and construction paper.

3. Fill the empty center of the jar with paper towels and wet thoroughly until the construction paper has been moistened also.

4. Place in a warm spot and add water daily.

5. Watch your seeds to see how they grow. What emerges first, the root or the leaves? (the root) Which way does the root grow? (down) Do your seeds need light? Place them in a warm and dark place and observe what happens. (At this stage, they do not need light to grow.) About the time your seeds in the viewer send forth leaves, you will notice the stem and leaves sprouting from the seeds in the soil.

To Be a Seed

A dormant seed, one that has been lying in the cold, winter soil for months, is gently touched by the warmth of spring. Its new life is released and it begins to grow! Only once did you have this experience of awakening with new life and growing into consciousness,

> *"It is important that you know you are planting seeds even if you don't see them bloom."*
> VIVIENNE VERDON-ROE

but you were probably too small to remember! Have your children pretend to be seeds, curled up and silent in the cold Earth. Lower the lights in the room and read this story. Ask them to listen carefully and act out what happens.

The Earth that surrounds you is frozen solid. Above the ground, the winter winds are blowing snow all around and it piles in drifts above you. You don't notice it because you are deeply asleep. Several months pass and the harsh wind turns into a light breeze. Instead of gray clouds, the golden sun brightens the sky. The ground begins to absorb the warm rays of sunshine and the snow begins to melt and slowly seep into the Earth. The moisture touches you and you begin to drink it in. You are so thirsty that you drink until you are puffed with water! Your coat softens and splits as you swell. The soil becomes warm from the sun and you can feel its heat. You begin to tremble and tingle as the warmth awakens you from your slumber. Very slowly, your tiny root reaches into the soil to absorb more water. It digs straight down, growing longer and longer each day. You drink the water and eat the food from your seed lobes, and soon you are strong enough to push your tiny stem and leaves through the ground into the bright daylight. *(Brighten the lights in the room.)* Your two little leaves spread open and catch the warmth from the sun. You no longer need the food from your seed, because you can make your own! Your green leaves combine the water from the Earth and the energy from the sun to make delicious sugar and starch for your growing body. With each day, you grow bigger and stronger!

In the hot, summer sunshine, you grow into a beautiful flower. The honeybees come to visit, tickling your petals with their tiny legs and fluttery wings. Some of your pollen sticks to their furry bodies and as they turn to leave, they brush off some of the pollen they have collected from other flowers. A couple of weeks go by and you begin to weaken. Your colorful petals droop and finally fall to the ground. You soon begin to wilt and slowly sink toward the Earth, taking your newly formed seeds with you.

The cooler autumn winds begin to blow and you are soon covered with dry leaves and dirt. The ground begins to get hard and cold, so you know it's time again for a winter's rest.

Build a Plant Game

This game is easy to make using construction paper and other scraps from your Recycle Craft Box. Your children will enjoy putting it together as much as playing it!

Each player will need: a light blue piece of construction paper, a tiny seed cut from scrap paper, a brown crayon, roots (cut from scrap felt or paper), a 4-inch piece of green pipe cleaner, two leaves, flower head (these can either be taken from discarded silk flowers or cut from construction paper), a sun and a rain cloud (cut from construction paper).

To Make the Game:

1. Take the blue construction paper and color the bottom half brown (blue for sky, brown for Earth). Glue the seed in the brown "Earth." This is your game board. Make a board for each player.

2. Make a chart on a piece of scrap cardboard to display in the middle of the playing table. It should say:

1 = **sun**
2 = **rain cloud**
3 = **roots**
4 = **stem**
5 = **leaf**
6 = **flower**

If your child can't read, draw pictures to depict playing pieces.

Directions for Play:

1. Give each player a game board. Lay the rest of the playing pieces and number chart in the center of the play area.

2. Roll a dice to see who will go first.

3. The first player rolls the dice and looks at the chart. If, for example, the player rolls a 2, he chooses a rain cloud from the playing pieces and places it in the sky of his playing board.

4. Continue around the circle, each player receiving one roll per turn. If a child rolls a number that corresponds to a playing piece he already has, his turn is forfeited and play continues with the next child.

5. The game continues until all the players have built a plant with a root, stem, two leaves, and flower with the sun and rain cloud in the sky.

How do we understand the green miracle of life?

The Dandelion

The common dandelion is a member of the chickory family. Its parts are used in many ways.

Roots: The roots can be roasted and ground for use as a substitute for or additive to coffee.

Leaves: Early in the spring, some people pick the tender, young leaves and toss them in a salad.

Flowers: Dandelion flowers are used for making wine.

More Than Just a Weed

City kids and country kids have seen the common dandelion. Most probably, the first fistful of flowers they joyfully gathered and presented to you were golden dandelions! It's about time these pesky lawn invaders were put to good use. Dandelions grow at such an incredible pace that they are excellent for demonstrating the life cycle of a plant to young (and impatient) children. Some good selections for reading about dandelions appear at the end of this chapter. (See *Hello, Dandelions!* by Barbara Williams and *Dandelion* by Barrie Watts.)

1. Find a young dandelion plant on your lawn or in your school yard. Place a marker, such as a stick or old ruler, next to the plant to measure its growth.

2. Every day or two, as the dandelion grows taller, make a mark on the stick.

3. Once the flower of the dandelion opens, you might notice that the bloom closes up at night and on cloudy days. To demonstrate this to your child, place a bucket over the plant and it will gradually close.

4. After the flower has been pollinated, it no longer needs to attract insects and will close up. The seeds develop inside the closed head and within a few days will open into a fluffy ball. The wind will blow the seeds across your yard, each one equipped with a feathery parachute.

5. Pick up one of these seeds and look at it through a magnifying lens. Notice that the seed has tiny burrs that will help anchor it to the ground wherever it lands. If a gliding seed settles into a spot and it receives enough water and sunlight, the growing process will begin all over again!

There Are Giants in the Garden!

Sunflowers are another fast growing plant. It will amaze your child to watch such a large flower grow from such a small seed! And at harvest time your family or the birds can enjoy a crunchy snack!

Prepare the Soil: Sunflowers need a lot of food and sunlight to grow tall. Spread several inches of compost on the soil and dig it in well before planting. Remember that they grow very tall, so make sure they are planted in a spot that won't shade your garden later.

Plant the Seeds: The seeds should be planted about a foot apart at a depth of ½ inch. Water the area thoroughly.

Care for Your Plants: The seeds should sprout in a week or two. At that time, pull out every other seedling (so the plants are two feet apart) to allow room for growth. Water the seedlings often because they get very thirsty! Pull weeds occasionally or mulch the soil so your sunflowers don't have to compete with the weeds.

Watch It Grow: Your sunflowers will grow quickly. You might want to make a growth chart by measuring the same plant every week and graphing its progress. After a flower forms, have your children compare their height to that of the tall bloom. Which is taller? Have your child paint a life-size picture of his sunflower.

Harvest Time: When the petals have dropped off and the birds begin to peck at the seeds, cut off the heads with a foot of stalk. Hang them upside down in a dry and airy place. When the seeds are dried, rub them off with your hand and store them in an airtight container.

A Lilliputian's View

Did you know that sunflowers are cousins to the daisy? It's easy to see their resemblance. However, a daisy stands as tall as your child's knee or hip, while a sunflower towers over him like a giant! What a wonderful fantasy situation this can create for your child! Have him pretend that your sunflowers are regular daisies and that he is half their size!

• Pretend that a "giant" child walks near you (whose knees will be the same height as the flower head!). Can you imagine how tall he or she would be? Have an imaginary conversation with him.

• Have your child draw a picture of himself as a "tiny" person under the sunflowers. Include other common objects, nearby plants, and insects as they would appear from this new perspective.

• Have your child help prepare a picnic to be eaten near the sunflowers. As you eat, use your imaginations and exchange stories about how different things would be as tiny people. For example, the apple you might be eating would be as large as a basketball, a strawberry as big as a grapefruit, or a carrot as long as a baseball bat!

Your point of view depends entirely on whose skin you are inside.

Seed Snacks

To Toast Sunflower Seeds: Spread shelled seeds in a single layer on a baking sheet and bake in a 350° oven for 5 minutes. Shake the pan once or twice and watch them carefully (they can burn easily). Sunflower seeds can also be toasted in a skillet on top of the stove, over moderate heat.

"No Bake" Seed Candy: Mix together 1 cup of sunflower nuts, 1 cup honey, 1 cup peanut butter, and 1 cup cocoa powder. Shape into one inch balls. Spread 1 cup of toasted sesame seeds on a plate. Roll each piece of candy in the sesame seeds. Chill before serving, if desired.

Granola Crunch: In a very large mixing bowl, combine 2½ cups rolled oats, ½ cup slivered almonds, ½ cup coconut, ½ cup toasted wheat germ, ½ cup sunflower nuts, ½ cup toasted sesame seeds. Stir together ½ cup dark corn syrup *or* honey and ⅓ cup orange juice. Pour over oat mixture and stir until well coated. Spread on a greased baking pan and bake in a 300° oven for 45 minutes, or until browned. Stir every 10-15 minutes. Remove from oven and stir in ½ cup raisins, if desired. Cool. Store in an airtight container for up to one month. Tastes great with milk in the morning or sprinkled over ice cream or yogurt. Makes 5 cups.

Make a Seed Catalog

After learning about plants and their seeds, let your child create his own catalog. Instead of discarding any garden magazines and seed catalogs, put them in your Recycle Craft Box. They provide wonderful pictures of plants, vegetables, and flowers!

1. Put a booklet together by placing several pieces of drawing paper on a piece of construction paper. Fold in half and staple on the folded edge.

2. Let your child collect seeds from the backyard, or from fresh fruits or vegetables. On each page glue one seed and a picture of its parent plant from an old gardening catalog. Help your child label each page with the name of the plant and write any comments that he may wish to add.

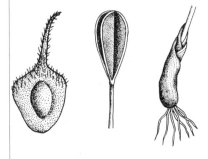

Growing Without Seeds

It may interest your child to know that not all plants need seeds to grow. A variety of plants will root themselves in water; some examples are sweet potatoes, carrots, beets, and some vines. Your child will enjoy witnessing this garbage garden!

Sweet Potato: Fill a jar about three-fourths full of water. Hold a sweet potato in the water so only the bottom third of the potato is covered. With your fingernail, make a mark on the potato at the rim of the jar. Stick toothpicks into four sides of the potato at the marked level. Place it in the jar; the toothpicks will keep it partially above water. Add water from time to time as necessary to keep it at its original level. Place the jar in a well lighted spot, but not in direct sunlight. Soon your potato will grow roots!

Carrot or Beet: Cut the top off each carrot or beet, leaving about one inch of vegetable. Place in a shallow pan filled with water or sand. Add enough water so that the vegetables are covered, but the crowns are above water. Make sure the water is kept at this level. Place the dish in a well lighted spot, but not in direct sunlight. In about a week, your veggies will sprout new leafy tops!

Mint: Place a bouquet of fragrant mint (either from a garden or purchased from a store) in a glass of water. Place in a well lighted spot. Within a week, the mint will grow roots! When it is well established, the mint can be planted in a pot or in the ground.

Eat the Fruit and Plant the Pit!

You don't need a big backyard to grow a tree. Even an apartment dweller can grow an avocado tree indoors! First, make guacamole or toss an avocado in a salad. Then, keep the huge seed to sprout a tree!

1. Let the pit dry for a day or two. Peel off the brown coat. Insert three toothpicks so that the seed can be suspended in a jar of warm water (base down, pointed end up).

2. Place the jar in a warm, dark spot. Add warm water to keep the bottom third suspended in water. After several weeks, roots will form.

3. Place the jar in a sunny spot and wait for a stem to push out of the seed. When it is about four inches high, you can plant your tree in soil!

Guacamole

To make a delicious dip for toasted corn tortillas, peel two to four fully ripe avocados, then mash with a fork. Salt and pepper to taste. To this basic mixture, add any of the following to taste:

~ Minced raw onion

~ Fresh tomato, chopped, peeled and seeded

~ Lemon juice

~ Dried hot red pepper flakes

~ A little olive oil

~ Cracked black pepper

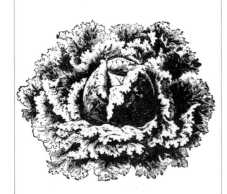

Happy Veggies, by Mayumi Oda. Parallax Press, Berkeley, CA, 1986.

"Do you want to meet Mother Nature? Come into my vegetable garden." Take a stroll through the garden all year long. The bright watercolor illustrations burst forth from every page. (ages 3 - 8)

Growing Vegetable Soup, by Lois Ehlert. Harcourt Brace Jovanovich, NY, 1987.

This book presents vegetable soup from its very beginning to its conclusion in a soup bowl! A father and child begin with the tools, planting the seeds and sprouts, watering, waiting for the sun to help them grow, weeding, and finally harvesting, washing, cutting, and putting the vegetables in a pot to cook. The recipe is included. (ages 3 - 6)

4. Place some gravel in the bottom of a flower pot. Let your child hold the pit in place while you fill the pot with potting soil. (Let about one-half inch of the pit stick above the soil.) Water well. Keep your plant in a sunny place in the winter. In warm weather it can be placed on a balcony, patio, or fire escape.

The Vegetable Garden

Many young children believe that food "comes" from a supermarket, not realizing that it must be grown out of the ground first. The following stories and activities focus on gardening for food production. Gardening adventures with children provide a special opportunity for them to see, firsthand, how vegetables and fruits are grown. It will dispel the idea that food just "appears" on the grocery shelves.

Making Dirt

"Where does dirt come from?" It's one of those things we can take for granted because it has always been there and there is so much of it! The first project of gardening is making the soil ready for planting. An effective way to build up your soil is by composting. Composting is the method by which organic material is reduced to humus, a rich fertilized soil most suitable for fortifying plants. Your children will enjoy helping you create the compost for your garden or house plants from discarded food scraps, leaves, weeds, and grass clippings. Within a month or two (depending on the size of your pile), you will have luxurious, fertilized soil to feed your plants. Before undertaking this project, you might want to read *The Compost Heap* by Harlow Rockwell to your children. Here are several easy methods of creating compost.

The Compost Pile: Dig a hole in the yard about 3 feet deep and 3 feet wide. Layer soil and plant matter, such as grass clippings, leaves, twigs and tree branches, fruit and vegetable scraps, eggshells, coffee grounds, and tea leaves. Water with each added layer. (Layers can be 6-8 inches.)

Build a Compost Bin: Create a bin using easily available materials: scrap lumber, concrete blocks, bricks, chicken wire, etc. First lay down a layer of coarse material, such as twigs, hay, or wood chips. Then add a layer of grass clippings and leaves. Top it off with a layer of garden soil. Sprinkle the materials with water as you build the pile. Repeat layers until your pile is several feet high. (The minimum size required to sustain the necessary biological reactions is about 3 feet wide by 3 feet high.)

The Compost Bucket: If you don't have a yard or large enough space to have a compost pile, this is a good alternative. Start with a large trash container (plastic or metal) and drill very large holes in its sides, up, down and all around to allow air to penetrate the pile and deliver oxygen to the bacteria and fungi in the soil. Layer soil or peat moss and plant matter in the container. If you don't have access to grass clippings, shredded newspapers can be used. Sprinkle with water and don't allow it to dry out. Stir every two weeks, as this helps to prevent strong smells from building up.

Gardening is Fun!

Growing vegetables is the most fun for children because they get to eat the finished product! Besides, planting a family garden can be a wonderful experience for every member of your household, young or old. Decide the best way to include your children. You can assign them a row, a corner of the garden, or small plot of their own. If you are a first time gardener, start small. You can always expand your garden next year. Or if you live in an apartment, plant in large pots. Just remember the main objective is sharing fun gardening experiences with your children.

There is not enough space in this chapter to include a step-by-step guide to gardening. But here are some basic tips to help you start a garden. A few excellent resources can be found at the end of this chapter.

Choosing a Site: When choosing a spot for your garden, remember that vegetables need:
- a lot of sunlight: at least 8 hours per day.
- water: situate it near an outdoor faucet.
- good soil structure: use lots of rich compost to build up the soil.
- good drainage: avoid low spots that tend to pool rainwater.

The Soup Garden Song

Tune: Home On the Range

My garden is full of ripe vegetables

That are tasty and nutritious to eat. *(rub tummy)*

I planted each seed *(pretend to plant seeds)*

And I pulled every weed *(pretend to pull weeds)*

The cool rain was water to drink. *(let fingers rain down)*

Oh, my garden so green!

There's corn and peppers and beets. *(count on fingers)*

The bright sun did shine *(make ball with hands over head to represent sun)*

On this garden of mine

That will soon be hot vegetable soup!

Slurp! Mmmm! *(pretend to eat soup)*

Resources for Young Gardeners (and their parents)

Books About Gardening:

Let's Grow: 72 Gardening Adventures With Children, by Linda Tilgner. Storey Communications, Inc. Pownal, VT 05261, 1988.

The Victory Garden Kid's Book, by Marjorie Waters. Houghton Mifflin, Boston, 1988.

Seed Companies:

Gurney's will send a free, tabloid-sized catalog with colorful photographs of people (and children) showing off their produce. 1224 Page Street, Yankton, SD 57078.

Burpee Seeds has a colorful catalog. 300 Park Avenue, Warminster, PA 18991.

Plan Ahead! To avoid having to dig up sod for your garden plot, several months before planting season cover up the desired area with a thick layer of newspapers, black plastic, or cardboard boxes opened flat and weigh down with stones or firewood. When the area is deprived of sun, the grass and weeds under the cover will die, decompose, and enrich the soil. Just remove the cover at planting time and you will discover the digging to be less strenuous!

What Will You Plant? There are so many choices, but the best vegetables are the ones your family will eat! Sit down with a seed catalog and allow your children to help decide what will be planted in the family plot or in their own. Some good "starter" crops include beans, carrots, radishes, cucumbers, lettuce and greens, peas, peppers, squash (including pumpkins), potatoes, and tomatoes.

"How Can I Help?" You should include your children as much as possible in the garden planning, cultivating, and planting. They will find much to interest them: earthworms and other insects that make their homes underground, watching the process of grass, leaves, and other plant matter gradually turn to "dirt" in the compost pile, and being invited to dig with you in the garden!

Waiting for Your Garden to Grow

After the seeds have been planted, the long wait begins. It can take a couple of weeks for the plants to begin growing, then several weeks before they flower and vegetables begin to grow. Here are some activities to keep them focused on the garden after planting and before harvest.

Make A Secret "Treasure" Map: Tell your child that the seeds are like vegetable "treasures" that will be buried in the ground, but only you and your family know where they are planted. So, after planning what foods will be grown, help your child to cut pictures from the seed catalogs and make a map of where the "treasure seeds" will be "buried" in the garden.

Wacky Garden Markers: From the scraps of cardboard in the Recycle Craft Box, let your child make creative row markers for the garden. He could draw imaginative vegetable pictures or cut pictures from catalogs to illustrate the signs. Write any comments on the signs that your child might want to say, such as something the vegetable might say or a silly jingle. Encourage creativity!

Earthworm Relocation Officer: As you are digging up the ground, you will undoubtedly disrupt the homes of helpful earthworms. Give your child the job of relocating them to an undisturbed part of the garden.

How Does Your Garden Grow?: You and your child could keep a Garden Diary to record events. The entries should be brief and can be accompanied by drawn pictures or snapshots. For example, "Today was planting day! We planted corn, peas, beans, and squash. Tomorrow we will plant herbs and flowers." Or "Squash is the winner! It is the first plant to sprout in the garden." Be sure to record successes and failures so that you will remember for next year.

Water Monitor: Your garden will need lots of water and you know how children love to play with the hose. Whenever your child is interested, it could be his job to water the garden.

Create a Scarecrow: If birds and small animals enjoy your garden as much as you do (or even if they don't), help your child create a scarecrow! First, make a skeleton by tying two thick sticks or poles together in a cross fashion. Stuff a pillow case for the head and stick it on the top. Then dress him up in old discarded clothing and stuff his body with straw. He can be as modest or elaborate as your child likes! Don't forget to name him. Also, your child could write a story about him in his garden diary. Developing a personality for your scarecrow can be great fun!

Organic Gardening

The term organic gardening has come to mean "without insecticides," but really there's more to it than that. It's a process in which you build and rebuild the soil, and encourage populations of "helpful" insects and birds to support the garden year after year. Another important reason to grow vegetables without chemicals is that young children tend to sample right from the garden. If you haven't applied harmful insecticides, you won't need to worry! Here are some successful ways to garden organically:

• Use compost to fertilize your soil. There's no need to apply chemical fertilizers; they are expensive and can weaken the soil for future plantings as well as contaminate the ground water supply.

This Year's Garden, by Cynthia Rylant. Illustrations by Mary Szilagyi. Bradbury Press, NY, 1984.

The anticipation is an exciting part of gardening, the waiting and watching as the brown Earth comes alive with green shoots. This book is a song of seasons as reflected in the growth, life, and death of the garden of a large rural family. (ages 4 - 10)

Way Down Yonder in the Pumpkin Patch!

Tune: In the Paw Paw Patch

Where, oh where is *(name)?*

Where, oh where is *(name)?*

Where, oh where is *(name)?*

Way down yonder in the pumpkin patch!

Pickin' ripe pumpkins, puttin' them in a barrow.

Pickin' ripe pumpkins, puttin' them in a barrow.

Pickin' ripe pumpkins, puttin' them in a barrow.

Way down yonder in the pumpkin patch!

Cuttin' off the top and scoopin' out the seeds.

Cuttin' off the top and scoopin' out the seeds.

Cuttin' off the top and scoopin' out the seeds.

There are so many, I'll be countin' all night!

Carvin' a jack-o-lantern and toastin' up the seeds.

Carvin' a jack-o-lantern and toastin' up the seeds.

Carvin' a jack-o-lantern and toastin' up the seeds.

They'll make a special treat for Halloween!

• Pulling weeds can be a tiresome chore. To discourage weed growth, apply a thick layer of grass clippings, leaves, or hay between plants and around seedlings.

• Bugs will eat the leaves of many plants. Don't be discouraged, because you can lose up to a third of the leaf area without harming yields. There are several ways to control the insects without using commercial insecticides:

1. When possible, pick the bugs off of the leaves by hand. Put them in a bucket of water and add them to the compost pile.

2. Lay boards between the rows and go out early every morning to turn the boards over. During the night, many bugs will have accumulated there, so just dispose of them and add them to the compost pile.

3. Many bugs can be washed off the leaves with a spray from the garden hose.

4. Companion planting helps to discourage bug populations. Plant herbs, marigolds, nasturtiums, onions, and garlic between and around the vegetables. (For a more detailed list of companionable herbs, see one of the suggested gardening books.)

Have a Nibbling Picnic!

Harvest time is an exciting time for children that have waited patiently for weeks to sample their home-grown veggies. Well, don't wait any longer! Go out into the garden and enjoy your produce right from the vine! (The vegetables will not require much washing if you have not used chemical insecticides.) Take a pan or bucket of water to rinse your vegetables, spread out a blanket next to the garden, and enjoy a variety of foods that are still warm from the sun.

A Pumpkin Patch

Pumpkins are a symbol of harvest time. Their brilliant, orange color very closely matches the autumn leaves on the trees. Every child will enjoy watching pumpkins grow plump and round in the garden. To harvest Halloween pumpkins, be sure to plant the seeds in mid-summer (not spring). Check on the seed packet for growing time or check with an agricultural center for advice.

Tips for Growing Pumpkins:

1. Soak your pumpkin seeds overnight in warm water.

2. Prepare the soil by fortifying it with lots of compost.

3. Poke holes in the patch about one inch deep. Drop a seed in each hole and cover with soil. Press down the soil with the palm of your hand.

4. Water the seeds well. Pumpkins need a lot of water to grow, so sprinkle with water often.

5. Your seeds should sprout in about a week or two. After the seedlings have grown a bit, cut off all but about three or four of the strongest. Mulch with hay or grass clippings to prevent weeds from growing and competing with the pumpkins.

6. To grow extra-large carving pumpkins, pick off the small flowers that form at the ends of the vines. This will allow more food for the pumpkins growing near the base.

7. Pumpkins are ready to harvest before the first hard frost when their skin is tough and bright orange. When you cut it from the vine, leave a 3-4 inch stem so it will not spoil.

Personalize a Pumpkin: After your vines flower, pumpkins will start to form. When one looks like it is well established, take a pencil and let your child write his initials or name on its skin. Then, an adult should go over the initials with a paring knife to slightly break the skin surface. As the pumpkin grows, so will your child's initials!

Pumpkin Math: There are many fun activities to do with pumpkins that also teach math concepts. After harvest time, try some of these suggestions:

Pumpkins Are Heavy! Take several pumpkins and weigh them. You can compare their weight and make a chart or graph. Compare your child's weight to the largest pumpkin.

Big and Round. Just by looking at your pumpkin, can you guess how big around it is? Measure out a length of string that you think will be the size of your pumpkin. Hold it around your pumpkin to see if you were right!

How Many Seeds? At carving time, save the seeds, wash and dry them, then count them to see how many there are. For young children, whose counting is limited, prepare a counting sheet with ten circles on it. Have them put a seed on each circle, then place the ten seeds in a pile or cup. Continue filling "10-cups" until all seeds are counted. Leave any last few seeds on the counting sheet that

Hidin' a few seeds and stuffin' them in my pocket.

Hidin' a few seeds and stuffin' them in my pocket.

Hidin' a few seeds and stuffin' them in my pocket.

To plant next spring in the pumpkin patch!

Pumpkin, Pumpkin, by Jeanne Titherington. Greenwillow Books, NY, 1986.

Jamie plants a pumpkin seed and watches it grow, picks it, carves it, and saves seeds to plant in the spring. The soft, almost luminous illustrations are soothing to the eye and the simple text will delight any child who loves this big, orange squash! (ages 3 - 8)

aren't enough to fill a 10-cup. Help your child count ten piles of ten, and put them in a "100-bowl." Continue filling 100-bowls until the seeds remaining aren't enough to fill a 100-bowl. Count the 100-bowls, 10-cups (or piles), and remaining single seeds. How many do you have?

Seeds to Eat: First, wash and dry your pumpkin seeds. Mix about 2 cups of seeds with 2 teaspoons of vegetable oil and sprinkle with salt. Spread the seeds on a cookie sheet and roast in a 300° oven for 30-40 minutes, stirring every 10 minutes. Let cool before eating.

Let's Grow Sprouts!

This activity has the same purpose as the seed viewer, but with one difference: your child can enjoy a snack within a few days! Sprouted seeds are tasty in salads or sprinkled over cream cheese on crackers or sandwiches, and they are high in protein. Some types of seeds to use are alfalfa, wheat, barley, garden cress (spicy and hot), lentils, or soy.

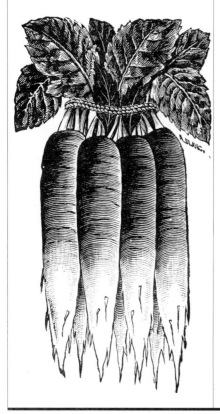

1. Place about one tablespoon of seeds in a clean glass jar. Cover the top with a clean nylon stocking or several layers of cheesecloth and secure with a rubber band.

2. Soak them in warm water overnight.

3. Drain and rinse them (without taking off the net covering). Keep the jar on its side in a warm place.

4. Every morning and evening, run fresh water on the seeds and drain them.

5. Sprouts should appear within five days. Place them in indirect sunlight until the tiny leaves turn green (about a day). They will keep in the refrigerator for several days or you can enjoy them right away!

Visit a "Pick-Your-Own Produce" Farm

Not every family (or classroom) has a backyard in which to grow a garden, but you can still have the experience of harvesting directly from growing plants. Many roadside vegetable stands are located next to the farm and offer the choice of choosing from their baskets or picking from the field. (Or you can call ahead and make that arrangement in advance.)

• Where can you find "pick-your-own produce" farms? If you look in a rural area and come up empty-handed, check with your State Department of Agriculture. They may have a list of farms that are set up to let customers harvest their own produce.

• When is the best time to go? Strawberries are a very popular small farm crop and can be harvested in June or July. For vegetables, mid-July to August is usually peak harvest time. Apples can be picked in the fall, usually around late September or October. (These times are quite general, because climate is the major determinant.) Also, keep in mind that certain vegetables or fruits are harvested at different times in the season, so if fresh corn is what you want, call ahead!

• Be prepared! You won't find much shade while you're out in the fields, so bring a hat, wear gloves, and put on sunscreen. Since it will be hot and children get thirsty, take along a thermos of drinking water. Also, bring your own strawberry baskets, boxes, or bags. Some farms will charge you for the boxes you take.

Hooray for Herbs!

You can't go wrong by planting an herb garden. Herbs are aromatic plants that are easy to grow and can be used in many ways. It has already been suggested that these plants will be an asset to a vegetable garden, but even grown separately or in pots, they are useful and tasty plants.

Plant a Pizza Garden: Choose herbs that will enhance a homemade pizza, such as oregano, parsley, sage, chives, and basil. You could even make a circle-shaped garden, like a pizza pie!

Potpourri Planting: There are many craft projects that call for herbs, especially the sweet smelling variety such as lemon balm, mint (even chocolate mint!), thyme, and rosemary. Dry them and mix them with dried flower petals to make a delicious smelling potpourri. It makes a nice gift for someone special, too!

Sun and Shade Gardens: Plant two small herb gardens, one for the sunlovers, like thyme, sage, basil, parsley, borage, and dill, and another for the herbs that like some shade, such as the many kinds of mint, pennyroyal, and violets.

A garden, no matter how well known by daylight, is a magical place on a summer night.

Herb Recipes for Every Day

Herbal Bug Repellant:

Why soak your children with chemicals to repel bothersome mosquitoes and other biting insects? You and your children can try this natural and environmentally-safe remedy instead.

1. Boil 1 cup of water and add 2 teaspoons of dried camomile.

2. Take the pot off the stove and let the mixture cool for 5-10 minutes.

3. Pour the liquid through a strainer and into a jar.

4. To use: Sponge the herbal liquid onto the exposed parts of the body (neck, arms, and legs) to repel pests.

Herbal Shampoo:

Herbal shampoos can clean your hair or body beautifully, but usually are quite expensive to purchase. For fun, you and your children can whip together this recipe for your family or to give as a gift.

1. Pour into a container:

~ bottle of castile soap (may be purchased at a drug or health products store)

~ 1 tablespoon of olive oil

~ 2-3 teaspoons of herbs (rosemary, ginger, violet, thyme, or lemon balm)

2. Mix together and seal the container.

3. Store for 1-2 weeks in a cool place.

4. Pour the liquid through a strainer and return it to the container. It may be used as a hair shampoo or body soap.

Herbal Moth Bags:

The smell of moth balls linger on sweaters and blankets long after they've been allowed to air. This is a sweet smelling alternative to moth balls when storing wool clothing.

1. Make sachet bags by sewing two small pieces of cloth (right sides together) along three sides. Turn inside-out.

2. Mix together a collection of herbs (such as mint, rosemary, thyme, sage, lavender, or marjoram) and crushed cinnamon.

3. Fill the sachet bags and sew to close. Pack these with your blankets and clothes to keep moths away. Next spring, you will open your trunks to an herbal fresh scent!

The Air Cycle Relay

Plants are the air filters of the world. The leaves use the energy from the sun to combine the by-product of our breathing (CO^2) and water from the soil to make sugar and starch to nourish the plant. This process is called photosynthesis. As a result, the plant releases oxygen (O^2) into the air, which we in turn breath to begin the cycle again by exhaling carbon dioxide (CO^2). This dramatization of the air cycle will help teach children how humans and other animals depend on plants for the oxygen they need to live.

Things you will need: Cut circles from black and blue construction paper. You will need five black circles for every blue one. Label the black circles CARBON and the blue ones OXYGEN.

To Play:

1. Divide the players into three groups: plant, animal, and air. The plants should stand opposite the animals. An air player should be assigned to each pair. Give each animal player one blue circle marked OXYGEN and five black circles marked CARBON.

2. Have the players act out the air cycle. To begin, have an "animal" hand a black and a blue circle to an air player. This represents the carbon dioxide (carbon + oxygen) that is released when animals breathe into the air.

3. Next, "air" carries both circles to a plant player. The "plant" takes the circles, keeps the black one (carbon) and returns the blue one (oxygen) to the air player.

4. Finally, the air player returns to the animal player and hands him the blue circle. This starts the cycle again. The animal breathes, releases CO^2 (carbon dixoide), which is carried to the plant. The plant absorbs it, keeps the carbon to help make food for itself, and releases the oxygen back into the air. Continue the relay until the animal player runs out of black circles.

5. At this time, the animal player must fortify himself by "eating" some food, in this case a plant. He should go over to the plant and gently tag him. The plant must then hand over all his black circles and curl up on the floor to represent a seed. After a brief time, he "grows" into a plant and joins the relay again.

6. Let the children exchange places and repeat the air cycle relay until each child has played every part of the cycle.

The Reason For a Flower, by Ruth Heller. Grosset and Dunlap, NY, 1983.

Not only are flowers beautiful to look at, they have a very important purpose in the life of the plant: they manufacture the seeds necessary to continue the circle of life. What happens to the seeds? They travel in various ways or become food for animals or people. This story is beautifully illustrated and reveals to the very young child the importance of plants and explains their cycle in a simple and delightful rhyme. (ages 3 - 8)

Rosy's Garden, by Satomi Ichikawa. Philomel Books, a division of Putnam and Grosset Group, NY, 1990.

Flowers seem to attract as many children as bees. Woven into the story of a young girl who visits her grandmother is a celebration of flowers. Rosy learns facts and folklore about flowers as she presses flowers, gathers seeds, and makes potpourri. This sumptuously illustrated volume captures the detail and beauty of a country garden. (ages 6 - 12)

The Flower Garden

Vegetable and fruit gardening is not the only kind: we cannot forget the beauty and importance of flowers to our yards, parks, and meadows. The following stories and activities will teach your children about their role as attractive and useful plants.

Plants Around the House

Most households have at least one potted plant sitting on a table or shelf to brighten up a room. There are some homes that have so many plants you would think you were visiting the botanical gardens! Toddlers are best taught to stay away from all house plants, since some leaves can be harmful if swallowed. But an older child can learn the basics of plant care by helping with the day-to-day maintenance and care of house plants.

Plant "Care Cards": Let your child help you keep a record of the plants in your home. Make a "care card" for each plant and write down basic information, such as the amount of sunlight and water required. Keep track of repottings, fertilizer feedings, pruning, etc. Teach your child to recognize improper care or diseases and how to remedy any growth problems.

How Do You Make a Flower Blush?

Answer: color some water with red food coloring and place a flower in it! This experiment will teach your child the route of water through a plant.

1. Take a glass of slightly warm water and add several drops of red food coloring. Mix together, adding more coloring if necessary to make the water quite visibly red.

2. Take a white daisy, white carnation, a stem of Queen Anne's Lace, or a stalk of celery with leaves. With a knife or scissors, cut the bottom of the stem diagonally and place the cut end into the colored water.

3. The water will gradually be sucked up into the stem and the veins that carry the water will be visibly red (especially noticeable in the celery stalk). Finally, the water will reach the petals or leaves turning them a rosy, red color!

Designate a Wildflower Plot

Wildflowers are some of the easiest flowers to grow and need very little care. Choose a sunny spot in your yard and designate it as a "Wildflower Plot." A variety of seeds can be purchased at a low cost. Then, in the spring, prepare the soil with compost and follow the package directions for planting. Very soon you will have a colorful patch of hearty flowers that will attract insects and butterflies all summer long!

Gardening on the Windowsill

If you don't have a yard or just want another place to grow plants, make a window box! It's easy, but it will require your adult supervision every step of the way.

1. Let your child help you find a box that will fit on your windowsill or make one from wood scraps. *Adult:* Drill drainage holes in the bottom of the box.

2. First, lay down a layer of small stones or gravel. Then fill with potting soil or compost.

3. Plant seeds, seedlings, or sink potted plants directly in the soil.

4. Help your child move it to the windowsill and secure it in place. To improve drainage, set it on two pieces of wood so that it is raised off the sill an inch or so.

5. To create tools for gardening in the window box, attach spoons and forks to sticks with packing tape or wire. These long-handled tools will remove the need for leaning out of the window. (To prevent accidents, always supervise your child while he is tending plants in a window box.)

Planting Spring Bulbs

The fall, before the ground freezes, is the time to plant bulbs. Before they can bloom, they must lay dormant in the cold ground for several months. When the warm weather comes, they are some of the first plants to announce, "Spring has arrived!"

1. In early fall, choose from a variety of spring-flowering bulbs at your local nursery or gardening department.

2. Check the package for planting instructions because depth and distance from other bulbs can vary for different types.

"The Earth laughs in flowers."

RALPH WALDO EMERSON

Planting a Rainbow, by Lois Ehlert. Harcourt Brace Jovanovich, NY, 1988.

This book begins, "Every year Mom and I plant a rainbow." In bold and exuberant pictures, a mother and child plant flowers in the family garden. Bulbs, seeds, and plants sprout and grow into a rainbow of colorful blooms. All summer long, the flowers are picked and carried home. And next year, a rainbow can grow all over again! This is a wonderful beginning book about plants. The illustrations show what is happening under the ground to the vibrant finished product. (ages 3 - 6)

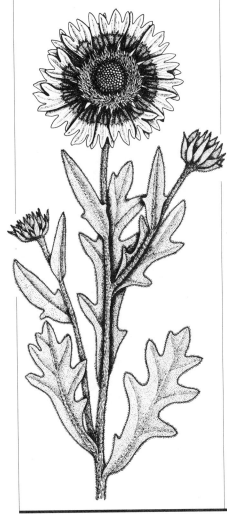

3. Mix some compost into the soil to fortify it. Dig the holes, drop a spoonful of bonemeal into each, and place a bulb (point up) firmly in the bottom of each hole. Cover with soil and water lightly.

4. That's all. It's so easy! You might even forget about them during the cold winter months. But just about when cabin fever has run its course, their green shoots poke out of the ground and bring color and life to your barren winter garden! They bloom year after year and if you cut them just before they fade, their beauty can be preserved by pressing.

Preserving The Beauty of Flowers

Spring flowers fade so quickly. Wouldn't it be nice to capture their beauty to enjoy any time of year? You can! Many flowers can be pressed or dried to be used in craft projects or flower arrangements. Here's how:

Make a Plant Press Book: The easiest way of pressing flowers is to slip them between two pieces of clean paper, then close them among the pages of a fat book. An alternative is to help your child make this portable plant press.

1. *Adult:* Cut two pieces of masonite or quarter-inch plywood into the size rectangle that you want. (If your child plans to tote it along on picnics or hikes, make sure it is a proper size for his small hands.) On one long side of each board, drill a hole in each corner. On the remaining long sides, drill three or four holes to bind the "book."

2. Help your child cut several pieces of heavy scrap cardboard that are the same size as the press. (The corners will need to be trimmed to allow for the bolts.) In each piece of cardboard, punch holes along one long side to match the holes on the binding edge of the "cover."

3. Bind the edge of the pressing book together with string. Attach the remaining two corners to long bolts that have wing nuts.

4. Allow your child to decorate the cover of his pressing book with paint, markers, pictures cut from magazines, etc.

5. Collect leaves and flowers, lay them between pieces of newsprint and slip them into the cardboard pages of the plant press. Tighten the bolts and leave for a week or two. The string may need to be tightened occasionally as the cardboard compresses with use. Use the pressed plants in craft projects or for making gifts.

Drying Flowers: Some flowers or their stems are so thick that they can't be pressed flat, so drying them calls for another technique. Air drying is certainly the easiest method. Simply gather your bunches of flowers or grasses into small bundles, secure with a rubber band, and hang them upside-down to dry. Or you can try these techniques:

Sand Drying:

1. Wash and dry some sand or locate clean, white sand at a gardening center. Sandpit sand can also be used and may be purchased at some toy stores.

2. Pour a layer of sand into a box. Gently place the flowers face down into the sand. Carefully sift sand over the flowers until they are completely covered.

3. Place the box in a warm, dry place for a couple of weeks, or until the drying process is complete.

4. To store dried flowers, glue some florist foam in the bottom of a large box. Carefully poke the flowers to be stored into it. Cover with plastic wrap to keep out the moisture and store in a dark place.

The Glycerine Method:

1. A bottle of glycerine can be purchased for a few dollars at a drug store. Mix one part glycerine with two parts water in a saucepan. Adult: Bring the mixture almost to a boil.

2. Pour the liquid into a tall glass and place your foliage stems into it. Let them sit in a cool, dark place until the leaves and petals begin to deepen in color.

3. Hang the flowers upside-down in a dark, dry closet to finish the drying process.

4. You may have to gently wipe the leaves with a tissue. The petals and leaves will look moist or shiny and will remain a bit pliable. Arrange your flowers in a vase and you will have a lovely centerpiece!

"The weight of a petal has changed the face of the world and made it ours."

LOREN EISELY

The Lady and the Spider, by Faith McNulty. Illustrations by Bob Marstall. Harper and Row, NY, 1986.

Live, for a while, a tiny spider's existence. She has made her home in a head of lettuce. She has no idea that her home is in a woman's vegetable garden and that the lady intends to eat the head of lettuce for lunch! The lettuce is pulled, taken to a faraway place called a kitchen, and washed. Luckily, the lady notices the little spider. But instead of throwing it down the drain, she carefully takes it back to the garden and places the spider in a new plant home. The woman's concluding thoughts are, "Isn't it wonderful that a creature so small can live and love life, find food, and make a home just like me!" This book beautifully points out the oneness of all creatures, no matter how small. (ages 3 - 8)

Tiny Garden Visitors

Your garden is a neighborhood for a wide variety of insects and other creatures. Instead of running for your swatter, join your children in observing and learning more about these fascinating creatures! You can keep a counting record or write a story about the bugs, snails, and worms that you and your child find.

Among the Flowers: You will see many nectar-eating insects such as caterpillars, moths, butterflies, and bees.

In the Vegetable Garden: Many different larva, insects, and other creatures can be found feasting among the vegetable and fruit plants. Some are eating the leaves and fruit, causing great distress to the gardener. But there are some that are quite welcome because they are feasting on the harmful insects! For example, ladybugs keep down the aphid population. Their bright red and dotted wings make them easy to spot and they are a favorite of youngsters. (See a gardening guide for more information on "helpful" garden insects.) Some other insects and creatures you might see are beetles, snails, slugs, ants, grasshoppers, bees, caterpillars, praying mantis, earwigs, and spiders.

Under the Soil: Another "helper" that lives underground is the earthworm. These wriggling creatures tunnel through the soil making it easier for water and air to seep in and reach the thirsty roots. The best time to find worms is after a rain when many can be seen on the surface of the ground.

Make a wormery by filling a glass jar with soil (you can make layers of different soils, such as sand, compost, and garden soil). Top with decaying material such as leaves and put in a few worms. (Keep the dirt moist, because earthworms will die if they dry out.) Cover the outside of the jar with dark paper to simulate their dark environment and let the worms go to work! After a while, remove the cover to observe the tunnels created by the worms. Be sure to return the earthworms to the garden after a few days, so they can continue their good and necessary work.

Through the Eyes of a Bug

It is difficult for humans, being such large animals, to get an insect's perspective of the world. There is a tool that can make it easier to look under leaves and through grasses. It is a dental mirror! One can be purchased at a drug store for only a couple of dollars and will double as a plaque finder and a bug pretender! (Please wash between uses!)

Give your child an inexpensive dental mirror and invite him to be a bug! Encourage him to use it to get close to the ground and "see" what an insect might see. Without disturbing the plants, your child can view the underside of leaves, inside a wide-mouthed flower, through grass and clover, behind patches of bark, etc. Here are some role-playing activities and questions to ignite your child's imagination. If you see that your child is inspired, ask him to illustrate some of the things he saw as a bug and write an experience story.

• Pretend you are a honeybee or butterfly sipping nectar from a flower. What do you see, smell, and feel as you crawl into the petals of a flower? Are there any other tiny bugs living there? Which kind of flower is your favorite? Why?

• Imagine you are a green grasshopper hiding in the tall grass. Take a look around you and describe what you see.

• On a rainy day, you might be a butterfly searching for a dry place to wait out the storm. Look there! It's nature's umbrella growing from the ground. Find a mushroom and discover the beautiful pattern on its underside. Would this be a good spot to get out of the rain?

Bug Cages

Your child can learn a lot about insects by closely observing them; but some are quick or fly away. Try catching some in a glass jar (poke plenty of air holes in the top) or construct this simple insect cage. Bugs are usually content to visit for a day or so, but after a time return them to the outdoor world.

1. Wash and dry the inside of an empty, half-gallon, paper milk carton.

2. Cut two large windows on opposite sides of the carton and open the top flap.

3. Take a pair of clean nylon panty hose and cut off one of the legs. Slip the bug cage into the stocking leg, leaving the top open.

4. Go bug hunting! When you capture an insect, be sure to include some source of food: the leaves of the plant on which you found the bug or a nearby plant will be fine. Sprinkle a cotton ball with water and add it to the cage so the insect can have a drink. Fold the carton closed and secure the nylon with a twist-tie or string.

5. Watch the creature for a little while, then let him go near the spot where he was found.

DREAM STARTER

In a garden, under the broad green leaves, little creatures crawl or fly from plant to plant looking for food. Imagine you are someone very small clinging to a vine in a pumpkin patch. The sun has come up and you begin to search for something to eat. You crawl under leaves, over the vines, and finally spy a tender new pumpkin forming under a withering flower.

The excitement of seeing food makes you unaware of the danger looming above. You head straight for the tiny green pumpkin and as you dart out into the sunlight, a large animal pecks at the vine with its beak. You scramble away as quickly as you can and hide on the underside of a leaf. The animal pokes and searches, brushing against the leaf several times. You hold on tight, hoping you won't be found. After a while, he loses interest or finds another tasty morsel and it is safe for you to move about once more.

Cautiously, you look around. All is clear! Again, you make a path toward the delicious pumpkin. It's been a long morning and you are hungry. All of a sudden, whoosh! You are washed off the vine by a stream of water. You are dazed by the suddenness of the rain when only minutes ago the sun was high and bright in the sky. Whoosh!

Miss Rumphius, by Barbara Cooney. Viking Press, NY, 1982.

The message given to a little child by her grandmother was that, "you must do something to make the world more beautiful." The story follows that little girl to womanhood as she travels to exotic places and grows older. But there is one more thing she must do! She decides to scatter lupin seeds over the countryside and along roadways to make the world a more beautiful place. Gardeners and flower-lovers of all ages will enjoy the outcome of this book. (ages 3 - 8)

You are splashed with water again and find yourself struggling in a muddy puddle. You look up to see a tall creature holding the end of a rain storm. Whoosh! You realize that if you don't find shelter soon, you could drown. So, with much effort, you pull yourself out of the sticky mud and climb under some broad, strong leaves to sit out the downpour, never loosing sight of the scrumptious meal waiting for you at the end of the vine.

Finally, at dusk the large puddles have dried enough for you to venture safely across the vine. Even without interference, it takes you a long time to reach the juicy pumpkin. You dig into its skin with your many legs and carve out delicious chunks to satisfy your hunger. As the sun sets, your body and legs get stiff. The breezes of the night are too cool for your tiny body, so you crawl into the flower bud that still holds the warmth of the mid-day sun. The petals close behind you, tucking you into a cozy bed until the sun returns to bring another day.

Get Involved!

Miss Rumphius Has Something To Say!

The story of Miss Rumphius is a true one. Along the southern coast of Maine, gorgeous lupin bloom every summer for residents and visitors to enjoy! Some people in the area have followed her example and have continued to sow lupin seeds over the sloping hills. Your family and friends could organize a project to beautify some neglected areas of your community. An easy way would be to scatter native wildflower seeds along highways, on roadway islands that are usually unkept, or on vacant lots. Not only will these areas be attractive to look at, they will also provide homes, shelter, and food for many types of wildlife.

A Crack in the Sidewalk

Have you ever thought that a crack in the sidewalk could be a mini-garden? It is amazing how well some plants can grow in such a small area! Try to beautify that crumbling cement by planting seeds in the cracks. Some seeds to experiment with are nasturtium, morning glories, alyssum, and mint.

The Story of Johnny Appleseed, by Aliki. Prentice-Hall, Inc., Englewood Cliffs, NJ, 1963.

In young adulthood, John Chapman headed west, clearing land and planting apple orchards along the way. Today people are proud to say that Johnny Appleseed passed through their land. Here is the story of that gentle pioneer who has become an American legend. (ages 4 - 8)

Organic Gardening Information Sources

Let It Rot! The Gardener's Guide to Composting, by Stu Campbell. Garden Way Publishing, 1975.

"Organic Gardening for a Healthier Planet," by Robert and Maria Rodale, *The Green Lifestyle Handbook,* ed. Jeremy Rifkin, Henry Holt and Co., NY, 1990.

The Rodale Guide to Composting, by Jerry Minnich, Marjorie Hunt, and the editors of Organic Gardening. Rodale Press, Emmaus, PA 1979.

Common Sense Pest Control Quarterly. Bio Integral Resource Center, P.O. Box 7414, Berkeley, CA 94704. Membership, including quarterly: $30/yr; publication catalogue $1 plus legal-sized self-addressed envelope.

The Organic Garden Book: The Complete Guide to Growing Flowers, Fruit and Vegetables Naturally, by Crown Publishers, Inc., NY, 1987.

Observe May Day

The origin of May Day goes as far back as the Roman times. It was a day filled with flowers, dancing, and song to celebrate the arrival of spring. Plan to honor the day with your family in some way. Your children can make baskets, fill them with flowers, and hang them on your neighbor's doorknobs. It's a nice way to remind friends that we all need to take the time to enjoy the beauty in our lives!

Help a Neighbor In Need

If you know of an elderly or handicapped individual in your neighborhood who could use some assistance for yard work or gardening, why not lend a helping hand? Not only will you be aiding someone who needs help, you will be teaching your children the importance of reaching out and caring for other people.

Share the Beauty of Plants

You can fill the gardens of your neighbors and friends without spending a penny! All you need is to make new plants from the cuttings of your existing ones. Many types of plants can be grown from this method such as herbs, some house plants, cactus, flowers, and vines. After you have started some new plants, give them to friends and relatives. Here are some starter tips:

Water Method: Take cuttings from vines or herbs and place them in a glass of water. Set it on an indoor windowsill and wait until roots form. When they are well established, transfer the plant to a pot. First, put in a layer of gravel to allow for drainage, then fill with potting soil or compost. Firmly pack the compost around the roots and sprinkle with water.

Sand Method: Cut a shoot from a healthy houseplant and strip the lower leaves from the stem. Insert it into a pot of clean damp sand and place the pot in a cool spot with lots of light. Keep the sand moist and in about six weeks the stem will have sent out roots. (If the cutting wilts, invert a liter-sized soda bottle that has been cut off at the top over it to help retain the evaporating moisture.) The cutting then can be transferred to a pot (see above).

Start a Junior Garden Club

If your child is active in the Scouts, Campfire Kids, or any other organized club, suggest that they develop some plant and gardening activities for the club members. Or, if several of your children's friends are involved in gardening at home, help organize a Junior Gardening Club. The members can exchange seeds, make plant crafts, learn about flower arranging, study backyard wildlife, and plant trees.

Eating Closer to Home

Whether it's your own backyard, a farm down the road or maybe in another county – you and your child can build an appreciation for the food the Earth provides by looking into these suggestions.

Grow Your Own Food: Plant a backyard vegetable garden. If you need information on such a project, contact Rodale Press, 33 East Minor Street, Emmaus, PA 18098. They publish the following books that would be of particular help: *How to Grow Vegetables Organically, High Yield Gardening,* and *The 60-Minute Garden.* They also publish *Organic Gardening Magazine.*

Eat a "Local Diet": It creates jobs in the region, lowers energy consumption and transportation costs, and encourages local, small-scale agriculture. For more information, write to The Cornucopia Project, Rodale Press, 33 East Minor Street, Emmaus, PA 18098.

Join Your Local Food Co-op: For the name and address of the one closest to you, contact the National Cooperative Business Institute, 1401 New York Avenue, N.W., Suite 1100, Washington, D.C. 20005. They have listings on-line in their computer and will be happy to help you.

For information on junior garden clubs, write

**The Junior Gardeners Chairman
National Council of State
Garden Clubs
205 Cobil Drive
Water Valley, MS 38965**

More Books to Share With Children

Apricot ABC by **Miska Miles.** Illustrations by Peter Parnall. Little, Brown and Co., Boston, 1969. A ripe apricot falls from a knobby and tall apricot tree. And with each letter of the alphabet, a creature or plant somehow interacts with the fallen fruit. At the end of the book, the seed inside takes root and a young tree is born to repeat the cycle. (ages 3 - 7)

The Seed the Squirrel Dropped by **Haris Petie.** Prentice-Hall, Inc., Englewood Cliffs, NJ, 1976. From the seed of a cherry comes a new tree that is cared for by a little boy until he is finally able to pick the cherries to make a pie. (ages 3 - 6)

Now I Know All About Seeds by **Susan Kuchalla.** Illustrations by Jane McBee. Troll Associates, Mahwah, NJ, 1982. With a brief text and colorful illustrations, this book presents several kinds of seeds and shows how they grow into plants. (ages 3 - 6)

The Little Red Hen by **Paul Galdone.** The Seabury Press, NY, 1973. This traditional story is a good illustration of the planting cycle. (ages 3 - 9)

Rabbit Seeds by **Bijou Le Tord.** Four Winds Press, NY, 1984. A delicately illustrated chronicle of the toils and satisfactions of a gardener's year. (ages 3 - 6)

Hello, Dandelions! by **Barbara Williams.** Holt, Rinehart and Winston, NY, 1979. A celebration of a common, yet much misunderstood flower. (ages 3 - 9)

Dandelion by **Barrie Watts.** Silver Burnett Press, Morristown, NJ, 1987. Simple text and clear photographs show how a dandelion changes from a flower to a dandelion clock. (ages 3 - 9)

Plant Experiments by **Vera R. Webster.** Children's Press, Chicago, 1982. A basic introduction to plants with simple discussions of algae, fungi, roots, stems, leaves, flowers, and seeds. (ages 3 - 9)

Science Fun With Peanuts and Popcorn by **Rose Wyler.** Illustrations by Pat Stewart. Julian Messner (a division of Simon and Schuster), NY, 1986. Learn about seeds: how they grow, what's inside, and how roots form and grow. Afterward, have a peanut and popcorn party! (ages 3 - 9)

My First Nature Book: A Life-size Guide to Discovering the World Around You by **Angela Wilkes.** Knopf, NY, 1990. Projects for the young nature lover, including a bottle garden, a worm farm, a caterpillar house, and more. (ages 6 - 10)

The Compost Heap by **Harlow Rockwell.** Doubleday and Co. Inc., Garden City, NY, 1974. This simply written picture book explains how a compost pile is made and how it turns into soil. (ages 3 - 7)

How My Garden Grew by **Anne and Harlow Rockwell.** Macmillan Pub. Co., NY, 1982. With pride and pleasure, a child describes growing a garden by himself. (ages 3 - 5)

Grandpa's Garden Lunch by **Judith Caseley.** Greenwillow Books, NY, 1990. Grandpa and Sarah planted seeds, watered, watched, and waited. Then one day Grandma invited Sarah for a very special lunch. (ages 4 - 9)

Too Many Hopkins by **Tomie de Paola.** G. P. Putnam's Sons, NY, 1989. Who has the biggest and finest garden on Fiddle-Dee-Dee Farms? The Hopkins family of rabbits wins that prize. (ages 3 - 7)

Your First Garden Book by **Marc Brown.** Little, Brown & Co., Boston, 1981. A storehouse of garden-related projects for beginners. (ages 3 - 10)

Look, Mom, It's Growing: Kids Can Have Green Thumbs Too by **Ed Fink.** Illustrations by Louise J. Mueller. Countripide Books, Barrington, IL, 1976. This is a wonderful book for the child who is beginning to develop an interest in gardening. (ages 5 - 10)

The Victory Garden Kid's Book by Marjorie Waters. Houghton Mifflin, Boston, 1988. Step-by-step instruction based on a whole season of gardening, from ground breaking in the spring to closing the plot in the fall. (with help, age 5 and up)

From Seed to Salad by Hannah L. Johnson. Lothrop, Lee and Shepard Co., NY, 1978. Salads taste best fresh from your garden. This book presents a straight-forward account of a small salad garden that is planned, planted, cared for, and harvested by the children of a family. (ages 6 - 10)

In My Garden: A Child's Gardening Book by Helen and Kelly Oechsli. Macmillan Pub. Co., NY, 1985. Solid and easy to follow advice about growing seven popular vegetables. (ages 4 - 8)

The Garden Book by Wes Porter. Edited by Sally Kovalchick. Workman Pub., NY, 1989. This book, which comes with a miniature greenhouse, is an excellent guide for parents and children to use together. (age 6 and up)

Strawberry by Jennifer Coldrey. Photographs by George Bernard. Silver Burdett Press, Englewood Cliffs, NJ, 1988. Photographs, drawings, and text on two levels of difficulty describe how the strawberry plant produces juicy strawberries and sends out runners to start new plants. (ages 3 - 10)

The Herb Growing Book by Rosemary Verey. Illustrations by Barbara Firth and Elizabeth Wood. Little, Brown & Co., Boston, 1980. This beginning guide shows you different herbs to grow indoors, on a sill, or in a garden. (age 5 and up)

The Herb and Spice Book for Kids by Alice Siegel and Margo McLoone. Illustrations by Gwen Brodkin. Holt, Rinehart & Winston, NY, 1978. Here are ideas for growing herbs, making herbal gifts, crazy cure-alls, and easy food recipes. (ages 5 - 12)

Desert Giant: The World of the Saguaro Cactus by Barbara Bash. Sierra Club Books, Little, Brown & Co., Boston, 1990. The ecological importance of the saguaro cactus as a habitat for many desert creatures is captured in the author's colorful illustrations and illuminating yet simple text. (ages 6 - 10)

The Biggest Pumpkin Ever by Steven Kroll. Illustrations by Jeni Bassett. Holiday House, NY, 1984. Once two mice fell in love with the same pumpkin. One watered and tended the plant during the day, the other repeated the care during the night, unknown to each other. A warm and delightful tale. (ages 3 - 6)

The Remarkable Plant in Apartment 4 by Giulo Maestro. Bradbury Press, NY, 1973. Imagine that! A plant that grows overnight! And we mean grows! This is a fun-filled fantasy story. (ages 4 - 9)

In My Garden by Ron Maris. Greenwillow Books, NY, 1987. Step into a little child's garden. Follow the path to see (in extremely colorful and detailed illustrations) the frogs in the pool, the glorious variety of flowers, and a big surprise at the end. (ages 3 - 6)

The Flower: An Ecology Story Book by Chris Baines. Illustrations by Penny Ives. Crocodile Books, NY, 1990. Two children plant a flower and learn how it grows and thrives in harmony with the ladybugs, ants, bees, and other creatures. (ages 4 - 8)

A Rose in My Garden by Arnold Lobel. Illustrations by Anita Lobel. Scholastic, Inc., NY, 1984. Beginning with one rose in the garden, the verses in this book build in the "House that Jack Built" style to include the flowers in the garden, a mouse, and a cat. (ages 3 - 6)

A Flower Grows by Ken Robbins. Dial Books, NY, 1990. Using beautiful hand-tinted photographs, this book follows the life cycle of the rough and ugly bulb of an amaryllis plant until it bursts into a perfect and delicate bloom. (all ages)

More Than Just a Flower Garden, photos and text by Dwight Kuhn. Silver Burdett Press, Morristown, NJ,

1990. Stunning microphotography shows the hidden world of the flower garden and the creatures whose lives depend on the colorful plants growing there. (read aloud, ages 6 - 9)

More Than Just a Vegetable Garden, **photos and text by Dwight Kuhn.** Silver Burdett Press, Morristown, NJ, 1990. Beginning with sprouting seeds, children are able to observe all phases of plant growth and to see in stunning photos the creatures that live in the hidden world of the vegetable garden. (read aloud, ages 6 - 9)

Linnea's Windowsill Garden **by Christina Bjork.** Illustrations by Lena Anderson. R & S Books, distributed by Farrar, Straus & Giroux, NY, 1978. Linnea grows plants all over her room - in pots, crates, even in glass jars – and she takes you on a tour of her indoor garden. (all ages)

Bugs **by Nancy W. Parker and Joan R. Wright.** Illustrations by Nancy Winslow Parker. Greenwillow Books, NY, 1987. This first book of entomology (the study of bugs) presents sixteen commonly known insects. (ages 6 - 10)

Backyard Insects **by Millicent E. Selsam and Ronald Goor.** Photographs by Ronald Goor. Four Winds Press, NY, 1981. Through simple text and clever photographs, discover common garden insects and learn about their protective appearance. (ages 6 - 10)

The National Gardening Association Guide to Kid's Gardening **by Lynne Ocone.** John Wiley and Sons, NY, 1990. This clearly written and useful guide will enable parents and teachers to assist their children through any gardening project they wish to tackle. (ages 6 - 12)

Resources for Parents and Teachers

Ladybugs and Lettuce Leaves, Center for Science in the Public Interest. Though this is primarily designed as a text for elementary school children (it has a Teacher's Guide to go with it), it could easily be used by parents. It is available for $6.95 from CSPI, 1501 16th Street, NW, Washington, D.C. 20036.

A Garden for Children by Felicity Bryan. This lovely book presents ideas about how to draw children into the garden by creating secret places as well as more utilitarian projects. It is published in England, but it is distributed in this country by Smith and Hawken, 25 Corte Madera, Mill Valley, CA 94941.

Gardening with Children Brooklyn Botanic Garden, 1000 Washington Ave., Brooklyn, NY 11225. The museum also offers a video called *Ready Set Grow* for children who have had no exposure to gardening. It comes with companion booklets and costs $29.95 plus $2.50 postage and handling.

The Youth Gardening Book is available from the National Gardening Asso., and copies are $8.95. Write the association at 180 Flynn Avenue, Burlington, VT 05401.

Gurney's catalog features snapshots of children showing off what they have grown. It offers the "Giant Jumble Seed Packet," which costs one cent. The catalog states that "we've kept the price a penny so children can buy it with their own money." Write Gurney, 1224 Page Street, Yankton, SD 57078.

Clyde Robin offers a canned kit called "*A Child's Garden.*" The brightly decorated can contains six vegetables from giant pumpkins to Indian corn, five bright flowers, planting stakes, and a book about gardening written for children. Write to Clyde Robin Seed Co., P.O. Box 2855, Castro Valley, CA 94546.

"The Privilege of Gardening with Children" by Carolyn Jabs. *Orion Nature Quarterly* (Autumn 1987): 33-41.

"Missouri's Garden of Consequence" *National Geographic* (August 1990): 124-140. The Missouri

Botanical Garden has been called to the front lines in the war to save plant specimens from the rapidly disappearing tropical rainforests.

A pack of "Special Kids' Salad Garden Seeds" can be ordered from Butterbrooke Farm. Send $1.00 to 78-K Barry Road, Oxford, CT 06483.

Watch It Grow offers "A Child's Garden Seed Collection," a combination of vegetable and flower seeds especially for a kid's garden. Send $1.00 to 2560 Nickel Place, Hayward, CA 94545.

The National Gardening Association is a national clearinghouse of information on youth gardening. They have created *Growlab,* an 8-foot-square indoor gardening center, designed for classroom use, in which children can grow plants from seed to maturity in less than three months. The NGA also presents training workshops and has published a curriculum guide entitled *GrowLab: Activities for Growing Minds.* Write to the Association at 180 Flynn Ave., Burlington, VT 05401.

W. Atlee Burpee Co. carries "Kinder-Garden" with seed packets, stakes, and how-to booklet. Write to 300 Park Ave., Warminster, PA 18974.

The American Horticulture Society publishes a Garden Books catalog. It is free and it contains a large selection for "Young Readers." For your copy write to AHS, 7931 East Boulevard Dr., Dept. PR-490, Alexandria, VA 22308.

The Windstar Foundation has developed a Biodome Project, a solar-heated dome structure which provides an environment for high-yield food production. This method of food growth conserves energy, soil, water, and recycles nutrients between aquaculture and horticulture. The project began in 1982 as an experiment in the utilization of renewable energy resources to produce fish and vegetables year-round in a harsh climate. For more information on the project, send a stamped, legal-size envelope to The Windstar Foundation, 2317 Snowmass Creek Road, Snowmass, CO 81654.

"A Child's Garden," a booklet which lists a bounty of ideas for planting projects both in the classroom and out, can be obtained by sending a postcard to Chevron Chemical Co., Public Affairs, 575 Market Street, San Francisco, CA 94119.

Let's Grow: 72 Gardening Adventures with Children by Linda Tilgner. Storey Communications, Inc., Pownal, VT 05261, 1988. This book presents dozens of exciting projects to help parents and teachers make gardening more fun for children.

The Butterfly Garden: Turning Your Window Box or Backyard into a Beautiful Home for Butterflies by Mathew Tekulsky. Harvard Common Press, 1985.

The Country Diary Book of Creating a Wild Flower Garden by Jonathan Andrews. Henry Holt & Co., NY, 1986.

Cucumbers in a Flowerpot by Alice Skelsey. Workman Pub., NY, 1984.

Banquets for Birds, National Audubon Society, 950 Third Avenue, New York, NY l0022, 1983.

The *Necessary Catalog* is full educational information on organic gardening, "how-to" publications, and a list of relevant books. The cost of the catalog is $2.00, which is refundable with your first order. Write 422 Salem Avenue, New Castle, VA 24127. The Gardeners Supply Co. also sells almost everything needed for organic and environmentally sensitive gardening. To receive a copy, write to them at 128 Intervale Road, Burlington, VT 05401.

CHAPTER FOUR

Trees Are Terrific!

Trees are the earth's endless effort to speak to the listening heavens.
RABINDRANATH TAGORE

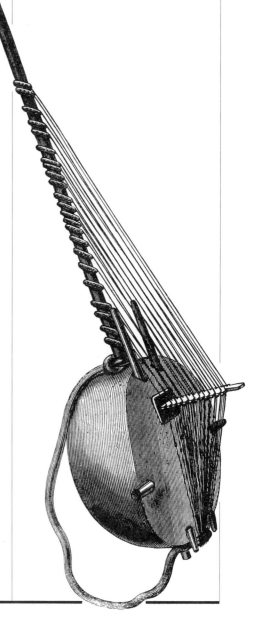

T rees may be the most important and useful plants on our Earth. They provide us with oxygen we need to breathe, water that is vital to all living things, food for both animals and people, wood that we depend on for our houses, furniture, and paper products – not to mention the oasis of shade on a steamy summer's day.

Children are naturally drawn to the majesty and adventure of a tree. They want to climb high in its branches, pick at the bark to expose the tiny insects living there, and build secret hiding places to escape from the ordinary world. As parents, we sometimes get caught up in our daily duties of bill paying, car pooling, food preparation, or household chores and we forget to take time to enjoy the beauty that surrounds us. We can become tuned to the natural world again through shared exploration with our children.

A Tree is Nice, by Janice May Udry. Illustrations by Marc Simont. Harper and Row, Pub., NY, 1956.

Trees are beautiful. They fill up the sky. If you have a tree, you can climb its trunk, roll in its leaves, or swing from one of its limbs. This is one of those books which tickles children with the realization that the everyday world can bring beauty into their lives. (ages 3 - 7)

Apple Tree, by Peter Parnall. Macmillan Pub., NY, 1987.

With vivid prose and detailed illustrations, this book endows a simple, beloved apple tree with a voice that echoes the miracle of life's cycles. Beginning in the spring, the apple tree is visited by bumblebees, ants, and flies busily gathering pollen and laying their eggs. Summer brings a robin and her nest, as well as many apple eaters such as ravens, deer, and raccoon. Winter snows arrive and it is too cold for visitors, so the apple tree stands alone. As nature's cycle unfolds, young readers and adults will discover the wonder and wisdom in the life cycle of the apple tree. (age 7 and up)

Take a moment and put yourself into the "remember when" mode. Imagine what it was like as a child pulling yourself higher and higher into a treetop. Maybe you found solitude there away from homework or younger siblings; no matter the reason – it was an adventure! As you share these picture books and simple activities with your children, remember the rapture you felt as a youngster and relive some of those experiences. Children love to hear about their parents as kids. So go ahead and tell them about the time your mother found you almost at the very top of a magnolia tree with your four-year-old sister following your lead! Luckily for the four-year-old, your mother was there to guide her down safely. But for you, it was like climbing Mount Everest, almost reaching the summit, only to be called down because of supper. Similar experiences will remain in your memory always. Share them with your children as you go together to explore the complexity, necessity, and beauty of trees.

Awareness

From Furniture to Buttons: We Need Trees!

Our lives would be very different if it were not for trees! Trees give us everything from the pages of this book to the eyeglass frames you might be wearing on your nose! This activity is meant to help your children discover their dependency on trees in their everyday lives. Walk through your house or building and identify all of the "tree objects" you can find and place a token (such as string tied in a small bow) on each item. When you are finished, you will be amazed at the great number of "tree gifts" that will be tagged!

We build with wood. People build many things with wood and these items will be the most obvious: furniture, doors, window frames, stairs, building blocks, baseball bats, tennis rackets, handles for brooms and mops, etc.

We use paper every day. To turn a tree into paper, the bark is first stripped from the trunk and the wood is chopped into very small pieces. The wood chips are "cooked" with other chemicals until they turn to pulp (which has an oatmeal consistency). Next the pulp is washed, sent through machines to flatten the fibers, and dried into smooth sheets. Most paper products are easy to spot: for example, drawing or writing paper, cardboard boxes, books, magazines, milk cartons, postage stamps, toilet tissue, paper towels, napkins, paper plates, etc.

We use tree "ooze." Tree saps, called resins and gums, are used to make many things, such as paint, varnish, mouthwash, some cosmetics, and soap. Rubber trees produce a liquid called latex which is used to make rubber hoses, tires, rubber gloves, rubber bands, and some balls.

Cork is a spongy bark from the cork oak tree. Do you have a cork bulletin board in your home? Also, some balls (like baseballs) use a cork center.

Do you eat food from trees? There are many delicious foods that come from trees, such as fruits, nuts, spices, and syrup. (For a more complete list, see "Tree Treats to Eat" in this chapter.)

Cellulose is everywhere. The major component of the tree's cell walls is called cellulose. It is used to make paper and many other useful products that we have around our home. Imagine life without these: buttons, toothbrushes, combs, carpeting, cellophane, photographic film, synthetic cloth (rayon, for example), plastic eyeglass frames, etc.

The Tremendous Tree Book, by May Garelick and Barbara Brenner. Illustrations by Fred Brenner. Four Winds Press, NY, 1979.

This book celebrates the tree, one of the most useful plants on Earth. A raccoon and squirrel act as guides to help introduce children to the excitement of trees that reads like fiction, but is all absolutely true! The authors have sifted through the vast information available to make the science of trees understandable and appealing to young children. This is a great read-aloud book and an ecologically-minded choice for storytime. (ages 3 - 9)

When Dad Cuts Down the Chestnut Tree, by Pam Ayres. Illustrations by Graham Percy. Alfred A. Knopf, NY, 1988.

The prospect of seeing the chestnut tree cut down makes a child think of all the good things that will come from its removal: a rocking horse, a fort for toy soldiers, a wheelbarrow, stilts, and blocks. But then come thoughts about all the reasons for letting the tree stay where it is: shade, a place for a treehouse, piles of leaves to jump into, kindling for a winter's fire, and a branch for a swing. Also, where will owl and squirrel live if the tree is removed? Finally a decision is reached: "Dad, don't cut it down at all!" The story in rhyme and bright illustrations will appeal to the youngest tree huggers. (ages 3 - 6)

Getting to Know a Tree, Personally!

Select a tree in your area to "adopt." Some criteria to consider will be size, type, and location. Size is an important factor because the tree you choose must be sturdy and well-rooted, so you and your child can observe your adopted tree for many years to come. The type of tree is a personal choice. Do you want it to be a fruit or nut tree? Is it a good climbing tree? Does it provide lots of shade for hot, sunny days? Ask your child these questions before a final selection is made. Also it needs to be a tree that will be easy for you and your child to observe in all seasons.

When a tree has been chosen, here are some sensory experiences to help create a bond between you, your child, and the adopted tree.

Look Closely: Carefully observe its physical characteristics (size, color, and texture of bark, leaf shape and distribution on tree, etc.) Have your child describe how the tree looks, and record his description in a "tree diary." For a more focused and detailed observation, give your child a magnifying glass to look more closely at the bark and leaves. Do you see any signs of insect or animal life? Do you see any seeds lying about or attached to the tree?

Listen: Does your tree make any sounds? Watch and listen as the wind moves through the leaves. You might want to spread a blanket under its branches and quietly listen with your eyes closed. Do you hear any birds or animals that might live in your tree? Put your ear up to the bark and listen to the inside of your tree. Do you hear any sounds? If you have access to a stethoscope, listen to the inside of your tree with it to magnify any sounds of sap running in spring or tiny insects chewing wood under its bark.

Touch: Slowly run your fingers up and down its bark. How does it feel? Is it all rough? Can you find some smooth patches among the rugged scales? Carefully feel the leaves. How do they feel different from the bark? If seeds are about, touch them and describe how they feel. Are they a type of nut (pecan, acorn, chestnut, walnut, etc.)? How do they travel from the parent tree in order to sprout elsewhere? Do they float or twirl? Are they carried by hungry animals? Play this game with your child: have him close his eyes as you place different parts of your adopted tree into his hands. Encourage him to describe how it feels and identify the tree part.

Take a Sniff: Smell the different parts of your tree to find out if they have an odor; for example sniff the bark, new and old leaves, and seeds. If it is spring and your tree is in bloom, also smell the blossoms.

*Do not taste any part of your tree. If your tree is fruit or nut bearing, check with an agricultural center before harvesting it.

Keep a Tree Diary

Since a tree can change from season to season, keeping a record of its yearly cycle and growth can help a child become more aware of seasonal changes and how plant life adapts throughout the year.

After the adoption process is complete, you will want to keep a journal of some kind in which to record seasonal changes, write stories and poems, or draw pictures. To begin, write the official date of adoption, choose a name for your tree, and write that in the diary. Have your child tell you why this particular tree was chosen and record his words. Take a photograph of your child with his tree or allow him to draw a picture. Repeat visits throughout the year, compare observations made each time, and make an entry in your tree journal. Here are other suggestions for journal entries:

• Have an imaginary conversation with your adopted tree. How does your tree feel, hear, smell, and see the things around him? Have your tree describe what he feels like to be covered with cold, wet snow. How did he feel during the violent wind and thunderstorm last night? In winter, when he appears to be sleeping, what does your tree dream about?

• Pretend you are the parent tree of your adopted tree. Describe how the seed traveled from you to its current location. What was it like seeing your offspring sprout from the ground as a seedling? Could you give the young sapling any advice about how to grow into a strong, sturdy tree?

• Draw pictures of your tree in different seasons. Have your child tell you a story about the adventures your tree experiences in each season, and record his words next to the illustration.

• Do any insects or animals live in your adopted tree? Have your child draw pictures of any creatures that he observes and briefly describe why this tree is a good home for them.

Tree Treats to Eat

It's amazing how many foods come from trees. Besides fruits and nuts, people enjoy eating the sap and even tree bark.

Plan and prepare a Tree Treats Party for friends or extended family. Here are a few tree foods to munch on at the party:

• Fruits: apples, apricots, avocados, cherries, coconuts, dates, figs, grapefruits, lemons, limes, olives, oranges, peaches, pears, and prunes.

• Nuts: almonds, cashews, chestnuts, pecans, and walnuts.

• Candy: maple sugar candy and chocolate.

• Spices: allspice, cinnamon, cloves, and nutmeg.

• Food from sap: syrup

Picnic Under a Shady Friend

Visit your adopted tree on a pleasant day and bring a picnic to eat under its shady branches. (Don't forget to bring a drink of water for your tree!) Include several "tree treats" (for example applesauce, maple sugar, pecans, and walnut fudge – all things kids will love!). As you eat, point out the different foods we receive from trees.

The Giving Tree, by Shel
Silverstein. Harper and Row,
Pub., NY, 1964.

This is a tender story about
giving and a quiet acceptance of
another's capacity to love in
return. "Once there was a
tree...and she loved a little boy."
Every day the boy would come to
play among her branches, eat her
apples, and sleep in her
shade...and the tree was happy.
But as the boy grew older he
began to ask more of the tree,
and the tree gave freely, until
there was nothing left of her but
a stump. This is a lesson about
all the gifts we receive from trees
and, hopefully, it will make us
think about how we care for
them in return. (all ages)

• After reading *The Giving Tree* by Shel Silverstein, talk about the
gifts that the tree gave to the little boy in the story. Does your
adopted tree give you and your child any gifts? Make a list and
illustrate them in your journal (don't forget oxygen and water).

• Write a thank you note to your adopted tree expressing your
appreciation for the special gifts that it gives to you.

Are We Really so Different from Trees?

Your first impression, when you compare yourself to a tree, might
be that you are very different creatures, but that is not true.

During a visit to your adopted tree have your child consider these
comparisons:

1. What does your tree need to survive? (It needs water to drink,
clean air to "breathe," and sunshine to grow. It combines part of the
water and part of the air and uses the energy from the sun to make
sugar for food.) You and your tree have these needs in common
because humans need water to drink, clean air to breathe, and food
to eat in order to survive.

2. Look at your body and compare it to your adopted tree.

• As we stand, our feet and toes keep us firmly in touch with the
ground. A tree's roots are buried in the ground.

• Our skin protects our insides and is a barrier against illness and
germs. A tree's bark serves the same function. Also, right under the
bark, the sap is channeled to all parts of the tree, much like the way
our blood is channeled through our veins.

• The trunk of our body is similar to the trunk of a tree, as it
keeps us straight and tall.

• Our arms can be compared to the branches of a tree.

• Leaves of the tree grab the sunshine in the same way that our
fingers can grab an object.

3. Pretend you are a tree. Stand up straight and tall, dig your toes
into the ground, hold your arms high over your head and spread
your fingers out to grab the sunshine. (One thing that trees can do
that we cannot is to create their own food from water, air, and
sunshine. This happens in the green leaves and the sugar is sent to
all parts of the tree to feed it.) Pretend that your fingers are making
food and let that sugar flow to all parts of your hungry body.

To Be a Tree

What does it feel like to be a tree? Trees are really the only ones who know. But, with their vivid imaginations, your children can magically transform into trees and experience those feelings. Ask your children to walk slowly in a circle and listen carefully as you read this short story. As the story progresses, ask them to act out what happens. The first part of the story is always the same, although you may select the ending you desire or act out a different ending on subsequent days.

One glorious, summer day you are walking through a meadow filled with dandelions. All around you there is a warm tingly feeling in the air. Without warning your toes begin to grow! You look down at them and watch as they grow right out of your shoes! You can no longer use your legs to walk as your toenails dig deep into the soft Earth. You feel them growing longer and reaching deeper until you are anchored in this spot. Your skin is turning hard and scaly. As each second passes your body and arms are becoming stiff. You can move them a little, such as when a breeze pushes against them, but that's all! Your fingertips and hair feel electric and they begin to dance in the wind. Soon your mouth closes and you can no longer talk; the only noise you make is the rustling of your leaves and an occasional creak of your trunk. All of this excitement has made you very thirsty. So you soak water into your roots and slowly push it up through your trunk, down each limb to feed the leaves on each branch and twig. . . .

. . .You can tell from the position of the sun that it is well past the noon hour and, because you didn't have any lunch, you begin to feel quite hungry. You know it will be impossible to eat in your usual way, since you have no mouth or teeth to chew! As you try to think through this problem, you realize your leaves, now full of water, are grabbing the rays of sunshine. They are using the sun's energy to make food! Your leaves use part of the water and part of the surrounding air to make sugar. Slowly the sweet food is pumped down the branches and through the trunk to every part of your body. It tastes good and satisfies your raging hunger. You think to yourself, "Now, that's a good lunch!"

Tree of Life: The World of the African Baobab, by Barbara Bash. Little, Brown and Co., Boston, 1989.

The baobab is an African tree that is filled with mystery and is even considered to be an honored elder of the tribe. It can measure up to forty feet across and sixty feet high! The Africans call the tree "mother" because it provides shelter and food to an incredible variety of creatures. The engaging, easy-to-read text and stunning watercolor illustrations document the relationship between the ancient baobab tree and the many life forms it helps to support. (age 6 and up)

. . .Since you can no longer move your head from side to side, it's difficult to look around. But with your eyes you spy a little brown squirrel searching for food near your roots. As he scampers up your trunk his claws tickle your bark, as if someone is lightly scratching what was once your back. He finds a nut on one of your branches and plucks it away. Oh, you felt that! It didn't hurt, but felt like something was being lifted away. He tickles you again as he runs down your trunk and scampers away. You listen for him, but instead you hear crows calling from the distance. *(Quietly, then louder.)* "Caw...caw...caw." They are heading this way! You feel a pinch, then another, and another. . .three large, black crows perch themselves on your branches and begin to quarrel. Suddenly, the wind picks up and you sway back and forth in the breeze. This startles the crows and they noisily fly away. *(Louder, then softer.)* "Caw...caw...caw!" until you can no longer hear their piercing calls. Soon you and the golden dandelions are alone in the meadow swaying in the delicate breeze that is so welcome on this warm day.

...It isn't long before you notice the sun has been covered up by dark rainclouds. "Pitter, patter, drip, drop, splash!" The raindrops begin to fall. Now your leaves are spreading out to catch the droplets and protect you like an umbrella. The soft, cool water is comforting after standing in the hot sun all afternoon. The rain washes the dust from your leaves and branches, in the same way that water used to bathe you in the shower at home. You see a crack of light streak across the sky. Then, CRASH; you hear the rolling thunder. That sounded close! You watch the lightning dance across the darkening sky; it's like a fireworks display on the Fourth of July! Look, there's one. . . and another. All of a sudden...zap! "Eee-Ouch!" You feel a sharp pain in one of your branches and you want to scream, but you can't! The lightning has severed the branch from your trunk and it falls to the ground, smoking on the cut edge. After a while, the pain subsides as the rain cools what's left of your burning branch. Finally, you realize how fortunate you really are: it's only with luck that you were not split in two! Over a long time your wound heals and new branches grow to take the place of the fallen one.

Dressed in Splendor

Children enjoy make-believe and dressing up can make it even more fun. With help, your young child can make this simple costume from a brown grocery bag, a crayon, fallen leaves, and seeds. Put the whole outfit together and your child instantly becomes a tree, and several children become a forest!

Tree Trunk Vest: Lay a brown paper grocery bag, folded, flat on a table. Cut down the two long sides about one-half inch from the edge. Cut a hole at the top of the vest that fits over your child's head. If there is printing on the sack, turn it inside out. With string, tie the vest on a real tree's rough bark and rub over the paper sack with a wax crayon to reveal the pattern of the bark.

Leaf Crown: Take one of the strips that was cut from the side of the vest and fit it around your child's head like a headband. Holding the measurement, remove the band from your child's head, and secure with tape. Glue fallen leaves (or leaves cut from construction paper) and fallen seeds or nuts onto the headband and allow to dry.

Leaf Bands or Bracelets: Using the remaining cut strip, measure around arms and/or wrists. Secure with tape and decorate with fallen leaves in the same fashion as for the headband.

Making Music from Wood

Create musical instruments from tree-derived products. Let your child rummage through the Recycle Craft Box to find materials. This will also help show how trashable items can become fun and useful creations.

Percussion Instruments:

• Clap wooden blocks or sticks together. To add variety, glue pieces of sand paper to two wooden blocks and rub together.

• Make drums from cylindrical cardboard containers, such as oatmeal and cornmeal boxes, or empty ice cream containers. Place a piece of waxed paper over one of the containers, secure with a rubber band, and brush with straw to create a delicate drum sound.

String Section:

• Take a piece of cardboard and cut notches on opposite edges. Stretch rubber bands or pieces of twine across the cardboard and pluck with fingers.

The Voice of the Wood, by Claude Clément. Paintings by Frédéric Clément. Dial Books, NY, 1989.

This book is breathtakingly beautiful. It is the story of a Venetian instrument maker who loved a great, old tree in his garden. One winter, the old tree dies and it has to be cut down. But the wood is saved to craft a magical cello - an instrument that would only give forth beautiful music if "the musician's heart was in tune with the wood." The outcome of the story is incredibly surprising and moving, an ending that points out the oneness of all nature. (age 8 and up)

Voice of the Wood

After reading *The Voice of the Wood* by Claude Clément, immerse yourselves in the rich and entrancing sound of the cello. Ask your children to close their eyes and listen for the deep voice of the cello. Here are some suggested recordings to choose from:

1. J. S. Bach - Suite No. 3 in C Major for Unaccompanied Cello, BWV 1009.

2. Shostakovich - Cello Concerto in E Flat Major, Op. 107.

Who Lives Here?

Tune: The Itsy Bitsy Spider

This is a riddle song. First, sing each verse separately to your children and ask them to guess which tree creature you are pretending to be. Later, they can learn the words and even add new verses to the song.

I scamper through the branches gathering my dinner,

If I am disturbed, you will hear me sharply twitter.

A hollow in the trunk becomes my treasury,

So be kind to the tree; it is a home for me. *(the squirrel)*

You might find me asleep on a bright and sunny day.

When nighttime comes around, it's time to wake and play.

Mice taste delicious, I'm sure you will agree.

So be kind to the tree; it is a home for me. *(the owl)*

After flying high, I need a place to rest.

On the branch of a tree is where I build my nest.

Squishy worms and grubs I munch on eagerly,

So be kind to the tree; it is a home for me. *(the bird)*

• Take an empty shoe box and make about four cuts on each of the shorter top edges (match snips across from each other). String rubber bands or twine between notches and pluck. This instrument makes an interesting, hollow sound different from that of the cardboard "guitar."

Woodwinds:

• Use cardboard tubes (such as paper towel rolls) to make "flutes."

A Tree Is a Home

This activity will help your children recognize that a tree is a home to plants, animals, birds, and insects. Keep in mind that you will probably not see all of these creatures in one afternoon's visit, as some are nocturnal or very shy. But you can look for evidence, such as a hollow in the tree or an opening to an underground tunnel. Look closely at and around your adopted tree and other nearby trees. Make a pictorial list of all the insects, birds, or animals that you see living in or using the trees in some way. Keep a slash mark count of each type of creature or plant observed. You might see:

On the Branches: Many birds use trees as resting spots or as places for nests in spring. (If you find a nest, do not disturb it.) Animals such as squirrels, raccoons, or frogs might live in or near your tree. During the evening hours in July and August, you can hear the buzzing of cicadas (commonly called locusts). They periodically shed their skins and you might find their brown, discarded casings attached to the branches or trunk of your tree.

On or Under the Bark: Look very closely to find the insects that live here because their color or markings help them blend into their background, camouflaging them as protection from enemies. (A magnifying glass may aid you.) You might see spiders, flies, ants, woodlice, beetles, moths, or fungi (shelf fungi is easy to spot).

On the Leaves: Caterpillars, insect larva, walking sticks, and aphids feed upon leaves. In the spring, honey bees often can be seen collecting pollen and nectar from blossoms.

Around the Roots: Fallen leaves that collect in drifts provide shelter and food for many creatures, such as woodlice, earthworms, slugs, snails, and mites. Some small animals dig tunnels beneath the roots, so you might see traces of chipmunks, mice, rabbits, or moles.

DREAMSTARTER

One cool, autumn evening you go walking through a beautiful forest. The last rays of sunshine peek through the forest canopy to make golden pictures on the moss-covered ground. Everything is so calm in the forest. You close your eyes and listen to the rustling leaves and pine needles as the breeze passes through the branches.

Suddenly, something darts out from behind a tree. You turn your head, but it's gone! "What could move so quickly?" you ask yourself. Being a curious child, you immediately set out to follow. You run in the direction of its sound, darting among trees and fallen branches along the way. Then you stop and listen again. . .*(pause, then snap your fingers)* there it is over by that rotting log. Quietly, you creep toward the log. You do not notice that with each step you are becoming smaller. . .and smaller. . .and smaller.

By the time you reach the log you can easily step into the hollow end, without even ducking your head! You stand at the opening to let your eyes adjust to the darkness. Around you are bits of debris from the forest floor, leaves, pine needles, twigs, feathers, pine cones, and a huge pile of acorns and seeds. Outside you hear a clatter as someone approaches, so you quickly hide behind the nearest pine cone and wait. Cautiously, a striped chipmunk enters the log, sniffing and looking for signs of an intruder. Satisfied, he runs over to the pile of nuts with a quickness you've never seen before! He empties his stuffed cheeks, adding a load of nuts to the mountain. With incredible speed he darts from one end of his house to the other, tidying the piles of material.

You watch him for a long time. Everything he does is fascinating, from nibbling on a seed to rearranging his soft bedding! It has been a long time since you've eaten and your stomach begins to rumble

I hide in the branches and look just like a stick.

If you don't look closely, I'll give your eyes a trick.

You might not even notice I'm chewing on a leaf,

So be kind to the tree; it is a home for me. *(the walking stick)*

The Dead Tree, by Alvin Tresselt. Illustrations by Charles Robinson. Parents' Magazine Press, NY, 1972.

The death of a mighty oak provides food and protection for the insects and animals of the forest. This story describes the final chapter in the life cycle of a tree and its importance to the creatures that live among its branches and within its wood. The great oak tree returns life to the Earth through its death. Witness the process of decay and understand the necessity of this life cycle to the forest and its creatures. (ages 5 - 12)

Forest Log, by James R. Newton. Illustrations by Irene Brady. Thomas R. Crowell, NY, 1980.

A majestic fir tree crashes to the moss-covered forest floor. The tree, which has lived for hundreds of years, will begin the long process of decaying. Now it will become a nurse log and provide homes and nourishment to thousands of plants and animals. The precise, detailed drawings and intriguing text tell about a unique, biological community and the role that every tree plays when it falls. (ages 4 - 9)

loudly. The chipmunk becomes alert to your presence and noses about until he finds your hiding place. Instead of being afraid, he chatters at you happily and hands you a nut to eat. The two of you share a delicious meal and chat joyfully to each other. Before long, you realize the daylight is fading and soon the night creatures of the forest will begin to hunt. You decide it will be safer to stay in the chipmunk's house until morning. After a long day of storing food, the tired chipmunk curls up on the soft feathers and pine needles to sleep. You snuggle down beside him and soon begin to dream about gathering plump acorns and tasty pine cones for the long winter.

Make a Seed Collector

One of the main purposes of a tree's cycle is to produce precious seeds to perpetuate itself. Most trees will produce millions of seeds in their lifetimes. Many of these seeds are eaten by animals or fall on inhospitable soil and fail to grow. Luckily, an occasional success produces another magnificent tree and more seeds!

To Make a Seed Collector: Gather together a clean, used pair of panty hose and tissue paper. Stuff the hosiery with the tissue and secure with a knot. Drag the seed collector on the ground under your adopted tree. Examine the acquired material for seeds and other interesting tree or plant parts. Look closely, using a magnifying glass, to see any evidence of animal or insect life such as chewed leaf parts or cracked and eaten seeds.

1. How are your adopted tree's seeds dispersed? Are they twirlers, floaters, hitchhikers, nuts, or berries?

2. Listen to your child as he makes up an adventure story about a tree seed. Have him illustrate it in his tree journal.

The Final Phase

A tree's value does not diminish after its death — instead it becomes an environment for thousands of earth-making insects. They chew, tunnel, live in, and decompose a fallen log for many years and gradually the tree turns to humus, a rich soil that will supply nutrients for the new plant life that takes its place in the forest.

Leaf Rubbings

Leaves are not only pleasing to look at. They serve a vital function for the tree: the chlorophyll (which gives them their green hue) uses the power of sunlight to combine water and air, resulting in sugars and starches to feed the plant. This process is called photosynthesis. In the fall, when the leaves turn bright orange, red, and gold, they no longer make food for the tree and it "goes to sleep" for the cold winter. This activity celebrates the uniqueness of leaves. It is an easy project for young children and results in a beautiful collage. Sturdy leaves with strongly defined veins work best.

Collect a variety of fallen leaves (remember, pine needles are also leaves) and arrange them face down on a table. (For younger children, tape the leaves to the surface for better results.) Place a piece of drawing paper over the leaves and rub evenly with the side of a wax crayon. Try a mixture of colors. An impression will come through to create a stunning leaf collection.

Dead or Alive?

Have your children take a close look at an old tree stump or dead log. (Offer a magnifying glass or dental mirror to enhance their viewing ability or vary their perspective.) Try to find creatures and plant life on the log, beneath the log, and under the bark. Some creatures that you might see are termites, beetles, centipedes, ants, woodlice, pill bugs, spiders, algae, mosses, fungi, tree seedlings, or wildflowers. All of these insects tunnel, eat, and excavate through the dead tree and help to decompose or break it down. It takes many years to turn a tree into the dark, rich soil called humus.

Here are some questions to think about during your exploration:

• Are dead trees and live trees inhabited by different populations of creatures? Give some examples.

• What value does a dead tree have to the forest and its creatures? What "gifts" does the tree give after it dies?

• Is it possible to tell what may have caused the death of this tree? Tell a story about what might have happened.

• If you could be any of the creatures working and living in this stump, which would you prefer to be? What would be some of your activities?

It's A Rottin' Home for Me

Tune: Old MacDonald Had a Farm

I am a termite in a log,

Living peacefully.

I bore through wood and eat my fill,

It's a rottin' home for me!

With a crunch, crunch, gulp!

And a crunch, crunch, gulp!

Plywood, firewood,

Any kind of wood would

Suit me fine and always be

A rottin' home for me!

There Is Life in Litter

Rake leaves into a pile, water them, and let them sit for a week or two. When you visit again, turn over the moist leaves and observe the busy, earth-making insects in action.

Celebrate the Jungle

Have your children dress up as creatures of the rainforest (to learn more about animals of the rainforest, see Chapter Seven). Here are some activities to incorporate in your rainforest celebration:

Make A "Tropical Products" Display: Help your children become aware of their dependency on the rainforests by creating a display of Rainforest Products.

Serve a Rainforest Smorgasbord: Create a snack tray full of treats from the rainforest. Include cashews, Brazil nuts, macadamias, peanuts, banana slices, pineapple, tropical fruits (mango, papaya, and guava), orange sections, chocolate chips, and coconut flakes for dipping.

Make Jungle Punch: Puree a banana in a blender. Add 1 cup orange juice, 1 cup pineapple juice, and blend. Before serving, add 1 can of lemon-lime soda and mix well. Place a scoop of lemon or lime sherbet in each glass and fill with punch.

Sprout a Tree

After visiting, observing, drawing, and writing about your adopted tree through the four seasons, you and your child will have developed a relationship with this beautiful plant and a concern for its welfare. To grow a tree from a seed is another experience that will foster these feelings of kinship. Ask your child if he or she would like to try to grow another tree from your adopted tree. Together, you can care and nurture the new seedling and, finally, plant it in a special place or give it as a gift.

Place rocks or pebbles in the bottom of a planting pot. Find a seed or seedling from your adopted tree. Mix potting soil with some soil from around the area of your tree and place it in the pot. Plant your seed, water it, and care for it until the new tree is well established. If you need extra guidance, contact your local agricultural center for assistance. When the seedling is sturdy enough to transfer, choose a spot and determine that it is well suited for the young tree's survival (plenty of room to grow, adequate sunshine, etc.).

Tropical Rainforests

In many parts of the world, tropical forests are being destroyed at an alarming rate; half of the world's rainforests are already gone! With the loss of these valuable jungles, we will lose half of the world's life forms (plant and animal) and thousands of useful products that come from them. As a parent or teacher, you have a unique opportunity to shape the attitudes of the future. By talking and reading to your young children about the current situation and getting them involved in conservation activities, you can make a difference!

We Can Learn from the Lorax!

After reading *The Lorax* by Dr. Suess, think about the message it is trying to send. Here are some ideas for you and your children to talk about:

• How do you feel about the Lorax? What was he trying to do? Did anyone listen to him?

• How do you feel about the Once-ler? When the Once-ler was young and making thneeds, how did he treat the trees? When he became old, did he regret what he had done? How can you tell?

• Why did the Once-ler keep making thneeds? Think of a way that he could have made thneeds without permanently destroying the Truffula forest. (He could have cut down some Truffula trees to make thneeds, but replanted the trees that were cut. Or he could have discovered another way to make thneeds that didn't require tree parts.)

• What could you (as a buyer of thneeds) have done to prevent the destruction of the trees? (You could have protested by writing letters, by not buying thneeds, and organizing the other buyers to quit purchasing them until the Once-ler began a tree conservation program.) Write a pretend letter to the Once-ler and tell him what you think.

• Imagine a favorite outdoor setting (such as a park, camping area, or nature center) that has many trees. Have your child draw a picture of it. Afterward, pretend that all of the trees in this special place are cut down. What would happen to the wildlife? How would this place change? Draw a picture of this favorite spot without trees and compare the two pictures. Which is a nicer place to visit?

Where in the World?

Unless you live in an area that has large expanses of undisturbed forest, the Earth's rainforests may be a concept too far removed for your young children to visualize. A globe (or world map) may help them understand where they are located.

If your children have never been introduced to a globe, that lesson should precede this activity. Here is a simple explanation for your children. Explain to them that the globe is a model of Earth. Locate the continent, country, state, and, if possible, city where you live and point them out to your children. Locate any other places that would interest them, such as cities where other relatives or friends live, vacation spots they have visited, the place(s) your children were born (if different from your current residence), your birthplace, etc.

The Lorax, by Dr. Suess (Theodor S. Geisel). Random House, NY, 1971.

The Lorax speaks for the trees in this impressive story about a fantasy land that is exploited by a greedy thneed manufacturer. The outspoken little Lorax helps us to see how vital it is to protect our wooded lands from clearcutting and pollution. The theme is a perfect parallel to the current plight of our planet's rainforests. The Lorax has recently become the symbol for the effort to save ancient forests in the Pacific Northwest. (all ages)

Once There Was a Tree, by Natalia Romanova. Illustrations by Gennady Spirin. Dial Books, NY, 1983.

Originally published in the Soviet Union, this edition is exquisitely illustrated and the message of the story is vital to environmental education today: that we humans no more own the Earth than each and every other creature which inhabits it. (age 4 and up)

Where the Forest Meets the Sea, by Jeannie Baker. Greenwillow Books, NY, 1987.

Baker's lifelike collage illustrations take the reader on an extraordinary visual journey through a tropical rainforest. Each picture is rich with life and, through careful examination, animals can be discovered hiding within the lush vegetation. The final page poses the question, "Will the forest still be here when we come back?" (ages 3 - 8)

First, read the story *Where the Forest Meets the Sea* by Jeannie Baker or *Rain Forest* by Helen Cowcher (see "Going, Going...Gone" chapter).

Then, using a globe, point out to your children where these beautiful jungles can be found near the equator in South America, Africa, Asia, Indonesia, and the Pacific Islands. You and your family probably use products from the rainforest –rubber, tropical fruits, nuts, spices, chocolate, some medicines – every day. Some of these have already been discovered in the "From Furniture to Buttons" and "Tree Treats" activities earlier in this chapter. In the following activities, you and your children will learn more about the products that are harvested from tropical forests and will come to realize the impact they have on your lives. On the map below, the solid areas represent tropical rainforests.

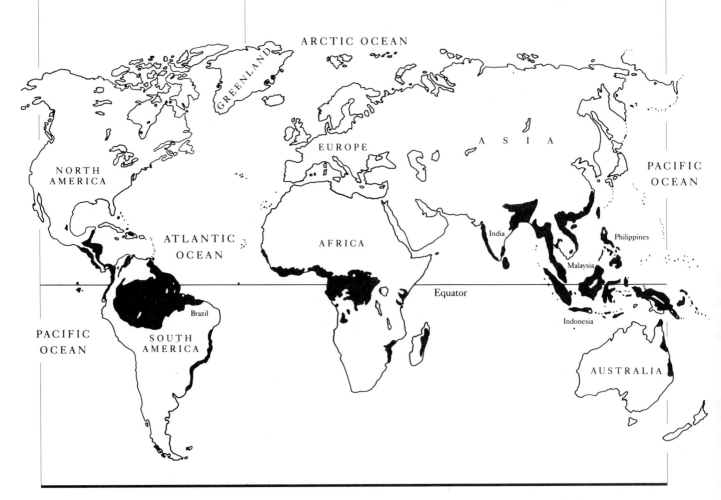

Good Things to Eat from the Rainforest

Look in your spice cabinet and collect all the spices which originate in the rainforests: allspice, cardamom, cloves, cinnamon, ginger, mace, nutmeg, chili powder, black pepper, paprika, and vanilla. Allow your child to sniff each one to see if he can guess what it is. Afterward, make spice cookies!

1¼ cups brown sugar, packed

¼ cup shortening

1 egg

1¾ cup all-purpose flour

½ teaspoon salt

¼ cup margarine, softened

½ teaspoon ground ginger

½ teaspoon cinnamon

¼ teaspoon allspice

½ teaspoon nutmeg

Heat oven to 375°. Mix brown sugar, margarine, shortening, and egg. Stir in the remaining ingredients. Shape the dough into one-inch balls. Place about 2 inches apart on an ungreased cookie sheet. Using a fork, flatten dough slightly with a criss-cross pattern. Bake until lightly browned, 10-12 minutes. Makes about 4 dozen cookies.

Rainforest Panorama

1. Take a large box and cut out one of the long sides for easy access.

2. Paint the inside of the box to look like a rainforest backdrop (lots of green plants, trees, ferns, and blue sky peeking through branches). Allow to dry.

3. Meanwhile, make trees from green construction paper. Roll paper into a tube and secure with tape. Cut the tubes into strips from top to about half way. Elongate tubes and curl "leaves" around a pencil. Glue trees to the floor of the panorama. Find and glue twigs, rocks, and grass to complete the jungle scene. Allow your children to place pretend insects and stuffed rainforest animals in their "rainforest."

Chocolate originated in tropical forests but is now grown in other areas. However, if the rainforests are destroyed, chocolate will become too expensive for average people. After singing this song, give each child a small piece of chocolate candy.

Kiss Chocolate Goodbye!

Tune: I've Been Workin' on the Railroad

Oh, my favorite food is chocolate.

I could eat it all day long.

I use it for dipping in my french fries

And I eat it with pecans.

It just tastes great with spaghetti,

I ate it for lunch one time.

If the rainforest disappears,

You can kiss chocolate goodbye! *(blow a kiss)*

Chocolate goodbye, (wave)

Chewing gum too,

Spices, vanilla, and bananas for you.

Rainforests must stay,

Let's not chop them away.

So, chocolate can be my dessert!

Yum! Yum! *(rub tummy)*

Gifts from the Tropical Rainforest

You might be surprised to discover some of the items that are gifts of the rainforest. Here are a few: chewing gum (chicle), tropical fruits and plants, bamboo and rattan, chocolate, nuts, spices, rubber items, coffee and tea, pharmaceuticals (insect repellent, bath oil, coconut oil soap, and musk perfume), tropical wood products (teak, mahogany, balsa, rosewood, and sandlewood).

Can your children or your classroom group add to the list?

A Rainforest in a Soda Bottle

Another reason the rainforests are vital to us, even though we may live many miles from them, is the part they play in regulating the flow of water on Earth. They soak up the abundant rains that fall in their regions and release it into the air as clouds. These clouds travel hundreds of miles and release the water (as raindrops) to other areas of our globe that are drier and in need of moisture. This terrarium will demonstrate to children that plants can generate enough moisture to satisfy their great need for water.

Things You Will Need: a two-liter plastic soda bottle, scissors, plastic wrap, gravel, charcoal (sold for use in fish tank filters), potting soil, and two small tropical plants such as a philodendron, prayer plant, fittonia, artillery plant, etc. These can be purchased at a nursery, florist, or variety store.

What to Do:

1. Take the label off of the soda bottle and remove the black plastic bottom. Rinse the bottle well with warm water.

2. Cut the top off of the bottle where it begins to curve. (This should be done by an adult.)

3. Line the detached black plastic bottom with a piece of plastic wrap that has been folded several times.

4. Spread about one-inch of gravel over the plastic wrap. Spread a thin layer of charcoal over the gravel and fill with potting soil.

5. Dig a little hole in the potting soil for each of your plants. Carefully remove the plants from their containers, place them in the holes, and press lightly.

6. Water the plants with about one-third cup of water. Invert and place the plastic cover over the plants forming a dome. The terrarium should be placed in a spot that will receive a lot of light, but not in direct sunlight (the heat will dry up the water that accumulates in the dome). Watch your rainforest terrarium to see the water released from the plants form droplets on the inside of the dome. These will rain down on the plants and continuously water them. (Since this container is not airtight, over time the water will evaporate. You will need to add a small amount of water to the soil every few weeks.)

Get Involved!

Like the Lorax, someone must speak for the trees on our planet. The conservation of trees begins at home and school. Young children and their families can make an impact by changing their usage habits, initiating some conservation projects, and speaking out against deforestation.

1. When you grocery shop, bring the paper or plastic bags saved from previous shopping trips. When the clerk asks you if you want a bag, reply, "No, thank you. I've brought my own to save a tree!"

2. If your purchase is small, refuse a paper bag by saying, "No, thank you, I don't need one."

3. Collect scrap paper. Use it before using new sheets of paper. Save empty cardboard containers to make craft projects.

4. Always use both sides of a piece of paper before discarding it or add it to your scrap paper box.

5. Make your own greeting cards out of scrap paper.

6. Only use paper plates or napkins when necessary (for picnics or camping trips), and not because you don't want to wash dishes.

7. Dry your hands on a cloth towel instead of using paper towels.

8. Recycle old magazines by using the pictures for art projects or donate them to a nursing home or doctor's office.

9. Wrap gifts in the comic section of your newspaper instead of buying fancy wrapping paper.

10. Collect newspapers and give them to a recycling center to be made into new paper. (Call and find out where centers are located.)

What About Christmas Trees?

Millions of evergreen trees are cut down every year at Christmas time. While these trees are grown on farms specifically for this purpose, here are two ways to observe holiday traditions that can make them "live" on - or at least make better use of discarded trees than simply putting them out with the trash.

Buy a Living Christmas Tree: Many nurseries sell live conifers that are ready to be planted a few days after Christmas. (If you are planning to buy a live tree, take into account your climate and dig a hole sometime in mid-November, if necessary, before the soil

Here are some organizations that are fighting to save the rainforest. They can also send you detailed information or classroom materials:

Friends of the Earth
530 7th Street, SE
Washington, D. C. 20003

National Wildlife Federation
1412 16th Street, NW
Washington, D. C. 20036

Rainforest Action Network
466 Green Street, Suite 300
San Francisco, CA 94133

World Resources Institute
1735 New York Avenue, NW
Washington, D. C. 20006

Recycling a 3-and-a-half-foot stack of newspapers saves one 20-foot Southern pine.

freezes.) Keep your tree outside until just before Christmas and be sure to keep it well watered. Drastic changes in temperature can cause the needles to fall off, so place it in an unheated garage for a day or so before bringing it into your house. Inside, place it in a spot with plenty of light, away from heaters or fireplaces, and keep the soil moist. After about a week, place the tree in the garage again to let it get used to the cold before planting it in your yard.

Recycle Your Christmas Tree: Save any edible ornaments (popcorn, cranberry garlands) for the winter birds. Then place the tree in a corner of your yard to provide shelter for animals or birds, or strip the needles from the branches and use them as garden mulch or compost, and chop the branches for kindling. If your children have never had the experience of counting the rings of a tree to determine its age, this would be a good opportunity. Saw straight across the trunk. (It is easier to count the rings if you lacquer the wood. Most conifers are 8 to 12 years old when they are cut for Christmas trees.)

The Children's Rainforest

Sharon Kinsman, a biology professor from Bates College, began traveling around to schools with her "Save the Rainforest" message in 1986. Through her impassioned message about Costa Rica's Monteverde Cloud Forest, Kinsman has inspired many school children to raise thousands of dollars to acquire and preserve over 10,000 acres of Monteverde's luxurious ecosystem. She comments that "once children sense how endangered all these wonderful species are from clearcutting and burning, their response is simple and straightforward. They want to save it." Kinsman is currently mobilizing kids in the United States through the Children's Rainforest, a nonprofit organization that she founded in 1988. For further information, send a stamped, self-addressed envelope to The Children's Rainforest, P. O. Box 936, Lewiston, Maine 04240.

Put on a Play!

"Save the Lofty Trees," a play for grades 1 - 3, is available for free! To obtain a copy, send first class postage for two ounces and a gummed name label to Leslie Mills, 1300-8 Richmond Avenue, Staten Island, NY 10314.

Money Raising Ideas!

Bake Sale: Bake brownies, cookies, or other goodies using spices from the rainforest. Have a bake sale and donate the proceeds to rainforest preservation groups.

Penny Days: It is estimated that over 50 billion pennies are sitting uncirculated in bottom drawers or in piggy banks across the country. Organize "Penny Days" at your church or child's school on which the children will bring pennies and wrap them in paper penny holders. Use the money to purchase acreage in tropical rainforests.

Cash for Trash: Recycle paper, glass, plastic, and aluminum for cash. Set up recycling bins at your school and church or arrange to pick up your neighbor's recyclables once or twice a month and take them to a Recycling Center and redeem them.

Organize a "Tree Saving" Carnival: Plan a neighborhood or school carnival in which the proceeds will benefit tree conservation organizations. Some activities to include are a cake walk, face painting, races, bean bag toss, water balloon catching contest, egg and spoon race, go fish, ring toss, etc. Don't forget to sell drinks, popcorn, hot dogs, and baked goodies.

Sell Candy to Save the Rainforest: Order nuts and candy to help save the Amazon Rainforest. All proceeds will be divided among indigenous groups working to save the Amazon. To Order: Candy is $3.50 postpaid per 8 oz. box (12 box minimum order). Payment must accompany order - no returns. Payable to Cultural Survival, 11 Divinity Avenue, Cambridge, MA 02138.

Children for Old Growth

The old-growth forests of the Pacific Northwest have almost disappeared. These ancient groves provide homes and food for wildlife, enrich the soil, release water into the air, and act as air filters. *Children for Old Growth* is a non-profit group working to save the remaining 3% of virgin trees. With a donation of $10.00 or more, your child will receive a nature poster to color, just a small token to thank him for caring and helping to save the trees. Send donations to Children for Old Growth.

Did You Know? The rainforest provides more than just good things to eat. One out of every four medicines comes from a tropical plant!

Any fool can destroy trees. They cannot run away.

JOHN MUIR

Children for Old Growth
Box 1090
Redway, CA 95560

The National Arbor Day
Foundation,
100 Arbor Avenue,
Nebraska City, NE 68410.

My Brother, the Tree

There is an old Indian custom in some tribes in which a parent will plant a tree for each child born and give the tree the same name as the child. It would be difficult to imagine a more beautiful gesture and it is easy to visualize the bond that would develop between that child and its brother or sister tree. You might want to begin a similar tradition in your family.

Observe Arbor Day

Arbor Day is a special day that has been set aside for planting and caring for trees. The first Arbor Day was celebrated in Nebraska on April 10, 1872. Today, all fifty states and many Canadian provinces celebrate this holiday every spring. (The actual date varies from state to state due to climate.) The National Arbor Day Foundation offers a wide variety of trees, plants, and flowering bulbs at special low prices, and a free membership with each purchase. For a catalog, write to the National Arbor Day Foundation.

Arbor Day News

Write for an extremely informative and simply written newsletter, filled with facts and activities having to do with tree-related themes. The National Arbor Day Foundation will send you a single free issue free. Write to The National Arbor Day Foundation.

Arbor Day Ideas

Allow your child to help select a tree to be planted in his or her name. You may wish to plant it on your own property or choose a public site. If you choose the latter, first ask for permission from your city. Possibly they will suggest an area in need of beautification. Bring your camera along at planting time each year, take photographs of your family planting the special trees, and keep a photographic album of Arbor Day celebrations. If you plant the tree on your own property, you may wish to photograph it each Arbor Day – wtih your child beside it – to record the progress of growth of both child and tree in photo album pictures.

More Books to Share With Children

The Peach Tree by **Norman Pike.** Illustrations by Robin and Patricia DeWitt. Stemmer House Pub., Inc., Owings Mills, MD, 1983. The Pomeroy family plants a peach tree on the hill near their house. This is a fine lesson in ecology, making its points with quiet charm. (ages 3 - 8)

Guy and the Flowering Plum Tree by **Robin Stemp.** Illustrations by Carolyn Dinan. Atheneum, NY, 1980. After eating plums, Guy counts the seeds. Oh, no! One is missing. He asks his mother what happens to a person who eats a plum stone. He will probably grow a tree inside, she says! In this enchanting fantasy Guy begins to imagine what sort of tree he will become. (ages 4 - 8)

A Tree With a Thousand Uses by **Aileen Fisher.** Illustrations by James R. Endicott. Bowmar, Los Angeles, CA, 1977. Two children search for a tree with a thousand uses. Although the other types of trees are very useful, the children conclude that the coconut tree must be the tree with a thousand uses. (ages 3 - 7)

The Tree by **Judy Hindley.** Illustrations by Alison Wisenfield. Clarkson N. Potter, Inc., Pub., NY, 1990. This book explores not just the shapes and textures of trees but their lore, their places in history, their uses, and their personalities. (ages 6 - 9)

Woodpile by **Peter Parnall.** Macmillan, NY, 1990. Each page of this thoughtful picture book leads to new uses for wood. (ages 5 - 9)

Our Tree by **Herbert Wong and Matthew Vessel.** Illustrations by Kenneth Longtemps. Addison-Wesley Pub. Co., Reading, MA, 1969. In *Our Tree*, the reader soon finds out what a tree is for; it's for exploring, investigating, and learning. Discover a world of animal life in and around it. (ages 3 - 7)

The Oak Tree by **Laura Jane Coats.** Macmillan Pub. Co., NY, 1987. The growth of a tree is so slow that, in a day, we cannot see it, but we can see and participate in the movement around it. This is a loving tribute to nature and the beauty of living that occurs every day. (ages 3 - 7)

The Apartment House Tree by **Bette Killion.** Illustrations by Mary Szilagyi. Harper and Row, NY, 1989. In this story young readers are introduced to the inhabitants of one special tree. (ages 3 - 6)

Animals That Live in Trees by **Jane R. McCauley.** National Geographic Society, Washington, D.C., 1986. Wherever trees grow, you will also find many animals. Meet the koala, owls, birds, insects, porcupine, howler monkey, bats, and other fascinating animals that depend on trees for survival. (all ages)

Tree Trunk Traffic, **text and photos by Bianca Lavies.** Dutton, NY, 1989. The photos in this book capture all of the action and beauty during one full day in the life of a tree and the animals who live there. (ages 3 - 8)

Know About Wood by **Rainer Sacher.** Wrens Park Publishing, Barton under Needwood, Staffordshire, 1978. A beautifully illustrated volume that covers many topics, such as different kinds of trees, how a tree is born, grows, and lives. (ages 4 - 7)

Look at a Tree by **Eileen Curran.** Illustrations by June Goldsborough. Troll Associates, Mahwah, NJ, 1985. The cheerful illustrations and simple text help a child learn about the different animals that can be seen in or around various types of trees. (ages 3 - 5)

The Life Cycle of a Tree by **John Williams.** Illustrations by Jackie Harland. The Bookwright Press, NY, 1989. The growth and life of a tree is described from seed to maturity. (ages 3 - 8)

Eat the Fruit, Plant the Seed by **Millicent E. Selsam and Jerome Wexler.** William Morrow & Co., NY, 1980. Directions for growing plants from the seeds found inside avocados, papayas, citrus fruits, mangos, pomegranates, and kiwis. (ages 3 - 7)

Arbor Day by **Aileen Fisher.** Illustrations by Nonny Hogrogian. Thomas Y. Crowell Co., NY, 1965. The story of J. Sterling Morton, founder of Arbor Day in 1872. (ages 6 - 9)

Plants in Winter by **Joanna Cole.** Illustrations by Kazue Mizumura. Thomas Y. Crowell Co., NY, 1973. Written in a read-aloud style, this book explains what happens to trees during the winter season. (ages 5 - 9)

Rain Forests by **Lynn M. Stone.** Rourke Enterprises, Inc., Vero Beach, FL, 1989. A non-fiction book with brief, but informative, chapters on aspects of a rainforest. (ages 6 - 9)

Rain Forest Secrets by **Arthur Dorros.** Scholastic Inc., NY, 1990. Information about the fragile ecosystem of the rainforest for young readers, with a resource list of organizations trying to curtail the cutting of these forests. (ages 6 - 9)

Forests: A Fact-filled Coloring Book by **Bettina Dudley.** Running Press, Philadelphia, PA., 1989. This is not your typical coloring book! It is full of fascinating information that any child interested in forests and trees would love to read. (ages 5 - 9)

The Fall of Freddie the Leaf by **Leo Buscaglia.** Charles B. Slack, NY, 1982.

How Freddie and his companion leaves change as the seasons pass – the author's way of showing that death is part of the cycle of life. (all ages)

Resources for Parents and Teachers

Ranger Rick's Nature Scope: Rain Forests: Tropical Treasures. Vol. 4, No. 4. National Wildlife Federation, Washington D.C., 1989.

Ranger Rick's Nature Scope: Trees are Terrific! Vol. 2,

No. 1. National Wildlife Federation, Washington D.C., 1988.

"The Wild, Wet World of Wonder," *Otterwise* (Fall 1989). *Otterwise* is a quarterly newsletter for "kids who love animals." A one year subscription is $4.00 and it can be ordered from P.O. Box 1374, Portland, ME 04104.

The Global ReLeaf Program is a national campaign with the specific goal of promoting reforestation. Writing to Global ReLeaf, The American Forestry Association, P.O. Box 2000, Washington, D.C. 20013.

The American Forestry Association offers detailed information on tree planting and care in several publications. Write to Tree People, 12601 Mulholland Drive, Beverly Hills, CA 90210.

The National Arbor Day Foundation offers ten free seedlings with a membership. A Teacher Package is also available. Write to 100 Arbor Avenue, Nebraska City, NE 68410.

Man of the Trees: The Life of Richard St. Barbe Baker is a video which shows how one man's vision is helping to heal the Earth. (25 minutes color) This video can be ordered from Music for Little People, P.O. Box 1460, Redway, CA 95560.

World Rainforest Report is published six times a year by the Rainforest Action Network. Write to 300 Broadway, San Francisco, CA 94133.

The New York Rainforest Alliance is committed to expanding awareness of the crucial role the United States plays in the fate of the tropical rainforests. Write to 496 A Hudson Street, G-11, NY, NY 10014.

Disappearance of the Great Rain Forest is a video narrated by Walter Cronkite. Available for rent or purchase from Arthur Mokin Productions, Inc., P.O. Box 1866, Santa Rosa, CA 95402.

An animated film of *The Lorax* by Dr. Seuss is available for rent from Population Reference Bureau, Inc., 774 14th Street, NW, Washington, D.C. 20005.

The Singing Tree (film # 03790) is a musical film about trees by Bill Brennan. It is available for rent from the Bureau of Audio Visual Instruction, The University of Wisconsin, P.O. Box 2093, Madison, WI 53701.

The National Geographic Society has many filmstrips, films, and videos about trees for rent or purchase. Contact Educational Services, Dept. 89, Washington, D.C. 20036.

Hug a Tree and Other Things to Do with Children Outdoors is an activity book that contains many tree-related activities. It is by Robert E. Rockwell and and is published by Gryphon House, 1983.

Project Learning Tree, sponsored by the American Forest Institute and the Western Regional Environmental Education Council, is filled with forest-related activities for elementary and secondary students. Write the American Forest Institute, Inc., 1619 Massachusetts Ave., NW, Washington, D.C. 20036.

Children of the Green Earth is committed to "regreening" the Earth by helping young people plant and care for trees. It publishes educational materials, a periodical newsletter, *Tree Song,* and promotes tree-planting efforts by young people all over the globe. Write to P.O. Box 95219, Seattle, WA 98145.

The Sierra Club has a pamphlet entitled "What You Can Do to Help Save Tropical Rainforests." Write 730 Polk Street, San Francisco, CA 94109.

Forest, Jake Page and the editors of Time-Life Books. Time-Life Books, NY, 1983.

The Illustrated Encyclopedia of Trees, Timbers, and Forests of the World by Herbert Edlin and Maurice Nimmo, editors. Harmony Books, 1981.

The International Book of Trees by Hugh Johnson. Simon and Schuster, 1973.

The Man Who Planted Trees by Jean Giono. Chelsea Green Pub. Co., Chelsea, VT, 1985.

The Simple Act of Planting a Tree: Healing Your Neighborhood, Your City, and Your World by Andy and Katie Lipkis. Treepeople, Jeremy P. Tarcher, Inc., Los Angeles, CA, 1990. A citizen forester's guide.

Wonders of the Jungle edited by Howard F. Robinson, National Wildlife Federation, 1986.

Environmental Education About the Rainforest by Klaus Berkmuller. World Wildlife Fund, Washington, D.C., 1984.

In The Rainforest by Catherine Caufield. Alfred A. Knopf, NY, 1985.

Saving the Tropical Forests by Judith Gradwhol and Russell Greenberg. Earthscan, London, 1988.

The Enchanted Canopy by Andrew Mitchell. Macmillan, NY, 1986.

Disappearing Rainforests by Robert Prosser. Dryad Press Limited, London, 1987.

The Primary Source, Tropical Forests and Our Future by Norman Myers. WW Norton and Co., NY and London, 1984.

Tropical Forest Education Package, Global Tomorrow Coalition. Washington D.C. 1985.

"Chewing Up the Jungle" by James D. Nations and Daniel I. Komer. *International Wildlife* (September/ October 1984): 14-l6.

"Is it Too Late for the Rain Forests?" by Richard Nalley. *Science Digest* (April 1986): 56-61.

"Last Days of Eden" by Loren McIntyre. *National Geographic* (December 1988): 800-817.

"Tropical Forests: Nature's Dwindling Treasures" by Peter White. *National Geographic* (January 1983): 2-65.

CHAPTER FIVE

Wet and Wonderful!

The frog does not drink up the pond in which he lives.

INDIAN PROVERB

Splash! Children are naturally drawn to water. In summer, kids of all ages throng to the neighborhood sprinkler. Some children spend so much time in the tub that their parents wonder if they are part fish! But enjoying the physical properties of water is only the beginning of a journey toward understanding this magical liquid and the crucial role it plays in our lives.

Of all the natural resources that people take for granted, none is more plentiful – or more fragile – than water. The surface area of Earth's oceans is much greater than that of land, and the volume of water between the waves and the ocean floor (in places several miles deep) is almost impossible for us to comprehend. Yet, if the Earth's total supply were represented by a gallon of water, only a few drops would be naturally drinkable. It is possible to melt polar ice or take the salt out of seawater; but managing these processes on a large scale requires massive amounts of energy.

The Paint-Box Sea, by Doris Herald Lund. Illustrations by Symeon Shimin. McGraw-Hill Book Co., NY, 1973.

Everyone knows that water is blue. Or is it? When a young girl makes pictures of the sea with the paints she receives for her birthday, she finds that the water can look gold, or red, or even dark brown depending on the conditions of the day. Jane and her brother turn an ordinary summer vacation into a special time of exploration and discovery. As they study the different moods and colors of the sea, they come to know the ocean as a living thing. (ages 5 - 9)

Since the beginning of time, the human population has increased, but the amount of water on the Earth has not. It is constantly in motion about the planet. First, the oceans, lakes, and streams evaporate into water vapor, form clouds, and eventually fall back to Earth as rain or snow. In winter, we see water freeze into ice and then melt back into water in the spring. We vitally depend on this continuous cycle to provide us with rain to grow our food and water to drink.

To keep our planet and its creatures alive and healthy, clean water is essential. A person can live for many weeks without food, but cannot survive without water for more than a few days; it's that important! Your children will learn that water is not only the main element on the Earth's surface, but it is also the key ingredient in their bodies. Staying healthy depends upon keeping all water as clean as possible. Pollution can come back to us as drinking water and it presents a danger to fish and other creatures that live in the sea. This chapter provides a variety of experiences that will introduce your children to the problems associated with water pollution. By becoming aware of their close relationship with water, your children will develop a respect for this precious resource and take an active role in conserving and preserving it.

Awareness

The Importance of Water Play

From a very early age, children are intrigued by water. Even an infant, wiggling and splashing in the bath, realizes that water is special stuff. It is fluid. It can easily change its shape to fit exactly whatever container it is poured into, it's wet, and just plain fun! For very young children, provide the opportunities and containers (such as scoops, cups, sponges, and sieves) for uninhibited water play. You can fill a wading pool for outdoor fun or allow extra time in the bath for exploration. Preschool-age children also enjoy water-related household tasks such as dish washing or doll bathing. Water play not only provides enjoyment, but also mathematic and physical science learning experiences for your young children.

Rain, Rain, Don't Go Away

You've heard this rhyme: "Rain, rain, go away. Come again some other day." Well, there's a new twist to the old tune! Instead, put on your rain gear and go outside for some rainy day fun. As you and your children jump from puddle to puddle, sing this little song and enjoy what the day has to offer.

Rain, rain, don't go away.
I'm so glad you're here today!
Little *(your child's name)* wants to play,
I just love a rainy day!

From a Mermaid's Point of View

Water has a special feel to it. Dip your hands into cool, clear water and experience the sensation. As you move your fingers through it, you can feel the coolness between each finger and hear the gentle rippling sound. The following guided imagination journey presents an enjoyable experience for children, as well as adults (a mixed group of adults and children works best). Provide a large bucket or tub of water for everyone to feel while you read this story. Ask them to close their eyes and imagine themselves immersed in the cool liquid. When the story is finished, remind the children

The Wet and Sandy Day, by Joanne Ryder. Illustrations by Donald Carrick. Harper and Row, Pub., NY, 1977.

"It feels like rain later," her mother warns. "I've got sunny feelings for today," the young girl replies as she skips out the door and runs to the nearby beach. After a brief swim, she discovers that her mother was right; a summer shower comes and chases all of the sunbathers away. Only the little girl stays to enjoy the pleasant rain. It becomes a special day to wiggle wet toes and watch fingers turn into raisins as a million raindrops wash over her, making her feel cleaner than if she had taken a hundred baths! This book invites young readers to share in the joy that a rainy day at the beach can bring. (ages 4 - 8)

that it was only pretend and that people cannot really breathe underwater without special equipment, such as an oxygen tank and air hoses.

The oceans, lakes, rivers, and ponds are full of water. As a matter of fact, water covers most of the Earth's surface. Imagine what it would be like if you could live underwater. As you dip your feet into the cool, clear water, your legs melt together to form a large tail. Instead of skin, scratchy scales cover your powerful tail. You wiggle it in the sunlight and watch it glimmer and shine with many beautiful colors. You let yourself slowly sink into the water and, as it covers your head, several gill slits appear on your chest. You find that you don't need a snorkel or oxygen tank, instead you can breathe the oxygen from the water through your gills. The water is cool and the waves tickle your skin and scales. As you sink lower, your hair floats all about your head, sometimes gently stroking your face. It feels silky, like the web of a spider, as you let it run through your fingers. You gracefully curl your tail behind you and begin to move it up and down. You lean forward and are soon swimming through the water. As you swim faster, you feel the water stroking your cheeks, streaming through your hair, and tickling your sides and back. Everything around you is silent, except for an occasion swishing sound as your tail stirs up the water.

Take a few minutes and enjoy your underwater adventure. Imagine yourself meeting the many fascinating creatures beneath the waves. After you come back to shore, plan to tell us something about your underwater fantasy that was exciting or made you feel good.

After a few minutes, ask everyone to return home. As soon as all hands are out of the water, have everyone sit in a circle and take turns describing something they saw or experienced during their imaginative journey. As an extension, you might ask that they draw a picture and write a brief quote about their underwater adventure.

Water Words

There are many words that describe water and how we perceive it: smooth, flowing, silvery, tinkling, crashing, velvety, slippery, cool, musical. We can dive into water and hear the splash, feel its coolness, taste its saltiness (if it's seawater), and see the sunlight shimmering through it.

After an experience with water, ask your children to choose one word to describe it. Record their responses and, as a group, write a story or poem that use all of the words.

As an alternative, you might have each child illustrate his or her water word and bind all of the pictures together into a big book called simply, "Water."

The Three States of Water

Very young children may not realize that water can exist in different states: as a liquid, a solid, and a gas. The best way for children to understand this concept is to experience it firsthand. First, allow some time for your children to explore water in its liquid state. Then take the same water and freeze it. After the block of ice has melted back into water, pour it into a pot and boil it. Your children will notice the bubbling of the water, but may not realize that the steam rising from the pot is their water changing into a gas (water vapor). One way to show them is to carefully hold a cold, unbreakable plate or pan over the boiling water, allowing the steam to condense into droplets. Let them feel the water that has formed on the bottom of the plate.

Extend your children's kitchen experiment by pointing out the changes of water in nature. Ask questions such as: "What happened to the puddle on the driveway?" or "What is snow?" Try these same experiments using rain or snow.

(Note: To explain how rain or snow is formed, see "Where Does Rain Come From?" Although the activity is similar, it will be better understood if children have had the experience of experimenting with the different states of water at an earlier time without the connection to weather conditions.)

Rain! whose soft architectural hands have power to cut stones, and chisel to shapes of grandeur the very mountains.

HENRY WARD BEECHER, 1887

Raindrop Stories, by Preston R. Bassett with Margaret F. Bartlett. Illustrations by Jim Arnosky. Four Winds Press, NY, 1981.

These stories about raindrops were told by P. R. Bassett to his four children when they were young. M. F. Bartlett, then working as a science teacher, heard the stories. She was convinced they had imaginative appeal, as well as being educational. So they corresponded for over a year to transform the oral stories into suitable prose. Follow Johnny Raindrop through a gentle spring shower, a hailstorm, a summer thunderstorm, an autumn rain, and an ice storm. The delightful text helps children imagine themselves as one of the droplets sailing high in the clouds anxiously awaiting an adventure. (ages 5 - 9)

The Importance of the Water Cycle

Take a Rain Walk

A rain shower offers a multi-sensory experience for your children. First, there is the comforting sound of falling rain. It begins as a pitter-pat, as the first few drops start to fall. Slowly the pounding of raindrops increases, followed by lightning and a clap of thunder as the clouds burst. Gather your children near a window or sit on a porch and listen to the rain. Take a deep breath and smell the Earth soaked with water. Try to observe any wildlife to see what they do during a rainstorm. If it is not too cold, go out with your children into the rain and feel the thousands of drops tap lightly on your head, shoulders, arms, and legs. Turn your face upwards, close your eyes, and let the rain wash over you. Open your mouth and taste the water. Jump into the puddles and hear the splash of water from your feet. Afterward, warm yourselves with a mug of cocoa and share stories about the best part of your rain walk.

Become a Thunderstorm

You and your children have the potential to sound just like a real thunderstorm, and it's great fun! Have your children sit in a circle and carefully listen to this story as they act it out. An excellent musical selection to use as a backup to your rainstorm is "Little April Shower" (3:52) from the Walt Disney movie *Bambi.* It can be found on *The Disney Collection,* Volume Two (distributed by Vista Records and Tapes, Burbank, CA 91521).

The grey clouds roll across the sky. They cover the sun and suddenly you are surrounded by the darkness of night, even though it's the middle of the day. *(turn down the lights)* The birds and animals can smell the damp Earth in the distance and realize that a storm is coming. So, they fly and scamper for shelter and, in the safety of their burrows and nests, they will wait out the storm. Softly, the first drops begin to fall. *(Have your children begin by lightly tapping the floor or their legs with their fingertips.)* Pit - pat - pit - pat - pit - pat. . . *(first slowly, then faster)* Soon it is raining very hard. *(As the intensity of the rain increases, have them change from tapping to slapping the floor.)* Do you hear the wind through the trees? Whoo-oo-oo-oo-oo! Flash! *(flick the lights).* . . then a few seconds later, crash! *(have the children clap their hands together)* The limbs on the trees are being tossed about by the strong winds, Whoo-oo-oo. Flash! *(flick the lights).* . . then crash! *(clap hands)* Finally, the rain slows down. *(Slowly slap the floor, then gradually return to tapping.)* The harsh wind turns into a gentle breeze. *(go from saying, "Whoo-oo" to just blowing air)* The last drip-drops fall from the wet leaves. *(slowly stop tapping)* The dark clouds move on. *(turn on the lights)* One by one, the birds and animals leave the safety of their homes. They drink from the puddles and watch the steam slowly rise into the sky. They are happy because they know that the life-giving rain will return another day.

Where Does Rain Come From?

Have you ever been asked that one before? It's hard to explain to a young, curious child in words, but quite easy to show him. By conducting this simple kitchen experiment, you can show your children how rain or snow is made.

1. Fill a saucepan or tea kettle with water and bring it to a rolling boil. Let the children observe the bubbles and rising steam. Ask them, "Do you think the steam is hot or cold?" (Because it is hot, use your judgment to decide whether your children should place their hands high over the steam to feel it. If so, carefully assist each child, keeping his hands and arm far from the hot pan.)

2. Place about ten ice cubes in a pie pan and let the children feel the bottom of the pan. Ask them, "How does it feel?" Hold it over the rising steam. (Do not let a child hold the pie pan; this needs to be done by an adult.) Allow the children to observe the bottom of the pan. As the water is heated, it turns into a gas (or steam) called water vapor. Your children can see that as soon as it hits the cool pie pan, it changes back into its liquid state and forms into water droplets. Ask them, "What happens to water vapor when it is cooled?" Let them feel the water on the bottom of the pan.

> **I**t will talk as long as it wants, this rain. As long as it talks, I am going to listen.
>
> Thomas Merton

The Water's Journey, by Eleonore Schmid. North-South Books, NY, 1989.

The water's journey begins high in the mountains in the form of snowflakes. As the ice melts, it becomes a brook flowing down the mountainside. It moves down the valley and then becomes a stream. The stream becomes a river, until it finally reaches the wide, blue ocean. From there, it will evaporate and begin the whole process again. Lovely paintings and simple, poetic text give children a greater understanding of the water cycle and its important role in supporting life on Earth. (ages 3 - 7)

3. Explain that on the Earth, water is heated by the sun and is changed into water vapor. It rises into the air, forming clouds. When the clouds become cold enough, the vapor changes back into water and falls back to the Earth as raindrops. Or, if it is really cold, the raindrops freeze and fall to the Earth as hail or snowflakes.

Breathe a Cloud

A cloud is just a huge collection of tiny water droplets (called water vapor) floating in the sky. On a very cold morning, you can make a small cloud by blowing your warm breath into the air. Your warm, moist breath comes in contact with the cold air and forms into minute water droplets. This process is known as condensation. In nature, real clouds happen in a similar way. The warm, moist air above a lake or ocean rises into the sky. There it meets cold air and forms into tiny droplets of water. These droplets cluster together to form the puffy clouds that we see floating across the sky.

Rest Upon a Cloud

Clouds are dynamic. They seem to be effortlessly floating in the sky, but they are actually tumbling through the air, constantly changing their size and shape. On a pleasant afternoon, clouds can be a source of entertainment for children and adults. It is an absorbing activity to watch a cloud change from an elephant, to a human face, to a turtle, to a flower, and so on. Instead of an ordinary rest time, take your children outdoors to watch the clouds roll by. Give each child a private space of his or her own and encourage everyone to find pictures in the sky. A wonderful book about the diversity of clouds, *It Looked Like Spilt Milk* by Charles G. Shaw, will stimulate their imaginations.

Tear a Paper Cloud

Your children can imitate the random artistry of real clouds by creating their own out of paper. Have each child tear a piece of white scrap paper into any shape he or she desires. When they are finished tearing, paste their "clouds" onto pieces of blue paper. Have each child carefully study his or her cloud picture and decide what it looks like. If someone can't decide, show the picture to the group

Stars, darkness, a lamp, a phantom, dew, a bubble. A dream, a flash of lightning, or a cloud: Thus should one look upon the world.

VAJRACCHEDIKA, A BUDDHIST TEXT

and allow them to offer suggestions, although the final decision should belong to the child. Let the children label their pictures with a sentence about their cloud and, if desired, bind all the pages together into a book to be shared by all.

The Raindrop's Relay

This relay demonstrates to young children the long and formidable journey taken by a raindrop in the water cycle. And when it's all over, the whole adventure starts again!

1. Since you'll need a lot of space, this relay is best done outdoors. Divide the children into groups of five. On each team, assign one of the paths taken in a raindrop's journey to each child: the mountain, the stream, the river, the ocean, and the cloud.

2. The children should line up in this order, with enough distance between them to mark a lengthy traveling path: the mountain child, the stream child, the river child, and, finally, the ocean child. For younger children, map out a path for each player to run by marking it with chalk or masking tape. Allow older children to draw their own path from their starting point to the next player, taking into account the part that they play. For instance, the path of the stream child will be much straighter than the river child's path. The ocean child does not require a path, but its boundaries should designated. The cloud child needs no path, but will "float" around the other players throughout the relay.

3. For each team, fill a balloon with water to represent a raindrop and ask each player to stand on his or her starting spot. Hand a raindrop (balloon) to each cloud child and ask him to "float" about until he reaches the mountain child. Start the relay by saying to the children that "the water falls from the cloud in the form of a snowflake onto the mountain." Have the cloud child hand-off the raindrop to the mountain child.

4. Continue by saying that "throughout the winter, the drop of water is frozen. When spring arrives, the snow melts and the raindrop begins his journey down the mountainside." Have the mountain child carefully run along his path and hand-off to the stream child.

5. "Many drops of water come together to form a stream. The

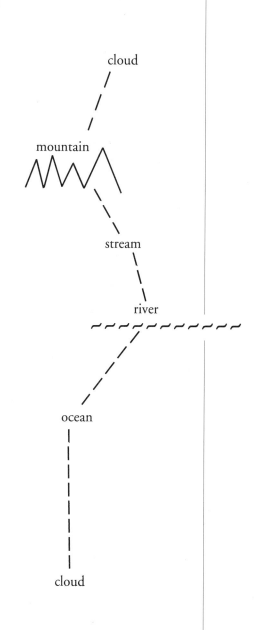

Humphrey, the Lost Whale: A True Story, by Wendy Tokuda and Richard Hall. Illustrations by Hanako Wakiyama. Heian International, Inc., Union City, CA, 1986.

Humphrey, the humpback whale entered San Francisco Bay on an October night in 1985. This was unusual in itself, but then Humphrey did something no whale has ever done. Instead of swimming back out to sea, he took a wrong turn and headed up the Sacramento River. It was clear that Humphrey was lost! It took 26 days, more than 500 concerned people and a large sum of money before the whale found his way back to the ocean. This book recounts the whole adventure for children, pointing out that often other creatures need our assistance and we must be ready to help. (ages 5 - 10)

stream rushes down the side of the mountain until it meets the river." Have the stream child run along its path and hand-off to the river child.

6. "Many mountain streams empty into the river. The river twists and turns until it meets the ocean." Have the river child travel along its path and hand-off to the ocean child.

7. "Many rivers empty into the ocean, where the water sloshes and is pulled back and forth by the moon. The sun warms the water and it changes into water vapor." Have the ocean child hold the raindrop and rock it back and forth in his arms, finally giving it to the cloud child.

8. "The vapor rises into the sky and forms clouds. The clouds travel over the land and eventually the raindrop falls onto a mountain top." Have the cloud child "float" back to the mountain child and hand him the raindrop again. Have the children repeat the relay, but this time let them tell the story of the raindrop as it travels to the ocean.

The Rain as Artist

The random splashing of raindrops creates a beautiful effect on this "rain picture." Have your child take a large piece of scrap paper and cover its surface entirely with watercolor paint. It can be a solid color or many colors. Dry completely, then during a light rain shower place it outdoors for a brief time and allow the raindrops to splash and partially wash away some of the paint. Bring it indoors and allow it to dry again. The drops of water will have created an interesting work of art. Since no two pictures will be exactly alike, encourage your children to try other designs and attempt leaving them in the rain for different periods of time. As you can imagine, this makes an entertaining rainy day project!

Life Underwater

There are many fine books that depict life under the water and you will discover a nice selection listed at the end of this chapter. The two featured here were chosen because they are true stories that show the relationship that humans have had with our very different, but highly intelligent "cousins" of the ocean, the dolphin and the whale. These and other beautiful mammals of the water (such as the seal, manatee, walrus, etc.) share a kinship with us that should be explored and understood. It is through this understanding that our children will develop a love and respect for these animals and realize that they are deserving of our concern and protection in the future.

Who Lives There?

In any body of water, you and your children will discover a wide variety of interesting creatures. In a pond you may find toads, turtles, snails, insects, crayfish, or small fish. In a lake you might see larger fish and an assortment of birds, ducks, and geese. While visiting the ocean, you will uncover even more intriguing creatures such as scallops, mussels, clams, jellyfish, crabs, and shrimp. And if you are really lucky, you might even spot a whale or dolphin in the distance. Not everyone lives near an ocean, but most everyone lives near some body of water, even if it's a small river or marsh. Take your children to explore the unique collection of birds, insects, and animals that make their home near or in it. Take along a sketch pad and have your children draw their favorite underwater friend. Ask them to discover something about that animal that makes the water the best place for them to live.

Make an Underwater Viewer

Have you ever tried to open your eyes underwater? Most of what you'll see is a big blur. That's because light behaves differently in water than it does in the air. Our eyes are especially designed to see in the air, but the eyes of fish and other sea creatures are designed to see underwater. You and your children can help make your under-water exploration clearer by making this simple viewer out of scraps from your Recycle Craft Box.

Take an empty and cleaned half-gallon milk carton and cut off the top and bottom. Cover one end with a piece of clear cellophane and secure with a rubber band. For clearer underwater viewing, simply place the plastic covered end into the water and look through the carton. You'll see many things you never noticed before!

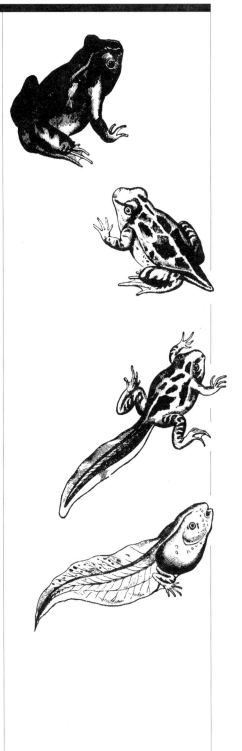

Visit an Aquarium

If your city has a public aquarium or if your local zoo has an aquarium building, plan a visit to learn about all of the interesting underwater creatures that live in different parts of the world. You might see an electric eel, live coral and beautiful coral fish, lobsters, or piranha. Many aquariums have displays of fish or other creatures that are not commonly known, so it will be a day of new discoveries.

What's for Dinner?

Sea creatures need the same things we do to live and grow – water, food, oxygen. In this underwater food chain story, your children follow the sunlight energy as it travels first through the water to the sea plants, then to the underwater animals.

The sun shines down upon the Earth and the glistening ocean waves absorb some of its light. *(Have the children pretend to be the rays of sunlight.)* A microscopic plant, drifting near the ocean's surface, grabs the sunlight filtering through the water and combines it with nutrients from the sea to create food for itself. *(The sun's energy is now part of the tiny plant, called phytoplankton. Have the children pretend to be a tiny sea plant.)* This plant floats along with the waves until suddenly, a tiny animal with a feathery body, called zooplankton, swims near and gulp! It eats the plant. *(Since the sun's energy is now part of the zooplankton, have the children pretend to be a tiny sea animal.)* This tiny feathery animal swims from the surface of the water down several feet where it meets a small fish. The small fish quickly snaps its jaws and swallows a mouthful of water, including the tiny animal. The zooplankton is eaten by the fish. *(Pretend to be the small fish.)* Far in the distance, sunning himself on a rock is a seal. That afternoon, he gets hungry and dives into the water in search of food. One of his favorites is squid, but today he can't find any, so instead he swims into a small group of anchovies. He swallows the small fish and several others in one gulp. *(Pretend to be the seal.)* Many weeks later, the seal is swimming near the surface of the ocean. Again he is looking for food, unaware of the danger below. The light of the sun surrounds his body making a shadow. An orca whale sees his silhouette, silently swims under him and snap! He eats the seal. *(Pretend to be the orca whale.)* The sunlight energy is now in the orca whale and becomes part of his body. He lives for many years in the cold waters of the ocean. One day, while taking a boat trip, you see the orca whale surfacing for air. You shout a greeting to him as he stops briefly to watch your boat speed by. Although he quickly disappears below the water, you know that he takes a bit of the sun and your greeting of friendship with him wherever he goes.

Our Cousin, the Whale

Although they live underwater, the bodies of whales, dolphins, and seals are similar to those of humans in many ways. At first glance they look like big fish, but they are not a fish at all. Whales, dolphins, and seals are mammals, just like a squirrel, a mouse or a person. They need to breathe air and their babies are not hatched from eggs but are born alive, just like human babies. In this activity, you and your children can become aware of the body parts that you have in common with whales and pretend that what once was your arm and hand, is now a strong flipper helping you navigate through the deep, blue ocean.

Through a Whale's Eyes: A whale has an eye on each side of its head which helps it see in almost every direction at once, but that also presents a problem. Because its eyes are so far to the sides, it has a blind spot in the front. (Unfortunately, whalers know this and always try to approach a whale head on. Since it can't see the ship coming, the whale is not aware of the danger until it is too late.) You can "see" through the eyes of a whale by holding three or four fingers of one hand between your eyes and over your nose. Keep your head still and with your other hand wave something in front of your face. You will notice that you can see the object when it's to the left or right, but not when it's directly in front of your face.

What's It Smell Like Underwater? A whale couldn't tell you, because it doesn't have a sense of smell. Instead, its blowhole, similar to our nose, is only used for breathing. When the whale is underwater, it holds his blowhole closed to keep the water out. When he reaches the surface, he blows out the old air and breathes in new air before going under again. An interesting difference is that a whale can hold its breath underwater for thirty minutes or more, while humans can hold their breath for about a minute. Try holding your breath for a minute; it's hard to do! Also, the whale's blowhole isn't located right above its mouth. Take your finger and trace from your nose, over your head, until your reach the back of your neck; that's where your nose would be if you were a whale!

Ears and Hearing: A whale's ears are hard to see. From the outside, all you can see are small holes right behind his eyes. His sense of hearing is very keen, and he can sometimes communicate

<blockquote>
E ven sleepers are workers and collaborators in what goes on in the universe.

HERACLITUS, 500 B.C.
</blockquote>

with other whales miles away. Like a bat, a whale uses echolocation to "see" in murky or dark water. Whales make special sounds and listen to the echoes, and in that way they can tell how far away and how big something is. To experience echolocation, play this game: blindfold one player and stand him in the middle of the group. Whenever he says "whale," everyone must respond, "here." By listening to his "echo," the blindfolded child can seek out and tag another player. Repeat until all players have had the opportunity to be the whale searching for his dinner.

Shake Your Flipper: On the sides of their bodies, whales have flippers to help them steer as they swim. The most interesting fact about them is that their skeleton has five "fingers," just like a human hand! Pretend to be a whale swimming through the ocean. Spread your fingers apart and use your strong flippers to help you twist and turn in the water.

DREAMSTARTER

P retend that you are swimming in the shallow water on the edge of the ocean. The sun feels warm on your shoulders and the sound of the waves crashing against the sandy beach fills your ears. The cold waves break on your chest as you walk into the deeper water. Far in the distance you see a whale surface, blowing a plume of water and steam into the air. After taking a deep breath, he rolls on his side and signals to you with his flipper. His invitation is enchanting, so you dive beneath the waves and swim out to meet him.

As you approach, you can see that he is a very large animal. You feel as tiny as a mouse next to his huge flipper. You lightly touch his skin; it feels smooth and rubbery against your fingertips. You gently stroke his back as he swims just beneath you. Soon, he begins to swim away. "I wish he wouldn't go," you think to yourself. As if he can hear your thoughts, he gracefully turns around and heads toward you. You see his enormous dark eye look directly into yours as he carefully sweeps past you. His giant flipper gently touches your leg and, not wanting to hurt you, he quickly pulls it near his body until he has safely passed.

Inside your head you hear a deep voice. "What kind of creature are you that I've never seen you before?" You suddenly realize that it is the whale talking to you. You discover that just by thinking thoughts, you can talk to your new friend. "I am a human being," you reply. The whale hears your thoughts and soon you are exchanging stories about your different lives. You tell him about the many creatures that live on land and he tells you about the ocean and what it is like to live beneath the waves. You swim together for most of the afternoon, sharing thoughts, diving, and playing tag. When it is time for you to return home, you are sad thinking you may never see your special friend again. He feels your sadness and says, "Although we may live in different worlds, we can always be friends. Whenever you want to talk, come to the ocean and sit quietly. Listen to what the sea has to say, because it will be me."

After saying good-bye, you reluctantly swim back to the beach. As you dry yourself with a towel, you watch the ocean and listen but you hear nothing except the breaking waves rolling on the sand. You wrap yourself in your towel, tuck your knees under your chin, and listen until the sun finally sets. You begin to wonder, "Did I just imagine him?" But, just as you turn to go, you hear a deep whisper on the wind that says, "Remember, you and I will always be friends."

The Largest Animal Ever

You might think that the great dinosaurs were the largest animals ever to have lived on this Earth. (See the "Going, Going. . .Gone?" chapter for an activity.) Although their huge size is hard to imagine, there are some species of whale that are even larger! Just to say that a Blue whale can reach a length of 100 feet isn't the same as seeing it from head to fluke. This activity will help you and your children visualize the enormity of some whales.

Dolphin Adventure: A True Story, by Wayne Glover. Illustrations by Jim Fowler. Greenwillow Books, NY, 1990.

This book offers young readers a you-are-there description of an almost unbelievable incident between a man and a family of dolphins. A mother and father dolphin bring their baby to the author/diver to remove a large fishing hook imbedded in his tail. Through desperate non-verbal communication with the parents of the wounded baby, the author is able to remove the hook while the parent dolphins scare off charging sharks. This touching story shows the level of communication and cooperation that is possible between animals and humans. (read-aloud, ages 5 - 12)

1. Have your children help you count out a length of string about 100 feet (30 meters) long. Have a child hold one end while another child stretches the string to its full length. Lay it down on the ground and have your children see how long it takes to race from the head to the fluke of a great blue whale.

2. Give a guided tour of your imaginary whale. As you walk along, point out where the different parts of his body would be. Start at the head and walk about twenty-five feet, and that's how big his jaws would be; also his eyes, ears, and blowhole would be located at this distance. Walk another fifteen feet and his flippers are located about there, each extending out about twenty feet. Have enough children lie head to toe to measure twenty feet. How many children long is a whale's flipper? Continue walking another twenty-five feet or so to see where his dorsal fin is located. Finally, walk along his tail about twenty to twenty-five feet. The final ten to fifteen feet measure the length of his two tail flukes; they would be approximately twenty feet wide (extending about ten feet to each side). If you are doing this activity on concrete, attempt to draw a rough outline of your whale with chalk using the above approximations to determine the location of body parts. (His mid-section would be about twenty feet wide.)

3. Have a picnic or take an imaginary ride on your whale's back. For a quiet time, have your children lie comfortably on the whale's back as you read the "Dream Starter" in this chapter.

Become a Whale

After learning about whales, your children can cooperatively become a magnificent whale and share an imaginary underwater adventure. To accompany your trek through the ocean, play a recording of actual whalesong or *La Mer* by Claude Debussy. Before you begin, assign a body part to each child or group, as suggested below. In this dramatization, your children should remain stationary while acting out their parts. Have them imagine that they are swimming through the ocean. After a time, have them switch places and experience the other parts of the whale.

Mighty Jaws: Have one child stand at the head and move his arms as if he were scooping up great mouthfuls of water. If you

Listen to the Whales

Whales Alive, a recording by Paul Winter and Paul Halley. Narration by Leonard Nimoy. With *Voices of the Humpback Whales, A Living Music Recording, c/o* Moss Music Group, 75 Essex Street, Hackensack, N.J. 07601.

would like, have him prepare a simple prop to represent baleen (the long, one-fourth inch thick plates that strain seawater and trap food). Just take a piece of scrap paper, about the length from his wrist to his elbow, and cut narrow strips along one edge. Make the cuts about one-half inch apart and don't cut all the way through. Tape the uncut edge to the child's inner arm so that it looks like a fringe hanging from his arm.

Blowhole: You'll need a group of three children for this. Have two children stand and face each other while holding hands. When it's time to breathe, have them open their arms into a big circle. At that time, the third child jumps up through the circle with his hands overhead and makes a spewing sound. After releasing the old air, he takes a big gulp of air and squats down again. Then the "blowhole" should close until the next breath.

Flippers: Choose one child to be each flipper. They should be situated to the side and a bit behind the blowhole. Have them extend their outside arm and gently sweep it from side to side, as if swimming.

Tail: Choose one child to be the tail. Have them lie on their stomach, with their arms to their sides, and gently lift their legs up and down in a smooth motion.

Save the Whale Game

Many countries are concerned about the future of whales. Over time, many species of whales are near extinction due to whale hunting. Although synthetic products make whaling unnecessary, there are still some countries that hunt these irreplaceable creatures. This dodge ball game makes it possible for your children to experience some of the emotions that whales and the protectors of whales might feel about hunting. Be aware that this game is not suitable for very young or immature children. Also, it is important to sit with the players after the game and talk about some of the feelings they experienced during play.

1. Choose several children to be the whales and assign the other players to be whale protectors. Form two large circles, the whales making up the outer circle and the protectors the inner one.

2. First, have the whales pretend to swim around their circle.

During play, tell them that they will not be able to run, but must walk or walk quickly in order to dodge a ball.

3. Tell the whale protectors that it will be their job to try to protect the whales from harm. To do this they must try to block the ball being thrown before it hits a whale.

4. To play, the adult stands in the middle of the circles and attempts to toss balls at the whales. (It is important that only an adult should throw balls. The object of the game isn't to see how many whales can be hit, but to have the children rally together in order to protect the whales from harm.) During the game, encourage the children to protect the whales as best they can.

5. Allow the children to exchange places occasionally to experience both points of view, the whale's and the protector's. At some times, you might want to have more whales than protectors and visa-versa. After everyone has had the opportunity to play both parts, gather the children together and talk about their experiences and their feelings about whale hunting.

Questions to Ask

• How did it feel to be a whale? What went through your mind when you saw a ball coming towards you? As a whale, how did you feel about the protectors?

• How did it feel to be a whale protector? When a ball was thrown, what thoughts went through your mind? Was it ever difficult to stop a ball from hitting a whale?

• Have any of you ever seen a real whale swimming in the ocean? Tell us about your experience and how it felt.

• Share your views about whale hunting. Do you think that all countries should stop hunting whales? Why or why not? What are some ways that people and government are trying to protect whales? Can you think of any other ways that you can help to stop the killing of whales? (See the "Get Involved" section of this chapter for some ideas.)

Teach us to walk the earth as relatives to all that live.

FROM A SIOUX PRAYER

Water for Life

We Use Water Every Day

In the home, water is used in many ways. Probably the most important use is for drinking; water is needed in our bodies for almost every purpose to keep it working properly. Other uses include cooking, bathing, cleaning, and flushing. Have your children help you discover all of the water outlets in your home. Cut large raindrops from blue scrap paper and attach one to each faucet (including outdoor, laundry room, and garage faucets) and toilet. Every time your children see this label, it will remind them of their dependency on clean water.

Where Does Your Water Come From?

Most children would simply answer this question, "The faucet, of course." They don't think about or even realize that the water has to come from somewhere before it can go through the pipes and out of your faucet. Some cities depend on underground water, or surface water (such as a lake or river), while other cities must have water piped in from a distant source. Where does your city get its water? To find out, call your Water Department and ask. If it is possible, visit the original source with your children and talk about the trip the water must take before reaching your house. Also, for older children, plan a visit to the waterworks in your community to learn about how it is cleaned and treated.

Take the Water Challenge

Do your children know how much water they use in a day? Probably not. Try this exercise to help them become aware of the many uses of water and the importance of conservation.

Save a gallon milk jug or two half-gallon milk cartons after use. Clean them thoroughly with soap and rinse carefully. Ask your children to take the "Water Challenge" by requesting that they try to get by on a gallon of water for a day (per child). They must use this water in place of faucet use such as for drinking, and rinsing teeth, toothbrush, hands, face, dinner plates, and so on. The only

The Magic School Bus at the Waterworks, by Joanna Cole. Illustrations by Bruce Degen. Scholastic, Inc., NY, 1986.

Who could imagine that a trip to the waterworks could be so much fun? With a teacher like Ms. Frizzle and the magic school bus, anything is possible! Humorous and educational, this story is written in a comic book style. Take a journey into the reservoir and through its purifying process to learn how drinking water is cleaned and treated before coming through your pipes at home. (ages 6 - 10)

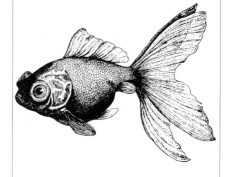

The Seal and the Slick, by Don Freeman. Viking Press, NY, 1974.

A young seal is caught in an oil slick spilled from an off-shore drilling rig. Covered with oil, he barely makes it to a beach where he is helped by two compassionate children. They scrub him with a special cleaning fluid and, happily, he is able to swim back to his family. (ages 4 - 8)

Jack, the Seal and the Sea, by Gerald Aschenbrenner. English adaptation by Joanne Fink. Silver Burdett, NJ, 1988.

Jack spends his days sailing the sea and taking in nets full of half-dead fish. He ignores the polluted condition of the water until he finds an ailing seal and receives a message from the sea itself about its sorry state. He gives up his life as a fisherman to carry the sea's message to mankind so that our oceans can be saved. (ages 5 - 10)

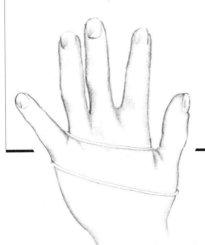

liquid they will be allowed to drink for the day is water, or if they want juice, it must be made from this water. (The rationed water must be used for everything, except flushing.) Can they do it? Let them try it for a day. They will discover that, indeed, it is a challenge!

Have a Mock Community Meeting

What if suddenly your water supply was severely limited and rationing of water was necessary. In many cities, during periods of drought, this is exactly what happens. Let your children act as community council members and decide on a water rationing program for your home or school. After discussing the problem, allow them to make a list of water conservation rules. Encourage them to choose rules which they can follow, such as taking five minute showers instead of baths or turning off the faucet while brushing their teeth. (For more ideas, see "Easy Ways to Conserve Water at Home" located in the "Get Involved" section of this chapter.) Also, discuss a plan of action to enforce the new rules. Create a poster to display the water rules. Reward certificates of merit or buttons to those that are exceptional water conservationists, such as the "Shortest Shower Award" or "Water Miser of the Week." Check your water bill to see if water consumption is actually lower.

Help! I Can't Get It Off!

That's exactly what animals are thinking when they become entangled in litter, such as a plastic six-pack ring over their heads. They don't have fingers and arms, so they are unable to lift it off. There have even been some reported cases in which baby seals have gotten their heads accidentally through six-pack rings and as they grew the ring tightened and eventually choked them. What's it like to become entangled in debris and unable to free yourself? This simple hand exercise will help demonstrate this to you and your children.

Take a rubber band and loop it around your thumb, stretch it over your hand (not the palm), then loop it around your little finger. Pretend that your hand is an animal entangled in a piece of litter. Without using your other hand, any other part of your body, or nearby object, try to free yourself from the rubber band. You can move it in any fashion, attempt to use the fingers on the entangled hand, twist it, etc. As you will soon discover, it is almost impossible to remove. This is the kind of helpless feeling that many entangled animals experience, and what's worse is that the more they struggle, the more entangled they become. That's why it is important to keep our oceans, lakes, and rivers free from debris, especially plastics that do not disintegrate and are harmful to the creatures living there.

The Turtle's Mishap: A Puppet Show or Play

Another name for trash is litter or garbage, but as soon as it hits the water it is known as "marine debris." This short puppet show (or play) illustrates to young children the potential harm their litter can pose to innocent creatures living beneath the waves.

List of Characters: Sea Turtle, Fish, Cormorant, Octopus, Seal, and Lobster.

Things You Will Need: puppets (or simple costumes), simple underwater background scene (if desired), and a small collection of trash: plastic six-pack rings, aluminum cans, plastic sandwich bags, a plastic milk jug, a wad of dental floss to represent fishing line, a foam cup, and various containers.

As the curtain opens, a sea turtle is swimming around in circles. On one side of his body, make it obvious that his flippers are entangled in a plastic six-pack ring. They are so tangled, they cannot move. His other flippers, though, are free and are paddling back and forth. Because of this, he is only able to swim in a circle.

Turtle: Help! Please, help. My flippers are stuck.

(He continues to struggle and swim in circles. Then along swims a fish and he stops to watch the turtle.)

Fish: What a strange thing to do. Why are you swimming in circles?

Turtle: Oh, please Mr. Fish, can you help me? My flippers are stuck and I can't get them free.

(Have the fish try to help the turtle by pulling on the plastic ring with his mouth.)

Fish: Oh, you really are stuck! Tell me, how did this happen?

A Tale of Antarctica, by Ulco Glimmerveen. Scholastic, Inc., NY, 1989.

One spring, as the sun begins to warm the air, the frozen landscape of Antarctica begins to change. Oil drums and garbage litter the beaches. This poignant story is about a father penguin who sees his family and companions becoming entangled in the debris. While hunting for food one day, he is unable to avoid the oil slicks that cover the water and is soon desperately in need of help. His family climbs over piles of trash to alert a team of people who are concerned for the wildlife. Eventually Papa penguin is treated with powdered clay to absorb the oil. As winter begins to set in, the oil tankers leave and the animals are left to wonder if their home will ever be the same again. (ages 5 - 9)

Turtle: I was swimming along and I just didn't see this plastic ring floating in the water. Before I knew what had happened, it was looped around my flipper. I tried to get it off, but then I got my back one stuck too.

Fish: I remember when something like this happened to me. I was poking my head in the rocks on the bottom looking for food, and all of a sudden it was stuck in a old, rusty tin can. It took me quite a while before I was finally able to shake it off. *(looking behind him and rushing off, he says:)* Woops, I've got to run or I'll be somebody's dinner. Good luck!

(A cormorant, a dark sea bird that swims underwater to catch fish, swims by and is perplexed by the circling turtle.)

Cormorant: You'll never get anywhere going around in circles like that.

Turtle: Maybe you can help. My flippers are stuck in this plastic ring. With your pointed beak, I'll bet you could get a good grip on it.

Cormorant: I'd be happy to try.

(So the cormorant tugs and pulls on the ring, but is unable to free it.)

Cormorant: I'm sorry, I can't budge it! You know, this reminds me of something that happened just last week. I was paddling on the surface when all of a sudden my legs were tangled in some fishing line. As I was trying to get free, it must have caught on something and I was pulled underwater. I could have drowned, but I was lucky enough to get out of that tangled mess just in time. Speaking of that, I need to go catch a breath. I'm sorry I couldn't help.

(The cormorant swims off, leaving the turtle alone. He continues to struggle and swim in a circle. After a time, along swims an octopus.)

Octopus: Is this a new dance or something?

Turtle: No, it's not a dance. I'm going around in circles because my flippers are stuck in this plastic ring. Say, you have a lot of strong legs. Could help me by pulling it off?

Octopus: Let me see what I can do.

(So the octopus tries many different ways to pull the ring off, but his efforts are unsuccessful.)

Octopus: This trash is really a problem. There have been many times I thought I was picking up a clam, only to discover it was the top of a jar or a hunk of glass.

(Along swims a seal.)

Seal: What's going on here? Are you two fighting?

Octopus: No, not at all. I'm trying to pull this plastic ring off Turtle's flippers. Would you care to help?

Seal: I'd be happy to.

(So the two of them tug at the ring, but it doesn't come free.)

Turtle: Ouch! It is so tight, my flippers are really beginning to hurt. Is there something else we can try?

Seal: Once I got caught in an old fishing net. I chewed and chewed until I cut it enough to break free. But this ring is much thicker, I don't think I could chew through it.

Octopus: That gives me an idea, I might know someone who could help.

(The octopus swims off to search for his friend and returns with a lobster.)

Octopus: See, here's the turtle I was telling you about. Do you think you could use your claws and cut through that plastic ring?

Lobster: I'm not sure, but let me try.

(The lobster cuts the plastic ring with his claws and the turtle is free.)

Turtle: Oh, thank you so much. I was beginning to think I would have to swim around in circles for the rest of my life.

(The cormorant and fish return.)

Fish: I just came back to see if you were all right.

Cormorant: I see you got free of the plastic ring. You were lucky this time!

Turtle: I know. I'll try to be more careful. But sometimes it's impossible to see the trash, especially those plastic rings or bags. Sometimes I wonder if humans think our ocean is just a big garbage can!

Seal: Everybody, listen. What's that noise?

(A faint rumbling sound and be heard and then it gets louder. All of the creatures watch as a motor boat passes overhead. As it goes by, a bunch of trash is thrown overboard and rains down on the animals.)

Turtle *(gravely)*: I just wish they'd stop and think!

(All of the creatures nod in agreement and then the curtain closes.)

Oil and Water Don't Mix

Although children are unable to do much about oil spills along the coast, they can learn about the devastation and difficulty that result from such spills. As you may have gathered from news broadcasts or newspapers, cleaning an oil spill is no easy task. First, the oil must be contained. Next, people must locate and clean each animal and release it to an unaffected area. And finally, chemicals are added to the water to dissolve the oil. It takes a long time before the contaminated area is safe for animals again. To help your children understand how hard it is to remove oil from water, let them try this experiment.

Fill a pan with water and pour a small amount of vegetable oil into it and allow your children to watch as it forms an oil slick on the surface. Assign them the task of removing the oil from the water as best they can. Offer them materials such as a baster bulb, cotton balls, an old towel, large spoons, cornstarch or another absorbent powder, a sponge, etc. When they are finished, talk about the possibility of using some of their methods on an actual oil spill. Would they be workable solutions? Did any of your methods do more harm than good? It is important to remember that the effective methods used for cleaning an oil spill also need to leave the environment safe for any wildlife.

An Ocean of "Goo"

By dramatizing an oil spill, your children can understand the effect it has on existing wildlife. In a single spill, thousands of birds, fish, otters, and other sea creatures die. When fish become coated with oil, their gills become clogged they can no longer breathe. Birds and otters suffer in other ways. When their feathers and fur become coated, they lose their insulating qualities and the animals are unable to stay warm in their cold environment. Also, the oil kills the small marine animals that eat food or drink water contaminated with it, thus killing the larger animals that feed on them. In this game, your children can pretend to be the animals or wildlife specialists at an oil spill. They will learn that animals harmed by an oil slick need special assistance before they are able to return to the ocean and that it is the responsibility of humans to provide that help.

1. Locate an old king-size sheet or parachute to represent the oil spill. Divide your children into groups. First, assign one group to be the wildlife specialists. Then ask the remaining groups to choose what kind of marine animal they will pretend to be. Some suggestions are: otter, seal, pelican, cormorant, and fish.

2. Have each group decide on a restricting form of movement. For example, the otters could walk on hands and feet facing upwards like a swimming otter. Fish could take small steps, while wiggling back and forth. Sea birds could pretend that their wings are stuck and walk in circles.

3. To play the game, have all of the animals hold the edges of the sheet or parachute. The wildlife specialists should stand on the outside of the sheet waiting for injured animals to rescue. At a signal, the children should raise the sheet. At that time, call out one or two animal names. Those animals should let go of the sheet and, using their movement, go under the raised sheet to the other side as quickly as possible. As the sheet/oil slick floats down, some animals might become trapped. They must stop moving and remain under the oil spill.

4. Repeat, again calling animal names, but this time the wildlife specialists can enter the raised sheet and "rescue" an injured animal by tagging him. Together they run from under the sheet and to the side where the specialist will pretend to clean the oil from the animal. Once cleaned, the animal can return to the game.

5. Continue playing in this manner until the players are tired or the oil slick is so full of "injured" animals that other animals are unable to move under the sheet. After the game, gather the children and talk about the real difficulties that animals face in an oil spill.

Check the Ingredients

Water makes up about 75% of our bodies and clean drinking water is necessary to keep us healthy. Throughout the world, polluted water is responsible for many forms of illness and every year many people die from these diseases. So it is easy to reach the conclusion that polluted water can make people sick. In this activity, since the Earth's surface is also about 75% water, you and your children can draw the same conclusion; that polluted water will

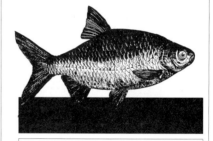

The care of rivers is not a question of rivers but of the human heart.

TANAKA SHOZO

Keep It Clean!

Tune: Bingo

We use water every day

In many, many ways.

Refrain (clap): W-A-T-E-R,

W-A-T-E-R, W-A-T-E-R,

We need to keep it clean.

Falling, falling from the sky

It rains upon the Earth.

(repeat refrain)

Clean water is a thing we need

To keep our bodies healthy.

(repeat refrain)

So next time that you take a drink,

There's something to remember!

(repeat refrain)

make the Earth sick as well.

You've seen ingredient labels on the back of food cans or cereal boxes; they list the contents of the food in order of quantity. For example, they might read: whole wheat, sugar, assorted chemicals, added vitamins, etc. Well, you and your children can make ingredient labels for a human body and the Earth's surface, and compare their contents. First, have your children make a poster with a picture of a human being and the planet Earth. Under each write a list of ingredients in order of quantity. Human: water, bones, muscle, body organs, skin. Earth's surface: water, rocks, iron, soil. In big letters, label the poster with a slogan such as, "We both need clean water to stay healthy."

Get Involved!

10 Ways to Help Stop Pollution

1. Never leave your trash on a beach or throw it into a body of water such as a lake, stream, or an ocean. Your garbage can be harmful to the animals that live there.

2. Cut the loops from plastic six-pack rings and other plastic items before throwing them away.

3. If your community has a recycling center, sort your aluminum, plastics, paper, and glass to be recycled. If it doesn't have a center, do what you can to get one started!

4. Whenever you are boating, keep trash secured on board (including unwanted fishing line) and dispose of it properly when you return to shore.

5. Toilets should not be used as garbage cans. Never flush plastics, but recycle them or place them in a trash can.

6. Have your family join a river or beach clean-up. Check with your local nature center to see when one is planned.

7. If you have older children that help with chores, instead of allowing them to dump household toxins down the drain (such as furniture polish, window cleaners, bleach, toilet cleaner, oil-based paint, and paint remover), teach them how to dispose of them

safely. First, use it all up. Then you'll need to wrap the container in newspaper, put it into a plastic bag, and put it out for the trash collector. Or store it safely away and turn it in on toxic waste collection day.

8. Try using "natural" cleaners, instead of store-bought ones. Allow your children to help with simple household jobs using these safer solutions. (see "Cleaner Alternatives" below)

9. When gardening, instead of using fertilizers or pesticides, enrich your soil with compost. These chemicals often find their way into ground water and can poison drinking water supplies. (See "Wonders in a Garden" chapter for ideas about keeping bugs from destroying your plants.)

10. Instead of using salt to melt icy sidewalks, use cat-box litter or sand. Salt can enter and pollute the water supply.

Cleaner Alternatives

We lock up our cabinets because they are full of toxic and potentially harmful cleaning products, but we think nothing of pouring them into the sink or toilet, which is to say, into our drinking water supply. You might think that by pouring a substance down the drain, it goes away. That is not true, because from there it enters the water supply and eventually it returns to your faucet as water for drinking or cooking. Let your children help you make these easy recipes for environmentally-safe household cleaners and allow them the opportunity to use them with your supervision. *(Note to adult: although these are made from common ingredients found on your kitchen shelves, they should not be ingested.)*

For Abrasive Cleaning: Use baking soda or salt, or a mixture of both.

Glass Cleaner: Mix a tablespoon of vinegar into a quart of water.

Wood Polish: Mix together one part lemon juice and two parts olive or vegetable oil.

Tile Floor Cleaner: Mix one-fourth cup vinegar into a gallon of water.

Bleach: For a gentler alternative, try using borax. It is a naturally occurring form of the element boron. It cleans, disinfects, whitens, and softens water without being as harmful to the environment.

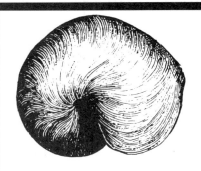

Center for Marine Conservation
1725 DeSales St. NW,
Suite 500
Washington, D.C. 20036

The Izaak Walton League of
America
1401 Wilson Blvd., Level B
Arlington, VA 22209.

Beach Cleanup Days

Did you know that beach cleanup days are organized all over the nation? If you live in a state that borders an ocean, check with your State Department of Wildlife, Fish and Game or Coastal Management for dates and details. (Most cleanup days are scheduled in September or October each year.) Get your family involved in keeping the beaches safe and clean for wildlife and visitors. To receive a newsletter and other information that promotes beach cleanup events, contact the Center for Marine Conservation. Ask for a copy of "Coastal Connection." They also have a Marine Debris Elementary School Information Packet.

Form a Stream Team

The description "babbling brook" brings to mind a clean, undisturbed mountain stream bubbling down a mountainside. Unfortunately, many small streams or creeks have become polluted or are lined with litter. How can you tell if a stream is polluted? If you can smell it, that's a bad sign. Also, its color can tell you something. For instance, if the water is brown and muddy, too much soil is washing into the water. Green water is a sign that too much algae is growing. Algae overgrowth makes it difficult for other animals to live in the stream. If you see a colorful, shiny film on the water, oil is present, poisoning the plants and wildlife. You can help your children organize a "Stream Team" to walk along the stream bank and pick up all the litter they can find. Also, they can plant trees along the bank to keep the soil from washing into the water. If they locate any sources of oil or sewage being dumped into the stream, an adult should take action to have it stopped. To send for a free "Save Our Streams" pamphlet, write to the Izaak Walton League.

Easy Ways to Conserve Water at Home

The United States uses more of the Earth's resources than any other country, and that includes water. You might say that we are water hogs! We are compulsive about having shiny cars, green lawns, and sparkling white clothes. After a long day, we overfill the bathtub to soak our tension away. Here are some suggestions for curbing your family's water use (and reducing your monthly bill as well).

1. Take short showers instead of baths. Set an egg timer for five minutes and see who can beat the clock! Offer a reward for the quickest shower.

2. Turn off the water while brushing your teeth or washing dishes.

3. Fill dishwashers and washing machines completely before doing a load. And, if possible, use an energy-saving cycle.

4. Fill half-gallon plastic milk jugs with water, fill partway with rocks to weight them down, and place one in the back of each toilet. You can save as much as ten gallons a day!

5. Collect the water that drips out of your air conditioner and use it for watering house plants.

6. Thoroughly clean an empty milk or juice jug. Each morning, fill it with water for drinking and put it in the refrigerator. That way you don't have to stand at a running faucet waiting for the water to cool, and you and your children will always have cold drinking water.

7. Letting the kids play in the sprinkler and watering your lawn can be accomplished at the same time. On a sunny day, choose to water a shaded area, or wait until evening when less evaporation will occur.

8. When children want to play with water, instead of letting the hose or faucet run, fill buckets with water and provide paint brushes. They will enjoy painting everything in sight and might even clean something along the way.

Adopt A Whale

What would children think about having the biggest "pet" on the block? You and your family (or class) can adopt a whale and feel good about supporting the efforts of the Wildlife Coalition in helping whales and other endangered animals. It isn't a lot of money, especially when you consider the importance of saving whales for the Earth's future. It also makes a thoughtful gift for someone. You can even choose a particular whale from a photograph. For $15 you will receive an official Whale Adoption Certificate, a photograph of your whale, and a year's subscription to the *Whalewatch* newsletter for updates on the activities and whereabouts

Whale Adoption Project
P. O. Box 388
North Falmouth, MA 02556

The President of the United States
1600 Pennsylvania Avenue
Washington, D.C. 20501

His Excellency
Ambassador of Japan
2520 Massachusetts Ave., N.W.
Washington, D.C. 20008

His Excellency
Ambassador of Norway
2720 34th St., N.W.
Washington, D.C. 20008

of your chosen whale. If a class adopts a whale, the teacher will be sent a free *Whales of the World* teacher kit. For information, write to the Whale Adoption Project.

A Thought About Marine Shows

You've probably heard of places that have dolphins and killer whales performing tricks for an audience. Many feel that these animals should not be kept in swimming pools just so they can entertain us, but should be left to live freely in the big, wide ocean. If you also feel this way, tell other people what you think and do not support these places by visiting them. Instead, plan a vacation to the lake or ocean and encourage your children to discover the many wonderful underwater creatures living in their natural habitat.

Your Letters Might Save the Whales

In 1946 the International Whaling Commission was set up because many countries were concerned about the future of whales. In 1983 the commission voted to stop almost all whaling, except for the few whales taken by native peoples that depended on them for their existence. Unfortunately, not all nations stopped. Japan and Norway still continue to kill whales, although all whaling products have been replaced with inexpensive substitutes. Many people all over the world protest their actions, and you and your children can also voice your concern by writing letters. The people of the United States can do something to pressure Japan and Norway to stop the killing of whales by refusing to import fish from these countries. Write to the President and tell him what you think.

A Picture Is Worth a Thousand Words

Letter writing is a great way for children to get involved in environmental issues. If your children are too young to write, let them draw instead! A child's picture may make a greater impression than a ten-page letter from an outraged adult. Can letters really make a difference? Yes! For example, due to public pressure, many tuna companies have altered their fishing techniques, making the ocean a safer place for dolphins. You and your children can write or draw a letter and help change the world.

More Books to Share with Children

Better Not Get Wet, Jesse Bear by **Nancy White Carlstrom.** Illustrations by Bruce Degen. Macmillan Pub. Co., NY, 1988. Getting wet is okay – for everyone but Jesse Bear. But finally, it is Jesse Bear's turn to splash in his wading pool on a hot day. This is a perfect book to make very young children aware of all the fun that can be had in the water. (ages 3 - 6)

The Four Elements: Water by **Carme Sole Vendrell and J. M. Parramón.** Barron's, NY, 1984. This colorful book illustrates for the very young child all of the reasons man should be grateful for water's presence on the Earth. The other books in the series include *Earth, Fire,* and *Air.* Each book includes a special section to help adults answer children's questions. (ages 3 - 6)

The Sea is Calling Me, **poems selected by Lee Bennett Hopkins.** Illustrations by Walter Gaffney-Kessel. Harcourt Brace Jovanovich, Pub., NY, 1986. The fascination of sealife is celebrated in poems in this lovely anthology. (all ages)

Water, by **David Bennett.** Illustrations by Rosalinda Kightley. From the Bear Facts Series, Bantam Little Rooster Book, 1989. The Bear Facts bear invites young readers to discover the wonders of nature in a series for preschool age children. Other books in the series include *Air, Sounds, Fire, Rain, Day and Night, Seasons,* and *Earth.* (ages 3 - 6)

Water by **Alfred Leutscher.** Illustrations by Nick Hardcastle. Dial Press, NY, 1983. This beautifully illustrated book presents many aspects of water including its properties, its power, its changeability, and the reasons it is essential to all life. (ages 6 - 9)

It Looked Like Spilt Milk by **Charles Green Shaw.** Harper and Row, NY, 1947. "It looked like spilt milk, but it wasn't spilt milk. . . . It was just a cloud in the sky." Children can watch a cloud change from one shape into another as each page is turned. (ages 2 - 6)

Flash, Crash, Rumble, and Roll by **Franklyn M. Branley.** Thomas Y. Crowell, NY, 1985. All about thunderstorms. (ages 6 - 10)

Peter Spier's Rain by **Peter Spier.** Doubleday, NY, 1982. A wordless book in which a little boy and girl do all the things that can be done in the rain. (ages 3 - 7)

Weatherwatch by **Valerie Wyatt.** Illustrations by Pat Cupples. Addison-Wesley, Reading, MA, 1990. School age children see how to preserve a snowflake, create a cloud, make a rainbow, chew lightning, catch pollution, and be a weather watcher. (ages 7 - 12)

That Sky, That Rain by **Carolyn Otto.** Illustrations by Megan Lloyd. Thomas Crowell, NY, 1990. A celebration of the extraordinary magic of something as ordinary as a summer rainstorm, especially when it is shared with someone you love. (ages 6 - 9)

What Makes It Rain? The Story of a Raindrop by **Keith Brandt.** Illustrations by Yoshi Miyake. Troll Associates, Mahwah, NJ, 1982. Follow the journey of a raindrop through the water cycle. (ages 5 - 9)

All Wet! All Wet! by **James Skofield.** Illustrations by Diane Stanley. Harper & Row, NY, 1984. A boy spends a wet day noticing how the animals, insects, and birds react to the wetness of the day from dawn into the darkness of a summer night. (ages 4 - 8)

Rain Rain Rivers by **Uri Shulevitz.** Farrar, Straus & Giroux, NY, 1969. A beautiful book for bringing the water cycle to life in the mind of a child. (ages 4 - 8)

Listen to the Rain by **Bill Martin, Jr. and John Archamboult.** Illustrations by James Endicott. Henry Holt & Co., NY, 1988. This lyrical book, a poetic mixture of sound and sight, evokes the beauty and mystery of rain. (ages 4 - 8)

Rain Talk **by Mary Serfozo.** Illustrations by Keiko Narahashi. Margaret K. McElderry Books, Macmillan, NY, 1990. *Rain Talk* is a joyous book about the many sounds and very special pleasures a rainy day brings to a little girl and her dog. (ages 4 - 8)

The Clean Brook **by Margaret Farrington Bartlett.** Illustrations by Aldren A. Watson. Thomas Y. Crowell Co., NY, 1960. This book explains for very young children how a brook cleans itself in nature, without the polluting influence of man. (ages 4 - 7)

Bringing the Rain to Kapiti Plain by **Verna Aardema.** Illustrations by Beatriz Vidal. Dial Books for Young Readers, NY, 1981. The beautiful African plain grows barren and dry until Ki-pat, watching over his hungry and thirsty herd of cows, spies a cloud hovering above and comes up with an ingenious way to bring the rain. (ages 5 - 9)

Dark and Full of Secrets **by Carol Carrick.** Illustrations by Donald Carrick. Clarion Books, Ticknor and Fields, NY, 1984. Christopher didn't like to swim in the pond by his family's vacation cabin. It was too dark and full of secrets. But when his father gives him a mask and snorkel, he finds that beneath the water's murky surface lies a world full of wonders. (ages 7 - 10)

When the Tide is Low **by Sheila Cole.** Illustrations by Virginia Wright-Frierson. Lothrop, Lee & Shepard, NY, 1985. A child asks her mother all kinds of questions about the tide: how does it work, where does it go, what is left on the beach when it is low? All these questions are answered and beautifully illustrated in this graceful and informative book. (ages 5 - 8)

The River **by David Bellamy.** Illustrations by Jill Dow. Clarkson N. Potter, Pub., Inc. Distributed by Crown Publishers, Inc., NY, 1988. This timely book relates how plants and water creatures co-exist in a river and of their struggle to survive a man-made catastrophe: the dumping of waste into their habitat. (ages 6 - 10)

The Hidden Life of the Pond, **photographs and text by David M. Schwartz.** Crown Publishers, Inc., NY, 1988. Beginning with the rains in the spring, and ending with the coming of the winter season, this book offers a wide array of life forms (including photographs of single-cell creatures) that live in a typical pond. (ages 5 - 10)

Puddles and Ponds: Living Things in Watery Places **by Phyllis S. Busch.** Photographs by Arline Strong. The World Publishing Co., Cleveland, OH, 1969. This book invites the child to explore and to discover for himself the wonders and beauty of the life that lives in watery places. (ages 6 - 9)

At the Frog Pond **by Tilde Michels.** Illustrations by Reinhard Michl. J. B. Lippincott, NY, 1987. A whole world can be discovered in a small pond. From the frogs that lay their eggs, to the fish living there, to the birds circling over it, it is a busy, activity filled world. (ages 4 - 8)

Dive to the Coral Reefs **by Elizabeth Tayntor, Paul Erickson and Les Kaufman.** Crown Pub. Inc., NY, 1986. Beneath the warm tropical waters of the ocean lies a strange and beautiful world called the living coral reefs. It is the home of millions of creatures that can only survive in this delicate and unique environment. (ages 5 - 10)

Fish Calendar **by Siegfried Schmitz.** Illustrations by Jurgen Ritter. Silver Burdett, Morristown, NJ, 1986. *Fish Calendar* tells how and where fishes live, what they feed on, and what plants and other animals are part of their world. (ages 5 - 9)

What's Under the Ocean **by Janet Craig.** Illustrations by Paul Harvey. Troll Associates, Mahwah, NJ, 1982. This is a colorful introduction for very young children to some of the plants and animals that live in the ocean. (ages 3 - 6)

All About Whales **by Dorothy Hinshaw Patent.**

Holiday House, NY, 1987. This is a fine introduction by a noted zoologist to the largest animal that ever lived. (ages 7 - 10)

Ibis: A True Whale Story by **John Himmelman.** Scholastic, NY, 1990. This moving story relates the adventures of a humpback whale calf that gets tangled in a fishing net and is later freed by a team of helpful whale watchers. The book portrays in a poignant way how man can help, instead of destroy, these incredible creatures. (ages 6 - 9)

Sterling: The Rescue of a Baby Harbor Seal by **Sandra Verrill White and Michael Filisky.** Crown Publishers, NY, 1989. In the cold ocean off the coast of New England, a newborn harbor seal is abandoned by her mother. Fortunately, the Marine Mammal Network is alerted and the pup is brought to a facility at the New England Aquarium where she is nursed back to health and finally released back into the wild. (ages 5 - 8)

Sea Otter Rescue: The Aftermath of an Oil Spill, **text and photographs by Roland Smith.** Cobblehill Books (Dutton), NY, 1990. On March 24, 1989, the *Exxon Valdez* hit the rocks in Prince William Sound, Alaska letting loose into the water over 250,000 barrels of crude oil. All of the wildlife in the area was seriously threatened, especially the sea otters. This stirring account brings home to young readers the devastation to wildlife that can be caused by mankind. (ages 8 - 12)

Song of the Sea Otter by **Edith Thacher Hurd.** Illustrations by Jennifer Dewey. Sierra Club Books, Little, Brown and Company, Boston, 1983. In a snug little harbor on the shore of the Pacific ocean, a baby sea otter is born. There he lives happily with his mother until he grows a little older, and bolder! Young readers are led through a growing-up adventure they won't forget. (ages 7 - 10)

Joshua Disobeys **written and illustrated by Dennis**

Vollmer (age 6). Landmark Editions, Kansas City, MO, 1988. When Joshua, a baby whale, disobeys his mother and swims too close to the shore to visit with a friendly human boy, he becomes stranded on the beach. Many people try to save him, but it is his huge mother who finally rescues her baby. (ages 3 - 7)

Henry's Wrong Turn by **Harriet Ziefert.** Illustrations by Andrea Baruffi. Little, Brown and Company, Boston, 1989. In this story, based on an actual incident, Henry the humpback whale tries to find his way back to the ocean after mistakenly swimming into New York Harbor. (ages 5 - 9)

Whale Song by **Tony Johnston.** Illustrations by Ed Young. G. P. Putnam's Sons, NY, 1987. This is a beautiful and unusual counting book that is a celebration of "these gentle giants who communicate with each other over vast distances through the oceans of the world." (ages 4 - 7)

Davy's Dream: A Young Boy's Adventure with Wild Orca Whales by **Paul Owen Lewis.** Beyond Words Publishing Co., Hillsboro, Oregon, 1988. One day a boy named Davy dreams of sailing among a pod of wild Orca whales. This wonderful book teaches not only that animals and man have a natural affinity, but also that dreams pursued can come true! (ages 5 - 9)

The Dolphin's Journey by **Brita Orstadius.** Illustrations by Lennart Didoff. R & S Books, NY, 1989. A small girl visiting a Greek island ventures out too far into the sea and is rescued by a friendly dolphin. That night, out of her window, she sees a large dark shape down on the beach. The dolphin has washed ashore and he is dying. Now it is the villager's turn to try to save him. (read-aloud, ages 6 - 9)

A Thousand Pails of Water by **Ronald Roy.** Illustrations by Vo-Dinh Mai. Alfred A. Knopf, NY, 1978. A small boy's infectious determination saves the life of a whale beached near an oriental village. (ages 5 - 9)

The Dolphin and the Mermaid **by Ruth Carroll.** Henry Z. Walck, Inc., NY, 1974. The peaceful world of the mermaid, the dolphin, and their friends is rudely disturbed by divers looking for coral. This wordless picture book, rich in detail, portrays an appealing idea of life beneath the ocean and man's responsibility to keep it that way. (ages 4 - 8)

The Great Fish, **written and illustrated by Peter Parnall.** Doubleday & Co. Inc., NY, 1973. In words and pictures of great beauty and dignity, the author has created a fable that serves as a warning to us all - a warning to respect the Earth and all it has given to us before it is too late. (all ages)

One World **by Michael Foreman.** Arcade Pub., NY 1990.This story shows how careful each of us must be of our environment, and how we must repair what damage we cause. (ages 5 - 8)

The Stream **by Naomi Russell.** Penguin, NY, 1991. An engaging presentation of one of nature's most vital processes: the water cycle. (ages 3 - 6)

Resources for Parents and Teachers

The Sea Around Us by Rachel Carson. Oxford University Press, 1951. Like other Carson titles, such as *Under the Sea Wind* and *The Edge of the Sea,* this classic book combines literature and oceanography.

The Animal Protection Institute of America offers *Whales,* a 16-page brochure that outlines some of the myths associated with this great animal, describes their social lives, and communication patterns. (25 cents) Also available is *The Harp Seal,* a pamphlet that discusses the life, history, habits, and killing of Harp seals. (25 cents) Write 2831 Fruitridge Road, P. O. Box 22505, Sacramento, CA 95822.

The Center for Marine Conservation, 1725 DeSales Street N.W., Washington, D.C. 20036, publishes lists

of good books for adults and children on whales, sea turtles, and seals. They also offer many other games and activities for elementary school age children.

Form a HEART Council - (Help Endangered Animals-Ridley Turtles). Any group with an adult sponsor may form such a group. The project teaches involvement in government as well as information on a very endangered species. Write to HEART, Piney Woods Wildlife Society, Box 681231, Houston, TX 77268-1231.

Whale posters and fact packs can be obtained from the American Cetacean Society, P.O. Box 2639, San Pedro, CA 90731.

For a *Whale Watcher's Guide to the North Atlantic,* a two-sided, fold-out, laminated field guide to whales, seabirds, and other marine animals, write to the Massachusetts Audubon Society, Public Information Office, Lincoln, MA 01773. ($3.65 + postage)

The Animal Welfare Institute offers many free items for teachers. Please use school stationery and indicate grade level. Inquire about: *How to Liven Up Your Classroom with a Pod of Whales, A Whale of a Friend, What Dolphins are Teaching Us about Communication,* and *Save the Whales.* Write P.O. Box 3650, Washington, D.C. 20007.

"Plastic Reaps a Grim Harvest in the Oceans of the World," by Michael Weisskopf, *Smithsonian* (March 1988): 59-66.

"Plastic's Threatening Tide," by Bonni Price, *Science World* (May 20, 1988, Vol. 44, No. 18): 8-11.

"Preventing Marine Debris," (for elementary school children). Provided by the Center for Marine Conservation, 1725 DeSales St., NW, Washington, D. C. 20036. Also available is a booklet entitled "All About Beach Cleanups" and *Coastal Connection,* a newsletter produced by the CMC to promote beach cleanup events, "Citizen Pollution Patrols," and other efforts to eliminate marine debris that injures wildlife, fouls our beaches, and threatens boater safety.

An Adopt-A-Beach School Education Program binder and other marine science curricula are available from Project OCEAN, Ocean Alliance, Bldg. E., Fort Mason, San Francisco, CA 94123.

"The Dirty Seas," *Time* (August 1, 1988, Vol. 132, No. 5): 44-50. An excellent article that points out that across the globe, the seas have been sending urgent signals that they are perilously close to their capacity to absorb civilization's wastes.

The Marine Debris Information Office (operated by the Center for Marine Conservation) has an incredible array of educational materials available to parents and teachers, including many of the above listed items. They offer packets for elementary school students, middle, high school, and college students, teachers, and the general public. Write or call either of their offices for this free material: Pacific Coast office, 312 Sutter St., Suite 606, San Francisco, CA 94108, (415) 391-6204, or the Atlantic/Gulf Coast office, 1725 DeSales St., NW, Washington, D.C. 20036, (202) 429-5609.

For information on the condition of our wild and scenic rivers, contact American Rivers, 801 Pennsylvania Ave., SE, Washington, D.C. 20003.

The Clean Water Action Project is concerned with water pollution and toxins in our water. For more information write 317 Pennsylvania Ave., SE, Washington, D.C. 20003.

Greenpeace, USA, has material available on the destruction of the habitats of marine mammals. Contact them at 1436 U Street, NW, Washington, D.C. 20009.

For information concerning our ocean and coastal resources, write to the Oceanic Society, 1536 16th Street, NW, Washington, D.C. 20036.

The Whale Center can provide material about the state of the world's largest animal. Contact them at 3929 Piedmont Ave., Oakland, CA 94611. Another source of information on this subject is the International Whaling Commission, The Red House, 135 Station Road, Histon, Cambridge CB4 4NP, England.

If you write the Animal Welfare Institute, P.O. Box 3650, Washington, D.C. 20007, your child can receive a letter from a blue whale that describes in a child's language the plight of this magnificent animal.

The Cousteau Society is involved in many areas of protection for life in the sea as well as the bodies of water themselves. Two magazines are offered for members of the Society, one for adults and one for children. For more information about the Cousteau Society and its work, write 930 W. 21st Street, Norfolk, VA 23517.

The U.S. Dept. of Commerce, National Oceanic and Atmospheric Administration offers a booklet entitled "Our Living Oceans" for parents and teachers. Address your request to Rockville, Maryland 20852.

"Sea of Troubles: Are We Deep-Sixing the Oceans?" by Jim Hogshire, *The Animal's Agenda* (June 1990): 22-27.

The Rocky Mountain Institute offers a booklet entitled "Water Efficiency for Your Home" at $5.00 a copy. It contains tips on cutting your water and sewer bills, efficient outdoor watering, smart landscaping, and planning a water efficient home. Write 1739 Snowmass Creek Road, Snowmass, CO 81654-9199.

The Outdoor Biology Instructional Strategies (OBIS) offers teaching modules entitled "Streams and Ponds" and "Ponds and Lakes." Contact Delta Education, Box M, Nashua, NH, 03061.

Pond and Brook: A Guide to Nature Study in Freshwater Environments by Michael Caduto. Prentice-Hall, Inc., NW, 1985.

"Learning to Love Streams: Save Our Streams," is a collection of teacher lesson plans for stream activities and monitoring. It is designed to help students test stream water quality and pinpoint problems. (4th grade and up, $2 each) Write to the Izaak Walton League of America, Inc., 1701 N. Fort Myer Drive, Suite 1100, Arlington, VA 22209. The League also offers a free SOS Kid's Activities packet that explains the causes of pollution and describes activities kids can do to combat the problem. It is written for children ages 6 to 13.

Ranger Rick's NatureScope: Diving Into Oceans Vol. 4, No. 2. Available from the National Wildlife Federation, 1400 Sixteenth Street, NW, Washington, D.C. 20077-9964. This is an excellent resource for activities dealing with life in the ocean, the physical properties of the ocean, and people's relationship with the ocean.

Animals of a Living Reef (all ages) is available in film or video from Coronet Films and Video, 108 Wilmot Rd., Deerfield, IL 60015-5196.

Animals That Live in the Sea by Joan Ann Straker. National Geographic Society, Washington, D.C., 1978.

Mystic Marinelife Aquarium has available *The Classroom Ocean,* a guide for teachers with information on setting up and maintaining a classroom aquarium. It also offers *Schoolword,* an elementary level newsletter containing activities and facts about aquatic life. Contact the Education Dept., 55 Coogan Blvd., Mystic, CT 06355-1997.

Coastal Awareness Resource Guide is offered free to elementary teachers. Write to the U.S. Dept. of Commerce, NOAA, Coastal Zone Information Center, Washington, D.C. 20235, and be sure to specify the grade you teach.

Sea Grant Communications offers *Wavelets* which are brochures on different ocean topics. Each one contains background information, and some of them include a activity, puzzle, or game. Single copies are free. Write to them at the Virginia Institute of Marine Science, Gloucester Point, VA 23062.

The Education Department of the Monterey Bay Aquarium has available educational materials, slide sets, and a video. Contact them at 886 Cannery Row, Monterey, CA 93940.

Ocean-Related Curriculum Activities (ORCA) offers activity books for all levels on different ocean topics. Many hands-on activities are included. For more information write the Marine Education Project, Pacific Science Center, 200 Second Ave., N., Seattle, WA 98109.

Our Dirty Water by Sarah M. Elliott. Julian Messner (a division of Simon & Schuster, Inc.), NY, 1974. This book is helpful in helping parents and teachers to explain water pollution problems, their causes, as well as possible solutions.

A Sea of Troubles by J. J. McCoy. Illustrations by Richard Cuffari. The Seabury Press, NY, 1975. This informative book examines the present-day threats to the living and mineral resources of the world's oceans and the political and economic conflicts involved in trying to save the sea from irreversible damage.

Hazardous Materials, Water Resources Newsletter is available through the Sierra Club, 730 Polk Street, San Francisco, CA 94109.

Project WILD Aquatic Education Activity Guide (all ages) contains many ocean and water-related activities. For more information write Project WILD, Salina Star Route, Boulder, CO 80302.

A free water conservation packet for grades 3-5, "The World Around You," includes three activity sheets that can be mimeographed or photocopied. Emphasis is on the importance of water and water conservation. Contact The Garden Club of America, 598 Madison Avenue, New York, NY 10022.

The Department of Water Resources, Water Education Program, has several flannel board stories, workbooks, and teachers guides on water and all it does for our lives available for grades K-3. One free copy of each are available to non-California residents. (California residents are asked to review sample copies before ordering classroom sets.) Write to 1416 Ninth Street, Room 338, Box 942836, Sacramento, CA 94236-0001.

There are several sections having to do with water pollution and conservation in *Save Our Planet: 750 Everyday Ways You Can Help Clean Up the Earth* by Diane MacEachern, Dell Publishing, NY, 1990.

Can the Whales Be Saved?, by Dr. Philip Whitfield, Viking Penguin, Inc., NY, 1989.

"Whales & Dolphins: 'And Thanks for all the Fish'," by Kieran Mulvaney is the featured article in *Animals' Voice* (October 1990, Vol. 3, No. 4): 30-38.

Saving the Earth: A Citizen's Guide to Environmental Action by Will Steger and Jon Bowermaster, Alfred A Knopf, Pub., NY, 1990. Especially see "The Water," pp. 167-216.

Attractive, illustrated information sheets on coastal wetlands, the southern coast, and beaches/dunes are available for librarians, teachers and students from Shirley Taylor, 1414 Hilltop Dr., Tallahassee, FL 32303. Send a SASE legal size with first class postage.

The National Fisheries Education and Research Foundation, Inc., publishes a curriculum guide for home economics teachers called "Seafood Resources for Educators." It is free by writing the Foundation, M Street, Suite 580, Washington, D.C. 20036.

CHAPTER SIX

Home, Sweet Home

And the world cannot be discovered by a journey of miles, no matter how long, but only by a spiritual journey, a journey of one inch, very arduous and humbling and joyful, by which we arrive at the ground at our feet, and learn to be at home.

WENDELL BERRY,
THE UNFORESEEN WILDERNESS

A child makes a dramatic entrance into this world and within a few seconds calls upon the Earth for that first breath of air. At that moment, the newborn child develops an intimate relationship with the Earth; for without clean air to breathe, clean water to drink, the right kind of food, and space in which to live and grow, the child cannot exist. It is the same with all beings on our planet. To ensure survival, basic needs must be met.

When young children think about their homes, they usually think of the buildings in which they live. But a home is much more than a building. To begin with, the house in which you live is also a neighborhood for many kinds of creatures – the spider that sets up housekeeping in the corner of your bedroom and the

Walk With Your Eyes, text and photographs by Marcia Brown. Franklin Watts, NY, 1979.

"We can see from the time we are born. But looking – that's something else. Looking is walking through your eyes to a new world." Thus begins this extraordinary book, laden with stunning color photographs that are a visual delight. The poetic text will show the reader how to observe his surroundings carefully and see the everyday world in a new way. This book is a feast for your eyes and a lesson to carry around in your heart. Reading it will engage your imagination anew both with the simple, ordinary objects of your private world and with the kaleidoscope beauty of the great outdoors. (all ages)

mouse that lives in your attic share this environment with your family. Take a step outside and discover that your backyard is really the perfect habitat for an abundance of life, such as plants, squirrels, insects, birds, and maybe a rabbit or two. Take a step farther and explore the region of the world in which you live. It is full of plants and animals that live and grow in an environment that's just right for them, whether it's a desert climate or a wet, damp one. Each place in which a plant or animal lives is unique and provides the exact needs to sustain its life.

Although it may not appear so, the environment is fragile. If just one of the four basic needs is removed from a habitat, the animals and plants suffer. For example, if the air in your neighborhood became so dirty with smog that the plants were unable to receive light from the sun, the web of life in this interrelated community would break down, causing hardship or death to the creatures that live there. By the end of this chapter, you and your children will be aware that the biggest community of all, the whole Earth, can be seriously affected by such things as air, water, and waste pollution. For it's not only the homes of animals that are threatened, but our homes as well.

Awareness

Welcome to Planet Earth!

Mosts human beings perceive their surroundings primarily through sight. This unusual nature walk will encourage you and your children to explore your natural surroundings in ways other than through your eyes. Before you begin, divide your children into pairs: ask one partner to be the tour guide first, and explain that after a time they will switch roles. (It is important that the children are paired with people they know and trust.) Read the following introductory paragraph to prepare them for their first "sightseeing" tour of Earth.

Close your eyes and imagine that you are an alien from another galaxy. On your home planet there is very little light, so that over time you have come to rely less on your eyes and more on your fingertips, ears, and nose. The only time you use your eyes is when you flash an occasional picture of your immediate surroundings into your brain, like a camera taking a picture. Over the past year you've been exploring other galaxies and you've recently arrived at the Milky Way and are visiting Planet Earth for the first time. You have been greeted by the President and after his (or her) long and boring speech, you are to be given a grand tour of Earth. But since you cannot see well with your eyes, your tour guide will take you by the hand and let you experience the Earth through your senses of touch, smell, and hearing.

Have each tour guide hold their partner's hand and slowly take them on a nature tour while the partner (alien) keeps his eyes closed. He should be encouraged to feel, listen, and smell (not taste) his natural surroundings, such as green leaves, tree trunks, rocks, decaying leaves, tree stumps, puddles, grass, flowers, etc. Occasionally, have the tour guide position his partner so that he can flash a picture into his brain (open his eyes for just a few seconds). The "pictures" can be creative, such as the view up the trunk of a tree, on the ground looking through tall grass, or at the

Touch Will Tell, text and photographs by Marcia Brown. Franklin Watts, NY, 1979.

Explore the world around you with your fingertips and you will "see" things differently. The poetic text and brilliantly clear, color photographs will present a variety of ways to experience the world through the sense of touch. (all ages)

The Other Way to Listen, by Byrd Baylor. Illustrations by Peter Parnall. Charles Scribner's Sons, NY, 1978.

When you know the other way to listen, you can hear wildflower seeds burst open, the rocks murmuring, and the hills sing-ing. It seems like the most natural thing in the world, of course, but it takes a lot of practice. And you can't be in a hurry. . . in fact, most people never hear those things at all. This book tells you about two people who did - one who was very good at it and one who took a long time in learning. (age 8 and up)

underside of a flower. After a while, have the partners switch roles. After the tour, ask the "aliens" to share their most interesting or beautiful stops. Then, (quite diplomatically) shake each child's hand and tell them how honored you were by their visit. Finally, wish them well as you send them on their continuing voyage through the Universe.

Beautiful Dinner Conversation

Once there was a little boy who lived with his mother. Every morning, the boy had to walk alone a great distance to school. He constantly complained to his mother about how boring and long the walk was, hoping she would allow him to stay home. But, instead, she would send him on his way with a sandwich and apple for lunch.

Finally, one morning, after listening to his daily complaint, his mother asked him to find something beautiful on his walk and tell her about it that evening. Reluctantly, he left for school and thought about his mother's request as he walked. After a while, he looked up from his path and searched the sloping hill for something beautiful. To his surprise, he noticed an apple tree covered with delicate pink petals. A gust of wind rattled the branches and some of the petals floated to the ground. A snow flower-shower! Why hadn't he noticed it before? Surely the tree had been there all along! That evening, he rushed home to tell his mother about what he had seen. To his delight, they decided to make it a game for the following day as well. As each went through their daily routine, they were keenly aware of their surroundings and searched for something beautiful to share with the other that evening. The boy told his mother about a multi-colored lizard that had been sunning himself on a rock, and his mother told him about a butterfly that was sipping nectar from a flower. All of a sudden, the boy couldn't wait to walk to school because his journey was always full of interesting things to see and hear.

Epilogue: His only complaint now is that it is so hard to decide what, of the many beautiful things he experiences, he will tell his mother at the end of the day. (That's not much of a complaint! So, why not give it a try at your house?)

T he butterfly counts not months but moments, and has time enough.

RABINDRANATH TAGORE, 1916

Seeing Beauty in Small Things

It is breathtaking to stand at the foot of a mountain and look up to see boulders and jagged rocks towering over you, or to walk along the beach watching the neverending waves crash against the shore. It is difficult to gaze upon the powerful elements of nature without being overwhelmed by their beauty. Take your children outdoors and look around. What stands out in your minds: a nearby tree, the flowers in the garden, or maybe a huge, puffy cloud overhead? Imagine what you would see if you were as small as an inchworm. The large objects that you see would not even be noticed by such a small creature! Instead, they might look upon a pebble as we would a mountain, or puddle as we would a large lake, or a dandelion as we would a maple tree decked out in autumn splendor. To help your children imagine themselves as small as an inchworm, have them sit quietly in a circle, close their eyes, and listen to this adventure:

> The world is full of billions of creatures that are so small that we don't take the time to notice them. Many of them are under your feet this very minute! Imagine that one sunny afternoon you are lying in the grass watching the clouds float by. You pull on a particularly tall stalk of grass to chew on, but it won't give. You pull and tug, but the blade of grass seems to be anchored to the ground. Out of frustration, you get up to give it a yank with all of your might! You squat down and as you take hold of the grass, you feel a tingle run up your arm and through your body. All of a sudden, the tree overhead becomes larger and larger. Its branches seem to be flying away from you at a rapid pace, until you find yourself the size of a tiny beetle dangling from the blade of grass. The backyard you know so well looks completely different from a bug's point of view. Nearby, you notice what appears to be a trail and soon you set off to discover where it leads.

Allow each child to choose a small area of the yard and pretend that he or she is still as small as a bug. Have them complete the story by mapping out their insect nature trail. Ask them to mark the scenic landscape with little signs made from folded scraps of paper. They can make up names for each sight, such as Treeroot Mountain

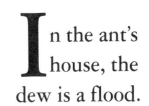

I n the ant's house, the dew is a flood.

PERSIAN PROVERB

Range, Parched Earth Canyon, Seed Boulder, or Giant Blade of Grass. Please ask them not to rearrange the objects in the area, but to find objects and vistas that occur naturally. (You might want to provide magnifying glasses and dental mirrors to help them view things from an insect's point of view.) When everyone is finished, ask them to visit each other's trails and pretend to be small insects on a nature tour.

DREAM STARTER

You love to do scientific experiments, observe nature, and learn about how things work. So naturally, the subject of science is your favorite at school. Imagine that one day the science teacher asks if you can stay and help clean up the laboratory. Since you like your teacher a lot and you don't have anything special planned, you tell her that you would be happy to help.

Later that day, after the bell has rung and everyone has gone home, you go to the science lab door and knock. No one answers, but you know that the teacher is expecting you, so you open the door and step in. Somehow the room is different when it is not full of kids: it is quiet and seems much more official and scientific. You quietly walk among the beakers of colored liquid, jars of chemicals, test tubes, rubber hoses, and safety goggles. You take a moment and admire your work station. You are currently working on a complicated solar-powered model and much of your class time has been spent finishing it. Since your teacher hasn't arrived yet, you decide you might as well get some work done and you go to the equipment drawer to get some tools to work on your project.

Next to the drawer you notice the cabinet marked with big letters, "KEEP OUT!" You've always wondered what the teacher keeps inside that is so secret. Well, today you might just get your chance, because there is a key stuck in the lock. You carefully look around to make sure no one is looking and you silently turn the key. To your delight, the cabinet door opens and you peer into the darkness. At first you think it is empty, but when your eyes adjust you see three pairs of glasses. "Big deal," you say under your breath. "What's so secret about glasses?" You pick up the pair nearest you and look closely at them. That's strange. Instead of clear glass, you notice that the lenses are dark gray. They are so dark that there's no way anyone could see through them. So, just out of curiosity, you try them on.

Instead of seeing tables and lab equipment, you see what appears to be bubbles floating in front of your face. "What's this?" you wonder. "Where are the bubbles coming from?" You pull the glasses down and look out over the rims. You don't see any bubbles in the air. "What's going on?" you say to yourself. You look through the lenses again and watch the bubbles floating and bumping into each other. You lower your head to look at the tabletop, but instead you see what looks like a forest of tangled vines. You run your finger along the table but you don't feel anything. You take off the strange glasses to have a look and all you see is dust on your fingertip. "Wow!" you say aloud, when all of a sudden you realize what's going on. The glasses act like a powerful microscope, enabling you to see things that are normally invisible to the human eye. Anxious to test them further, you search for something else to look at. You spy a jar marked with the words, "pond water" and immediately put on the glasses. Before your eyes, hundreds of bizarre creatures wiggle and swim about; some look like hairy monsters and others look like squiggly centipedes. Naturally, this makes you curious about the other glasses, so before your teacher returns you go to the cabinet to try them.

The next pair appear to be normal glasses with clear lenses. "These don't look very exciting," you comment. But when you try them on, instead of seeing a classroom, you see trees, grass, and a sky full of clouds. As you look around, you realize you are seeing outside the school building. In one of the trees you watch as a pair of birds feed their newly hatched family. "I never noticed that nest before," you remark. You decide to give that a closer look at recess tomorrow.

> *"There must be new contact between men and the earth; the earth must be newly seen and heard and felt and smelled and tasted."*
> WENDELL BERRY

A House is a House for Me, by Mary Ann Hoberman. Illustrations by Betty Fraser. The Viking Press, NY, 1978.

Written in a sprightly rhyme, this book describes the dwellings of various animals and objects. "A web is a house for a spider, a bird builds its nest in a tree. There is nothing so snug as a bug in a rug, and a house is a house for me!" Delightfully clever with colorful illustrations, this book will make you look upon ordinary places and objects in a new way. And in conclusion, you and your children will come to understand that "each creature that's known has a house of its own, and the Earth is a house for us all." (ages 3 - 7)

Keep Looking, by Millicent Selsam and Joyce Hunt. Illustrations by Normand Chartier. Macmillan, NY, 1989.

The house looks empty, the yard looks empty, and snow covers the ground. But is it really empty? Look closely and you will find all the animals living in their own homes. Children will enjoy seeing all the animals using one of our abandoned habitats for their own. (ages 4 - 8)

"I wonder about this last pair," you say as you pick them off the shelf. The lenses look like they've been painted with blue and green watercolor and when you place them on your nose, you aren't prepared for the scene in front of you. You can see far beyond the schoolyard. In fact, you can see farmland, cities filled with people, and large expanses of wilderness. You see tall mountains, deserts, dense forests, and blue ocean. When you turn your head to one side, you can see the plains of Africa and you watch as a pride of lions argue over a meal. In another direction, you see the frozen Arctic region and you marvel as a polar bear swims through the icy waters looking for fish. Next, you see a beautiful, lush forest dripping with rain and you follow a family of Howler monkeys swinging among the branches. You turn to the other side and watch with interest as a rare giant panda strips bamboo leaves from a long stalk.

You lose track of time as you stand there looking over the world. Suddenly, the door of the laboratory opens. You quickly remove the glasses and try to return them to the cabinet, but it's too late. Your science teacher walks over and gazes down into your eyes. You know she must be angry at you for opening the cabinet, so you try to apologize. "I'm sorry, but the key was here and I just couldn't resist." Your teacher says nothing, but the glint of understanding in her eyes gives you some relief. To divert her attention, you ask, "How do they work; are they magic?" "No," she responds hesitantly. "If they work, it's because there is magic inside of you. The true gift of 'seeing' is something that very few people have." You don't really understand what she is trying to tell you, but you realize it must be the secret behind the locked cabinet.

You immediately run to your best friend's house and tell her all about the special eyeglasses. After school the next day, the two of you sneak into the lab and quietly make your way to the secret cabinet. To your amazement, you find it unlocked. You reach in, pick up a pair of glasses and hand them to your friend. "Here, try these!" you say excitedly. She puts them on and you wait for her response. You watch as your friend turns her head from side to side. After a few seconds, she takes them off. "Well?" you ask anxiously. Your friend gives you a doubtful look as she shakes her head and shrugs her shoulders. Then she says, "I don't see anything!"

What's That, Habitat?

To illustrate the meaning of habitat for young children, they must first come to understand why they live in the place they do. Whether your family lives in an apartment building, house, hogan, or log cabin, your home provides these basic necessities: air to breathe, a source of nearby water, food, safe shelter, and enough space in which to live and grow. If your home excluded one of these basic needs, your family would suffer. (Unfortunately such inadequate living arrangements do exist and many people's lives are filled with hardship trying to provide these essential needs for themselves or their families.) Have your children ever thought about their home in this way? Probably not, especially if you have lived comfortably since they were born. This scavenger hunt will help your children become aware of how their homes fulfills their basic needs.

1. First, without your children present, set up the scavenger hunt by writing each of the following clues or riddles on a piece of scrap paper and hiding them (all but one) around your house in these suggested places:

• I'm something you need each day, especially after you run and play. I fill you up as you drink me down, so go to the place where I can be found. (water) *Do not hide this riddle, but hold it for the first clue.*

• Your empty stomach can wiggle and pull; I fill it up until it's full. Sometimes I'm eaten hot or cold. Where am I kept in your household? (food) *Place this riddle near the sink area.*

• Although I'm all around you, I can't be seen. To keep your body healthy, I must be clean. You breathe me in through your nose, but try to grab me and away I go. (air) *Place this riddle near the refrigerator.*

• From wind and rain I keep you safe – I'm very necessary in this place. Look all around you, for I'm sturdy and tall. You'll probably find me upon some wall. (shelter or building) *Hang this riddle from the ceiling or light fixture so that it is dangling in the air.*

• Take me away and you'd be cramped; no place to play and no place to stand. To find me you'll need a rocket, you might presume. What I'm talking about is elbow room. (space to live and grow) *Hide this riddle somewhere on the wall.*

The Old Boot, by Chris Baines. Illustrations by Penny Ives. Crocodile Books, NY, 1989.

At night, when we are asleep, there are all kinds of creatures hard at work in the long grass. Before the sun comes up, they need a safe, dark place to hide. In this story, a group of night crawlers have made their home in a discarded boot. One sunny afternoon, all the night creatures are asleep and the ants are collecting food for their nest. Suddenly, the Earth begins to shake, a foot crashes down beside the boot, and then the old boot is lifted into the air. A child shouts, "It's full of creepy crawlies!" and drops it to the ground again. The bright sun shocks the woodlice, millipede, and slug. They quickly scatter and vanish in the grass. This intriguing book illustrates that homes can be found in the most unlikely places and can easily be disrupted if we are not careful. (ages 4 - 8)

2. To begin the hunt, hand your children the first clue or riddle (the one you didn't hide). If they are unable to read, read it to them and let them guess what it is talking about - in this case, water. Go to the sink area and allow your children to hunt for the next clue.

3. After it is located, read it and continue the hunt until all of the clues are discovered.

4. To conclude, have your children recall their basic needs and where, in their house (or school), these needs can be met. If desired, have them draw pictures or maps of their houses including each.

Your Backyard is Somebody's Home

Most likely, the habitat in which you live (your home) is filled with human inventions, such as electricity, running water, a refrigerator to keep food fresh, and possibly environmental controlling devices to heat or cool the air in your home. This type of environment did not occur naturally, but was created to reduce the size of a human's habitat. For example, before running water a person would have to travel to a source of water (such as a river) every day to meet this need. In nature, animal habitats vary in size according to the needs of each animal. Their homes include not only their shelter (or nest), but a territory in which to gather food and water. To observe a natural habitat, simply go into your own backyard or to a park.

Have your children choose an animal to observe in nature and pretend to be that animal. Have them discover where their kitchen (source of food), sink and faucet (simply a puddle or morning dew), and house (shelter or nest) are located. Keep in mind this may take in a large area, bigger than your own backyard. Finally, have each child draw a map or picture of the home or habitat of his chosen animal which include these basic needs (don't forget to include air). When they are finished, point out that their whole picture represents how much space is needed for them to live and grow.

As an extension for older children, play "What If. . ." Ask each child to decide what would happen to him (as that animal) if the place in which he builds his nest were chopped down, for example. Or, what if the grass in which he feeds was sprayed with chemicals or died from lack of rain? How would these conditions change his map? To survive, what changes will he have to make?

Honey, I'm Home!

In the story, *The Old Boot* by Chris Baines, a group of bugs discovered that a discarded boot made a perfect daytime shelter. Never realizing it could be somebody's home, the child was taken by surprise when he picked it up! This simple action caused chaos in the bugs' peaceful lives. I'm sure this same kind of thing has happened to you and your children before, such as the time when you moved an object and a spider scurried away, causing you to jump back in surprise. Who would have realized that a spider had taken up residence there? All around you, in your own home and outdoors, animals and insects make their homes in the most unusual places. Because we are not thinking from their point of view, we are not aware of how perfect this unlikely place is to set up housekeeping. Next time you or your children accidently burst into (or destroy) somebody's house by mistake, take the time to view the world from that creature's eyes. Have your children draw a picture of that animal's home from inside (its point of view) or from its "front door." If the thought of having a spider as a roommate disturbs you, set an example for your children by carefully capturing it in a jar and releasing it outdoors so that it can find another place to call home.

This Place is Special

The area of the world in which you live is special. It has a climate and contains vegetation that is just right for the animals, birds, and insects that live there. This will become obvious to you and your children if you have the opportunity to visit different parts of the world. Whenever the chance presents itself, compare life in different habitats, such as a pond, meadow, desert, mountain region, urban area, etc. By learning about your region of the world (or biome), you and your family will come to appreciate the uniqueness of your special place on Earth.

"Creatures in Your Community" Party

You and your children can celebrate your particular place on Earth by having a "costume" party. Have each child create a board costume by cutting a face hole and two arm holes in a large, flat

> S eeing a thing involves assigning it a place in the whole.

piece of cardboard (the side of a packing box works well). Have each child decorate the front to look like a certain animal or plant found in your region of the world with paints, scraps of fabric, and other goodies from your Recycle Craft Box. To "wear" the costume, have him place his arms through the arm holes and put his face up to the face hole. (Or, if desired, design another type of costume.) At the party serve foods that are native to your region. Have one or two people pretend to be news reporters and interview each "creature" to discover why this particular habitat is the best place for him. To make it more realistic, use an audio or video recorder for the interviews. These interviews become a great source of entertainment later at the party.

Our Neighborhood, The World

The term "neighborhood" may bring to your child's mind the street where he lives, but actually it's much more than that. No community has everything it needs, so most depend on neighboring communities. For example, in nature a certain plant may depend on a particular insect to come from a distance to pollinate it. Or in the case of humans, we pack and ship food to places that cannot grow it because of climate; for instance, citrus fruits from Florida to colder regions. This activity will help your children see that they depend on the whole world for the things in their lives.

1. Go around your house (or school) and find items that have been grown or manufactured in another part of the world. This will not be difficult since many items and foods are imported from other regions and countries. For example you might find avocados from Mexico, books printed in Germany, a telephone made in Japan, cotton blouses from India, a basket woven in China, or mixed nuts containing brazil nuts from the tropical rainforest.

2. Spread out a large world map and set each item on its place of origin.

3. Now ask: Did you find anything that originated from your area? What item traveled the farthest to get to you? What is your favorite food and where does it come from?

When you are finished, it will be plain to your children that they depend on the world every day for goods and food.

Air Is Almost Everywhere!

Air. It's invisible. You can't taste it, hear it, and (hopefully) can't smell it, but it's there. Without it, we could not live. It is important stuff! Before you can talk to young children about air pollution and its effects, they need to know that air is a real substance. The following experiments will help you demonstrate the existence of air to your children. There is one place you can "see" air and that is when it's underwater. Next time your child takes a bath, try these simple experiments:

1. Hold apparently empty cups and containers underwater sideways and watch the bubbles. What are the bubbles? *(air)* Where did they come from? *(from the cup)* So was the cup really empty? *(No, it was full of air.)*

2. Give your child a straw and have him blow air bubbles into the water.

3. Blow up a balloon and ask your child what is in it. *(air)* Hold it underwater and release the air. What happened to the air in the balloon? *(It floated through the water and you see it as bubbles.)*

4. Take a clear drinking cup and stuff a wadded, dry rag or tissue into the bottom of it. Push the cup completely underwater, open end first. *(Be sure the cup is not tilted or the air will escape.)* Lift the cup out of the water and examine the rag or tissue. Did it get wet? *(no)* Repeat, but this time slightly tilt the cup so that some air is released. Ask your child to tell you what is happening. *(The air is leaving the inside of the cup and water is taking its place.)* Lift the cup out of the water and feel the rag or tissue: indeed, the water has replaced the air in the cup and dampened the rag.

Air Pollution

Air pollution is one of the biggest environmental problems facing the world today. Many people are attempting to find workable solutions, but there are no easy answers. The first step to correcting this problem is to be aware that there is a problem and be able to identify some causes. With your guidance, your children can take that first step.

The Sky Jumps Into Your Shoes at Night, by Jasper Tompkins. The Green Tiger Press, San Marcos, CA, 1986.

This fanciful book sets out to show small children all of the things the sky can do. It begins: "The air is the sky. The wind is the sky. The blue is the sky. The sky is a warm blanket around our house, the Earth." Very young children will love this book. (ages 3 - 6)

Michael Bird-Boy, by Tomie de Paola. Prentice-Hall Books for Young Readers, Simon and Schuster, NY, 1975.

A young boy, who always wears a bird suit, lives in the country. One day a black cloud drapes the sky causing the flowers to wilt and the white birds to become dirty. Michael is determined to find the source of the cloud. Soon he meets Boss Lady whose Genuine Shoo-fly Artificial Honey Syrup factory is polluting the sky. He persuades Boss Lady to make real honey and solves the pollution problem. This gentle lesson about air pollution is just right for very young children. (ages 3 - 7)

What is Air Pollution?

Most air pollution is the result of burning fuel, such as oil, wood, charcoal, or natural gas. There are times when pollution isn't immediately visible to our eyes, as is demonstrated in this experiment. *(Note: This experiment requires the use of a lighted candle and should be conducted by an adult.)*

Light an ordinary candle. Have your children stand back and observe its flame. What do they see? It is possible to see the currents of air moving above the flame, but no obvious smoke (or pollution) can be detected. Next, hold a clear or white glass plate (or any material that will not burn or break) several inches above the flame. *(This should be done by an adult.)* After a moment, soot will form on the glass. What you are seeing is the pollution that results from burning a fuel, which in this case is wax. Have your children look closely at the ring of soot. After the glass cools, allow them to run their finger through it and observe the "dirt" on their fingertip. Certainly a lighted candle doesn't produce much, but you and your children can see from this experiment that it does cause some air pollution.

Keeping An Eye on the Air

What are some causes of air pollution? Look around you, and you will notice that they are everywhere. When you are walking along an avenue and a bus goes belching by, that's air pollution. When you watch the circling smoke rising from a chimney, that's air pollution. When you see a jet trail streaked across the sky, that's air pollution. When you are whizzing along the freeway in your car, the resulting exhaust is air pollution. When you see sources of pollution, simply point them out to your children and soon they will be able to identify them too. That's the first step!

Putting It to the Test

What is the quality of the air that surrounds your home? You and your children can test it! The easiest way is to cut cards from white scrap paper. First, choose several areas to test, such as your backyard, basement, kitchen, nearby park, next to a road, etc. Label each card with its location and spread a layer of clear petroleum jelly on it. Tack the card (jelly side out) in place. After a couple of days (or a week), gather the cards and look closely at the accumulation on the jelly. What kind of debris can be observed? Which location produced the most dirt? You and your children might be surprised!

What Is Acid Rain?

So, you've been alerted to the devastating effects of acid rain in the newspaper and news reports, but what exactly is it? The acidic chemicals that are being pumped into the atmosphere combine with water to form strong acids. The acid falls on the Earth in all types of weather - not only in rain, but also in snow, dew, sleet, hail, or fog. The pollutants in the air make it dangerous for people to breathe. They also poison lakes and streams, kill trees and crops, and cause buildings and marble statues to erode. Still, after all that, the most serious effect of acid rain is damage to the soil. Do this activity with older children to demonstrate how acid rain can affect plants.

Take two equally healthy house plants. Place each in sufficient light. Sprinkle one daily with ordinary tap water. Sprinkle the other with a solution of one-half vinegar and one-half water (to represent acid rain). Make sure the liquid wets the leaves and soil. Do this for three to four weeks. Observe the plants during that period and note any growth differences. Discuss with your children the chain of events that could happen if, for example, acid rain were to damage an entire crop of wheat or soy beans (the main ingredient in livestock feed).

What is Your Pollution Quotient?

Most people like to think of themselves as friends of the environment and declare a deep concern for the future of the planet, but their actions can be in conflict with these values. Gather your family together and take the following test.

• If you walked somewhere, rode your bicycle, or rode public transportation (instead of driving in a car) in the last week, give yourselves 10 points.

• If you recycle newspaper, used computer paper, and some junk mail, add 10 points.

The Last Free Bird, by A. Harris Stone. Illustrations by Sheila Heins. Prentice-Hall, Inc., Englewood Cliffs, NJ, 1967.

This book is a beautiful and touching plea for the protection of the natural beauty and wonders of our land. It begins, "Once we were many living in quiet valleys and green fields. . . But that was long ago before people came; before people came and changed the land. . ." The bird's moving tale will inspire readers to take action and protect the "homes" of innocent birds and animals from pollution and pavement. (age 6 and up)

Do the Trash Rap

by Desirée Waidner (age 11)

There's a problem we've heard called the Greenhouse Effect,

It's gettin' warmer and warmer; what will happen next?

There's a hole in the ozone and its frying our planet,

And that's not the way that God would've planned it.

There's a box on our burger and it's called Styrofoam,

And it'll be here long after we're gone.

We've got to make a switch as fast as we're able,

To find something better that's biodegradable.

There's stuff in the air and it's makin' us sneeze,

Some days are so bad that a lot of us wheeze.

Let's all work together; let's all make a pact,

It's not too late for us to clean up our act.

So collect those papers, plastic bottles, and cans,

To recycle all that is part of the plan.

If we all make the effort and give what it's worth,

We can clean up our planet, we can save Mother Earth!

• If you picked up litter in the past week, add 5 points. If you littered in any way, subtract 20 points.

• If you planted one or more trees in the last year, add 10 points.

• If you drove your car (or had someone drive you) to a destination fewer than two blocks away in the last week, subtract 20 points.

• If you have taken your children to a natural setting, such as the woods, a stream, or a mountain trail in the past month, add 10 points.

• If you recycle aluminum cans and aluminum foil, add 10 points.

• If you burn or bag your leaves or grass clippings, subtract 10 points. If you compost, mulch, or leave your leaves or grass clippings alone to decompose, add 5 points.

• If you have a compost pile, add 10 points.

• If you have a family vegetable garden, add 5 points.

• If you have forgotten to turn off a light, television, or radio in an empty room today, subtract 5 points.

• If you have purchased a product packaged in a foam container in the past week (that includes food from some fast food restaurants), subtract 5 points.

• If you use both sides of a piece of paper before throwing it away, add 5 points.

• If you recycle glass and plastic, add 10 points.

• If you have volunteered your time for an environmental cause in the past year (such as a paper drive, trash pick-up, etc.), add 10 points.

How did your family score?
90 points or above: Indeed, you are a friendly family of the Earth!
80 - 89 points: You are a concerned family and doing OK!
70 - 79 points: Your family needs to make a plan and try harder.
Below 69 points: Your family is contributing to the problem.

Tons of Trash

Not too many people think about garbage, except to remember to put it near the curb on collection day. But more and more of it is being produced, and at such an alarming rate that it won't be long before there are no safe places left to put it all! So take some time and think about trash: your children's future depends on it.

The Four "R's"

You've heard of the three "R's" in school. When it comes to garbage there are four "R's": reduce, reuse, recycle, and reject! In this game, your children can think of lots of ways to put the four "R's" to work on an ordinary can of garbage.

1. Sit with your children and brainstorm about trash. On small pieces of scrap paper, have the children write the names or draw simple pictures of ordinary objects you might find in a garbage can: worn out or torn clothing, a glass bottle or jar, plastic sandwich bag, foam food container, paper napkin, an empty oatmeal box, old magazine, aluminum beverage can, apple core, banana peel, egg shells, milk carton, old toys, junk mail, a newspaper, an individual juice box, and so on. (If you have any trouble thinking of things, look in your own garbage!) Put all of the papers in a container; this will be the "trash can" during the game.

2. Reuse a soda bottle to make a spinner. Have the children sit in a circle, place the bottle in the middle of the group, and ask someone to spin it. Whomever it points to must go to the "trash can" and choose a slip of paper. Then he must tell the group how he could remove it from the garbage by referring to one of the four "R's" of trash: reduce, reuse, recycle, or reject. For example, he could choose to reduce by using a cloth napkin instead of a paper one, recycle a glass jar (or food waste by composting), reuse a torn shirt by making wash rags, or reject by refusing to purchase food packaged in foam containers.

3. When the game is finished, look and see if anything is left in the trash can. Most likely there will be a few things that must be discarded. Can anyone think of an alternative or use for these objects?

Just a Dream, by Chris Van Allsburg. Houghton Mifflin Books, Boston, 1990.

Walter is a young litterbug who thinks that sorting trash is a big waste of time, and that's not all! When he sees his neighbor watering the tree she receives as a birthday gift, he tells her it is "a dumb plant" and doesn't understand why anyone would be happy about getting one. With his birthday just a few days away, he is certain he doesn't want one! That night, Walter's dream takes him into the future that he is helping to create. It is one where his neighborhood is buried under a mountain of trash, the air is so polluted that it is difficult to breathe, no wilderness exists anywhere (even on Mount Everest), and the fish are virtually gone from the ocean. When he wakes up, he is a changed person who cares a great deal about the future of the planet and begins to mend his ways by choosing a tree as his birthday gift. (age 5 and up)

Take the Trash Out

Tune: Ninety-nine Bottles of Beer on the Wall

You've talked about garbage, now it is time for some habits to change. Have each person in your family or classroom decide on one way he will commit himself to reduce the amount of garbage he produces. Write their commitment on a piece of scrap paper. After each person states his intention, sing a verse of the following song (begin with the number of people in your family or class) and cheer his effort. Continue the count down until there are zero pieces left! After everyone has committed themselves, have each person sign the document and post it near the main garbage can in your house or classroom.

There are ten pieces of trash in the can,

Ten pieces of trash,

By taking one out,

We all can shout:

Nine pieces of trash in the can!

Become a Trash Basket for a Day

How much garbage do you produce in a day? You'd know, if you had to carry it with you wherever you went! What is it like to be a trash basket? It isn't a glamorous life! To become aware of how much garbage they create in a day, have your children strap a grocery bag on their belts and carry it with them for an entire day. Every time they would normally discard something, put it in the bag instead. At the end of the day, have each person look through his bag to see if anything can be reused or recycled. Have each person look at the remaining trash and decide on ways in which he can reduce his waste by making other choices, such as choosing a glass container that can be recycled instead of a plastic or foam one.

Take a Trash Walk

You and your children will be amazed how much garbage is produced in a single neighborhood in one week. Take a walk up and down your street on trash collection day and count the cans or bags lined up on the street. Do your children think there is enough to fill up their room? What about your entire house? It will boggle your minds to see the amount of garbage collected each week in your own neighborhood. Try to imagine how much is collected each month, or each year. Now, that's a mountain of trash!

Plant a Reverse Garden

Biodegradable. That's a big word for little kids. If you have a compost pile, it takes time, but your children can watch grass clippings, leaves, and food waste break down into humus or rich soil. If that is not available to you, try planting a garden, in reverse!

1. Fill a deep pan with soil. Gather together different types of garbage and plant them under the soil. Some items to include are dead leaves, food waste (like an apple core and banana peel), an old sock, a tin can, a wad of newspaper, a plastic container or bag, and a foam cup.

2. Sprinkle the soil with water every couple of days. After one week, dig up the garbage. What, if anything, is happening to the trash? Replant the objects and continue to sprinkle with water every other day.

3. Wait two more weeks and uncover the garbage again. Do you see any noticeable changes in the objects? Are some items beginning to decompose (or rot)? What items don't seem to show any change? Explain to your children the meaning of biodegradability (when an object is capable of being broken down by living microorganisms present in the soil). Is there any evidence that some items are biodegradable? Replant one more time and continue to water regularly.

4. After two more weeks, uncover the objects for the last time. Are there any items that have almost completely rotted away? Which items are still in tact? What can you conclude from this experiment? From your original list of items, sort the objects into two groups: biodegradable and not.

Visit a Recycling Center

Many communities have places where glass, aluminum, and/or plastic can be deposited for recycling. The objects are sorted, crushed, remelted, and used again. Young children are fascinated by the sorting machines and can become actively involved in separating the glass, plastic containers, and cans. It's like visiting a three-ring circus! Although this is just the first step in the recycling process, it can be an excellent learning experience for your children. You and your kids can have fun, make a little extra cash, and help the environment too. What a deal!

The Vanishing Wilderness

It's unfortunate, but after a beautiful, natural area is discovered by man, it usually is turned into a tourist attraction. A paved road is put in, a parking lot is built, restaurants and hotels are erected, and the natural beauty everyone comes to see is changed forever! By reading the following stories and participating in the suggested activities, you and your children will realize the impact you have on unspoiled wilderness and will develop a desire to protect it for future generations.

The Recycle Song

Tune: So Early in the Morning

This is the way we smash the cans,

Smash the cans, smash the cans.

This is the way we smash the cans,

For recycling.

This is the way we sort the glass,

Sort the glass, sort the glass.

This is the way we sort the glass,

For recycling.

This is the way we bundle papers,

Bundle papers, bundle papers.

This is the way we bundle papers,

For recycling.

The Mountain, by Peter Parnall. Doubleday and Co., NY, 1971.

This is the story of a mountain in the west that is teaming with plant and animal life. It is discovered by a group of people that claim to love the mountain and "want to keep it just the way it is." So, it is declared a national park and more and more people come until. . . . Although the illustrations are comical, they tell of a sobering lesson that we have yet to learn. (all ages)

The Lost Lake, by Allen Say. Houghton Mifflin Co., Boston, 1989.

This is the story of a boy and his father who set off for a camping trip to Lost Lake, the father's favorite spot as a boy. When they finally reach the lake after a long hike, they discover it has been "found" by too many people. Disappointed by the changes they find, they set off in search of a quieter place. This book effectively shows how some parks and wilderness areas can be ruined by people who don't care about the Earth. (ages 5 -10)

Please, Get Out of My House!

To enjoy the natural world, you can hike through the woods, walk along the seashore, or camp at a lake. Young children especially enjoy the outdoors but may not realize that it's like visiting somebody's home; in fact, that is exactly what it is. These habitats are home to many creatures. A good way to make children aware of the impact they have while visiting natural settings is to reverse the situation as in the following story.

Imagine that one Saturday morning you are sitting in your living room eating a bowl of cereal and watching cartoons. All of a sudden a group of strange people, whom you have never seen before, just walk into your living room! They are carrying blankets, tents, a kerosene stove, fishing poles, and a huge ice chest full of food, soda, and beer. They yell, "This looks like a good place!" and dump all of their stuff in a heap. They don't even notice that this is your house. They talk loudly to each other, making it impossible for you to hear the T.V. Their obnoxious kids start running around your house, climbing on the furniture, taking your toys, tearing your favorite books, and then they run right by you, knocking over your cereal! While the kids are doing this, the grown ups are slurping down drinks and throwing the empty cans on your living room floor.

Finally, you've had enough! You walk over to the adults. They point their fingers and call to their kids, "Hey, kids, look at this!" They don't even listen to you when you ask them to please leave your house. They just keep pointing and staring. When you take another step forward, one kid picks up an empty can, throws it at you, and screams, "You, get out of here!" They all chime in, "Yeah, go on home! Get out of here!" And they start throwing things at you! One of the empty cans whips the side of your head, leaving a stinging bruise. You decide it would be safer to hide until these strangers decide to go. So you creep into the hall closet and quietly shut the door. You know you are missing your favorite program, but you have no choice. And as you sit in the dark, listening to the strangers laughing and their kids yelling, you wonder if your house will ever be the same.

Playing Lightly on the Earth

The personal choices that we make each day all have an effect on our environment. For children, even something as simple as having fun outdoors or playing a game can cause some damage. In this activity, they can learn to recognize the impact they can have on the quality of their environment.

Ask your children if they like to play outdoors and you will hear a resounding "yes!" Do some of the games they play cause damage to the environment? The answer is yes. To convince your children, you may have to do some investigating. Go outdoors to a park or playground and see if your children can find any evidence of damage – for example, soil stripped of grass under a swing or on a baseball diamond. Some children think it is fun to carve their initials on tree trunks or write graffiti on walls. To them it may be just a game, but it causes damage to plants and, many people believe, creates a kind of pollution. Is there any way to play without causing damage? Maybe not entirely, but children can be aware of it and try to choose games that don't have a lasting effect on the environment.

Treading Lightly on the Great Outdoors

Camping and hiking in a wilderness area is an excellent way to become a part of the natural world, especially if you live in an urban area most of the year. You and your children will carry the feelings and memories of an outdoor experience with you long after you've returned to town; and with the slightest recollection, a yearning for another encounter with nature beckons you to go back. But do the plants and animals that live in that area want to see you again? Here are some suggestions to follow so that you and your family will always be welcome visitors to the Great Outdoors. Compared to the old school of "it's here to use as I please" outdoor etiquette, low-impact camping takes some extra planning and effort; but you and your family can feel a sense of pride knowing you are doing it the right way and ensuring the continued access to beautiful and healthy wilderness areas.

1. Probably the most important part of a low-impact camping or hiking trip is to plan it well. Since you will need to pack out every scrap of your litter (plus any litter that you find along the way),

Farewell to Shady Glade, by Bill Peet. Houghton Mifflin Co., Boston, 1966.

From the top-most branch of the sycamore tree, raccoon can see the huge machines coming towards Shady Glade, home to sixteen varied animals. He knows that the opossums, rabbits, frogs, and skunk will have to join him in finding a new home that, hopefully, will be safe from "progress." But where to go and how to get there - that is the problem! The solving of this problem will delight young readers while, at the same time, making them aware of how "progress" can disrupt the habitats of many creatures. (ages 5 - 10)

"Come forth into the light of things. Let nature be your guide."

WILLIAM WORDSWORTH

begin the trip by minimizing it. Food should be removed from cans and containers, then measured into portions to eliminate any leftovers. This is where resealable plastic bags can be helpful. They then become a light weight, waterproof way to carry out your garbage on the return trip.

2. By walking quietly through wilderness areas, not only will you provide an atmosphere in which you and your family will be more aware of your surroundings, but also the animal life and any other visitors will be appreciative of your manners.

3. An undisturbed landscape provides a visitor with a sense of discovery. Be considerate of future travelers and do not harm the ecology by leaving your mark. Examples would be carving on tree trunks, building rock monuments, or etching your name in the dirt. Also, please leave any plant life, rocks, and other natural objects as you found them.

4. If you are lucky enough to encounter wildlife, try not to disturb it by keeping downwind and avoiding any sudden movements. Although it may be tempting, resist feeding any birds or animals since it can alter their natural feeding habits.

5. Naturally, when choosing a campsite, try to find an area that will not be damaged by your stay. For example, pitching a tent and setting up your kitchen on surfaces that are void of any plant life will provide a durable area for you and your family while making it easy to remove any evidence of your visit. (Gravel, snow, rock, or uncrusted sand are some suggestions.)

6. Wear soft-soled shoes while at camp and try to take a different route each time you fetch water in order not to wear a path through the vegetation. If you are camping with a scattered group, avoid creating a path between campsites.

7. When you are ready to leave an area, make sure that it is left exactly as it was found. For example, if you have cleared the area under your sleeping bag, replace any twigs, pine cones, or rocks to their original place. And, of course, remove all traces of your campfire.

The Shrinking Habitat Game

As soon as people encroach on a wilderness area and build houses, shopping malls, or highways, the animals living within that area must compete for fewer and fewer resources. This game will help illustrate to your children some of the hardships faced by these animals when an area is "claimed" in the name of progress.

1. Have your children choose a familiar habitat. How is the quality of life for the animals in that undisturbed habitat? Before starting the game, sit together and exchange stories about the birds, animals, and insects that could live there.

2. Have each child choose an animal from that habitat that they would like to portray. To simulate the area, place a long rope in a circle on the ground. Have all of the "animals" step inside the circle.

3. Begin the game by calling out a shrinking habitat influence, such as a forest fire, building a dam, erecting houses or a shopping mall, clear-cutting trees, farming, livestock grazing, mining, etc. Each time you call out an influence, have one of the children tighten the rope to shrink the habitat.

4. After a while, the children will begin to compete for space. If their animal is to survive, they must remain inside the circle. As the habitat shrinks, the children will start falling or being pushed out.

5. When you run out of ideas, end the game and gather the players together. Some questions to ask are: when the habitat became so crowded that it was almost impossible to stay in, how did you feel? What would you say is one of the most habitat-threatening influences that wild animals face today? How can humans be more considerate of animal life when expanding into new areas?

A Day Can Make the Difference

As soon as you wake up in the morning, although you may not realize it, you begin to make choices that have an impact on the Earth. This game will give your children the opportunity to recognize some of their own living habits that might be changed to better the environment.

Divide your children into two groups and have them sit facing each other. Choose one group to go first and, as you read one of the

Robins, Rorioles, and other birds are natural recyclers, sometimes using bits of our trash such as thread, string, and paper, as materials for their nests.

following vignettes, ask the children to listen carefully and act it out for the other team. After watching, have the other group decide if the situation has a helpful or harmful effect on the environment and, if it is harmful, decide how it could be changed for the better. Switch groups and repeat.

• Your alarm goes off, telling you it's time to wake up and get ready for school. You pull back the covers and feel a chill in the air. Instead of looking for your robe and slippers, you adjust the temperature setting of the heater.

• In the bathroom, you turn on the faucet in the tub to let the water warm up for a while. Meanwhile, you gather together your towel, soap, shampoo, and washcloth.

• You love to sing in the shower, so you stand bellowing a long tune while you let the warm water wash over you. Twenty minutes later, you emerge from the shower.

• It's time to brush your teeth, so you turn on the water and let it run while you scrub your pearly whites. Finally, you rinse your toothbrush and mouth before turning off the water.

• By the time you reach the kitchen, you know there isn't much time for breakfast. You pour yourself a big bowl of cereal, smother it with milk, and within minutes your mother tells you it's time to go. So you dump the cereal down the drain.

• You grab the sandwich your mom has made and stuff it into a plastic bag. Then you quickly jam it, along with your papers and books, into your backpack. Finally, you jump on your bicycle and pedal as quickly as you can to school.

• At school, you are asked to draw a picture and write a story about your favorite animal. You decide that your favorite animal is a tiger, so you get a piece of paper and start drawing. After you've started, you change your mind and decide to make up a story about a gorilla instead. You throw your paper in the trash, get a new piece, and begin again.

• At recess, you and your friends decide to play pirates and pretend that the jungle gym is your ship. "But we'll need some swords," someone says. So you go to a tree on the playground and break off several long limbs that will be just right for pretend swords.

- After school, you and your friend ride your bicycles to a convenience store to buy some chewing gum. You walk into the store and buy the gum. Just before you get back on your bike, you unwrap a piece and put it into your mouth. You look around for a garbage can, but don't see one, so you drop the wrapper on the ground.

- Back at home that afternoon, you turn on your radio and listen to music while you lie on your bed doing your homework. At four o'clock your favorite television program is on, so you jump up and run to the living room, leaving the light and radio on in your room.

- Every night, right after dinner, is the time you have trash duty. So, you walk through the house and empty all of the trash baskets into a big plastic bag. It is also your duty to sort through the garbage to make sure that nothing that is recyclable is thrown out, but is sorted into separate bins (for glass, plastic, newspapers, or aluminum cans). Well, tonight there is a TV program you don't want to miss, so you just throw everything into the garbage can and put it out for the trash collector.

- At bedtime, you go into your room, put on your night clothes, turn off the radio and light, and crawl into bed. After a busy day, it is not long before you are fast asleep.

The Council of All Beings

Think about all of the animals and plants with whom we share this planet. Now focus on just one. How does that creature feel about the things that are happening to its Earth? In this activity, you and your children are asked to "become" a creature or plant of the Earth and "speak" for it. (This is adapted from the ideas presented in *Thinking Like a Mountain: Towards a Council of All Beings* by John Seed, Joanna Macy, Pat Fleming, and Arne Naess, New Society Publishers, Philadelphia, PA, 1988.) By developing an empathy with the Earth, you and your children will discover a greater understanding and commitment toward it.

To prepare for a Council of All Beings, you must first explain to your children what the council is: it is a meeting of the creatures, plants, and beings that live on Earth. Explain that they will "become" (in their imaginations) an animal, plant, or ecological feature

All I See Is Part of Me, by Chara M. Curtis. Illustrations by Cynthia Aldrich. Illumination Arts Pub. Co., Bellingham, WA, 1989.

A little boy discovers that all creation is part of him and he is part of all creation. "I am part of all I see, and all I see is part of me. I am my hands, I am my feet, I am the puppy across the street. I am the moon, I am the stars, I'm even found in candy bars!" In this journey that carries the reader beyond the printed page, a child discovers his common link with all of life. (ages 4 - 8)

"What pattern connects the crab to the lobster and the orchid to the primrose and all four of them to me? And me to you?"

GREGORY BATESON

(such as a mountain or a river) and take part in a meeting to discuss their feelings about the Earth and its future. The human part of themselves will be asked to listen to the other beings of the Earth and learn from them.

Choosing: Give each person time alone to reflect about the plants, animals, birds, insects, and other ecological features that share our Earth. Tell them to think and listen, because after a while, a "being" will choose them to speak for it in the council meeting. (It is important that the participants and beings choose each other; they should not be assigned.)

Becoming: After they have been chosen, the beings should prepare for the meeting by creating a mask or costume. The materials can be provided, but each child must design his own. Make this a quiet experience so that each person can think about his or her chosen being. Tell them that, little by little, they will "become" their chosen beings as they create their masks or costumes. Once their costume is completed and worn, they will no longer be who they are, but will, as if by magic, really "become" another being.

The Council of All Beings: The leader of the meeting should take on the role of Chief Seattle and open the council with this brief speech. (Although some of the words have been changed so that children can better understand his message, the ideas are Chief Seattle's. They are taken from a speech that was given to his tribal assembly in the Pacific Northwest in 1854.) To begin, have all of the beings sit in a circle facing each other. Throughout the meeting, remember to refer to participants by the name of the beings they represent, not by their actual names.

Every part of this Earth is sacred. Every shining pine needle, every sandy shore, every mist in the dark woods, every meadow, and every animal, bird, or humming insect is holy. You are part of the earth and it is part of you. The perfumed flowers are your sisters; the deer, the horse, the great eagle, these are your brothers. The tall mountain, the stream in the meadow, the body heat of the pony, and man – all belong to your family.

The earth does not belong to you; you belong to the earth. All things on this earth are connected, like the blood that connects one family; so that whatever happens to the earth, also happens to you.

We have gathered here today to speak of our Earth. We want you to hear our words and learn from them.

Allow the beings to come to the center one by one, identify themselves, and tell the council how they feel about what is happening to the Earth and how it is affecting them. (If, for example, they speak for an endangered animal, they can tell the council what is happening to threaten their existence.) Then ask each being to express some hope or goal for the future. Before closing the council, have each participant commit himself to some form of action to accomplish the goals expressed. To end the meeting, have Chief Seattle close with these words:

This we know. Whatever happens to the earth happens to the people of the earth. Try to imagine the whole earth as a spider's web. Man did not weave this web of life, he is merely a strand in it. So, whatever he does to the web, he does to himself.

Get Involved!

Make Earth Conservation a Family Project

There are a lot of things you and your children can do to help keep our Earth safe and clean right in your own home. Here are some suggestions:

1. Make an effort to use your family car less. Walk, ride a bicycle, carpool, or use public transportation whenever you can. The less your car is used, the more you and your family contribute to clean air!

2. Start your own forest! Plant as many trees and shrubs as you can. You may be able to get free (or inexpensive) seedlings from the Forest Service, the Arbor Day Foundation, or your state agricultural office. Or grow your own seedlings in milk cartons. Trees help clean the air, create oxygen, prevent soil erosion, and help cool the Earth.

3. Turn off lights, televisions, radios, and other such appliances when you are not in the room. By using less energy, less fuel is burned and less exhaust is released into the air.

Brother Eagle, Sister Sky: A Message from Chief Seattle. Illustrated by Susan Jeffers. Dial Book, New York. 1991.

The words of Chief Seattle capture the Native American belief that this Earth and every creature on it is sacred. This beautiful book sends an important message to people young and old to care for and preserve the environment. (age 6 and up)

4. On a cold day, wear a sweater instead of turning up the heater.

5. Recycle everything you can: newspapers, aluminum foil and soda cans, glass, plastic, motor oil, and scrap metal.

6. Avoid using disposable cups, utensils, and plates. If you must use them, choose paper products instead of plastic since paper doesn't take as long to break down in the environment.

7. Make a compost pile in your backyard to recycle grass clippings, leaves, food scraps (except meat), and weeds. (See "Wonders in a Garden" chapter to find out how.)

8. Seek out fast food restaurants that wrap their food in paper or cardboard instead of plastic foam containers. If your favorite restaurant hasn't gotten the word, let them know how you feel by writing a suggestion to the main headquarters.

9. Instead of throwing away your old magazines, take them to a doctor's office, homeless center, nursing home, barber shop, laundromat, or place where more people can enjoy them.

10. When toting your lunch to work or school, reuse paper bags or invest in a lunchbox and thermos. Wrap food in wax paper or reusable plastic containers (like butter tubs), instead of plastic bags.

11. Give unwanted toys, clothes, or other reusable items to a charitable organization (such as Goodwill or Salvation Army). Or, for a little extra cash, sell them at a consignment shop.

12. When you see litter on the street, pick it up. Make a conscious effort to pick up at least one piece of litter each day. Challenge your family members and friends to do the same. Imagine if everyone picked up just one piece of litter each day how much cleaner our streets and towns would be!

Make Some Fancy Cans

Decorate used drums or barrels and place them around your school and community. (Used drums or barrels can sometimes be found at hospitals, supermarkets, manufacturing plants, or schools.) Decorate them with Earth-saving messages and slogans. Make some for litter and others for recyclable items. If a local business is willing to place one of your fancy cans for recyclables in their shop, every couple of weeks collect the recyclables and take them to the recycling center in your community.

Create a Pollution Pin-up Board

How is your community and your world handling the pollution problem? Keep abreast of the situation by creating an ecology bulletin board. Anytime you see an article or picture in a magazine or newspaper that shows areas that have been spoiled by pollution or tells of efforts that are being made to clean up polluted areas, pin it on the board for all to see. Make any new additions part of your dinner conversation so that your whole family becomes aware!

Junk Mail

Every day you get your mail and sort through it. What do you end up with? A huge pile of junk and a few pieces of real mail. It's a problem! There are several ways to deal with this problem. First, give your children the junk mail, ask them to keep any nice pictures and photographs, and put them in your Recycle Craft Box; they make great decorations for card making and other projects. If you want to do something to reduce the amount of mail you throw out each day, write to companies and tell them to take your name off of their mailing list. Or, if you write to the Direct Marketing Association and ask to be removed from their mailing lists, their Mail Preference Service will stop your name from being sold by most large mailing list companies. It won't stop the mail you receive from companies that already have your name, but it will stop future mailings by about 75%. It's worth a try!

Direct Marketing Association
6 East 43rd Street
New York, NY 10017

Trash Treasure Chest

One man's trash is another man's treasure. In your home or school, set up a box for reusable items. It will be a special place where children can come to pick and choose from discarded riches! (In a school, this is best placed near the art room so the art teacher can have first choice of the goodies.) Your box can be created to hold scrap paper or a collection of interesting objects that would have otherwise ended up in the trash, such as old greeting cards, scraps of fabric, unwanted toys, containers, wheels, etc. The box will act as a central place for exchanging such bits of treasure!

Create Your Own Backyard Wildlife Refuge

Make your backyard or school ground come alive by gardening for wildlife. You can attract birds and other wildlife from your region by planting specific shrubs, flowers, and trees. The National Wildlife Federation puts out a brochure filled with helpful suggestions, a list of books to help you get started, and an application to have your wildlife refuge certified as an official Backyard Wildlife Habitat.

Write:
**National Wildlife Federation
Dept. FB
8925 Leesburg Pike
Vienna, VA 22184-0001**

Melissa Poe
Kids FACE
P.O. Box 158254
Nashville, TN 37215

Adopt a Highway

If you have ever traveled across the country, you might have noticed the "Adopt-A-Highway" signs posted along the roadside. This program has been set up in approximately 75% of the states to help keep our highways free of litter. Organizations such as church groups, scout troops, schools, and businesses volunteer time three or four times a year (for a minimum commitment of two years) to pick up any litter along their assigned mile of highway. The Department of Transportation provides the trash bags, road warning signs, safety vests, and caps. They also conduct a safety meeting for all new participants. For more information about this program and how to volunteer, write or call your State Department of Transportation.

Saving a Place for Wildlife

Is there a natural area near your home in danger of being destroyed? There are some steps you and your family can take.

• First, and most important, read the local newspaper and listen to news broadcasts to gather all of the information you can about the project. It is necessary to be well informed.

• Call or write your government officials and tell them what you think. You might even write a petition and get the signatures of other people in your area that have the same concerns.

• Check with any local nature centers, wildlife groups, or citizen groups and join their ranks. Find out ways your family can help.

Start Your Own "Kids FACE Club"

This is an organization that was started by a 9-year-old girl named Melissa Poe. She was very concerned about pollution and wrote to the President of the United States. The reply letter didn't address the issues that she had raised, so she went into action. She had her letter blown up and placed on 250 billboards around the country and she even made an appearance on the "Today" show to talk about pollution. Since then, she has founded "Kids for A Clean Environment" (or Kids FACE) and currently there are over three hundred Kids FACE clubs in the United States. Your children can start a chapter in their community! For information, write to Melissa Poe at Kids FACE.

More Books To Share With Children

Your Own Secret Place by **Byrd Baylor.** Illustrations by Peter Parnall. Charles Scribner's Sons, NY, 1979. Almost everyone has his or her own private, secret place to sit, dream, and plan. This book will help readers consider the pleasures of their own secret place, whether it be in a tree, a sandy gully, or an undiscovered cove. (age 7 and up)

"If I Built a Village. . ." by **Kazue Mizumura.** Thomas Y. Crowell Co., NY, 1971. In this eloquent story, a young child, building with blocks, creates a village, town, and city that welcome the animals to share the land and sea. (ages 3 - 7)

Winter Barn by **Peter Parnall.** Macmillan Pub. Co., NY, 1986. As winter closes in, a centuries-old barn becomes a world apart, a refuge for creatures great and small. (age 8 and up)

At Home in Its Habitat: Animal Neighborhoods by **Phyllis S. Busch.** Photographs by Arline Strong. The World Publishing Co., NY, 1970. This book tells the story of how living organisms depend upon each other and their environments. (ages 6 - 12)

A Walk in the Woods by **Carolyn Arnold.** Illustrations by Freya Tanz. (from the First Facts Series) Silver Burdett Press, Westwood, NJ, 1990. Each book in this series explores the wonders of a particular habitat that can be discovered in a simple nature walk. Other titles in the series include: *A Walk in the Desert, A Walk Up a Mountain,* and *A Walk by the Seashore.* (ages 3 - 6)

Animals Everywhere by **Ingri and Edgar Parin D'Aulaire.** Doubleday and Co. Inc., Garden City, NY, 1954. In this book, your young child will be introduced to the animals from the tropics to the Arctic region in their native habitats. (ages 3 - 6)

Under the Moon by **Joanne Ryder.** Illustrations by Cheryl Harness. Random House, NY, 1989. Mama Mouse teaches her little mouse how to recognize her particular home in the meadow by reminding her of its special smells, sounds, and textures. (ages 3 - 5)

Life Underground by **Maria Rius and J. M. Parramón.** Barron's, NY, 1987. In this colorful book, Papa Bunny explains to his little bunny rabbit how their underground home was built by digging through various layers of Earth. The illustrations clearly show plants and other animals that grow and live beneath the ground. Other books in the series include: *Life in the Air, Life on the Land,* and *Life in the Sea.* (ages 3 - 6)

Under Your Feet by **Joanne Ryder.** Illustrations by Dennis Nolan. Macmillan, NY, 1990. Under your feet, deep in the Earth, small creatures are living out their life cycles. In this lyrical story, Joanne Ryder offers thoughtful parallels between the boy above the ground and the animals under his feet. (ages 4 - 8)

Earth Calendar by **Una Jacobs.** Silver Burdett, Morristown, NJ, 1985. In just one handful of Earth there are millions of tiny plants and animals. This book describes some of these animals and plants that live and grow in the Earth. (ages 5 - 10)

When I'm Sleepy by **Jane R. Howard.** Illustrations by Lynne Cherry. E. P. Dutton, NY, 1985. A little girl wonders what it would be like to sleep with the animals wherever they sleep. (ages 3 - 6)

Where Do Birds Live? by **Ron Hirschi.** Photographs by Galen Burrell. Walker and Co., NY, 1987. This introduction to all the special places where birds make their homes offers young readers a perfect book to enjoy while bird watching. (all ages)

Urban Roosts: Where Birds Nest in the City by **Barbara Bash.** Sierra Club Books, Little Brown and

Co., Boston, 1990. This fascinating book explores the world of birds and other creatures who have adapted to life in the city. (ages 6 - 10)

Air All Around by Tillie S. Pine and Joseph Levine. Illustrations by Bernice Myers. McGraw Hill, NY, 1960. You cannot see it, taste it, smell it, and - you cannot live without it! This book illustrates many of the things that air does for our lives. (ages 4 - 8)

The Air We Breathe by Enid Bloome. Doubleday and Co, Inc., Garden City, NY, 1971. With photographs and an easy-to-read text, this book enumerates the ways that air becomes polluted and what can be done about the problem. (ages 4 - 8)

The Pearl by Helme Heine. Atheneum, NY, 1985. Beaver's excitement at finding a mussel that undoubtedly contains a pearl is tempered by the realization that such a treasure could stir feelings of greed in his friends. (ages 4 - 9)

Heron Street by Ann Turner. Illustrations by Lisa Desimini. Harper and Row, 1989. "In the beginning they lived in a marsh by the sea - herons, ducks, geese, raccoons. . ." But then men, women, and children came and everything began to change. An effective tale of "progress" and the losses it has caused in nature. (ages 4 - 8)

I Like Old Clothes by Mary Ann Hoberman. Illustrations by Jacqueline Chwast. Alfred A Knopf, NY, 1976. This is the delightful story of a child who likes wearing hand-me-downs and enjoys imagining the history behind these old clothes. (ages 4 - 8)

The Wump World by Bill Peet. Houghton Mifflin Co., Boston, 1970. This book tells of a fictitious world inhabited by Wumps, simple grass-eaters well suited to their small world. One morning their peaceful existence is shattered when they are visited and taken over by the Pollutions from the planet Pollutus. *The Wump World* is truly a fable for our time. (age 4 and up)

Where Can the Animals Go? by Ron Wegen. Greenwillow Books, a division of William Morrow & Co., NY, 1978. This story forcefully dramatizes the endangered future that many animals face due to man's encroachment on grasslands, waterways, mountains, and forests. (age 5 and up)

The Web in the Grass by Berniece Freschet. Illustrations by Roger Davoisin. Charles Scribner's Sons, NY, 1972. The little spider spins a web as delicate as lace and as strong as a trap. Her way is one of nature's many ways and her habitat is as precious to her as ours is to us. (ages 5 - 9)

ABC of Ecology by Harry Milgrom. Photographs by Donald Crews. Macmillan Co., NY, 1972. A unique alphabet book in which each letter represents some aspect of our environment. (age 5 and up)

The Little House by Virginia Lee Burton. Houghton Mifflin Co., Boston, 1942. *The Little House* has spoken to generations of children on the importance of one's home. It points out in a most effective way how habitats can be lost by the encroachment of industry and "progress." (all ages)

Garbage! Where it Comes From, Where it Goes by Evan and Janet Hadingham. Simon & Schuster, NY, 1990. Every day Americans throw out enough garbage to fill 63,000 trucks! This book examines the health and environmental impact of landfills, dumps, and incinerators, and shows how everyone can contribute to a cleaner, less polluted planet. (ages 8 - 12)

About Garbage and Stuff by Ann Zane Shanks. Viking Press, NY, 1973. This is an excellent introduction to the concept and process of recycling waste materials. (ages 4 - 8)

The Planet of Trash: An Environmental Fable by George Poppel. Illustrations by Barry Moyer. National Press Inc., Bethesda, MD, 1990. Two astronauts from outer space land on a polluted, lifeless planet.

Discovering that the planet's inhabitants have vanished mysteriously, they excavate in search of clues of this lost civilization. As artifacts of our own world emerge, the reader realizes that the dead planet is Earth. (age 8 and up)

Loving the Earth: A Sacred Landscape Book for Children by Frederic Lehrman. Illustrations by Lisa Tune. Celestial Arts, Berkeley, CA, 1990. Breathtaking photographs, colorful illustrations, and easy-to-understand narrative convey to readers that our planet is deserving of our respect and is in need of our care. (age 5 and up)

A Place to Live by Jeanne Bendick. Parent's Magazine Press, NY, 1970. *A Place to Live* describes in a clear and logical text how all things on Earth are connected and what every animal needs in his particular habitat to survive. This is an excellent book to introduce the concept of bioregionalism to young children and to help them become aware of their particular place on Earth. (ages 6 - 12)

Soil Erosion and Pollution: A New True Book by Darlene R. Stille. Children's Press, Chicago, 1990. This addition to the *New True* series presents material about the erosion of the soil and the harmful effects of these processes on the planet in a way that even a small child can understand. (ages 6 - 9)

The Indian Way: Learning to Communicate with Mother Earth by Gary McLain. John Muir Press, Santa Fe, NM, 1990. This is an environmental awareness guide that contains many projects to open young minds to nature's wonders and shows how we can live in harmony with our environment. (age 8 and up)

The Adventures of Checker by Janet Sheldon. The Environmental Literacy Group, 33770 Woodland Drive, Evergreen, CO 80439. In this whimsical story, a small creature learns the environmental impact of choices made during common daily activities. Children discover immediate and long-term consequences for each action or choice made. (ages 6 - 9)

Good Planets Are Hard to Find! by Roma Dehr and Ronald M. Bazar. Illustrations by Nola Johnston. Earth Beat Press, Vancouver, Canada, 1989. This book is an environmental information guide, dictionary of ecological terms, and action book for children (and adults). (ages 7 - 12)

Going Green: A Kid's Handbook to Saving the Planet by John Elkington and Julia Hailes with Joel Makower. Illustrations by Tony Ross. Puffin Books, a division of Penguin USA, NY, 1990. This guide introduces young readers to the concepts of ecology and features many environmental activities and experiments. (ages 8 - 12)

50 Simple Things Kids Can Do to Save the Earth by The EarthWorks Group. Andrews and McMeel, 4900 Main Street, Kansas City, MO 64112, 1990. Projects, experiments, and games to teach kids that the planet and all objects and beings on it must be handled with care. (ages 8 - 12)

Earth Book for Kids by Linda Schwartz. Illustrations by Beverly Armstrong. The Learning Works, P. O. Box 6187, Santa Barbara, CA 93160, 1990. *Earth Book for Kids* offers children and their families a wide variety of ways to learn about the environment while having fun. Between its covers are fascinating facts and creative ideas for activities to help kids become better acquainted with their environment and learn to care for the Earth. (ages 8 - 12)

The Window by Jeanne Baker. Greenwillow Books, NY, 1991. A wordless book about our changing environment and what is happening to our wilderness throughout the world. (all ages)

Look Inside the Earth by Gina Ingoglia. Grosset & Dunlap, NY, 1989. In this book young children learn about the Earth's layers, resources and why people must keep it safe for all living things. (ages 4 - 7)

Save the Earth: an Action Handbook for Kids by Betty Miles. Alfred A. Knopf, NY, 1991. This handbook offers many projects, activities, and information to help kids help to save the earth. (ages 8 - 12)

Resources for Parents and Teachers

The Institute for Earth Education in Warrenville, Illinois offers several programs in environmental awareness, such as *Sunship Earth* and *Earthkeepers,* which approach this subject in an integrated manner, one that fosters in children a deep connection to the Earth. The best place for teachers of Earth Education to begin is by reading Steve Van Matre's book, *Earth Education...A New Beginning,* published by the Institute in 1990. For their catalogue and information about joining the Institute, write P.O. Box 288, Warrenville, IL 60555.

The Natural Resources Defense Council has a family newsletter, *tic,* which has features for both children and adults. Write to the council at 40 West 20th Street, New York, NY 10011.

ECO-KIDS Club is an ecology-based program for kids in grades K through five that features projects, newsletters, and other suggested activities having to do with the environment. Write the club c/o Animal Rehabilitation Center, Inc., Box 629, Midlothian, TX 76065.

For an incredible list of free and inexpensive material on many environmental subjects, order *Green Guides* from the Environmental Education Committee of the Sierra Club for $6. *Green Guides* covers 67 topics ranging from acid rain, endangered species, toxics and pesticides to wetlands. Send a check made out to Sierra Club, Environmental Education Committee, c/o Pat Suiter, Box 557953, Miami, FL 33255.

The Acid Rain Foundation, Inc. offers a wide range of educational materials for elementary grades. Contact them at 1410 Varsity Drive, Raleigh, NC 27606.

Rain Rain Go Away is a coloring-activity book about acid rain featuring wildlife characters to make complex issues understandable for children in grades K-3. The book is $1.95 plus postage from Public Focus, 92 Shaftsbury Avenue, Toronto, ON M4T 1A5, Canada.

The American Lung Association offers "Charlie Brown Cleans the Air," a cartoon story about the environment and the need to keep it clean. To obtain this free story, write 1740 Broadway, New York, NY 10019.

America the Beautiful Fund publishes environmental education materials. Contact them at 219 Shoreham Bldg., Washington, D.C. 20005. Keep America Beautiful also has education materials, so write them at Mill River Plaza, 9 West Broad Street, Stamford, CT 06902.

The National Wildlife Federation publishes a booklet entitled "You Can Do It" which gives kids many suggestions for what one person can do to help the environment. They have also produced the *CLASS Project,* a series of environmental investigations for use with kids in grades 6-9. Write 8925 Leesburg Pike, Vienna, VA 22184-0001.

"A-Way with Waste" is a curriculum guide for grades K-12. Write to Washington Dept. of Ecology, 350 150th Ave. NE, Redmond, WA 98052.

Living Lightly in the City: An Urban Environmental Education Curriculum consists of four volumes: K-3, 4-6, 7-9, and 10-12. Write to the Schlitz Audubon Center, 1111 East Brown Deer Rd., Milwaukee, WI 53217.

Project Learning Tree has several recycling and energy activities. Write the American Forest Council, 1250 Connecticut Ave. NW, Washington, D.C. 20036.

Project WILD offers several pollution-related activities. Write to the Western Regional Environmental Education Council, Salina Star Route, Boulder, CO 80302.

"Saving Energy" is a *Wonders of Learning Kit* that includes 30 student booklets, a read-along cassette, and activity suggestions. It is available from National Geographic Educational Services, Dept. 90, Washington, D.C. 20036.

The Lorax by Dr. Seuss is an animated film about destruction of natural resources and pollution. It is available for rent from The Film and Video Library, The University of Michigan, 400 Fourth St., Ann Arbor, MI 48103-4816, or from Population Reference Bureau, Inc., 777 14th St. NW, Suite 800, Washington, D.C. 20005.

Were You a Wild Duck, Where Would You Go? by George Mendoza. Illustrations by Jane Osborn-Smith. Stewart, Tabori and Chang, NY, 1990. Although this book is advertised as a children's book, we feel that it is one that adults should read as well. The captivating watercolor illustrations and teat of this book evoke the once lush natural world and show what has become of it through the carelessness of mankind.

Sierraecology is written for teachers and Sierra Club leaders involved in youth education. It publicizes innovative environmental education programs, curricula, and materials. Each issue features announcements of new environmental education materials available as well as descriptions of successful environmental education programs from around the United States. It is published four times a year and is free. Write to *Sierraecology,* Sierra Club Public Affairs, 730 Polk St., San Francisco, CA 94109.

The Education Department of Marine World Africa USA offers a exciting selection of materials for teachers. Write Marine World Parkway, Vallejo, CA 94589.

The Environmental Action Coalition publishes *Eco-*
News, an informative, cartoon-illustrated newsletter about the environment for grades 4-6. The membership fee is $15. The coalition also offers a film library for free loan to EAC members.

An SOS Kids' Activities Kit is offered by the Izaak Walton League of America. The kit explains the course of pollution and describes activities for kids 6-13. Contact them at 1701 North Fort Myer Drive, Suite 11090, Arlington, VA 22209.

The U.S. Environmental Protection Agency serves as a clearing house for free and inexpensive information about the environment. One of their many offerings is an environmental coloring book entitled "Once There Lived a Wicked Dragon." For a list of educational materials, write 401 M Street, SW, Washington, D.C. 20460.

Cobblestone: The History Magazine for Young People, Vol. 10, No. 8, (August 1989) is devoted to environmentalism and has many articles on people in history who spent their lives to protecting the Earth such as John Muir, Rachel Carson, and David Brower.

Zephyr Press has recently published a series entitled "Our Only Earth: A Global Issues Curriculum." Some of the books in the series include: *The Future of Our Tropical Rainforests, Our Troubled Skies, The Ocean Crisis,* and *Endangered Species.* For information contact Zephyr Press, 3865 East 34th Street, #101, Box 13448-W, Tucson, AZ 85732-3448.

Milliken Publishing Co., St. Louis, Missouri, offers *Environment and Pollution,* a collection of twelve teaching units, each one introduced by a full-color transparency which emphasized the basic concept of the unit. (Grades 5-9).

The Greenhouse Crisis Foundation has published *101 Ways to Help Heal the Earth: A Citizen's Guide.* Write to 1130 Seventeenth Street, NW, Washington, D.C. 20036.

For Our Kid's Sake: How to Protect Your Child Against Pesticides in Food by Ann Witte Garland, 1989. From Sierra Club Books, 730 Polk Street, San Francisco, CA 94109.

Nontoxic, Natural & Earthwise by Debra Lynn Dadd, 1990, from *The Earthwise Consumer,* Box 279, Forest Knolls, CA 94933. This is one of the best how-to-live-without-toxics books.

Ecologue: The Environmental Catalogue and Consumer's Guide for a Safe Earth by Bruce Anderson, Editor. Prentice Hall Press, NY, 1990.

Whole Earth Ecologue: The Best of Environmental Tools & Ideas, ed. by J. Baldwin. Harmony Books, NY, 1990.

EarthPulse Handbooks by Susan Hassol and Beth Richman, are published by The Windstar Foundation, 2317 Snowmass Creek Road, Snowmass, CO 81654. Each booklet in this series concentrates on a single subject such as recycling or energy.

The Global Ecology Handbook is compiled by The Global Tomorrow Coalition. Beacon Press, Boston, 1990. This book is the official backup for the PBS *Race to Save the Planet* series. An activity and teacher's guide is also available. Write to WGBH, Print Projects, 125 Western Avenue, Boston, MA 02134.

Since its start in 1974, *Planet Drum* has been a major influence in developing interest and action in the areas of bioregionalism and "reinhabitation" of the land. Membership includes a subscription to their review, *Raise the Stakes.* Write Box 31251, San Francisco, CA 94131.

An annotated list of educational materials on environmental issues is available from the U.S. Environmental Protection Agency, Office of External Relations and Education, Youth Programs, Room 823 W2, 401 M Street, SW, Washington, D.C. 20460.

A 64-page publication offering hundreds of resources for classroom use is available from PBS Elementary/Secondary Service, Dept. PR, 1320 Braddock Place, Alexandria, VA 22314. Ask for the "Environmental Resource Compendium."

Keepers of the Earth: Native American Stories and Environmental Activities for Children by Michael J. Caduto and Joseph Bruchac, Fulcrum Press, Golden, CO, 1988. Although this book is more appropriate for grades 4-8, many activities can be modified for younger students. A teacher's guide to the book is also available.

Pollution: Problems & Solutions, Ranger Rick's *Naturescope,* 1990, published by the National Wildlife Federation, 1400 16th St. NW, Washington, D.C. 20036-2266. This is an excellent collection of activities dealing with trash, air pollution, water pollution, as well as choices and challenges.

The Environmental Literacy Group has developed a unique series of educational materials designed specifically to empower environmental responsibility in children five through seventeen. Their publication *Impact!* contains over 30 activities that involve children in decision-making on environmental issues. Each activity presents the objective, classroom time, materials needed, and learning skills strengthened. All activities are suitable for the primary grade levels. Write to 33770 Woodland Drive, Evergreen, CO 80439.

The Sierra Club offers a pamphlet entitled "21 Ways to Help Stop Global Warming by the 21st Century." For information on this and other Sierra Club publications, such as those on clean air, toxics, the arctic national wildlife refuge, and global warming, write Sierra Club Public Affairs, 730 Polk Street, San Francisco, 94109.

Rush to Burn: Solving America's Garbage Crisis? Island Press, Washington, D.C., 1989. (Articles on solid waste disposal that originally appeared in the newspaper *Newsday.*)

"Recycling Plastics: A Forum," *Environmental Action* (July/August 1988): 21-26.

"Buried Alive. The Garbage Glut: An Environmental Crisis Reaches Our Doorstep," *Newsweek* (November 27, 1989): 67-76.

The National Wildlife Federation has published a booklet entitled "Your Choices Count" which deals with overflowing landfills, toxic trash, water pollution, ozone depletion, loss of habitat, endangered species, and other environmental problems. Write 1400 Sixteenth Street, Washington, D.C. 20036-2266.

Saving the Earth: A Citizen's Guide to Environmental Action by Will Steger and Jon Bowermaster. Alfred A. Knopf, NY, 1990. This book is an excellent report on the state of our environment, an encouraging call to action, and a source of practical information for those who wish to do their part in saving the Earth.

50 Simple Things You Can Do to Save the Earth, The Earthworks Group. Andrews and McMeel, NY, 1989. Also *50 Simple Things Kids Can Do to Save the Earth* by the same group, 1990. Both books offer experiments, facts, and exciting things to do to keep the Earth a safe, healthy place.

P3: The Earth-based Magazine for Kids is a great environmental magazine that focuses on the very things kids are interested in. It is full of games, activities, ideas for getting involved, and letters from kids. Write Box 52, Montgomery, VT 05470.

Thinking Like a Mountain: Towards a Council of All Beings by John Seed, Joanna Macy, Pat Fleming, and Arne Naess. New Society Publishers, Santa Cruz, CA, 1988. This is a collection of readings, meditations, poems, and guided fantasies by experienced workshop leaders and activists to help the reader develop empathy for the Earth and find new clarity, inspiration, and commitment.

Audubon Adventures has published a special issue entitled "Recycling our Resources: The Garbage Crisis" for Earth Day, 1990. The teacher's guide for this issue also contains a reading list having to do with this problem. Contact the National Audubon Society, Route 4, Box 171, Sharon, CT 06069.

Away With Waste is a teacher's guide published by the Washington State Dept. of Ecology, Waste Reduction, Recycling, and Litter Control Program, Eikenberry Building, Mailstop PV-11, Olympia, WA 98504.

Here Today—Here Tomorrow: A Teacher's Guide to Solid Waste Management (K-12), New Jersey Dept. of Environmental Protection, Division of Solid Waste Management, CN414, 401 East State Street, Trenton, NJ 08625.

Let's Recycle: Lesson Plans for Grades K-6 and 7-12. RCRA Docket Information Center, Office of Solid Waste (OS-305), U.S. Environmental Protection Agency, 401 M Street SW, Washington, D.C. 20460.

Recycling Education—A Workbook for Teachers, from Keep America Beautiful, Mill River Plaza, 9 West Broad Street, Stamford, CT 06902. Also ask about *Waste: A Hidden Resource* (curriculum guide and Apple IIe software).

Habitat is Where It's At is a coloring book for all ages containing facts and fun. Available for $2.25 plus 75 cents postage and handling from Defenders of Wildlife, 2244 19th Street NW, Washington, D.C. 20036.

Knock the Four Walls Down, Environmental Education Investigations for the Elementary School, by B. J. Amundson. Fifty-eight inexpensive environmental teaching units covering a wide variety of topics. All of the pamphlets are very inexpensive. Write to P. A. Schiller and Associates, P.O. Box 307, Chicago, IL 60690.

CHAPTER SEVEN

Going... Going... Gone?

What is man without the beasts? If all the beasts were gone, men would die from a great loneliness of the spirit. For whatever happens to the beasts soon happens to man.
CHIEF SEATTLE, 1854

It is believed in the scientific community that the current rate of extinction on our planet is one to three species per day. In the world today, there are over five hundred federally listed threatened and endangered species, and many more are considered rare and might soon be listed. It is the alteration or the elimination of an animal's habitat that causes its populations to fall and endangers its survival. The most devastating impacts to their ecosystems are caused by man, through urbanization, timber cutting, wetland drainage, conversion of wild lands to agricultural fields, and pollution. When extinction is caused by natural forces at work over thousands of years, it is an uncontrollable event. When extinction is brought about by human intervention and environmental destruction, mankind has the responsibility to prevent it through careful stewardship of our planet and its inhabitants.

 This can be a frustrating topic for young children, who want to love and care for the creatures of our planet. For instance, when they learn about the rainforest and all the exotic plants and creatures currently being threatened, they simply reply, "So, why don't they just stop cutting the trees?" It's a beautiful and innocent question and voices a serious problem that they will be left to solve, if this generation doesn't find the answer. Now is the time for action. You and your children can become actively involved by learning about extinction and the events that lead to it. This chapter takes advantage of children's curiosity about dinosaurs to define this difficult concept: with their new knowledge of the past, they can step into the present. By relating some of the causes of extinction for dinosaurs to the plight of today's endangered creatures, children can better understand the current problems faced by these animals in our fragile and interconnected ecosystem.

The Dinosaur Egg Game

Young children are intrigued by dinosaurs and seek out as much information about them and their prehistoric environment as they can. This activity will provide an opportunity to explore and answer questions about these fantastic creatures, while satisfying your child's vivid imagination.

Things You Will Need: *plastic eggs (the large panty hose egg containers work well), a bowl of sand or grass, a poster or picture of a dinosaur (preferably a Duckbill, as depicted in Dennis Nolan's Dino-saur Dream), and the dinosaur questions printed on paper. Place one in each egg.*

1. Place the nest of sand or grass near the picture of the dinosaur. Place the plastic eggs (filled with questions) in the center of the room.

2. Explain that the mother dinosaur has lost her eggs! One at a time, have your children choose an egg, answer the question, and place the lost egg back in the nest, returning it to its mother.

Alternative: Instead of answering all the questions in one sitting, explain that the eggs will be returned to the mother dinosaur one egg each day. Write responses on paper and illustrate with crayons, markers, or paint. After all the questions have been answered, put the pages together to make a big book. Make a cover and add it to your collection of dinosaur memorabilia.

Dinosaur Questions To Ponder

• If dinosaurs were alive today, would that be a good thing? Why?

• What kind of dinosaur would you like to be?

• If you were as large as a dinosaur, what would be difficult to do?

• Do you think that dinosaurs ever got bored? What would they do for fun?

• If you could have a dinosaur for a pet, what would you name it? Why?

• What would you miss most if you lived at the time of the dinosaurs?

• If it lived today, what do you think a dinosaur would enjoy eating?

• What kind of noise do you think a dinosaur made when it was happy? Sad? Angry? Lonely?

• How was life different when dinosaurs lived on Earth?

• What do you think caused the dinosaurs to become extinct?

• Can you think of any animals alive today that remind you of dinosaurs? How are they the same?

Dinosaur Dream, by Dennis Nolan. Macmillan Publishing Co., NY, 1990.

At bedtime, as he's snuggling down to go to sleep, a little boy named Wilber discovers a young Apatosaurus in his backyard. He decides that the only thing to do is to return the dinosaur to its herd. Their walk takes them back through time; traveling through the Ice Age, the Age of Mammals, the Cretaceous Period, and finally to the Jurassic Period, where they find the huge baby's mother. This book presents interesting material about prehistory mixed with a nighttime adventure and beauti-ful paintings that make it all believable. (ages 4 - 8)

Maia: A Dinosaur Grows Up, by John R. Horner and James Gorman. Illustrations by Doug Henderson. Courage Books, a division of Running Press, Philadelphia, PA, 1987.

This is the story of Maia, a duck-billed dinosaur that lived 80 million years ago in what is now the Montana grasslands. It is a realistic account of the life of this type of dinosaur written by the first paleontologist ever to uncover an extensive nesting ground. It is a large, beautifully illustrated volume that will undoubtedly please every dinosaur querist in your house. (age 5 and up)

Dinosaur Eggs

What would it be like to hatch from a dinosaur egg? After reading the book *Maia*, create a paper maché dinosaur egg. Then have your children curl up on the floor and pretend to be baby dinosaurs as you read the story below.

To make dinosaur eggs:

1. Blow up and tie a balloon for each child.

2. Make a solution of glue and water. Have your children dip strips of newspaper into the glue solution and use them to wrap the balloons completely. Allow to dry for approximately two days.

3. Repeat the process and allow to dry.

4. When the "eggs" are dry, decorate them with paint. Encourage your children to create interesting patterns or designs on their eggs, such as cracking lines (as if the dinosaur were beginning to hatch.)

Your world is very small. There is just enough room inside your egg for you to grow into a baby dinosaur. Everything you know is dark and warm. Even when you open your eyes, there is nothing to see. Finally, after many weeks, the day has come. You feel restless. Something inside you says it is time to get out. So with your special pointed tooth, located at the end of your nose, you begin to peck at the hard shell that surrounds your body. It is slow work and you stop often to rest. First, you make a tiny hole. The light from outside sneaks into your dark world and for the first time you can see. Peck . . . peck . . . peck . . the hole becomes bigger. The cool air rushes in and you can feel the chilly breeze on your face. You stretch your legs and the hole becomes a crack. With one final push, you break the egg apart and slide out of your protective shell. At first you close your eyes to the bright light. The warmth of the sun is comforting and quickly dries the wet scales on your back. You can feel that everything around you is alive and moving. You are no longer alone in your world and, for the first time, you feel the touch of another dinosaur as one of your brothers or sisters steps heavily on your head as he makes his way out of the nest. For a brief moment you wish you could return to the peace and warmth of your egg, but instead you instinctively open your eyes and begin to crawl in search of food.

The Dinosaur Dash

A young child benefits from both quiet and lively activities in the process of learning. While playing the following game, your children can pretend to be the Stegosaurus and experience how it must have felt to move about or, when necessary, to run from danger.

Lay some obstacles in the middle of your playing area – chairs, pillows, blocks, tables, etc. Have your children line up on one side of the area. Ask them to get down on their hands and feet (with legs extended and bottoms in the air) to represent Stegosaurus dinosaurs. Explain that their forest is on fire and they must successfully clear the burning area and cross the river to safety. On your signal, have the children pretend to be a herd of Stegosaurus racing to the other end of the playing area, climbing over or under any obstacles in their path. Once everyone has reached safety, have them sit down and share any difficulties they may have had. What kind of difficulties do they think a Stegosaurus would have had moving about? Stegosaurus was a plant-eater. What types of vegetation do your children think they would have eaten, considering their size and mobility?

A Brontosaurus in the Living Room?

Even as an adult, it is difficult to visualize the immense size of one of the largest "giant lizards;" so imagine how impossible this must be for a child! Try this experiment; the process is a marvelous learning experience and the results will delight the whole family. Before you begin, tell your children that the Brontosaurus was one of the largest dinosaurs and present pictures to help them visualize its appearance.

1. Ask your children to guess whether a Brontosaurus could fit into your living room or classroom. Allow the children to help you measure a string about sixty feet long. The string may be precut, but the counting would be a good experience and will allow the children to accurately visualize the length of string. (If counting to sixty is too difficult, count by tens, six times.)

2. Hold the string to its full length in the room. Would a Brontosaurus fit in the room? If not, measure around the perimeter of the room. How many times does it go around?

3. Take the string outside and stretch it to its full length. How

Dinosaurs ranged enormously in size, from as small as two feet in length to as large as eighty feet! In general, the smaller ones appeared first.

Hungry Dinosaurs

Tune: **Frere Jacques**

Tyrannosaurus, Tyrannosaurus,

You eat meat, you eat meat.

Stalking through the jungle,

Searching for your dinner,

You're so mean, the Tyrant King!

Brontosaurus, Brontosaurus,

You eat plants, you eat plants.

Wading in the river,

Chewing on some algae,

You're so tall, the biggest of all!

Pterodactyl, Pterodactyl,

You eat fish, you eat fish.

Soaring through the air,

Diving in the water,

Catch that fish, your favorite dish!

Stegosaurus, Stegosaurus,

You eat plants, you eat plants.

Your boney plates protect you,

When you turn to fight,

Swing your spikes, with all your might!

many children long is a Brontosaurus? Allow the children to count their giant steps as they walk the length of the string. How many seconds does it take them to run from the head of a Brontosaurus to its tail? Have the children run from one end of the string to the other as you count aloud.

What Happened to the Dinosaurs?

Up to this point, the activities have stressed the lives of dinosaurs. Now it is important to talk about their extinction. This concept can be more complex for your young children to grasp. You might explain to them, "The dinosaurs could not adapt to the changes in nature, so slowly over many years there were fewer and fewer dinosaurs until there were no more." The following stories and related activities will aid in introducing and defining the finality of extinction.

The Dinosaur's Dilemma

Take any of the popular theories you believe could have caused the dinosaur's extinction and the deleterious event is always the same: the breaking down of the dinosaur food chain. This game will demonstrate to more mature children the events that led to the extinction of those giants that once roamed Earth.

Things You Will Need: *cups of equal size, a large tub or bucket, and a source of water, such as a water hose. You will want to play this game outdoors, since it is necessary to spill the water. Note: You can also play the game with sand in a sand pile.*

1. Divide your children into groups of five. Give each child a cup. Within each group, assign these parts to play: three of the children as "plants," two as "plant-eating dinosaurs," and one as a "meat-eating dinosaur." Each group should stand away from the tub in this order to create the shape of a triangle (or a food chain pyramid) with its base at the tub.

2. To begin, turn on the water hose and start to fill the tub or bucket. Explain to your children that the water represents the sun and/or favorable climate that feeds the plants. Ask the plant children

to come forward and receive the energy for food by filling their cups from the tub.

3. Their food energy can now be passed to the plant-eating dinosaurs. Have the three plant children pour all of their water into the cups of the two plant-eating dinosaur children. (Since three cups of water are being poured into two cups, some of the water will be spilled. This represents the energy that is released when a plant eater consumes its food, breathes, grows, moves about, etc.)

4. Continue the events in the dinosaur food chain by asking the plant-eating dinosaur children to pass on food energy by emptying their water into the single cup of the meat-eating dinosaur child. (Again, some water will be spilled.)

5. To complete the circle of events, ask the meat-eating dinosaur child to take his cup of water and return it to the tub. This represents the energy that will be returned to the Earth at the end of his life, which will feed the growing plants.

6. Have the children continue playing in this manner while you relate their actions to the circle of events in the dinosaur food chain. After awhile, abruptly turn off the water and announce that a catastrophic happening has just occurred (such as an asteroid hitting the Earth or a sudden change of climate). Your children will notice that some water will still be in the tub and they should continue playing.

7. Eventually, the water will run out. The "plants" can no longer receive the sun's energy and must.drop out of the game. When this happens, the food chain quickly collapses. There is no food for the plant eaters, who must drop out of the game. This leaves only one hungry meat-eating dinosaur without food.

8. Sit down with your children and talk about what this game means. How are the events similar to the current situation of many endangered animals?

An Archaeological Dig in the Backyard!

It is fascinating to children that such large and fantastic animals lived on our planet so long ago. But how do we know they were here? We know because fossils and dinosaur bones have been

The Last Dinosaur, by Jim Murphy. Illustrations by Mark Alan Weatherby. Scholastic, Inc., NY, 1988.

With spectacular lifelike illustrations and dramatic text, we see a glimpse of what life may have been like for one of the last dinosaurs to roam the Earth. This sometimes sad story focuses on a tiny herd of plant-eating Triceratops. We see them searching for food, making their way through an eerie, dark forest, and finally fleeing from a fire. Their journey concludes in a confrontation that produces an end to one world and the beginning of another. (age 7 and up)

Last of the Dinosaurs: The End of an Age, by David Eldridge. Illustrations by Norman Nodel. Troll Associates, Mahwah, NJ, 1980.

This dynamic book explores the various reasons that caused the extinction of the huge reptiles that once ruled the land and seas. The simple text takes the reader step-by-step through the breaking down of the food chain caused by geologic and climatic changes on the Earth. The book ends with an imaginary last few days of a dinosaur and its desperate search for food until time runs out. (ages 5 - 10)

discovered all over the world by archaeologists. To learn more about archaeology, read the book *Fossils Tell of Long Ago* by Aliki. Then let your children experience for themselves what role the archaeologist has in uncovering our ancient past. Encourage your children to pretend to be the first humans to discover dinosaur fossils. Bury shells and cleaned turkey leg bones under the sand. Provide digging tools and allow your children to discover the hidden fossils and "dinosaur bones."

What is a Fossil?

Let your children learn about fossils by making some! The hardening of the dough in this activity simulates how the minerals and dirt surrounding ancient plant and animal matter slowly turned to rock over many centuries to form the fossils that archaeologists uncover today.

1. First, make salt dough by mixing together four cups of flour, one cup salt, and one and a half cups of water. Knead for five minutes. (You may also use plaster or clay.)

2. Give each child a ball of dough. Have the children flatten their dough balls on pieces of waxed paper.

3. Provide items such as shells, twigs, cleaned chicken leg bones, leaves, and plastic toy dinosaurs. Allow children to use the items to make impressions in their dough.

4. Allow to air dry completely (possibly 2-3 days) or bake in a 325° oven for about 30 minutes. Let each child tell about his "fossil" and share a made-up a story about how its impressions came to be left in the "stone."

An Archaeologist's Delight

Things You Will Need: *a clear glass pan (8 x 12 inches), two flavors of gelatin (lime and raspberry or cherry), crushed graham crackers, two sliced bananas, raisins, and prepared whipped topping.*

1. Prepare the lime gelatin as the package directs. Pour it into the glass pan and chill. This represents a layer of limestone.

2. Drop the banana slices and raisins evenly over the chilled gelatin. These represent the fossils.

3. Prepare the raspberry or cherry gelatin as the package directs.

Carefully pour it over the banana slices and chill until firm. This represents a layer of sandstone.

4. Sprinkle the crushed graham crackers over the gelatin. This represents a layer of coal.

5. Finally, top with the whipped topping to represent a siltstone layer. Before serving, explain the various layers to your children. Serve the dessert in squares and allow your young archaeologists to "dig" through the layers to discover the fossils!

Five Gigantic Dinosaurs

This poem is a fingerplay or it can be dramatized with a glove puppet. To make a glove puppet, sew velcro tabs onto the fingers of one glove. Cut out five dinosaurs from scrap felt and sew the corresponding velcro tabs on their back sides. (Test to see if this is necessary, as the felt may stick to the tabs unaided.) Place a felt dinosaur on each finger. As you read each stanza of the poem, have your child remove the dinosaurs one at a time until they are extinct.

Five gigantic dinosaurs letting out a roar,
One went away and then there were four.

Four gigantic dinosaurs munching on a tree,
One went away and then there were three.

Three gigantic dinosaurs watching a volcano spew,
One went away and then there were two.

Two gigantic dinosaurs resting in the red-hot sun,
One went away and then there was one.

One last dinosaur, in the days of yore,
He went away and then there were no more.

Whatever Happened To the Dinosaurs?

The light-hearted book *Whatever Happened To the Dinosaurs?* by Bernard Most and this followup activity encourage the development of your children's imaginations and their creative thinking process. After completing this activity, talk with your children about the actual theories that scientists believe caused the dinosaur's extinction: change in climate, alteration in food supply, dust from a

Panda, by Susan Bonners. Delacorte Press, NY, 1978.

With soft-brushed pen and ink drawings, this story describes the life cycle of a rare giant panda living in a mountain forest in southwest China. Witness her birth and travel with her through adulthood until the time she is awaiting the birth of her first cub. The text is simple and will appeal to young children. Note: Mating is mentioned, but it is brief and sensitively handled. (ages 4 - 10)

The Panda, by Nadine Saunier. Illustrations by Marcelle Geneste. Children's Press Choice by Barron's Educational Series, Inc., NY, 1988.

This book presents a beautifully illustrated account of an endangered animal and its daily life. Some of the words have been replaced by clever miniature pictures, therefore making this a rebus reader. What better way to involve a beginning or non-reading child in sharing the story? They will anxiously await their cues and be more attentive in the process to make learning more fun! (ages 4 - 8)

comet's impact blocking out the sun, or a combination of several events.

1. Read the book to your children and discuss their ideas about what may have happened to the dinosaurs. Encourage creative and sometimes silly notions.

2. Have each child illustrate their idea on a piece of drawing paper. Write a quote on the bottom of each paper for a language experience story. Create a cover from construction paper and staple all the pages together to make a book. Add this to your dinosaur memorabilia.

Prehistoric Time Line

This is a cooperative project resulting in a stunning historical mural. Attach a long sheet from a roll of brown wrapping or butcher paper to the wall. Help your children plan and draw a story over the length of the mural from the beginning of the dinosaur era to their extinction. Decorate the mural elaborately with crepe paper for volcano eruptions, cut or real leaves and grass, and drawn or painted trees and ferns. Cut dinosaurs from coloring books or design some from scrap paper and paste them to the time line. Write a language experience story under your children's creation.

The Rare Giant Panda

Some of the same conditions faced by dinosaurs, such as alteration in food supply or habitat, are causing hardships for some animals alive today. But unlike the natural reasons involved in the extinction of the dinosaurs over millions of years, humans are often responsible for the destruction of animal habitats today. The present animals in danger of extinction are being studied and labeled "threatened or endangered" so that current laws will protect their habitat from further damage. There is hope that low animal populations will be able to reestablish themselves over time. In some areas of the world, such as the tropical forest regions, destruction of the fragile ecosystems is happening so quickly that our planet faces the real crisis of losing these precious forests within the next generation.

There is something you can do to help and there is no time to be wasted. Learn all you can about endangered animals and teach your children, so that they will be equipped to face these problems in their future. The giant panda will introduce the endangered species topic, not only because it is an endangered animal under protection today, but also because children are already familiar with the cuddly-looking dweller of the rapidly shrinking Chinese mountain region.

Panda Prints

Panda bears are very difficult to observe in the wild. Many scientists who go out to observe a giant panda in the mountain jungles of China will wait weeks or months before actually seeing one. One way they track them is by looking for their paw prints in the snow or mud. Have your children pretend to be scientists patiently waiting in the bamboo forest looking for a panda bear.

1. *Adult:* Cut a potato in half and draw a panda bear footprint on the cut side of the potato half. Carefully carve away the excess part of the potato with a knife. The footprint should stand at least one-fourth inch above the rest of the potato.

2. Have your children gently press the footprint in a shallow dish of paint and then press the print onto a piece of construction paper. Allow to dry before hanging to prevent drips.

"Save the Panda" Pendant

The first level of activism is to tell other people about your beliefs. A nice way for children to share their thoughts is by wearing a button or pendant so that others can know where they stand on the endangered species issue.

1. First, make salt dough by mixing together four cups of flour, one cup of salt, and 1½ cups water. Knead five minutes.

2. To make the head of a panda, roll some dough into a one and one-half inch ball and flatten with your hand or a rolling pin.

3. Roll two three-quarter-inch balls and flatten. With a drop of water, attach these ears to the top of the larger circle of dough.

4. At the top of your pendant, between the ears, make a small hole using a drinking straw.

Panda In The Forest

Tune: A Bear Went Over the Mountain

A panda roams the green forest,
(walk in a circle or in place)

A panda roams the green forest,
(look from side to side)

A panda roams the green forest,
(pretend to search for food)

Searching for bamboo stalks.

He finds one here and he eats it,
(pretend to pick leaves)

He finds one here and he eats it,
(motion to your mouth)

He finds one here and he eats it,
(make chewing movements)

Tasty, tender shoots.

5. Allow to air dry overnight or bake in a 325° oven for about 30 minutes. When dry, paint the ears, nose, and eye patches black. With a permanent marker, write "Save the Panda" on the back. String some yarn through the hole and wear as a necklace.

DREAMSTARTER

There is only darkness and a comforting dream swimming inside your mind. Bump! No. . . it's so warm and peaceful here. The soft fur of your mother and the sound of her breathing make you dig in closer and resist the morning. She nudges you with her black, wet nose, "Time to wake up." Reluctantly, you turn over and open one eye to look out of your den. There is a low-lying mist moving through the trees and soft snow is falling. You love to play in the snow, so all of a sudden you are in a hurry to go outside.

Your mother blocks the way and urges you to begin your morning wash. So you lick your paws and rub them gently over your eyes and face. In your tummy you feel the emptiness as air grumbles against nothing. It grumbles again because you need some food. After stretching your stiff legs one by one, you and your mother set out to find your favorite food - delicious bamboo.

The leaves from the forest floor rustle and crunch beneath your paws. This beautiful mountain forest has always been your home. Lately, you have heard stories from the birds that food is getting harder to find. Many of them have had to leave the forest hoping to find a new home. You hope there will always be enough food for you and your family. The sounds of the forest begin to sing in your furry, black ears as the birds awaken to greet the new day. Imagine the wonderful adventures you will experience today!

The first thing to do is to find a sacred place to live in.

PAWNEE TRIBE

The Hungry Panda Game

The main food in a panda bear's diet is bamboo leaves. Every fifty to one hundred years the bamboo plants flower and die. This has happened recently in the bamboo forests inhabited by the giant pandas. Many of them are having trouble finding enough food until new bamboo growth establishes itself. This game will help make your children aware of the food shortage faced by the endangered panda bear.

1. Cut out large green "bamboo" leaves from scrap construction paper, one for each player. Scatter them around the floor.

2. While you sing "The Hungry Panda," ask the children to pretend that they are hungry pandas looking for bamboo leaves. As the words are sung, randomly choose a bamboo leaf from the floor, and remove it from the playing area.

3. At the end of the verse, all the hungry pandas must seek out and stand on a leaf in order to "survive" to the next round. Continue playing until only one panda remains in the game.

4. After playing, sit with your children and talk about the giant panda's dilemma. What ideas do they have that might help the panda survive in the wild?

Pastry Panda Paws

Veggies can sometimes be difficult to disguise, but many children are excited to eat something they have helped prepare! As you are cutting the circles, ask your children to pretend that the pastry circles are the paws of the hungry pandas and that they will get to fill them up with delicious vegetables. Also, have them pretend that the spinach leaves are bamboo leaves, a panda's favorite food. And, who knows? Maybe "bamboo leaves" will become a favorite of your panda-loving youngsters too!

Things You Will Need: *1 cup butter, 1½ cups all-purpose flour, ½ cup dairy sour cream, ¾ cup shredded cheese, and assorted vegetables (cut into small pieces or shredded), such as spinach leaves, carrots, broccoli, onions, and mushrooms.*

Cut the butter into the flour until it is completely mixed. Stir in the sour cream until thoroughly blended. Divide the dough in half; wrap each and chill at least eight hours. Place all the shredded or

The Hungry Panda

Tune: London Bridge

The hungry panda quietly creeps

Hunting bamboo leaves to eat.

He grabs one quick and walks away

Munching tasty leaves all day.

chopped vegetables into a bowl. Add the shredded cheese and mix together. Roll the pastry on a well-floured board and cut into six-inch circles. Spoon one-fourth cup vegetable mixture into the center of each circle. Fold each over into a half-circle and press the edge with the tines of a fork. Bake in a preheated 350° oven for 20-25 minutes or until golden brown and puffed. Let stand for five minutes before serving because the filling will be hot.

Panda Bear Cookies

These cookies make great items for an "Endangered Species" fund-raising bake sale. The proceeds can then be donated to one of the many groups that work to aid animals in danger. (See the Resources section at the end of this chapter.) Your customers will be happy to know they are helping to aid the many animals at risk on our planet.

Things You Will Need: *a large and small circle-shaped cookie cutter, 1 pound of butter or margarine, 2 eggs, 5 cups all-purpose flour, 2 cups sugar, a pinch of salt, 1 tablespoon vanilla, 1 teaspoon baking soda in 3 tablespoons of milk, powdered sugar icing, raisins, and chocolate sprinkles.*

Put all of the ingredients, except raisins and chocolate sprinkles, into a large bowl and mix with your hands until a smooth dough is formed. (You cannot damage the final result by overmixing.) Form into a ball, dust with flour, wrap the ball closely to keep it from drying out, and chill it thoroughly.

Break the ball into convenient-sized pieces, adding a bit more flour to each ball of dough for easier handling. Roll out on a lightly floured surface. Using glasses or round cookie cutters, cut the dough into large circles (for the panda's head) and small circles (two small circles to be used as "ears" for each panda head). Place the heads on a cookie sheet and position a pair of ears on each one, circles slightly overlapping. Bake in a 350° oven for about 12 minutes or until light brown. Allow to cool on a rack for at least one-half hour. Meanwhile, mix together 2 cups of powdered sugar and 2 tablespoons of water. Spread on the panda cookies. Sprinkle ears and eye patches with chocolate sprinkles. Place a raisin in the center of each eye patch. (Makes about five dozen cookies.)

Learn More About Endangered Animals

After focusing on the rare giant panda, you can help your children expand their knowledge about endangered species by learning about other animals at risk of extinction. The book *Hey! Get Off Our Train* and related activities will introduce you and your children to other threatened species and inform you of their current situation.

Hey! Get Off My Train Game

After reading the story, allow your children to act it out. As conductor, they will have the power to extend sanctuary to the endangered animals they encounter on their journey. After playing the game, sit together as a group and talk about the current problems faced by these animals and brainstorm ways to help.

1. Line up chairs or old boxes to represent a train. Prepare a set of endangered animal cards by drawing or cutting pictures from magazines. On each card, briefly write why that animal is currently in danger of extinction.

2. Choose a child to be the conductor and have him sit at the head of the train. Let the other players choose from the pile of animal cards.

3. One by one, let the players approach the train to board. Each time the conductor should say, "Hey! Get off of my train," to which the player will reply, "Oh, please may I have a ride?" Then if the player can relate a reason why his species is endangered, the conductor allows him to board. Continue playing until all animals are safely riding on the train.

Identifying Endangered Animals

This simple game is excellent for introducing your children to some basic facts about endangered animals. Use the set of animal cards you created for the previous game and pass one out to each child. Say, for example, "I'm looking for a Loggerhead Turtle. The Loggerhead Turtle is a sea turtle. This turtle is the largest type of

Hey! Get Off Our Train, by John Burningham. Crown Publishers, Inc., NY, 1989.

A young boy and his faithful companion take a trip on a toy train around the world. Along the way, one by one, endangered animals board the train and plead for sanctuary. The boy takes them on as they explain what is happening to them and their habitats. Their fantastic lark ends up being quite a remarkable journey with a surprise ending that will leave both children and adults delighted. (ages 4 - 8)

> *"We reenact Noah's ancient drama, but in reverse, like a film running backwards, the animals exiting,*
> *ferret*
> *curlew*
> *cougar*
> *wolf*
> *your tracks are growing fainter."*
>
> JOANNA MACY

sea turtle and can grow to be as big as your daddy (actually up to seven feet). Those who have a picture of a Loggerhead Turtle on their card, please stand up and pretend to be swimming through the ocean looking for jellyfish and fish to eat." Go around the circle and say the names of the children pretending to be a sea turtle. Praise them for their creativity. Continue with other types of endangered animals until all have been identified. For younger children, you may wish for all the players to dramatize the movements together, so that they do not become restless waiting for their turns.

Endangered Animal Musical Chairs

This traditional game simulates the problem faced by many endangered species today, a shrinking habitat caused by man's increased demand for land. When species' hunting grounds are reduced, the food supply is also reduced, making the competition between animals great. Some animals do not survive and their population is slowly reduced until it is impossible to rebuild their numbers, causing extinction.

1. Set up chairs as if for regular musical chairs, but allow a chair for every player. Tape a picture of a dinosaur on the back of one chair (this chair is never removed from the game). Explain to your children that this group of chairs is their habitat and that the labeled seat is the "Chair of Extinction."

2. Divide the players into two or three groups and declare each group to be a different animal that will share the same habitat, such as bears, moose, and deer.

3. Have the children stand around the chairs. The players should begin walking when they hear the music or environmental sound effects. When the music is stopped, all children must sit in a chair (everyone should have a seat). The child that ends up in the "Chair of Extinction" leaves the game, as in regular musical chairs.

4. Remove one chair from the "habitat" and continue playing until one or two species have become "extinct." When the game is over, discuss with your children how it felt to watch their species become more rare or finally extinct.

For older children: For an added dimension, you may want periodically to set out another chair in the game called the "repopulation chair." It should be labeled with a picture of a baby animal. When a player sits in it, another member of his species is allowed to reenter the game. This chair is added or removed from the game as the adult desires. Eventually though, have the game end as above.

No More Room Game

This game will teach your children that people need to protect animal habitats if wild animals are to be preserved from extinction.

1. Have the children stand against one wall. As you place one piece of scrap paper for each player around the room or on each desk, explain to your children that each paper represents an island on an undiscovered planet. The planet has one animal living on each island (place an animal cracker on each paper). Tell the players that they are all visitors from outer space coming to live on this planet. Further explain that because of a limited food supply, each island can only support one person or three animals.

2. To begin play, ask a child to "land" on any island. Ask him if there is room for the animal. (No, not according to the rules of the planet.) Have the child move the animal to another paper. Is there room for it? (Yes, unless there is already three animals or one human on it.)

3. Continue in this manner until one of the animals has no place to go. Then you (the adult) eat the cracker. Explain that the animal just has become extinct and can never come back. Explain that maybe you just ate all the dinosaurs! The next animal might be all the dodo birds or passenger pigeons.

4. Continue the game until there is only one paper left with three animals on it and one human being waiting to land from outer space. Point out to your children that on Earth, we must decide if we are going to save a place for animals.

5. Luckily, on our planet, animals and people can share the same island, even the same yard. Sit down with your children and think of all the animals that live in your yard, including worms, insects, birds, pets, etc. Do they have a right to live there? Emphasize that we do need to think carefully before we disturb or destroy any animal's home, even if it's under a rock!

Rain Forest, by Helen Cowcher. Farrar, Straus and Giroux, NY, 1988.

Life is peaceful for the many animals of the rainforest, but a cry of alarm reverberates through the jungle. Something even more powerful than the jaguar is threatening this secluded and placid world. The animals of the forest sense a change is coming. The rich colors of the forest leap from the pages into your memory and heart to fill you with respect for the beauty of their untouched world and a sense of obligation for their fate. An excellent source for rainforest pictures. (ages 3 - 9)

The Great Kapok Tree: A Tale of the Amazon Rain Forest, by Lynne Cherry. Harcourt Brace Jovanovich, NY, 1990.

A young man is ordered to cut down a Kapok tree. He becomes sleepy and decides to take a rest under the tree before he begins his work. As he sleeps, he is visited by all the creatures who will lose their homes if he completes his task. Each animal whispers in his ear the reasons that they need the tree to sustain their lives. An anteater reminds him, "What happens tomorrow depends on what you do today." Finally, a Yonomano child of the rainforest pleads, "When you awake, please look upon us all with new eyes." When he awakes their whispers echo in his ears. He looks all around at the forest and its creatures and makes his decision. (all ages)

Creatures of the Rainforest

The rainforest of the tropical regions is an ideal home for many creatures. There is plenty of water, shelter, and food to support numerous species of insects, birds, reptiles, amphibians, and mammals. Rainforest destruction is one of the most pressing ecological problems on our planet today. It is estimated that 30 to 50 acres of forest is being destroyed every minute due to farming, logging, ranching, mining, and dam building. The unique habitat of these creatures is shrinking rapidly and the plants, animals, and insects of these regions are beginning to encounter some of the difficulties your children have already experienced in previous activities.

The following stories and activities will focus on the delicate ecosystem of the rainforest and will teach your children that the animals of the rainforest play a vital role in maintaining this important environment.

The Sounds of the Rainforest

After reading *Rain Forest* by Helen Cowcher to you children, talk about the many different voices and sounds you might hear if you were to visit such a jungle: the rustling of the leaves and branches, the buzzing and cries of the many animals, insects, and birds, and the pitter-patter of the rain on the forest floor.

Using homemade instruments such as tissue paper to rustle or a nail clipper to represent an insect sound, create a soundscape of the jungle and record it to use as background to your reading of the story, stick puppet show, and other rainforest activities.

Act Out the Story

After reading *The Great Kapok Tree* by Lynne Cherry, dramatize the story. Choose one child to be the man with the axe resting under the tree. Have the other children pretend to be the animals of the rainforest and quietly crawl near him and whisper in his ear. If you are alone with your child, allow your child to be the resting man first, then switch places and let your child be one of the animals in the story.

A Rainforest Jamboree

The animals, birds, and insects of the rainforest are unique only to these shrinking areas of the world; outside of this unparalleled ecosystem they would not survive. This activity will give your children the opportunity to learn more about these unusual creatures and to imagine what life would be like in a rainforest.

1. Let each child choose to "become" a creature from the rainforest. Before the dramatization, give them the opportunity to read about their particular animal, learning what they can about their habits, movements, food requirement, etc. They may also wish to create a simple costume or sandwich board vest to wear that will further help them to identify with "their" animal.

2. Out of scrap materials from your Recycle Craft Box, make simple props to represent a rainforest. Drape strips of green and brown crepe paper around the room to create a jungle ambience.

3. Using your rainforest soundscape or a commercial recording (such as *Rain Forest* produced by The Relaxation Co., Box 1011, Manhasset, NY 11030), have your children dramatize life in the rainforest. Have each child move about the room pretending to be their chosen animal. Afterward, sit together in the rainforest and allow each child to share some brief facts about their creature with the group.

For preschool age children: Make rainforest animal cards and give one to each child. The children should pretend to be the animal on their card when they hear the sound recording. When it is stopped, they must freeze in place until the recording is started again. Occasionally, let the children switch cards and pretend to be a different type of animal.

Stick Puppets

The story, *Rain Forest* by Helen Cowcher is very easy to dramatize using stick puppets. Using her illustrations as a guide, draw large pictures of rainforest creatures on scrap poster board or cardboard. Decorate with crayons, markers, or paint. Cut them out and glue a craft stick or cleaned Popsicle stick onto the back of each. When not in use, these make nice decorations for the rainforest environment described in the previous activity.

Toucan Toast

This is an entertaining and unique breakfast treat! While your children are painting their toucan beaks, show them pictures and comment on how beautiful this endangered bird is. Encourage conversation by asking questions. For example, what makes this bird different from the ones we see in our backyard? What do the colors of his beak bring to your mind? The toucan uses his beak to crush fruit to eat. Can you think of any hardware or kitchen tools that can be used the same way?

wheat bread (cut into circles and toasted)

small banana (cut in half then split lengthwise)

cream cheese

raisins

food coloring

and cotton swabs.

Place toasted bread circle (head) on a serving plate and spread with cream cheese. Position a raisin in the middle for an eye. Lay a banana slice (beak) cut side down and to one side of the head. Dip the cotton swabs into food coloring and paint the "beak" in a beautiful rainbow pattern.

Jaguar In the Forest Chant

Jaguar in the forest deep,

Swift and silently you creep.

No one knows that you're about,

But Howler monkey gives a shout!

Easel Art

Decorate your home or classroom with endangered species posters. Provide paint and large easel paper and ask your children to paint pictures of endangered animals in their natural habitats. Have each child dictate a short quote or slogan for their poster.

They're Bouncing Back

They're bouncing back, they're bouncing back, *(slowly flap arms)*

The whooping cranes are bouncing back! *(lift legs high)*

Tall and graceful birds that dance,

Now they have another chance.

They're bouncing back, they're bouncing back, *(stretch arms in front)*

The gators now are bouncing back! *(imitate jaws with arms)*

The Jaguar In the Forest

The jaguar is one of the most fierce predators in the rainforest. He is swift and silent of foot, often catching his prey by surprise. In this game, young children can pretend to be the creatures of the rainforest innocently going about their business when the Howler monkey sounds the call of alarm. It is the jaguar's ability to be unassuming as he cleverly moves through the rainforest that makes this activity as exciting as life in a real tropical jungle.

1. Before you begin, indicate a "safe" tree or other spot. Choose one child to be the Howler monkey, the only person that can call an alarm during the game. Play a sound effects recording and begin the game by chanting the rhyme at left. Ask the children to move about the playing area pretending to be creatures of the rainforest and busying themselves by crawling, climbing, searching for food, etc.

2. Inconspicuously walk among the "creatures" and quietly tap one of the players on the shoulder. That child becomes the jaguar and begins to silently creep toward the Howler monkey.

3. If the Howler monkey sees him coming, he sounds the alarm by screeching. All of the creatures then run to the safe spot while the jaguar attempts to tag some prey for dinner.

4. If the jaguar reaches and tags the Howler monkey before he is noticed, the Howler monkey cannot sound the alarm. The jaguar can then continue to tag players until they notice and run to safety.

5. After a round, choose another child to be the Howler monkey and continue playing in the same manner. Play until all of the children have had the opportunity to be the Howler monkey.

Commitment Cakes

These wholesome cupcakes make perfect child-sized birthday treats or special desserts! After learning about endangered species, you and your children can set aside a day to think and talk about what each of you can do to save animals from extinction. Then allow your children to commit themselves to some course of action, such as writing letters, raising money, etc. As they blow out the candles on their cupcakes, they can announce their intentions to the whole group.

Things You Will Need: *½ cup raisins, ¼ cup apple juice concentrate, 1 ripe banana (sliced), ¼ cup vegetable oil, 1 teaspoon vanilla, ½ cup unsweetened applesauce, 1 egg, 1 cup whole wheat flour, ½ cup wheat germ or bran cereal, ½ teaspoon baking powder, ½ teaspoon baking soda, ¼ teaspoon salt, 1 tablespoon cinnamon, and animal crackers.*

Heat raisins and apple juice concentrate in a saucepan until the raisins are soft (about 3 minutes). Pour into a blender and puree. Add the banana, oil, vanilla, applesauce, and egg; blend together. In a large bowl, stir together the dry ingredients (except crackers). Add the blender ingredients and stir together well. Fill greased or lined muffin tins three-fourths full and bake at 400° for about 20 minutes. Cool completely, then frost. Top each cupcake with an animal cracker before serving.

Frosting: In a small bowl beat 8 ounces of cream cheese until soft. Gradually beat in 3 tablespoons of apple butter and 2 tablespoons of apple juice concentrate.

Success Stories

Although the future for some endangered animals is bleak, we don't want to overlook the successful efforts that have been made in the past few years to save some endangered species of the world. The "They're Bouncing Back" chant offers an active way for your young children to learn about these success stories.

Get Involved!

Simple Things Can Help

Every small step you take to help the endangered animals of our planet helps all of us survive!

• Be careful not to disturb plants and animals when you're outdoors.

• Refrain from purchasing items made from wild animals.

• Never choose a wild animal, such as a tropical parrot, as a pet.

• Conserve energy by turning off lights and by using your air

Sharp-toothed beasts with scaly skin,

They're swimming in the swamps again.

They're bouncing back, they're bouncing back, *(arms straight out)*

Bald eagles now are bouncing back! *(lean side to side as if soaring)*

Soaring over lake and bay, Doing better every day.

They're bouncing back, they're bouncing back, *(Arms up in front)*

The polar bears are bouncing back! *(curl fingers and move forearms up and down)*

Snowy white with coal black eyes,

Their numbers now are on the rise.

Reprinted with permission from Ranger Rick's *Naturescope,* "Endangered Species: Wild and Rare" published by the National Wildlife Federation, 1990.

"I am in favor of animal rights as well as human rights. That is the way of a whole human being."

ABRAHAM LINCOLN

conditioning, furnace, or car less. Recycle paper and glass. By doing these things, you will use a smaller amount of the natural resources that animals depend on for survival.

• Have a lemonade stand, bake sale, or car wash to help raise money for organizations that aid endangered animals.

• Learn all that you can about endangered animals. Visit your local or school library to read more about them. Share what you learn with your friends.

Camera Safari

Make your next trip to your local zoo more than a sightseeing trip. Be aware of the exhibit signs, because most endangered animals will be labeled with a special logo and specific information about their current situation in the wild. Take along a notebook and your camera. List all of the endangered animals on exhibit at your zoo and take their picture. When you get home, have the photographs developed and make a book.

Organize a Voting Collection

Many zoos have "adoption" programs that allow you to donate money to help feed an animal for a year. Call and talk to the zoo personnel about such programs. Get your neighborhood, church, or school involved by organizing a "voting collection." Have pictures of several animals that can be chosen and allow the children and parents to pick their favorite by buying a vote for 10¢ or 25¢ each. Take all of the money collected and "adopt" the winning candidate!

An Endangered "Pet" Scrap Book

This is a simple project that you and your children can share. The memory of it will remain with them for the rest of their lives. This idea is simple, but it really allows a young child to do something about an animal that they've learned about and have come to cherish.

As a family, class, or individual, choose an endangered animal to learn more about. Create a scrap book to record information and chart progress of conservation efforts. Cut out pictures and articles from magazines, allow your children to draw and write stories about your chosen "pet," keep a list of all the books you and your children read about that animal, choose a special day to commemorate each year in honor of your "pet" and have a party. Get in touch with organizations that aid endangered animals and, when you write letters, take quotes from your children and allow them also to sign the letter.

Endangered Animals Don't Have to Live Far Away!

Are there any threatened or endangered animals, birds, or insects in your community? Contact the Nature Conservancy for more information. Involve yourself and your family in any conservation efforts that are currently underway.

Your Letters Might Save the Elephants

So many people want the ivory of the elephant's tusks that too many elephants are being killed. In fact, if the hunting continues at this rate, there won't be any elephants left in Africa when your children grow up!

• The people of Japan use more ivory than any other country and they have not joined the world ban on ivory. Help your children write a letter, on behalf of your family or school, asking the Ambassador of Japan to give your message to his country.

• America has joined the world ban on ivory, but only for a limited time. Does your family or class think the ban should be continued indefinitely? Tell the President of the United States what you think.

• You can help your children write a letter to the United Nations Environment Program and tell them that you want elephants to be around when they grow up and ask what you can do to help.

The Nature Conservancy
1815 North Lynn Street
Arlington, VA 22209
(703) 841-5300

His Excellency
Ambassador of Japan
2520 Massachusetts Ave., N. W.
Washington, D. C. 20008

The President of the United States
1600 Pennsylvania Avenue
Washington, D. C. 20501

UN Environment Program
P.O. Box 30552
Nairobi, Kenya, East Africa
(You'll need an overseas stamp.)

More Books To Share With Children

The Dinosaur Who Lived In My Backyard **by B. G. Hennessy.** Illustrations by Susan Davis. Viking Kestrel, a division of Viking Penguin, Inc., NY, 1988. A boy imagines what it was like long ago when dinosaurs roamed in what is now his backyard. (ages 3 - 7)

The Littlest Dinosaurs **by Bernard Most.** Harcourt Brace Jovanovich, NY, 1989. Simple text and colorful drawings combine fact and fantasy to relate the story of the small dinosaurs to the youngest dinosaur-lovers in this world. (ages 3 - 7)

Whatever Happened to the Dinosaurs? **by Bernard Most.** Harcourt Brace Jovanovich, NY, 1984. A humorous speculation of what really happened to make the dinosaurs disappear. (ages 3 - 7)

Fossils Tell of Long Ago **by Aliki.** Harper and Row, Publishers, NY, 1972 and revised in 1990. How fossils are formed and what they tell us. (ages 5 - 9)

The Dinosaur Hunter's Kit. Running Press, 1990. Now kids can hunt for dinosaurs the same way paleontologists do. This kit includes a hunter's handbook, a replica fossil of an Apatosarus, and the proper excavation tools. (ages 8 - 12)

As Dead As A Dodo **by Paul Rice and Peter Mayle.** Illustrations by Shawn Rice. David R. Godine, Publisher, Boston, 1981. A long overdue tribute to sixteen extinct animals in the form of short histories, each accompanied by a portrait. (ages 7 - 12)

The Modern Ark: The Endangered Wildlife of our Planet **by Claire Littlejohn.** Dial Books for Young Readers, NY, 1989. This book shows the variety of animal life that is threatened in eight different habitats: tropical forests, woodlands, mountains, grasslands, deserts, rivers, oceans, and polar regions. The idea behind the book is that if our wildlife is to survive, we have to turn our planet into a modern ark to preserve both the animals and their habitats. (ages 5 - 10)

Endangered Animals **by Lynn M. Stone.** Children's Press, Chicago, 1984. This non-fiction book discusses various endangered animal species in the world, why and how they became endangered, and what can be done to save them. (ages 7 - 10)

Wildlife in Danger **by Robert Burton.** Silver Burnett Color Library, Macmillan Publishing Ltd., NY, 1981. This spectacular volume looks at the animals and plants that are on the verge of extinction. (all ages)

Help Save Us: Sticker Book of Wild Animals (**Volumes 1 and 2**). Illustrations by Debby L. Carter. E. P. Dutton, NY, 1989. These books take children on a trip around the world, illustrating the different habitats of many endangered species. Children can then complete the pictures using reusable stickers. (ages 4 - 8)

And Then There Was One: The Mysteries of Extinction **by Margery Facklam.** Illustrations by Pamela Johnson. Sierra Club Books, Little, Brown and Co., Boston, 1990. This is a read-aloud book that examines the many reasons that animals disappear from the Earth. (ages 7 - 12)

Endangered Wildlife **by Martin Banks.** World Issues Series, Rourke Enterprises, Inc., Vero Beach, FL, 1988. This non-fiction book offers excellent information on the causes of extinction and compares natural extinction with the dramatic rate of extinction today due to man's influence. (ages 8 - 12)

Animals In Danger: A Pop-up Book **by William McCay.** Illustrations by Wayne Ford. Aladdin Books, Macmillan Pub. Co., NY, 1990. Eight of the most endangered animals are brought to striking three-dimensional life. (ages 4 - 8)

Giant Pandas by Ovid K. Wong, Ph.D. Children's Press, Chicago, 1987. Vivid photographs and an easy text describe the physical characteristics, habitat, behavior, and endangered situation of China's national animal treasure. (ages 6 - 9)

Nature Hide and Seek JUNGLES by John Norris Wood and Kevin Dean. Alfred A. Knopf, NY, 1987. Lurking in the bushes, clinging to the underside of a leaf, perched high in the branches of the rainforest, are countless fascinating creatures. (age 5 and up)

Rain Forest Secrets by Arthur Dorros. Scholastic, NY, 1990. This book invites children to explore the delicate balance of life in the rainforest. It also examines the threat to rainforests and provides a list of organizations children can contact for more information. (ages 6 - 9)

I Am Leaper by Annabel Johnson. Illustrations by Stella Ormai. Scholastic, Inc., NY, 1990. No one in the Environmental Research Center can believe it when the tiny kangaroo rat squeaks into a computer and her sounds come out in English! Her natural habitat is threatened and the reader will be stunned to discover the monster's identity. (read-aloud, ages 7 - 11)

Professor Noah's Spaceship by Brian Wildsmith. Oxford University Press, NY, 1980. The animals and birds of the huge forest were happy until the air in the forest began to smell and turned a nasty color. They had to devise a plan to save themselves. After a fantastic journey, they travel backwards in time to planet Earth, before it was polluted. They vow that this time they will keep their world clean, if only man will cooperate. (ages 4 - 8)

Antarctica by Helen Cowcher. Farrar, Straus and Giroux, NY, 1990. One year a new sound is heard in Antarctica, an unfamiliar sound. Helicopters whirring and ships crashing through the ice announce that man has arrived. The creatures hope that they can share this fragile world with man in peace. But will man let

them? This is a beautiful companion volume to the author's *Rain Forest.* (all ages)

The Bollo Caper by Art Buchwald. Doubleday and Co., NY, 1973. This short novel is written from the perspective of a leopard that has been captured and shipped to the United States so that his skin can be made into a fur coat. (read-aloud, age 7 and up)

The Call of the Wolves by Jim Murphy. Illustrations by Mark Alan Weatherby. Scholastic, Inc., NY, 1989. Winter is approaching and as the wolf pack nears the caribou herd they ready themselves to hunt. Suddenly, the undisturbed rhythm of their lives is shattered when a plane swoops down. (ages 7 - 12)

The Jungle is My Home by Laura Fischetto. Illustrated by Letizia Galli. Viking Press, NY, 1991. This book captures the beauty of the jungle and, through the animals' sad predicament, presents the tragedy of the jungle's destruction. (ages 3 - 8)

Resources for Parents and Teachers

The Endangered Species Handbook by Greta Nilsson. © 1986. One copy is free to educators, if request is written on school letterhead. Write to Animal Welfare Institute, P.O. Box 2650, Washington, D.C. 20007.

Life in the Balance by David Rains Wallace. (This is a companion to the Audubon television specials.) Harcourt Brace Jovanovich, NY, 1987. This is an invaluable primer on global ecology, with an emphasis on how all life forms are affected by mankind.

Audubon Wildlife Report published annually by the National Audubon Society. This excellent reference includes in-depth reports on individual animal and plant species, many of them endangered. Available from Northeast Audubon Center, R.R.1., Box 171, Sharon, CT 06069. $39.95 per year ($2 postage and handling).

Audubon Adventures Vol. 4, No. 3 (Dec. 1987/Jan. 1988). This is a newspaper for elementary age children published by the National Audubon Society. Packets of 32 issues are sent to "adopted" classes each month during the school year along with a Leader's Guide. Write 613 Riversville Rd., Greenwich, CT 06831. The issue cited deals with endangered species.

Endangered Species Issue Pac offered by the U.S. Fish and Wildlife Service and the National Institute for Urban Wildlife. Write to the National Institute for Urban Wildlife, 10921 Trotting Ridge Way, Columbia, MD 10921. $5 per pac, $3 postage and handling.

Endangered Animals Teaching Unit by Leigh Childs, Lois Schwartz, and Jeff Swenerton. 1984, $24.95. Zoo Books, Wildlife Education Limited, 930 West Washington St., San Diego, CA 92103. Includes teachers' guide, student readers, and activity sheets.

Write for free teacher's guides: *Rainforest, Vanishing Species,* and *Habitat* from Marine World Africa USA, Education Dept., Marine World Parkway, Vallejo, CA 94589. (Telephone 707-644-4000, ext. 434) Material contains excellent games, vanishing animal trivia cards, puzzles, and lots of helpful information.

Project WILD, developed by the Western Regional Environmental Education Council, Salina Star Route, Boulder, CO 80302, has activities dealing with endangered species.

World Wildlife Fund, an organization that works to protect endangered wildlife and wildlands, offers "Buyer Beware" brochures on illegal wildlife trade and a Wildlife Trade Education Kit containing background information, activities, and a slide program. Write to Traffic (U.S.A.), World Wildlife Fund, 1250 24th Street, NW, Washington, D.C. 20037.

In the Rainforest by Catherine Caufield. Knopf, NY, 1985.

Saving the Tropical Forests by Judith Gradwohl and Russell Greenberg. Earthscan, 1988. Agribookstore, 1611 N. Kent St., Arlington, VA 22207.

Ranger Rick's NatureScope Vol. 4, No. 4, "Rain Forests: Tropical Treasures," National Wildlife Federation, 1989. Also see Vol. 3, No. 3, "Endangered Species: Wild and Rare." 1987.

Defenders of Wildlife will provide information on endangered species. Write to 1244 19th Street, Washington, D.C. 20036.

The Preservation of Species by Bryan G. Norton. Princeton University Press, Princeton, NJ, 1986.

Man's Responsibility for Nature by John Passmore. Scribner's, NY, 1974. A useful discussion of the inherent right of species to exist.

What's Wildlife Worth? by Robert and Christine Prescott-Allen. Earthscan, Washington, D.C., 1982.

What is Happening to Tarzan's Jungle? How to build a model rainforest in the classroom. Send stamped manila envelope to Joyce Crebase, Griffin School, 26 Davis St, Oakville, CT 06779.

The Rainforest Food Web Game. 50 pages. For grades 3-8. Students play the part of a plant or animal (34 possible roles). Comes with Teacher's instructions, fact sheet, sample food webs, and "what if" web damaging situations. Send $6.50 to F. Sandford, Biology Dept, Coe College, Cedar Rapids, IA 52402.

Tropical Rainforest: A Global Issue. Fifteen minute filmstrip or video with teacher's guide. $22. Write the Appalachian Audubon Society, P. O. Box 15123, Harrisburg, PA 17105.

Tropical Rainforests - A Disappearing Treasure. Teacher manual and student activities. K-12. $11. Smithsonian (SITES), Attn. Publications, 1100 Jefferson Dr. SW, Room 3146, Washington, D.C. 20560

Excellent resources and information are available from *Save The Rainforest*, 604 Jamie St., Dodgeville, WI 53533.

Endangered species pamphlet is available from The Humane Society of the United States, 2100 L. Street, NW, Washington, D.C. 20037. (20 cents)

Endangered Species: Their Struggle to Survive by Micki McKisson and Linda MacRae-Campbell. This is part of the "Our Only Earth Series," a curriculum for global problem solving. Also in this series are *The Future of Our Tropical Rainforests, Our Troubled Skies,* and *The Ocean Crisis.* This series offers an integrated curriculum that explores real life issues, culminating with a "Summit" where students seek solutions to global problems and create action plans. The program is ideal for grades 4 - 12 and provides wonderful background information for teachers and parents. Contact Zepher Press, P.O. Box 13448-W, Tucson, Arizona 85732-3448.

Center for Environmental Education. *Endangered Species Issue.* Washington, D.C., Center for Environmental Education, 1982.

"On the Brink of Extinction: Conserving the Diversity of Life." Worldwatch Paper #78 (June 1987).

Endangered Species Animal Rummy Educational Card Game. Safari Limited, Box 630685, Ojus, FLA 33163.

Global Tomorrow Coalition. *Biological Diversity Education Packet.* GTC Education Services, 1325 G Street NW, Suite 915, Washington, D.C. 20005.

Environmental Education About the Rainforest by Klaus Berkmuller. World Wildlife Fund, Washington, D.C.

The Enchanted Canopy by Andrew Mitchell. Macmillan Pub. Co., NY, 1986.

"Rondonia: Brazil's Imperiled Rain Forest," by William T. Ellis. *National Geographic* (December 1988): 772-779.

"Woman in Love With a Jungle," by Mark J. Kurlansky. *International Wildlife* (September/October 1985): 34-39.

"Last Days of Eden," by Loren McIntyre. *National Geographic* (December 1988): 800-817.

"Is it Too Late for the Rain Forests?," by Richard Nalley. *Science Digest* (April 1986): 56-61.

Project Panda Watch by Miriam Schlein, Atheneum, NY, 1984, is an excellent resource for teachers that clearly explains the bamboo crisis.

The Sierra Club has a pamphlet which discusses the importance of biological diversity. Write the Sierra Club, Public Affairs, 730 Polk Street, San Francisco, CA 94109.

State of the Ark: An Atlas of Conservation in Action by Lee Durrell. Doubleday, NY, 1986. An authoritative atlas of the state of the living planet and its creatures - its systems, habitats, and species, prospects for survival.

How to Save the World by Robert L. Allen. Kogan Page, London, 1980. A superb presentation of a strategy for preservation.

Managing Our Wildlife Resources by S. H. Anderson. Charles Merrill, Columbus, Ohio, 1985.

Extinction, by Paul and Anne Ehrlich. Random House, NY, 1981. This book offers one of the best treatments of the value of wildlife and the causes of extinction.

Disappearing Species: The Social Challenge by Erik Eckholm. Worldwatch Institute, Washington, D.C., 1978. One of the best overviews of the need for wildlife conservation.

"What's New at the Zoo?" by David M. Kennedy, *Technology Review* (April, 1987): 67-73. An excellent discussion of the role of zoos in breeding endangered species.

CHAPTER EIGHT

Hurt No Living Thing

Most children have a natural affection for animals and are born with a sense of curiosity and fascination about animal life. One important way for parents and teachers to teach respect towards animals is to present consistent, positive role models. If the family or classroom pet is well cared for and it holds a place of importance in the lives of the adults that the children look to for guidance, then children will be more sensitive to the needs of the animals around them.

Across the course of history, human beings have formed relationships with other animals. Some of these have been mutually beneficial, but a great many have served human needs and desires at the expense of the animals involved. It is important that our children are made aware that they, as humans, are also animals and that they share many common traits with other members of the animal kingdom. This awareness leads

All the creatures of the earth are our kin. They sleep in our cosmic home, eat at our table, share our air and water, and play with our children. We are composed of their bodies and they of ours. Each of us represents but a brief manifestation of the flow and cycling of life here. In human families we speak of blood lines, but in reality, each of us is intimately related to all the creatures of the earth.

STEVE VAN MATRE
EARTH EDUCATION: A NEW BEGINNING

A Fairy Went a Marketing, by Rose Fyleman. Illustrations by Jamichael Henterly. E. P. Dutton, NY, 1986.

Illustrated with rich and detailed paintings, this rhyming story is about a fairy who treats her animal friends with love and respect. The text is brief; for example, "A fairy went a-marketing - she bought a colored bird; it sang the sweetest, shrillest song that ever she had heard. She sat beside its painted cage and listened half the day, and then she opened wide the door and let it fly away." As she meets other animals such as a little fish, a frog, and a gentle mouse, she does a kind favor for each one. (ages 3 - 7)

to a broader spectrum of concern: children who tell us how much they love their golden retriever, who care that so many animals are abandoned every day, who want to help orphaned or injured wildlife, will become the volunteers who offer their time at animal shelters, the adults who petition the government for sanctions against whaling nations, and the parents who pass on a compassionate attitude of broad sympathies to their children. Such an attitude can help children develop the insight and understanding they will need as adults to make personal and political choices beneficial to all creatures.

Animals and People Are Alike in Many Ways

The idea that human beings are animals, made of the same stuff as our pets and other animals in the wild, may be surprising to some children. We have set ourselves apart from the natural world by living in houses, buying food in supermarkets, and purchasing our clothes from department stores, so that it is difficult to see that people and animals have some of the same characteristics and needs as the other creatures of the Earth. These activities will show your children some basic characteristics that animals and humans share.

1. Have your child lie down on a large piece of butcher paper. Draw around his or her body, creating an outline on the paper. Have your child decorate his lifesize portrait with paint, crayons, or markers in any fashion he wishes.

2. On another piece of paper, draw the image of your pet or a favorite animal of your child. Allow your child to decorate it.

3. Cut out both pictures and tape them next to each other on a wall or bulletin board. Using string, connect similar body parts, such as heads, facial features, neck, trunk, stomach, legs and toes. As you do this, talk to your child about the similarities and differences between people and animals.

We All Have Needs

All creatures have the same basic needs for survival: food, water, and shelter. Children who are well cared for may never have given this much thought. Their meals are prepared for them when they are hungry; they turn on the faucet when they are thirsty; they have a house to come into when it rains and a cozy bed in which to sleep. Here's a hands-on project that will help children think about and illustrate the similarities between people and animals.

1. Take a legal-sized sheet of paper (8½" x 14") and fold the two ends into the center, making a folded piece about 8½" x 7." Open the paper to reveal three sections.

2. Provide old magazines, scissors, and paste. Ask your child to cut from a magazine a picture of a child that looks like himself and paste it on the left section. Next, cut out a picture of a cat or dog (these animals are suggested because they are the most familiar to young children) and paste it on the right section, leaving the large middle section blank.

3. Next, ask your child to look through the magazines and cut out pictures of items that he and the animal need each day and paste them in the middle section. For example, both need food and each would enjoy fish, meat, and milk; a house would provide shelter for the child and animal; water is essential to both. Other suggestions are sunshine, toys, a hair brush, and a place to sleep.

Another way you can help your children make the connection between the needs of people and animals is by commenting on daily pet (or animal) care, such as offering fresh water and food. You might say, "It's hot today, so before we get a drink, let's give Rover (or the birds) some cool water. That way we can all have a water break!" By providing a good example and allowing your children to help care for your pet or neighboring wildlife, you will help them discover that animals have the same basic needs as people.

Do Animals Have Feelings?

Like human beings, animals react physically and emotionally to their environments. It is important that children are made aware of these feelings and learn to recognize how an animal feels by its behavior. For instance, it is wise to teach young children how an

Where the Wild Things Shouldn't Be

by Beverly Armstrong

How would you like to live in a cage that was just about ten feet square,

With no toys to play with and nothing to do - just you and a bed and a chair?

Oh, sure you'd be fed (the same thing each day), you'd have water (unless they forgot)

And since you would never be going outside, you wouldn't get cold or too hot.

But oh, you'd be lonely just sitting alone with no one to talk to all day.

You'd remember the trees, and the grass and the breeze, the places where you used to play.

You'd remember your friends, you'd remember the sky, and the games and the strawberries and sun,

And you'd know you could never go skating again or go swimming, or ride bikes, or run.

You'd get mad and scream and throw things around; you'd kick and you'd pound on the wall,

And your owners would scold you, and say to themselves, "He isn't a nice pet at all!"

animal looks when it is threatened. A cat will arch its back and raise its fur and tail, and this is usually accompanied by hissing or spitting. If children understand the cat's "language," they will most likely back away to avoid a scratch. Besides anger or fear, children should learn to recognize other animal feelings such as pain, jealousy, affection, loneliness, or nervousness.

Role playing is a good way for children to put themselves into the animal's situation and understand their possible reactions. Some young children become quite attached to a particular stuffed animal and in negative situations will reach for their imaginary pets. For example, when the toy is dropped to the floor, the child will pick it up and comfort it as if it felt pain. Encourage this type of relationship with both imaginary and live pets.

If you are a teacher, invite your students to bring in their favorite stuffed animals and provide pet care supplies in the house-keeping area for dramatic play.

Animal Feelings Charade

Before playing, write some animal situations on scrap slips of paper and place them in a hat or container. Some suggestions are:

• You are a dog and your owner gets out your leash for a walk. How do you react? (happiness)

• You are a cat and you have been locked outside in the rain. How will you feel and what will you do? (sadness)

• You are a pet rabbit and you are sitting in your owner's lap being petted gently. Show what you are feeling. (affection)

• You are a dog and have been left alone all day with no toys. How will you feel and what will you do? (loneliness)

• You are a cat and someone has pulled your tail. How do you react? (pain)

To Play: Have your children take turns pulling a situation out of the hat and acting it out for the other players. As part of their role playing, have the child include any sounds (howling, purring, growling, barking, etc.) that would be appropriate. Then ask the group to guess which feeling is being demonstrated. (If it is necessary to provide a hint, you may read the situation to the group.)

Do Animals Have Rights?

There is a rising concern in our country today about the rights of animals. While there are laws that establish minimal standards for animal welfare, animals should be treated with kindness and respected as living creatures. As parents and educators, we have the opportunity to teach by example. For instance, the love and care we give family pets is an excellent place to establish the responsibility that people have toward domesticated and wild animals. The following activities can influence children and teach them to recognize the rights of other people and animals in their lives.

• Take this opportunity to talk with your children about the rules governing your household or classroom, including how you feel animals should be treated.

• Make and illustrate a list of house rules: for example, that toys must be picked up before bath time, crayons are to be used on paper (not walls), respect must be shown for each other and belongings. Then make another list of rules for the caring and handling of pets. For instance, a pet should be given fresh water at least twice a day, time should be taken every morning and afternoon to play with and exercise your pet, or that the dog should be walked each evening.

• Tell your children that rights are basic things to which all people are entitled in order to live a happy life. Brainstorm with your children about what rights they think all people should have: love, food, clothing, a place to live, water, etc. Also, young children might say toys and parents. Ask them if they think animals have any rights? Make another list next to the "people" list and compare. Are any the same?

Being Caged

As the poem "Where the Wild Things Shouldn't Be" by Beverly Armstrong suggests, being taken from your home and being put into a cage takes the fun and quality out of life. How do the animals in the zoo feel? This is a serious question for people who care about animal welfare. Some animals appear to be content while others seem restless or bored. This activity will help your children understand and experience some of the same emotions as captive wildlife.

1. Set up a "zoo" in your play area by sectioning off cages with

The more you'd get mad, the less they would like you, the less they'd remember to care

About if you had water or if you got fed or if you were lonely in there.

And then you would know what it's like to be kept as a pet when you're meant to be free,

And you'd listen when wild things are trying to say, "Please don't make a pet out of me."

Dream Wolf, by Paul Goble. Bradbury Press, NY, 1990.

This majestic book reveals the helpful and harmonious relationship between wolves and humans. When two children wander from their camp and become lost, they are befriended by a wolf. For his kindness, the wolf is forever honored by the Indian people. The conclusion points out the sad situation existing today between men and wolves. It states, "Hunters have killed and driven them away with guns and traps and poisons. People say that the wolves will return when we. . . have the wolves in our hearts and dreams again." (ages 4 - 10)

string. Assign one child to each cage and give them a bowl to represent water and food. Tell them they cannot chat with any neighboring child. You will notice that this will be fun at first, but very soon the children will become bored and restless.

2. After a while, give each child a toy. The toy will occupy them until they exhaust it of possibilities; soon boredom and frustration will set in. Take note of behavior difficulties the children are demonstrating so you can talk about it later.

3. Finally, pair the children by putting two in each "cage." Tell them they can play and talk with their partner. What a difference this will make! You will notice the mood in your "zoo" brighten considerably. But, most likely, by this time the children will be ready to be set free.

4. After the game, gather the children around and talk about the feelings they experienced at different stages of the role playing. How did it feel being alone with just a bowl of water? When they were given a toy, did it change their feelings? When they were caged with a partner, did their mood change and in what way? Conclude the discussion by talking about how zoos can make their exhibits more fun for the animals that live there.

The Simple Things

Even caring adults may not always show respect for other living creatures. It is easy to reach for a swatter and destroy a cricket or spider that has taken up residence in your home. But it is also easy to reach for an envelope and glass and return the creature to the outdoors. (Cup the glass over the insect, then slide the envelope slowly underneath, nudging the insect gently into the temporary trap.)

Language and the media matter too. Think about the phrase "Big Bad Wolf" taught to young children from infancy! Films too have given many animals an undeserved bad name, encouraging misinformation and ill treatment. Sharks, bears, black cats, and wolves have all been maligned in folk tales and films. By increasing our awareness to the simple daily things, we can help our children grow up to be sensitive to the rights of all creatures.

Have a "Big Good Wolf" Day!

Set aside a day to celebrate the specialness of wolves. Read stories and view a video, such as *Wolf* distributed by Media Guild, that show wolves in their natural habitat or engaged in a helpful relationship with humans.

Pets

Most of your children will have little exposure to wolves, but the influence of the stereotypes in many traditional stories about "villain" coyotes, wolves, bears, foxes, snakes, etc. are enough to establish the incorrect impression that some carnivorous species are inherently "bad". . . undeserving of habitat, food, or life. Animals that children do experience include a variety of pets, whether in their home or that of a neighbor or relative. Meeting the needs of a pet (such as food, water, warmth, grooming, and medical attention) can develop the understanding that adopting an animal is not the same as buying a toy - it's assuming responsibility for a living being that must be nurtured.

Pet Care Tips

If your family or classroom has a pet, or you are thinking about possibly getting one, there are many things that need to be considered. What are the needs of the pet? Who is responsible for feeding and caring for the pet? Where will it play and sleep? Many people don't think about the responsibilities of pet ownership until it is too late. It may be hard to believe, but there have been people surprised to find themselves burdened with a huge sheepdog in a one-bedroom apartment! You might hear them say, "He was so cute and little when we got him!" The needs of any pet have to be considered before accepting that animal in your home or classroom. When you involve your children in the decision-making process, they will learn about the great amount of time and attention that is necessary to raise a pet and what their responsibilities will be. Sit down and discuss the following points with your children.

• You will need to provide your pet with the love, food, water,

The Big Good Wolf Song

Tune: London Bridge

I'm not afraid of the big good wolf,

Big good wolf, big good wolf.

I'm not afraid of the big good wolf,

He doesn't do me harm.

He has a family and five cute pups

They roll and play, roll and play.

He treats them well so they will be

Big good wolves someday!

I Really Want a Dog, by Susan Breslow and Sally Blakemore. Illustrations by True Kelley. Dutton Children's Books, NY, 1990.

A boy has a deep longing for a dog to play with and to love. Along comes a canine conscience that asks the boy, "Who will be responsible for this dog; feed it, train it, bathe and care for it?" Each time the boy responds, "Me!" Then his wish is granted. But what kind of pet will be best? This is a good story for any child who sincerely wants a pet of any kind. It points out the reality of pet ownership in a humorous way. (ages 4 - 8)

A Rabbit for Easter, by Carol Carrick. Illustrations by Donald Carrick. Greenwillow Books, NY, 1979.

Paul is entrusted with the kindergarten's pet rabbit over Easter vacation. Due to his neglect, the rabbit is lost - and luckily found a few hours later. A much wiser Paul has learned the responsibilities of pet care. (ages 4 - 8)

shelter, exercise, and health care it needs.

• If you own a cat or dog, think carefully about letting your pet have babies. Many more kittens and puppies are born than there are homes for. Consult your veterinarian for information about spaying or neutering your pet.

• Does your pet know your name and address? To assure that your pet will be returned to you should it get lost, attach an identification tag to its collar.

• Keep your pet safe in your own house or yard.

• Take your pet to see a veterinarian regularly. Dogs and cats need yearly examinations and shots to prevent certain diseases. Also, at any time if your pet appears to be ill, call or visit your veterinarian.

• Be aware of any potential dangers in your home, such as poisonous plants or stored chemicals. Keep them out of reach of your pet or remove them altogether. Some poisonous plants are azalea, holly berries, iris flowers, ivy, philodendron, and dieffenbachia leaves.

• Holly, mistletoe, and poinsettia plants are festive additions to the home during the holiday season, but if digested by an animal can cause severe abdominal pain, vomiting, and diarrhea. It is best to seek alternatives or keep these plants well out of reach.

• A pet should never be left in a closed car in warm weather. Even with the windows partly open, the temperature can reach 160° within minutes! It would be best to leave your pet at home if you intend to leave the car at all.

• Please don't let your pet travel in the open bed of a pickup truck. Dogs can't hold on the way humans can and any sudden start, stop, or turn can knock them around violently, or even toss your pet onto the roadway.

"No Chemical" Pest Control for Pets

Fleas and ticks can be an annoying problem for pets and their owners, especially during warm weather. While lots of remedies are sold in stores, many long-term pet ailments can result from the frequent use of chemicals. Here are some alternatives to chemical sprays and shampoos:

Groom Daily With a Flea Comb: These metal combs with tiny teeth are available at pet supply stores. Comb through your pet's coat daily, concentrating on back, stomach, rump, and legs. Drop any fleas into warm soapy water.

Flea Sachet for Bedding: To repel fleas, put one cup of dried mint leaves into a handkerchief or fabric scrap. Bring the corners together and tie into a bundle with string or a rubber band. Place this in the pet's bedding or wherever your animal sleeps. Regularly vacuum areas frequented by your pet and discard the bag.

Food Supplement: Supplementing commercial pet foods with fresh meat, raw and cooked vegetables, fresh fruit, cooked grains (oats, cornmeal, and cracked barley), garlic, and raw eggs can help restore a natural resistance to fleas and other parasites.

Flea Spray: Mix together ½ cup fresh or dried rosemary and one quart boiling water. Steep 20 minutes, strain, and cool. Sponge or spray onto fur and allow to air dry.

Deluxe Dog Treats

Things You Will Need: *2 cups whole wheat flour, ¼ cup cornmeal, ½ cup soy flour, 1 teaspoon bone meal, 1 teaspoon sea salt, ¼ cup sunflower seeds, 2 tablespoons vegetable oil, ¼ cup unsulfured molasses, and 2 eggs mixed with ¼ cup milk.*

1. Mix dry ingredients and sunflower seeds together.

2. Add oil, molasses, and all but 1 tablespoon egg mixture. Add more milk if necessary to make a firm dough. Knead for five minutes and let dough rest for thirty minutes.

3. Roll out dough to ½ inch thickness. Cut into shapes and brush treats with the remaining egg mixture.

4. Bake on ungreased cookie sheets for 30 minutes in a 350° oven or until lightly browned. To harden the treats even further, turn off the oven and leave the tray in the oven for another hour.

Pet Lover of the Day!

Young children enjoy caring for the family or class pet, but may not be ready for the responsibility for its fulltime care. It will be quite an honor for your child to be chosen "Pet Lover of the Day" with the task of feeding, watering, and exercising your pet. You

Scat, Scat, by Sally Francis. Putnam Group, NY, 1978.

Once there was a cute white kitten without a home. She wandered around the neighborhood only to be hit with a stick, sprayed with a hose, and swept into the street by the people she meets. Also, a big dog gives her a fright and she finally ends up in a windowbox. Luckily for her, it belongs to a little girl who gently takes her into her arms, giving the kitten the security and affection she has been searching for all day. This story reveals the loneliness and danger that any stray animal faces on the street. Its simple text and happy ending makes it a good choice for very young children. (ages 3 - 7)

could create a special badge out of scraps from the Recycle Craft Box to be worn proudly all day. Be sure to praise him for a job well done!

But We Don't Have a Pet!

By having an animal in the home, children have firsthand experience of daily care, but for some families (or classrooms) this is not a possibility. There is another option: the imaginary pet. Allow your children to role play with stuffed animal toys. Provide bowls, brushes, small "pet" toys, strings for leashes, empty food containers, bedding, etc. Pretend with your children, so they have a good example to follow, and encourage them to treat their imaginary pets with affection and tenderness. Also, many of the suggested activities for live pets can be substituted with a pretend pet by just adding a little imagination!

A Special Pet of Mine

How can young children begin to grasp the enormous responsibility of pet ownership? Certainly, by helping with the family or classroom pet, they will learn some of the ways to care for an animal. Another way is to allow them to create and care for a "pet" of their very own, around the clock!

1. Mix together 4 cups flour, 1 cup salt, and 1½ cups water. Knead for 5 minutes. Allow your children to create "pets" from dough. Dry at room temperature or bake in 350° oven for about 50 minutes.

2. After the pets are dried, provide markers, paint, glitter, yarn scraps, etc. for decoration.

3. Have the children name their pets. Sit together and allow each child to tell what is special about his or her pet to the group.

4. Next, tell your children that they are going to be responsible for their special friends all day. They must carry their pets with them when they go to school, play, eat, everything! It will be their job to protect them from harm or injury, and not to lose them.

5. After your children have had the experience of caring for their "pets," sit down with them and discuss some of the difficulties they faced during the day.

Alternative: Older children may decorate hard-boiled egg "pets." Fragility will add a special dimension to their supervision, making the children even more attentive to careful handling. (Eggs are not recommended for young children for this reason, and because at the end of the day the egg will have to be disposed of, making it necessary to break a bond that may have formed during the day.)

Lost and Looking for Love

Scat, Scat Live!

The story of *Scat, Scat* by Sally Francis is very easy to act out, needing very few props. It's even more fun with a cat puppet, if one is available. Help your children organize a play for neighbors or schoolmates. They'll enjoy themselves and at the same time spread the word about proper pet care.

Help, I'm Lost

Children can understand the fear, confusion, and panic that result from being lost, even for a moment. These times are not quickly forgotten and can be a base of understanding for how a lost animal might feel in a strange neighborhood.

1. Ask your children to relate stories about a time when they were actually lost or couldn't find their parents in a store, at a park, in a large group of people, etc. Ask questions: How did you feel? What did your parents do?

2. Shift the discussion to the problems faced by lost or abandoned animals. Can they tell someone where they live? Talk about the importance of identification tags.

3. Encourage your children to write and illustrate a story about a lost pet. What dangers does it face while lost? Does the story have a happy ending?

Visit an Animal Shelter

Arrange to take your children to a local animal shelter to meet the people who work there and learn about animal care.

Pets Without Homes, by Caroline Arnold. Photographs by Richard Hewett. Clarion Books, NY, 1983.

Buffy is a lost and lonely puppy. Max is a cat whose owner has moved to a place where he cannot keep him. Buffy and Max are pets without homes. Here is a look at an animal shelter and the people who work there. What happens to animals like Buffy and Max? This book takes you through the step-by-step procedure from when a stray is picked up by "the pound" to when he is finally released to a new family. Before you decide to buy a pet, read this book and, chances are, you will want to "adopt" a dog or cat who needs a loving home. (ages 5 - 10)

My Lost Dog Song

Tune: Where, Oh Where Has My Little Dog Gone?

Where, oh where, has my little dog gone? *(hand over eyes, searching)*

Oh where, oh where can he be?

I forgot to close the garden gate, *(hands on head in despair)*

And he ran away from me. *(pretend hand is dog running away)*

I searched the park and I searched the school. *(hand over eyes, searching)*

Oh where, oh where can he be?

I called out his name in the neighborhood *(cup hands around mouth)*

And my dog came running to me! *(pretend hand is dog running to you)*

He jumped on me and I gave him a hug, *(pretend to hug dog)*

And I noticed the time was late. *(tap wrist)*

I attached his leash and we headed for home, *(pretend to walk)*

You can bet I closed that gate! *(shake index finger, pointedly)*

~ Prepare questions for the staff ahead of time.

~ Find out from the workers what items are most needed for the animals in the shelters.

~ Upon returning, write an experience story about the field trip. Afterward, send a letter to thank the staff for their time and helpfulness.

~ Talk with your children about what they saw at the shelter.

Have an Unbirthday Party!

After visiting an animal shelter, have a party for the lost and lonely animals! Bring any needed items such as blankets, pet toys, food, dog biscuits, collars, etc. You might want to view the movie, *The Incredible Journey* produced by Walt Disney Home Video, and afterward talk about a pet's great devotion to its owner. For refreshments make ginger cookies in the shape of dog bones.

Chain Story Circle

Have you ever been part of a chain story? It's entertaining to see how each player's imagination adds adventure or fantasy to the tale. Who knows where the story will lead? That's part of the fun! Gather your children in a circle and begin the game by reading one of these story starters, then let the children continue adding to the adventure one by one. (Encourage creativity but discourage violence in the story.) If one is available, pass a puppet from child to child so the group has a focal point.

• Yesterday, my owner took me on a ride in the car. I love to look out at the passing traffic and slobber on the window! She pulled into a parking lot and got out to mail a letter, and since she left the door open, I followed her. Someone had dropped an ice cream cone on the sidewalk so I went over to lick it up. I didn't notice that my owner had gotten back in the car, and I guess she didn't see that I was missing, because she drove off! Everything was unfamiliar around me, but I knew I had to find my way home. So I started walking down the street. . . .

• My favorite thing to do with my owner is to take an evening walk. He says that I am a very obedient animal, so he never puts a leash on me. This evening, we walked down to the supermarket to get some milk. He told me to stay near the door and wait for him. He went inside and was away for a very long time. I watched people coming and going, hoping he would return soon. Every time the door opened I peeked in to see if my owner was there. Finally, I couldn't wait any longer. . . .

• I thought it would be fun to go with my owners on their vacation. They packed their bags and talked excitedly about the trip on the plane. Then I realized that one of their bags wasn't a bag at all! It was a cage for me. This morning, when it was time to go, my owners had to chase me all over the house before they finally caught me and stuffed me into the small box and closed the door. I cried and scratched at the bars, but they wouldn't let me out. So, here I am at the airport, being bumped by luggage and heading down the conveyor belt. I'm so scared, what will happen to me? . . .

Share Some Quiet Time

Quiet time is a necessity, especially in a society where our time is structured from morning until night. All people need time alone to rest, think, plan, discover, and dream; children are no exception. These days, children with time alone usually spend it in front of the television, their minds filled with someone else's thoughts. As parents and educators, we need to make sure that we leave enough time free for our children to reflect about the world around them and discover its beauty and mystery. Only then will a bond be created with the natural world to be carried throughout a lifetime.

• Occasionally, take a rest period outdoors. Allow your children to take a mat or blanket and find a space for themselves. Tell them that this is a time for thinking and exploring with their eyes, and later they can share their experiences with you or their friends.

• For children who need a focal point, try lying in a fragrant and soft patch of clover. Ask them to quietly search for four-leaf clovers.

• Another exciting focal point is an anthill. Children are fascinated by the flurry of ants traveling to and from the mound.

• Take the story *Quiet* by Peter Parnall a step further. Allow your children to find a special spot in a natural setting and actually become a part of it! Have them lie down and cover their bodies with leaves, fallen twigs, or pine needles, leaving only their faces

Play With Me, by Marie Hall Ets. Viking Press, NY, 1955.

A little girl takes a walk through the meadow asking the animals to play with her. She tries to catch a grasshopper, a frog, a turtle, a chipmunk, a blue jay, a rabbit, and even a snake. But each time she approaches, they run away. Discouraged, she sits down by a pond to watch a bug and, one by one, the animals come out to sit with her. She remains very still, without making a sound, and soon a baby fawn comes near and licks her cheek. The little girl's example. will teach your children the benefits of blending into the scene when trying to observe nature. (ages 3 - 6)

Quiet, by Peter Parnall. Morrow Junior Books, NY, 1989.

This is a beautifully illustrated book about a boy lying quietly on the ground and waiting for animals to come near. After a while birds, a mouse, and chipmunks climb on him. (age 5 and up)

visible. The sensation of being part of the Earth will engage them even further into a relationship with their natural surroundings.

• Set aside an indoor location that belongs to your child and encourages quiet reflection. It might be the corner of an attic, a screened-off area, even a walk-in closet decorated by your child.

D R E A M S T A R T E R

Winter is coming. You can feel it in the cool morning hours. It takes longer each day for the warmth from the sun to heat up the air. Something inside of you whispers into your ear, "It's time to go." It is time to follow your flock south in search of warmer weather. You look around at all the delicious seeds and grubs. It's hard to believe the other birds when they tell you that soon the leaves will fall and food will be hard to find. You tell them you won't go. "There's no need to fly to a faraway place, because there's so much food right here!" You watch as the flock takes off one by one and falls into a large group, but you don't follow them. The mass of birds in the sky becomes smaller and smaller, until they are so distant that you lose sight of them completely.

Weeks go by and each day you fill yourself on all the juicy worms, grubs, and crunchy seeds you can find. You are not alone, because many birds decided to stay and you make many new friends around the bird bath. One night a chilling wind and freezing rain covers the city. Within days the few remaining autumn leaves fall from the trees. And it isn't long before a cold, wet snow falls and covers the Earth like a blanket. You remember their warning and discover the flock was right. Food is very hard to find and all of the birds begin to fight over the tiniest bits. You know you will have to find

Salt Hands, by Jane Chelsea Aragon. Illustrations by Ted Rand. Dutton, NY, 1989.

This is a simple but magic story of a moonlit night when a little girl wakes to find a deer in her yard. Cupping salt in her hands, she tiptoes outside and waits as the gentle creature comes closer and closer. This is a tale that captures perfectly a moment of communion between the human and animal worlds. (ages 4 - 8)

something to eat or you will starve. So you go off alone, away from the bickering, hoping to find a morsel to ease the gnawing inside your body.

You land on the edge of the bird bath and peck at the frozen water. Even a refreshing drink is hard to find! So you take gulps of snow and swallow, making your insides shiver with cold. Suddenly, you hear a peculiar sound. But where is it coming from? You look around and see a child spreading seeds upon his windowsill. He calls to you cheerfully, "Come here, birdie. Do you want some food?" He leaves the window open and stands nearby to watch.

Yes, you need food, but can this human child be trusted not to harm you? You cautiously hop closer, looking for signs of danger. You see the delicious, earthy seeds on the sill. You are so hungry you decide to take the risk. You fly to the ledge and begin pecking rapidly, keeping your eye on the child. He stands quite still, just watching you eat for a long time. After a while, you notice him step nearer, but the food is more important. Finally, his face is right next to yours and he reaches his soft hand out to stroke your wing. "There, sweet bird." His whispering voice calms your fear. You look directly into his eyes and chirp with gratitude. You know you've made a new, although very different, kind of friend today. "Come back tomorrow," he says quietly, "and you can have more!"

Bird Watching

In most communities, birds are probably the most abundant type of wildlife and can be easily observed. For young children, it isn't necessary to identify species and label them by name, but just enjoy watching them fly about, searching for food, and nesting in the spring. If your children are interested in learning the names of common birds, there are some identification guides written especially for children.

Natural Bird Feeders

For centuries it has been a custom to hang food for the birds on trees. Here are some ideas that you and your children can do together to provide much needed food and fat for hungry winter birds.

Anna's Rain, by Fred Burstein. Illustrations by Harvey Stevenson. Orchard Books, NY, 1990.

Outside it's cold and wet, and night is coming. Anna knows the birds are waiting to be fed even though it is raining. Her daddy carries her and the bird seed out to the feeder just as it begins to sleet. Back in the warm house, they know happily that the birds won't go hungry, thanks to Anna! (ages 3 - 6)

The Bird Tree, by Frans Van Anrooy. Harcourt Brace and World, Inc., NY, 1966.

This is a Christmas story but goes much beyond being a holiday book. A young boy and his grandmother have no money for ornaments, so they decorate their tree with only berries and nuts. When they awaken, they see the most beautiful Christmas tree they have ever seen, one absolutely filled with every color bird one could imagine. What follows perfectly illustrates the need to be kind and compassionate to all creatures, as well as the communion that can be reached between animals and humans. (ages 5 - 9)

• Pine Cone Feeder: Take a pine cone and spread suet or peanut butter on its sides. Roll it in bird seed and hang it on a tree branch, making sure that any visiting bird will have a perch to rest upon while feeding.

• Dried Fruit Garland: Dried fruit is a favorite of some birds. Using a blunt needle and dental floss, string some dried figs, apricots, apples, fresh cranberries, and toasted oat cereal. Drape the garland on a tree for the hungry birds.

• Suet Log: Find a small log. Adult: Chisel or drill holes up and down its sides or attach soda bottle caps with hammer and nails. Allow your child to help fill the holes or caps with suet. Another method is to melt the suet and pour it on a log. Allow to cool. Suspend from a sturdy branch.

• Sunflower Heads: Hang dried sunflower heads upside-down. The birds will peck out the tasty seeds.

Gather Your Own Bird Food

The common plants, referred to as weeds, provide food for many species of birds. Gather some from unweeded gardens, parks, meadows, and school yards. You can either hang a bunch of weeds from a tree or strip the seeds into your feeder. Some favorites are ragweed, knotweed, lamb's quarters, and dock.

Make Bird Boxes

Many cities have eliminated nesting sites for birds such as bluebirds, woodpeckers, tree swallows, and chickadees by removing the dead trees that these birds prefer. But there is a solution that is a fun and easy project for home or school: building and setting out bird boxes. Bird boxes must meet some specific building requirements, or birds will not use them. Here are some general rules to follow:

• Do not just make "bird boxes;" create them for a specific species, such as bluebird or chickadee. The opening holes must be a certain size to attract a specific species. This also provides protection from egg snatchers, such as raccoons or opossums.

• Bird "apartments" work best for martins. Most birds demand their privacy and will drive other birds away.

• The best material to use is wood. Never use any type of metal,

W hen the bird and the book disagree, always believe the bird.

BIRDWATCHER'S PROVERB

such as a tin can, because the heat will build up inside and make it too hot for the birds to survive.

• The houses should be hung from branches, attached to trunks or placed on poles. Don't crowd the houses, because only about three to an acre will be used.

• Houses should be cleaned after each season. So make certain that either the top or bottom of the box is hinged for easy access.

For more information about specific recommendations, contact the United States Department of Agriculture or The North American Bluebird Society, Box 6295, Silver Spring, MD 20906-0295.

Create a Bird Sanctuary

In addition to bird feeders and boxes, there are two other ways to attract birds to your backyard. First is by adding a bird bath and the second is to plant food shrubs of various kinds.

Bird Baths: Ceramic or concrete bird baths are available at garden centers or stores that sell outdoor furniture and ornaments. Another less expensive and more rewarding alternative is to make one with your children using scraps from the garage.

Things You Will Need: *a 4 foot long post (4" x 4"), a garbage can lid with the handle removed, rubber washers, and three long screws.*

1. Drive the post into the ground, making sure that it stands perfectly straight.

2. Fasten the lid to the top of the post with three screws. Place a washer on the screw before pushing it through the garbage lid. To prevent leaks, make sure the screws are tightened securely.

3. Find a large stone or brick to place inside the bird bath as a resting perch.

4. Fill with water and be patient, it may take a week or more for the birds to find their new watering hole. Change the water every few days.

Food Shrubs: To plant bushes that provide food for the birds, it is not necessary to have a large yard. A few shrubs here or there will do the trick. They furnish shelter and food for many types of birds and are attractive to the eye. Some suggestions are: dogwood trees, wild rose, blueberries, blackberries, and raspberries.

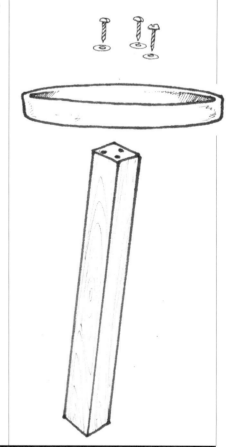

The Tiny Patient, by Judy Pedersen. Alfred A. Knopf, NY, 1989.

A young girl and her grandmother find a chirping sparrow with a broken wing. They carefully pick her up, wrapped in a handkerchief, and take her into their warm house to nurse her back to health. They make a sickbed nest for the bird and set it in a sunny window. They care for her day after day until her health is restored. Then one summer morning, she is returned to her friends in the wild. With luminous drawings and simple text, this story evokes a mood of tenderness as we witness the girl and her grandmother care for their tiny patient. (ages 4 - 8)

Sebastian Lives in a Hat, by Thelma Catterwell. Illustrations by Kerry Argent. Kane/Miller, 1990.

After the death of his mother, a baby wombat lives in a hat and is cared for by humans. (ages 3 - 6)

Orphaned Wildlife

In the spring, you may find injured or abandoned baby birds. It is a child's natural response to want to care for them and feed them until they are strong enough to be set free. But without training, many adults don't know how to care for the tiny and helpless creatures and wonder if they are better left alone. In fact, if you do take an injured or abandoned animal into your home, you need to be aware that you are responsible for its life. These stories and helpful hints may aid you if ever you are faced with this sometimes frustrating and precarious dilemma.

Wild Bird Care

• If you find a bird without feathers, locate the nest and replace the bird. The parents will continue to feed it, even if you have touched it. If you can not locate the nest, fill a strawberry basket with dried grass and nail it to the tree trunk, then place the bird gently in the basket.

• If you find a young bird with feathers, not apparently injured, leave it alone. In late spring and summer, many young birds are learning to fly and accidently find themselves earthbound during a lesson. The parents will return later and continue instruction, if the young bird is left alone.

• If the bird is injured, place it in a basket or box lined with tissue paper. Change the paper regularly. Keep the box in a warm place and away from drafts because birds are very susceptible to respiratory infections. If it is cool inside your house, you can place a heating pad on the floor of the box and set on low only. Call a veterinarian for assistance.

• To feed an injured bird, mix canned cat food with enough water to make a liquid. Feed it to the bird with an eyedropper directly into its mouth. Older birds can be fed small chunks with a pair of tweezers. Feed every 30-45 minutes, but don't worry about feeding at night. If the bird is young, encourage self-feeding by holding food in front of its face, then placing it directly on the ground. If the bird refuses to eat, take it to a veterinarian specializing in bird care.

How to Help Orphaned or Injured Wildlife

The best thing you can do with apparently orphaned birds and wildlife is to leave them alone. In most cases, the parents have left the nest in search for food and will return shortly. There are cases in which the mother will abandon its young because it senses some illness or defect and knows the baby will die. If you are certain that an animal has been orphaned or injured and you wish to help, here are some basic guidelines:

• If you find an injured animal, don't try to care for it yourself. It needs special attention from a trained professional. Seek out a wildlife rehabilitation center or call a veterinarian as soon as possible.

• Only if professional help is unavailable, line a box with a heating pad and tissue paper. Set the temperature on low only and place the animal in the box.

• To feed a baby mammal, mix together 1 part evaporated milk, 1 part water, and ½ teaspoon of corn syrup. Warm over low heat and test on your wrist (it should be the same temperature as for a human infant). Holding the animal upright, feed with an eye dropper or doll's bottle every four hours through the day and night. If it has no fur, it should be fed every 2-3 hours.

Death of a Pet

The death of a family pet is like the death of a much loved relative. For young children this time can be confusing. If they have never experienced a death in the family, they will not know what it is to grieve. Allow your children time alone to cry, sort their thoughts, and remember the happy times with their pet. Here are some ways to help your children express their feelings and, at the same time, honor the memory of a special family member:

• Help your children create a scrapbook full of photographs and drawn pictures to remember special moments with their pet. Write any comments your children may feel are appropriate, such as, "Here we are in the backyard playing ball. It was Rover's favorite game," or "Sandy loved the water and would jump right into the pool with us!" This project will help your child sort through sad feelings by focusing on happy occasions.

The bird of paradise alights only upon the hand that does not grasp.

JOHN BERRY

A Hunter and His Dog, by Brian Wildsmith. Oxford University Press, Walton Street, Oxford, 1979.

Though trained to retrieve fallen birds for his master, a dog finds he is too kind-hearted for this work. Instead, he sets up a medical station for the wounded birds and returns each evening to care for them. His master discovers what is going on and is overcome with compassion for the very animals which he has hunted. (ages 4 - 8)

The Gnats of Knotty Pine, by Bill Peet. Houghton Mifflin Co., Boston, 1975.

This book is dedicated by the author "to my young friends who love toy guns with the hope that you won't grow up to love real guns and real bullets that kill real things." The story illustrates in an amusing, but meaningful, way the plight of a group of forest animals the day before hunting season begins. It points out very clearly that man often takes advantage of the animal world in a brutal and unfair manner. But it ends on a happy note when the tiny gnats of the forest, cooperating as a unit, run the hunters out of the forest so that all the animals can resume their normal lives. (ages 4 - 10)

• Read a story about the death of a pet, such as *The Tenth Good Thing About Barney* by Judith Viorst or *I'll Always Love You* by Hans Wilhelm. After reading the book, talk and listen to your children about their feelings. Also, take this time to express your feelings of sadness so that your children realize that they are not alone in their grief.

• Help your children write a story or poem about the pet. Or, if desired, write a prayer thanking God for all the good times and for allowing the pet to be such a special part of your lives.

• Prepare a memorial ceremony. Have the family members stand or sit in a circle. Pass around a candle or a personal item of your pet, such as a collar or toy and allow each person to tell something about the pet they will always remember.

Attitudes About Hunting

Humane organizations and many individuals are taking a strong stand against hunting, encouraging instead non-violent alternatives such as bird watching, hiking, camping, and wildlife photography. There was a time when humans depended on meat and hides from animals for survival. Today, very few societies maintain their lives by hunting, and certainly in our society, it is rarely a necessity. Hunting is now primarily considered a recreational "sport," even to the hunters who use the meat of the animals they kill. We feel that this is a powerful subject for very young children, and suggest that parents and teachers use caution when approaching this topic. Several book suggestions in this chapter demonstrate quite well the animals' side of this issue. Be aware that children are very sensitive when hearing about or seeing an animal injured or killed. You need to take time to talk with your children about your views concerning this controversial subject.

Read and Decide

After reading *Harold and the Great Stag* by Donald Carrick, talk with your children about the events in the story. How did Harold feel about the Great Stag? How did the hunters view the stag? Was

Harold surprised to discover that the hunters wanted to hunt and kill him? What risk did he take to save the Stag? What happened to make Harold realize what it felt like to be hunted? How would you feel in that situation? How did Harold feel when he heard the Great Stag still ran free? What is this story saying about hunting? What does this story make you think about?

The Hunter vs. the Animals

To explore their feelings about hunting, children need to discover and understand both sides of the issue. Role playing is an excellent and safe technique for children to experience such a situation. *(Note: This activity is not recommended for very young children, immature children, or children with a tendency towards violence. In more mature children, it can evoke feelings similar to those experienced by hunters and hunted animals.)* The children must exchange places to experience both sides and, to complete this activity, discuss their reaction to the game.

1. Tell your children that this is only a game and that afterward, you will listen to their thoughts about their experiences. Divide the children into two groups: the hunters and the animals.

2. Designate a large playing area, and if possible, include some shrubs or trees for concealment. Tell the children that no one is allowed to leave these boundaries.

3. Give "the animals" about five minutes to scatter and hide.

4. At the signal, "the hunters" go out to tag any animals they can find. When "an animal" is tagged, they must lie down at that spot for the remainder of the game, pretending to be injured or killed.

5. After about 10-15 minutes, call the children back to the base. Switch the groups and repeat the game.

After the children have experienced both sides of the game, gather them around and talk about their feelings. Here are some suggested questions:

• How did it feel to be the person who hunted the animals? According to the rules, when you tagged "an animal," they immediately were injured or killed; how did that make you feel?

• How did it feel to be the hunted animal? When you were found and being chased, what emotions did you experience? Besides

Harold and the Great Stag, by Donald Carrick. Clarion Books, NY, 1988.

When Harold, who lives in England during the Middle Ages, hears that the Baron and his royal hunters are planning to hunt the legendary Great Stag, he devises a clever scheme to protect the animal. During the hunt, he climbs into the branches of a tree to hide himself from the men and their dogs. Having been covered with the Stag's scent, the dogs follow his trail and begin to bark ferociously and leap toward the branches. At that moment, Harold knows the terror and panic of being hunted. In the end, the plan works and the Stag continues to run free. (ages 5 - 9)

hiding or running, did you have any other way to protect yourself from the hunters?

• Who had the most power in the game, the hunters or the animals? Do you think the situation was fair? Why or why not?

• What is this game trying to teach you about hunting? (After the discussion, let the children silently draw their own conclusions about the hunting controversy.)

Where Does Fur Come From?

Many products are made from fur or hides from animals, such as gloves, shoes, coats, sweaters, hats, and even some expensive stuffed animals. Most children do not know where these items come from and are unaware that some animals are killed for their natural coats. In the case of a wool sweater, the sheep is not harmed since its coat is sheared. But for items, such as a raccoon tail cap, rabbit muff and hat, or fur coat, the animal must be killed for its fur.

There are two ways that the fur is taken – one, often painful to the animal, is by trapping. Other animals, such as mink and fox, are raised on "fur farms." If you think these uses of fur are unnecessary and cause cruel treatment of animals, here are some things you can do:

• Teach your children about the origins of clothing and accessories. Cut pictures from magazines of different types of clothing: cloth, wool, fur, leather, and exotic skins such as alligator or snake. Talk to your children about where these clothes originate, from plant or animal. Share your thoughts with your children about the fur controversy.

• Set an example for your children. Refrain from buying things made from animal fur or skins, such as alligator shoes or boots, fur coats, even something as small as a rabbit's foot key chain.

• If your friends or other family members don't know where fur comes from, tell them. For suggestions about alternatives to fur, see *Fuzz Does It* by Vicki Cobb in the "Resources" section of this chapter.

Get Involved!

Simple Things You Can Do

Just by becoming more aware of the animals and wildlife around them, children will learn to be more respectful of these creatures. Here are some very easy life changes that you and your family can make to benefit the well-being of animal life:

1. If you have a pet, make sure that its needs for food, water, exercise, and especially love are met every day. Take your pet to visit a veterinarian regularly.

2. Attach an identification tag to your pet's collar. To avoid losing your pet in an accident, never allow it to roam freely in the neighborhood. Always walk your dog on a leash.

3. Consider having your pet neutered or spayed to avoid bringing more animals into this world than there are people to care for them.

4. Learn to enjoy wild animals in their natural habitats. Never choose a wild animal as a pet, as they have special needs that humans cannot meet.

5. In most cases, you should not try to help an abandoned or injured wild animal. It could carry a disease that could make you ill or could hurt you out of fear. Call a local nature center, animal shelter, or veterinarian for assistance.

6. Build and take care of birdhouses, feeders, and baths. To find out how to recycle containers into bird feeders, write "Recycle for the Birds," National Wildlife Federation, Dept. FB, 8925 Leesburg Pike, Vienna, VA 22184-0001.

7. Fence off vegetable gardens. Grow extra lettuce, carrots, and greens in another part of the yard for small animals to eat, so they won't disturb your main crop.

8. Pick up discarded trash along streams, in woods, and on beaches. Garbage can hurt wildlife when it is swallowed or if animals become tangled in it. Always cut apart the plastic rings from soft drink six-packs.

9. Offer to walk a senior citizen's dog.

"Animals are not brethren, they are not underlings; they are other nations, caught with ourselves in the net of life and time."

HENRY BESTON

Animal Welfare Institute

The Animal Welfare Institute publishes two booklets on caring for pets called *Kittens and Cats* and *You and Your Dog*. These booklets cost 25¢ each, so just send a letter with the quarters taped to it to:

Animal Welfare Institute
P.O. Box 3650
Washington, D.C. 20007

Humane Society

The Humane Society of the United States is committed to the goal of ending animal suffering and provides brochures on many subjects concerning the welfare of animals. Membership is $10.00 a year and all donations are tax-deductible. Available titles include *Pets, Captive Wildlife, Hunted Wildlife, Farm Animals, Unwanted Animals*, and *Companion Animals*. Request a list of informational publications on the subject of animal welfare. Send a self-addressed and stamped envelope to:

The Humane Society of the
United States
2100 L Street, N.W.
Washington, D.C. 20037

10. Carry an insect outside instead of killing it.

11. Refrain from buying items made from fur or exotic animal skins; cloth items are a humane alternative.

12. Show respect and kindness to all animals, even the ones you don't like. Give your favorite animal friend a hug today!

Start a "Kind Club"

If you know of a teacher, scout leader, or librarian in your area that cares about animals, he or she can help you start a club to promote humane treatment of animals. First, organize a few friends and their children who are interested in animals. Here are some suggested activities to do with the children:

• Read stories or view videos that promote good feelings about animals in their natural habitat. Subscribe to *Kind News* through the Humane Society of the United States (see "Resources for Parents and Teachers") and use it as a focal point for your meetings.

• Invite a guest from the local animal welfare organization to speak to your group or take a field trip to the animal shelter in your area.

• Organize fundraising activities, such as a garage sale, used book and toy sale, or bake sale. Donate the money to an organization that supports the humane treatment of animals or make a donation to your local animal shelter.

• Provide paint and poster board. Allow the children to create posters that promote positive animal treatment and care to be displayed at the local library or in the hallways of the school building.

• Build bird boxes and feeders for the children to put in their own yards or on school grounds. In the winter, string dried fruit, berries, and cereal to drape on the bare trees.

• Learn about first aid for pets. Allow the children to role play emergency situations using stuffed animal toys.

Animal Lessons on Television

As parents and teachers, we need to choose programming for our children that will promote a healthy attitude about animals. For very young children, programs such as *Mister Rogers' Neighborhood*,

Sesame Street , and *Captain Kangaroo* on PBS are concerned about this issue and air segments about people and pets, wild animals in their natural habitat, and interviews with animal care professionals. For older children, PBS airs many regular programs and specials about animals, such as *Nature, Wild America,* and *The National Geographic Specials.* Sit down with your children and watch television together; then talk or answer any questions they may have regarding the program.

Action for Animals

If you and your family are concerned about animal rights, the fur and hunting controversy, ethical treatment of laboratory animals, etc. there is an organization that addresses these powerful issues. They publish an organization newsletter and a special version for grade school through high school age children called *PeTA Kids.* For more information, write PeTA (People for the Ethical Treatment of Animals), P.O. Box 42516, Washington, D.C. 20015-0516. Ask for *The PeTA Guide to Action for Animals* and the latest issue of *PeTA Kids.* They also provide information packets, cards, and fliers on subjects such as product testing, the fur industry, and factory farming.

Celebrate World Vegetarian Day

Every year on October 1st, picked because it is the day before Gandhi's birthday, World Vegetarian Day is celebrated. Gandhi practiced Hinduism, a religion whose followers are vegetarians and who try to live without harming any living thing - human or animal. Have a party featuring vegetarian, non-animal snacks (your guests probably won't even notice until you tell them) and explain that on this special day we eat lower on the food chain in honor of animals. Have party favors and games having to do with animals and the special place they hold in our lives.

Orphaned and Injured Wildlife, Inc.

Orphaned and Injured Wildlife, Inc. is a non-profit organization that cares for animals needing special medical attention or nurturing until they are able to care for themselves in the wild. They publish a newsletter twice a year and accept tax-deductible donations, and food or material donations. For more information, write:

Orphaned and Injured Wildlife, Inc.
Rural Route Box 5650
Spirit Lake, IA 51360

More Books To Share With Children

Otto the Bear by Ivan Gantschev. Translated from the German by Karen M. Klockner, Little, Brown and Co., Boston, 1985. Otto lives up in the mountains, but he frequently visits an old woodsman who gladly shares with him fruit from his garden. A new family moves in and builds a fence to keep Otto from the grounds. The story of how the new woodsman and Otto become friends is one example of harmony between man and the animal world. (ages 5 - 8)

Christmas Day Kitten by James Herriot. Illustrations by Ruth Brown. St. Martin's Press, NY, 1986. The famous veterinarian/writer shares the true story of how an independent-minded stray cat gives a woman and her three basset hounds a Christmas present. Other books by Herriot, all of which portray a compassionate attitude towards animals, include *Moses the Kitten, Only One Woof, Bonny's Big Day,* and *The Market Square Dog.* (all ages)

Where Does the Brown Bear Go? by Nicki Weiss. Greenwillow Books, 1989. This is a good-night book for preschoolers that will foster love of all animals. (ages 3 - 5)

Huge Harold by Bill Peet. Houghton Mifflin Co., Boston 1961. Huge Harold is no ordinary rabbit since he is the size of a cow! With no place to hide from hunters and dogs, he runs from one place to another looking for refuge. He finally ends up in a hayloft and is discovered by the farmer who then protects, feeds, and cares for him. (ages 4 - 8)

The Snuggle Bunny by Nancy Jewell. Illustrations by Mary Chalmers. Harper and Row, NY, 1972. "Once there was a snuggle bunny with no other bunnies to snuggle against." So he set out to find someone just for himself. He couldn't find any other bunnies, but he did find a lonely old man and he snuggled up against him making both of them happy. (ages 3 - 6)

Listen to Your Kitten Purr by Lilo Hess. Charles Scribner's Sons, NY, 1980. This is the story of Mindy, a female tabby cat, typical of thousands of homeless cats who wander streets and alleyways. It tells of the attempted drowning of her kittens by uncaring people and of her adoption, after being abandoned, by a family who cared for her and decided to do their part to stop the cycle by having Mindy spayed. This is a sensitive book that helps children to see and understand the tragic plight of abandoned animals and what people can do to help. (Documented by photos-including the birth of the kittens. For older children, ages 8 - 12.)

Cat's Nine Lives by Lilo Hess. Charles Scribner's Sons, NY, 1984. This story chronicles the nine lives of Misty, a purebred Persian cat, from her birth in a cattery through several owners, a stint as a show cat, a stay at an animal shelter, and a period of homelessness. Finally, Misty finds a good home with a loving family. (ages 8 - 12)

Lonesome Little Colt by C. W. Anderson. Collier Books, NY, 1961. The lonesome little colt has no mother and the other colts will not let him near theirs. His life becomes a little brighter when a little boy and girl notice his unhappiness and give him some extra attention and love. (ages 5 - 8)

The Nest: An Ecology Story Book by Chris Baines. Illustrations by Penny Ives. Crocodile Books, NY, 1990. We watch as two birds carefully build their nest in an apple tree just beginning to bud. They are sure the nest is safe, hidden in the lovely blossoms. Two children carelessly allow their kitten to climb the tree to the nest sending the entire bird family into an uproar. The book ends happily, but points out that we must be more thoughtful and aware of other creatures and their homes. (ages 4 - 8)

A Bag Full of Pups by Dick Gackenbach. Clarion Books, NY, 1981. You can see how we depend on and appreciate our pets in this simple story. (ages 3 - 6)

Lost in the Storm by Carol and Donald Carrick. Seabury Press, NY, 1974. When Christopher and his friend Gray are playing in the sand, Christopher's dog, Bodger, trots off down the beach. It begins to rain and the boys run to Gray's house, thoughtlessly forgetting about Bodger. The result, as the storm becomes fierce, is that the dog is left out all night as Christopher worries and frets about his pet's safety. The story teaches the need for a sense of responsibility in the care of a pet. (ages 6 - 10)

The Accident by Carol and Donald Carrick. Seabury Press, NY, 1976. It was getting dark by the time Christopher and his dog, Bodger, neared the lake to meet his parents. Then Christopher heard the pick-up truck coming down the road. The accident that followed wasn't anyone's fault, but later the grieving Christopher blamed himself. It was only when his father suggested that they find a suitable stone for Bodger's grave that Christopher found a satisfying way to express his grief. *The Accident* is a story of loss told with sensitivity and feeling. (ages 7 - 10)

The Foundling by Carol Carrick. Illustrations by Donald Carrick. Houghton Mifflin, Clarion Books, NY, 1977. Memories of his dog, killed in an accident, cause Christopher to resist his parents' efforts to adopt a puppy from the animal shelter. But while out on his bicycle, he finds a lost puppy and establishes a special relationship with him. It is only then that he can allow another pet into his heart. (ages 6 - 10)

Perfect the Pig by Susan Jeschke. Holt, Rinehart & Winston, NY, 1981. Perfect the Pig's wish for wings is granted but ends up causing him to be exploited by a greedy man. With the help of a young, sympathetic girl, Perfect finds out that some humans do care. (ages 4 - 9)

Nobody's Cat by Miska Miles. Illustrations by John Schoenherr. Little Brown & Co., Boston, 1969. Nobody's cat is tough, scrappy, and wise in the ways of city streets and fending for himself. He lives in a box in an alley and feeds himself from handouts and trash cans. His story will make young readers much more sensitive to the plight of abandoned animals. (ages 7 - 10)

Somebody's Dog by Miska Miles. Illustrations by John Schoenherr. Little Brown & Co., Boston, 1973. A big, silver dog becomes separated from his owner at the beach and goes searching for some dinner when his tummy feels empty. (ages 7 - 10)

Dogs and More Dogs by Bianca Bradbury. Illustrations by Robert MacLean. Houghton Mifflin Co., NY, 1968. It is the story of a group of boys and girls who decide they want to help the animals of their town by starting an Animal Welfare Club. The ups and downs of the club members, often quite funny, point out our responsibility for the welfare of the animals in our lives. (read-aloud, ages 6 - 10)

Much Ado About Aldo by Johanna Hurwitz. Illustrations by John Wallner. William Morrow and Co., NY, 1978. Aldo Sossi, eight years old, is a lover of animals and interested in everything. He is very excited when his teacher announces a project on the relationship of man and animals. The first phase of the project introduces crickets to carefully prepared terrariums placed in the back of the classroom. Then, however, chameleons also arrive, and Aldo realizes that the relationship they are studying is that between consumer and consumed. He is so shocked that he gives up eating meat and embarks on a desperate attempt to save the crickets. This is a wonderful read-aloud book. (ages 6 - 10)

A Wolf Story by David McPhail. Charles Scribner's Sons, NY, 1981. In this moving story of children's understanding of their animal brothers, a timber wolf is captured and taken from his home in the North Woods. The story tells how he regained his freedom and of the children who helped him. (ages 5 - 9)

Come With Me by Ashley Wolff. Dutton, NY, 1990. This story captures the joy and wonder of a boy's first walk with his new puppy - and of the world they will be sharing together. (ages 3 - 7)

The Mare on the Hill by Thomas Locker. Dial Books, NY, 1985. This book presents a beautiful story about a mare who previously has been abused and the two children who painstakingly gain her trust. (all ages)

The Dead Bird by Margaret Wise Brown. Illustrations by Remy Charlip. Young Scott Books, a division of Addison-Wesley Pub. Co., 1965. Some children find a dead bird, tenderly pick it up, and bury it. They show great respect for the bird by giving it a funeral and planting flowers around its grave. The mood of this book is very somber, but it is a good choice for a child who experiences the death of a wild bird. (ages 4 - 7)

The Tenth Good Thing About Barney by Judith Viorst. Illustrations by Erik Blegvad. Atheneum, NY, 1971. In an attempt to overcome his grief over the loss of his pet, a little boy tries to think of the ten best things about Barney, his cat who has died. (ages 4 - 8)

Rosalie by Joan Hewett. Illustrations by Donald Carrick. Lothrop, Lee & Shepard Books, NY, 1987. Rosalie is an old dog and she can't move or play the way that she used to. But she's still Rosalie and a very important member of the family. This book shows the special tenderness between a cherished pet and the family who cares for her in her old age. (ages 4 - 9)

I'll Always Love You by Hans Wilhelm. Crown Publishing Co. Inc., NY, 1985. Anyone who has or had an old dog in the family will be especially touched by this book. The narrator is a little boy who loves his dog, Elfie very much. One day Elfie does not wake up.

The boy, who has always told Elfie how much he loves her, finds comfort in the fact. (ages 4 - 8)

Be Nice to Spiders by Margaret Bloy Graham. Harper & Row, Pub., NY, 1967. A matchbox with a note attached is left on the steps of the zoo. The note reads, "Please look after Helen. . .I can't keep her anymore." Out of the box crawls a spider. The zookeeper tries to catch her, but with lightning speed she disappears into the zoo. The animals, once plagued with insects, become happy and contented - all because Helen is spinning webs and catching flies. (ages 4 - 8)

Thy Friend, Obadiah by Brinton Turkle. Viking Press, NY, 1969. Wherever Obadiah went, a certain sea gull would follow. One day, the sea gull is not there. Obadiah finally finds him on the wharf with a fishing line around his beak. He removes it and watches the gull fly far into the distance. (ages 4 - 8)

Helping Our Animal Friends by Judith E. Rinard. Photos by Susan McElhinney. National Geographic Society, Washington, D.C., 1985. In a clear text with wonderful photographs, this book illustrates the main things people (especially children) can do to help care for the animals in their lives. (ages 3 - 8)

Arion and the Dolphins by Lonzo Anderson. Illustrations by Adrienne Adams. Charles Scribner's Sons, NY, 1978. This story, based on an old Greek legend, is one of the earliest tales of friendship between dolphins and human beings. Arion makes friends with the dolphins and plays his lute for them day after day. When his life is threatened by wicked sailors at sea, the dolphins save him from drowning and carry him safely home. (ages 5 - 9)

Fiona's Bee by Beverly Keller. Illustrations by Diane Paterson. Coward, McCann and Geoghegan, NY, 1975. Fiona has no friends and she hopes every day to find one. But she finds a bee instead, drowning in a dog dish. She fishes him out to save his life and her kind act changes her life. (ages 6 - 9)

The First Dog by **Jan Brett.** Harcourt Brace Jovanovich Pub., NY, 1988. Kip, the cave boy, and Paleowolf each face hunger and danger on a journey in Paleolithic times. When they decide to join forces and help one another, Paleowolf becomes the first dog. (ages 6 - 10)

The Unhuggables: The Truth about Snakes, Slugs, Skunks, Spiders, and other Animals that are Hard to Love by **Victor H. Waldrop, Ed.** Ranger Rick Books. National Wildlife Federation, Wahington, D.C., 1988. This book tells how these unappealing animals contribute to the world. (ages 5 and up)

Amigo by **Byrd Baylor Schweitzer.** Illustrations by Garth Williams. Macmillan Pub. Co., NY, 1963. A Mexican boy named Francisco wants a dog more than anything in the world. Amigo, a furry prairie dog puppy, wants a human boy. The tale of how the two "tame" each other day by day, and how they grow to understand each other's ways, will delight children. (read-aloud, ages 5 - 9)

Winter Harvest by **Jane C. Aragon.** Illustrations by Leslie Baker. Little Brown and Co., Boston, 1988. This is an evocative picture book about a young girl's routine of feeding a family of deer in the winter. The simple story captures the tenuous relationship between human beings and wild animals. Illustrated with soft-edged watercolors, this book depicts the stillness of the winter season and then infuses it with flashes of color and life. (ages 4 - 8)

A Precious Life Jataka Tales Series. Dharma Publishing, Berkeley, CA, 1989. A deer shows compassion to the prince who would have hunted him down and killed him, thus effecting a change in the prince's attitude towards hunting. (ages 4 - 8)

The Hunter and the Animals by **Tomie de Paola.** Holiday House, NY, 1981. A hunter falls asleep in the forest. While he is sleeping, the animals take his gun and rearrange the terrain so that when the hunter awakes he is lost. But when the animals sense his fear they feel sorry for him and lead him home. Realizing that the animals are his friends, the hunter breaks his gun. (ages 3 - 8)

Every Living Thing by **Cynthia Rylant.** Bradbury Press, 1985. Twelve stories about the extraordinary relationships between humans and animals. (read-aloud, ages 6 - 10)

Horton Hears a Who by **Dr. Suess.** Random House, NY, 1954. Horton the Elephant hears a small noise one day while splashing in a jungle pool. He looks all around but can see only a small speck of dust flying through the air. The sound is coming from the speck! Horton decides that there must be some sort of small creature on the dust speck, a creature too small to be seen but, none the less important because "a person's a person, no matter how small." (all ages)

Charlotte's Web by **E. B. White.** Harper and Row, NY, 1952. Even though *Charlotte's Web* was written in 1952 - long before "animal rights" became a household term - its pro-animal message rings out loud and clear in the opening pages of the book. The concern shown for Charlotte and her friend, Wilbur the pig, shows the respect we should have for the point of view of the animal in its own world. This book is a must! (read-aloud, ages 6 - 12)

Resources for Parents and Teachers

The Humane Society of the United States' catalogue of publications, speciality items and audiovisual materials is a marvelous source for both parents and teachers wanting to further the cause of humane education. HSUS is a charitable, national animal-protection organization with headquarters in Washington, D.C. Through the catalogue, one can order pamphlets on pet care, public education material, pet overpopulation, trapping and fur, captive wildlife, animal exploitation, and humane education. Send for the catalogue by writing the society at 2100 L Street, NW, Washington, D.C. 20037.

The Humane Society also offers a four-page student newspaper (33 per bundle) with a teaching guide. *Kind News* teaches students respect for each other, animals, and the environment. It is produced in a junior edition for grades two through four and a senior edition for grades five and six. A subscription includes *Kind Teacher,* a teacher's guide with reproducibles, posters, games, daily calendar announcements, and lesson plans coordinated with *Kind News.* Editions are delivered each month of the school year. Many humane societies, as well as corporations, adopt an entire school system for $18 a year per class, the rate for several subscriptions. An individual can subscribe to *Kind News* (which includes the teacher's guide and nine months of bundles) for $25 per year. Order from the National Association for the Advancement of Humane Education (NAAHE), Box 362, East Haddam, CT 06423.

A Humane Teaching Guide for Project WILD, developed by the National Association for the Advancement of Humane Education. Humane Society of the United States, 2100 L Street, NW, Washington, D.C. 20037. This guide is designed for educators who are concerned about some of the biases evidenced throughout the *Project WILD* activity guides.

Otterwise: For Kids Who Love Animals, a quarterly newsletter for children, has many articles in past issues pertaining to humane treatment of animals. The Summer 1990 issue contains an article entitled "Do Animals Have Rights," and also offers 20 ways to help animals. Winter 1988 discusses using cruelty-free products and also deals with the fur issue. Tips for injured wildlife are found in Spring 1990. Order *Otterwise* from P.O. Box 1374, Portland, ME 04104.

"How to Raise a Puppy and Live Happily Ever After," is a 16mm film that can be obtained from AIMS Instructional Media, Glendale, CA.

The Boulder County Humane Society offers a filmstrip about abandoned pets entitled "A Home is Belonging to Someone." Write 2323 55th Street, Boulder, CO 80301.

Natural Health for Dogs and Cats, by Richard H. Pitcairn, D.V.M., Ph.D., and Susan Hubble Pitcairn. Rodale, Emmaus, PA, 1982. This guide helps you provide the same natural lifestyle for your pets that you can provide for yourself and your family.

Wolf, distributed by Media Guild, San Diego, CA. Part of a series called *Animals, Animals, Animals,* 22 minutes. Explores the world of this much maligned and unjustifiably feared predator.

Wolves and Coyotes, by Rosanna Hansen. Grosset Platt & Munk, NY, 1981. This book provides lots of solid information on the habits and behavior of wolves and coyotes. The images of wolves as evil, bloodthirsty animals is put to rest .

The Alaska Wildlife Alliance is dedicated to saving Alaska's wolves. It works to stop aerial wolf hunts, predator control, and other exploitation of wildlife in Alaska. For information write The Alaska Wildlife Alliance, Box 202022-D, Anchorage, AK 99520.

Other organizations engaged in trying to stop the killing of wolves include: Friends of the Wolf-USA, P.O. Box 16, Davis, CA 95617; Project Wolf USA, 6529 32nd Avenue NE, Seattle, WA 98115; and Voice of the Wolf, 1988 Damascus Rd., Rte. 4, Golden, CO 80403.

The Aspen Society for Animal Rights has available information on the fur issue and trapping. Send a stamped envelope to P.O. Box 2766, Aspen, CO 81612.

Fuzz Does It!, by Vicki Cobb. Lippincott, NY, 1982. Throughout the book, directions are given for spinning wool, cotton, or pineapple fibers by hand, making paper from dryer lint, and for testing wool for insulation. An interesting book to look at alternatives to fur.

Birds of North America: An Audubon Society Beginner's Guide. Text by George S. Fichter. Illustrations by Authur Singer. Random House, NY, 1982.

The Birdhouse Book: Building Houses, Feeders, and Baths, by Don McNeil. Pacific Search Press, Seattle, WA, 1979.

The Complete Book of Bird Houses and Feeders, by Monica Russo. Sterling Publishing Co., NY, 1976.

The North American Bluebird Society has available a pamphlet entitled "Where Have All the Bluebirds Gone?" Write to Box 6295, Silver Spring, MD 20906. The society, founded in 1978, is a non-profit organization determined to increase the populations of the three species of bluebirds on this continent. It also publishes a quarterly journal entitled *Sialia.*

1,001 Ways to Save the Planet, by Bernadette Vallely. Ivy Books, published by Ballantine, NY, 1990. See especially "Pets and the Environment," pp. 62-65.

The Animals' Voice Magazine, published bi-monthly by the Compassion for Animals Foundation, is an extremely comprehensive journal devoted to the welfare of animals in our society. Of special interest to parents and teachers are Vol. 2, No. 2 (April 1989) which features several articles on teaching children to have a compassionate attitude toward animals, and Vol. 1, No. 2 (Sept. 1988), an issue devoted in large part to the true nature of wolves. Write 3961 Landmark Street, Culver City, CA 90232.

The Animals' Agenda: The International Magazine of Animal Rights & Ecology is published monthly by the Animal Rights Network (except for combined issues in January/February and July/August). Offices are located at 456 Monroe Turnpike, Monroe, CT 06468.

Caring For Our Animal Friends is an annotated directory of teaching materials available from the California Veterinary Medical Association. Write 1024 Country Club Drive, Moraga, CA 94556.

Humane Education is a quarterly magazine for educators published by the National Association for the Advancement of Humane Education. The association's address is Box 362, East Haddam, CT 06423.

The Animal Welfare Institute promotes the welfare of all animals and works to reduce the pain and fear inflicted on animals by humans. Membership includes *Animal Welfare Institute,* a quarterly newsletter. Write P.O. Box 3650, Washington, D.C. 20007.

Friends of Animals is a group dedicated to eliminating human brutality to animals. Its many programs include working for the protection of animals used in testing and experimentation, breeding-control services, and a wild animal orphanage and rehabilitation center. The group also heads the Committee for Humane Legislation active in legislative affairs. Write P.O. Box 1244, Norwalk, CT 06856.

The Fund for Animals was founded to relieve pain and suffering in wild and domestic animals. Members receive a newsletter and "Action Alert" updates on legislation. For more information write 200 West 57th St., New York, NY 10019.

The American Society for the Prevention of Cruelty to Animals (ASPCA) offers "The ASPCA Guidelines for Student Experiments Involving Animals." It can be obtained from 441 East 92nd Street, New York, NY 10128. The organization's listing of acceptable animal-related projects may be found in the book, *Humane Biology Projects,* published by the Animal Welfare Institute (P.O. Box 3650, Washington, D.C. 20007).

It is available from the ASPCA Education Dept. for $1.50 per copy.

The Humane Education Committee (HEC) was formed for the purpose of institutionalizing animal-welfare/rights philosophies into educational school systems. Teachers are provided with staff development workshops and resource materials necessary to provide a humane approach in their teaching. Contact the committee at P.O. Box 445, Gracie Station, New York, NY 10028.

Zoos Without Cages, by Judity E. Rinard. National Geographic Society, Washington, D.C., 1981. The excitement of modern, humane, and scientifically designed zoos comes alive with informative stories and numerous colored photographs.

Song of Creation: An Anthology of Poems in Praise of Animals, edited by Dr. Tom Regan and Andrew Linzey, Abbey Books, 1988. Includes over 100 poems, spanning almost every period of literary expression.

"Special Section: Animals and Empathy," *Orion Nature Quarterly,* Vol 9, No. 2 (Spring 1990), pp. 8-31. Published by the Myrin Institute, Inc., 136 East 64th St., New York, NY 10021.

Vegetarian Times. P.O. Box 570, Oak Park IL 60303. A monthly magazine full of vegetarian news and recipes that promotes a healthy and tasty way to eat lower on the food chain.

For children who like to color, you can order the "I Love Animals and Broccoli Coloring Book." Send an envelope with your return address along with two twenty-five cent stamps to Vegetarian Resource Group, P.O. Box 1463, Baltimore, MD 21203.

The Animal Welfare Institute publishes a book that tells instructors how to teach children about first aid and care of mice, gerbils, rabbits, birds, opossums, and other small animals. Single copies are free, if requested on school letterhead. Ask for "First Aid and Care of Small Animals" and write Animal Welfare Institute, P.O. Box 3650, Washington, D.C. 20007.

The New York City Board of Education's *Humane Educational Resource Guide* is designed for classroom teachers who wish to incorporate animal welfare and environmental issues into their curriculum. The guide features lesson plans and student worksheets for kindergarten through sixth grades. For a copy send $6.00 (postpaid) to the NYC Board of Education, 131 Livingston Street, Brooklyn, NY 11201.

Your child can correspond with another child living across the globe and share his/her concern about animals. The England-based *Royal Society for the Prevention of Cruelty to Animals* has a pen-pal exchange in their children's publication *Animal World* for children ages 10 to 15. Send your full name, address, age, and a self-addressed and stamped envelope to Penfriends, *Animal World,* RSPCA, Causeway, Horsham, West Sussex RH12 1HG, England.

Animal Liberation, by Peter Singer. (Second edition). A New York Review Book, Random House, Inc., NY, 1990. This is a very important book that may change the way many of us look at animals and, ultimately, at ourselves.

Diet for a New America: How Your Food Choices Affect Your Health, Happiness and the Future of Life on Earth, by John Robbins. Stillpoint Publishing, Box 640, Walpole, NH 03608. This book is an extraordinary look at our dependence on animals for food, and the often inhumane and unhealthy conditions under which they are currently raised.

50 Simple Things You Can Do to Save the Animals, by Ingrid Newkirk, National Director, People for the Ethical Treatment of Animals. Warner Books, NY, 1990. Tips for everyday living, charitable giving, political action, and responsible consumerism.

Animals and Why They Matter, by Mary Midgley. University of Georgia Press, Athens, GA, 1984.

The Case for Animal Rights, by Tom Regan. University of California Press, Berkeley, CA, 1983.

Inhumane Society: The American Way of Exploiting Animals, by Dr. Michael W. Fox. St. Martin's Press, NY, 1990. This is a book that deals with the use of animals in testing for cosmetics, scientific experiments, and other uses made in the name of "progress" that the author finds cruel and often unnecessary.

Animal Rights and Human Obligations, Tom Regan and Peter Singer, eds. Prentice-Hall, 2nd ed., Englewood Cliffs, NJ, 1989.

Morals, Reason and Animals, by Steve Sapontzis. Temple University Press, Philadelphia, PA, 1987.

In Defense of Animals, Peter Singer, ed. Harper and Row, NY, 1986. Essays by leading activists and thinkers in the area of animal rights.

The Extended Circle: A Commonplace Book of Animal Rights, J. Wynne-Tyson, ed. Paragon House, NY, 1988. Hundreds of short extracts from humane thinkers down through the ages.

Man Kind?: Our Incredible War on Wildlife, by Cleveland Amory. Dell, NY, 1980. This is a critique of the way in which humans use animals in unnecessarily cruel ways.

The Green Lifestyle Handbook: 1001 Ways You Can Heal the Earth, Jeremy Rifkin, ed. Henry Holt & Co., NY, 1990. See especially "Cruelty-Free Living" by Dr. Michael W. Fox, pp. 71-77. This article provides a list of manufactures who carry only products that are not tested on animals.

A Bibliography on Animal Rights and Related Matters, by Charles R. Magel. University Press of America, Washington, D.C., 1981. A listing of over 3000 books, articles, pamphlets, symposia, and other publications on animal rights from Aristotle to modern times organized by topic.

Animals and Men, by Kenneth Clark. William Morrow and Co., NY, 1977. This is a lavishly illustrated history of man's relationship to nature as reflected in art. An excellent source of examples of the various interpretations of animals in western culture.

Animal Rights: Stories of People Who Defend the Rights of Animals, by Patricia Curtis. Four Winds Press, NY, 1980. A personalized account of people involved in the humane movement, written for young adults. It profiles such people as a medical student, a lawyer for a humane group, and a veterinarian.

The Teaching of Reverence for Life, by Albert Schweitzer. Holt, Rinehart, Winston, NY, 1965. Schweitzer's definitive work on the philosophy of reverence for life. This book should be in the collection of anyone interested in the humane movement and its intimate relationship with concern for peace and human rights.

The Handbook of Animal Welfare, R. Allen and E. Westbrook, eds. Garland STM Press, NY, 1979. A collection of articles dealing primarily with dogs and cats, focusing on problems of pet overpopulation, humane concerns in animal control, and our obligations to and responsibilities for pets.

Between Pets and People: The Importance of Animal Companionship, by Alan Beck and Aaron Katcher. G. P. Putnam's Sons, NY, 1983. Popularized review of the scientific literature on the relationship between people and pets.

Epilogue Let There Be Peace On Earth

If we are to reach real peace in the world we shall have to begin with children; and if they will grow up in their natural innocence, we won't have to struggle; we won't have to pass fruitless ideal resolutions, but we shall go from love to love and peace to peace, until at last all the corners of the world are covered with that peace and love for which consciously or unconsciously the whole world is hungering.

GANDHI

This we know to be true: the only person in the world you can change is yourself. "So," you might ask, "what good does it do to recycle my aluminum cans or walk to the drugstore instead of riding in a car? How can my single effort change the Earth?" Well, if it were up to you and your family alone to solve all of the problems facing our planet, the task would be overwhelming. But you are not alone. Throughout the world many people are altering their lifestyles and making environmentally sound choices; it is their collective effort that will bring about change. The world as a whole faces

Six Crows, by Leo Lionni.
Alfred A. Knopf, NY, 1988.

A farmer and six crows live near each other and disagree about who should have the wheat from a field. So, to scare off the crows, the farmer builds a scarecrow. Indeed, they are frightened and build a ferocious kite which in turn frightens the farmer. The crows and the farmer build a bigger and more vicious scarecrow and kite until their foolishness causes the wheat crop to wilt from neglect. Finally, a wise owl intervenes and helps the two warring parties reach a compromise. This story beautifully demonstrates to young readers that communication is the key to peacemaking. (ages 4 - 8)

these problems because air, water, and waste pollution cannot be contained within the boundaries of a country, but affect the entire planet. There are many obstacles to overcome before people can unite and bring about a better world for our children; it will take communication and cooperation with all peoples, in every part of the world.

Throughout the pages of *Earth Child,* you and your children have become more aware of the fact that our planet, filled with many beautiful and unique creatures and plants, is deserving of your respect. This concluding chapter will help you complete your circle of love and respect for the world by emphasizing that you cannot live in harmony with the Earth without also living in harmony with the people of the Earth. In the pages that follow, you will discover many suggestions and ideas that will foster an understanding between the members of your family or classroom and other people. If everyone could find room in their hearts for others, then our global problems would diminish rapidly.

Peace Begins At Home

If you say to a child, "What the world needs is peace," a likely response might be, "A piece of what?" This abstract concept is very difficult for a young child to understand and put into words. As a parent or teacher, you will find it easier to teach a child to do mathematics, play tennis, or bake a cake than to be a peacemaker.

Why? Because it isn't difficult to follow rules or a recipe, but to keep one's mind open to the differing opinions and needs of others takes respect and a belief that all people are worthwhile. Left to face these challenges on his own, a child can grow up to be a very unhappy, angry, or selfish human being. But with the example and guidance of a loving adult, that same child can become a caring individual who recognizes the beauty in people and in the world around him.

Towards a Peaceful Solution

Throughout this book, you and your children have been asked to "become" objects or animals in nature in order to empathize with their situations and understand their feelings. While it's one thing to think like a tree, it is quite another to take the viewpoint of another person, especially in the middle of a disagreement. When asked to speak from the other person's perspective, young children often will revise what they hear to more closely match what they think or want. But it is this role reversal that is the key to understanding. The following guidelines will help you and your children resolve personal conflicts in your home or classroom, and everyone will walk away with a better understanding of each other.

Imagine that you walk into a room and discover your children fighting. Your first instinct is to act like a referee at a wrestling match, right? An alternative is to allow your children to work it out among themselves, with your help. First, separate your children, allow some quiet time for them to calm down, and then take the role as mediator instead of judge. Working together towards a peaceful solution takes time, but you will be giving your children a valuable gift, the gift of communication and understanding. Here are some guidelines to follow:

1. **Listen to Each Other:** Most parents or teachers would immediately say, "Tell me what happened?" But that kind of questioning makes you the judge in the case. Instead, ask each child to state what he thinks is the problem while everyone listens, without interrupting. (That takes some self-control.)

2. **"Become" the Other Person:** After each child is given the opportunity to briefly state the problem as he or she sees it, ask each

"Lord, make me an instrument of thy peace. Where there is hatred, let me sow love."
Saint Francis of Assisi

person to take a moment to think about the other person's words. Then ask each child to "become" the other person and to state the problem from the other person's point of view. (This will be difficult, but is very important. It helps each child to understand the whole problem, not just one side.)

3. Brainstorm Solutions: So, how can the problem be solved and peace returned to your home or classroom? Have your children come up with several ways in which they might resolve their difference. (You might offer some ideas.) This step shows them that many options can result in a peaceful solution and that there is more than one right way. Finally, have them choose one or more of the suggestions and go about their business. . . and peace returns!

Peacemaking Practices At Home and School

Since very young children cannot recognize the consequences of their words or actions, often they are unaware of how they contribute to a disagreement. Because of this, working through a disagreement to a peaceful solution requires an adult's assistance and it may be a good idea to establish some ground rules for keeping peace in the home or classroom. Here are a few suggestions:

• **Following the Rules:** Establish a set of rules or defined processes to help your children work through their disagreements (such as the guidelines above). Post them somewhere in your home or classroom and be consistent about following them. Also, it is important that you and the other adult members of your family become examples for your children.

• **Using "I" messages:** In the middle of an argument, young children often point to each other to establish blame for the disagreement. This usually takes the form of name-calling and invariably somebody's feelings are hurt in the process. To help eliminate this problem, establish the rule that only "I" messages can be used in an argument. For example, you might hear your child scream, "You always take everything for yourself; you're just a hog!" Instead, an "I" message must always start with the word "I", such as, "I feel cheated because you got more candy than I did." It's a hard rule to follow. But once it's mastered, disagreements remain just that; they do not turn into an ugly and degrading war of words.

"The first peace, which is the most important, is that which comes within the souls of people when they realize their relationship, their oneness, with the universe and all its powers."
BLACK ELK

- **Words and Actions:** To help your children become aware of the consequences of their words and actions, point them out whenever possible. For example, you might say, "Look how happy Jennifer is when you play ball together," or "How is Brian going to feel if you take the truck away?"

- **Cooperative Games:** Set up your home or classroom to encourage cooperation and sharing instead of competition and conflict. Take a simple board game such as *Candyland*, for example. You can help your children focus on helping each other as they take turns by defining winning as "when all of the players get to the end of the path." Encourage your children to engage in dramatic play in which they take on interdependent roles such as in a grocery store, house, or restaurant. In the park, such activities as playing on a teeter-totter or tire swing also encourage children to cooperate.

Reaching Out to Help Others

If from a very young age your child learns to see life from differing points of view and is actively involved in helping others, he or she will be able to develop qualities of compassion and respect for other human beings. Children begin with the people that directly touch their lives: their family and their communities.

Getting to Know Your Neighbors

It's a good feeling to know that you have neighbors whenever you need a cup of sugar or someone to talk to. In our fast-paced society many families, consciously or unconsciously, have secluded themselves from their neighbors. It's unfortunate, but the days are quickly disappearing when neighbors can be seen chatting over the back fence or sharing meals together. There are many benefits to be gained from knowing your neighbors, from security to friendship. Try to make an effort to know the people who share your neighborhood and host an old-fashioned "Block Party" or barbecue! If you live in an apartment, invite your whole floor. It is great fun and, who knows? You and your children might even meet some new friends!

Captain Snap and the Children of Vinegar Lane, by Roni Schotter. Illustrations by Marcia Sewall. Orchard Books, a division of Franklin Watts, Inc., NY, 1989.

When the children run to the end of Vinegar Lane and shout, Captain Snap always comes out of his broken-down house and hobbles across his junk-cluttered yard to give a loud snap of his lip and chase them away. But one day there is no sign of him and Sody knows something is wrong. So she tiptoes up to the window and discovers Captain Snap stretched out on his bare bed, obviously very ill. As afraid as she is, she knows there is only one thing to do; she must help him. The next time the children visit Captain Snap they discover he has a special talent and a wonderful secret to share. (age 4 and up)

Lend a Helping Hand

We all need the security and friendship of other people to make our world a nice place in which to live. And in our own neighborhoods, knowing that someone is nearby when we need help can be comforting. Are you and your other family members available when others need your assistance? Is it possible that an elderly neighbor struggles to keep her lawn mowed, leaves raked, or house in good repair? Why not take it upon yourselves to help those in need, right in your own neighborhood. This kind of reaching out can foster a genuine concern for people and will set a good example for your children to live by.

Senior Friends

Due to medical reasons or for lack of relatives, many elderly people spend their last few years in nursing homes. These homes can sometimes be a lonely place to live, especially when few family members take time to visit. You and your children can brighten the lives of the elderly residents by becoming frequent visitors to nursing homes. Small children are usually uninhibited and accept the limitations of older people without problems. If you live away from your own parents, you might consider "adopting" grandparents for your children. Although they can never take the place of real grandparents, it can be a worthwhile arrangement for everyone involved!

Recycle for the Homeless

We have heard about the plight of the homeless in our country for some time now. In every major city, you can find people with no warm bed to sleep in, bathroom to bathe in, or house to come home to. Caring people all over the country are trying to do something to combat this difficult problem. You and your family or students can join the effort! Cash in recyclables and donate the money to centers for the homeless in your community. Better yet, set up Fancy Cans around your city – a great project for schools or churches. (See the "Home Sweet Home" chapter for details.) It may not add up to much, but every little bit will help, and it will certainly foster a caring and compassionate attitude in your children.

Have a Caring Carnival

This is a super money-raising idea! Help your children organize a neighborhood (or school) carnival and donate the proceeds to charitable organizations in your community. It can be simple or elaborate, and here are some suggested attractions: bean bag toss, raffle, cake walk, foot races, bake sale, craft booth, penny toss, face painting, white elephant sale (donated items and toys), ring toss, tricycle obstacle course, etc. If space is a problem, set it up at a nearby park. Don't forget to advertise in the neighborhood; get everyone involved in one way or another!

Community Garden

Are there people in your community with green thumbs to spare? Setting up a community garden for the homeless is a wonderful way to supply needed fresh vegetables and fruit to homeless shelters. There are two ways you and your family can get involved – either by helping to organize, plant, weed, and care for a community plot or by donating produce from your own garden. If you want to be an independent supplier, be certain to arrange your food donation with a specific center. (To fulfill health regulations, they may need to inspect your garden.) Either way, you will be helping the Earth to care for those in need.

Used Toys Can Help

There is an easy way for your children to become involved directly with helping others – by donating their unwanted (but still in good condition) toys and books. How about that game you bought them last year? Is it still sitting untouched on the shelf? Sometimes children want to save you hurt feelings (since it was a gift from you), rather than letting you know how they really feel about it. So, ease their minds by telling them how pleased you would be to have an unwanted toy or book donated to a charitable cause. A "Used Toy and Book Sale" can raise a lot of money for charity. Or you can donate the unwanted items to a center for the homeless or pediatric ward. And don't forget, used toys and books are an especially appreciated donation around the holidays.

Tele-pledging

It's getting late and you have only a couple of donations to show for your whole afternoon's work. "No, not today," you hear for the hundredth time. It can be disappointing to be rejected at every door when you are giving your valuable time to help other people. So, let your fingers do the work instead of your feet! Whenever you need to collect food, clothing, old toys, etc. for charitable organizations, instead of walking up and down the streets of the neighborhood, make telephone calls (or pass out flyers) and ask for donations beforehand. This will not only reward your efforts with better results, but will give people a little time to gather some things together. It will also provide you with a specific route to take on collection day.

DREAM STARTER

Many people struggle to provide the basic necessities for themselves and their families: good food to eat, warm clothing to wear, and a safe place in which to live. Maybe you've seen a homeless person walking along the street with torn or dirty clothes, unclean hair, and wornout shoes. Perhaps the person is sick, or has lost his job. Whatever the reason for his troubles, he needs other people to help him as much as possible. Let's imagine that one day you are walking along and you notice a family standing on the sidewalk. There is a mother, father, and a young girl. The first thing you notice is that although it is a chilly day, not one of them is wearing a coat. Their faces are dirty and their hair is uncombed. As you walk past them, the girl, who is about your age, looks at you with lonely eyes and says, "Hello." You acknowledge her with a quick, "Hi," and a nod of your head, but hurry past her heading for home. As you walk along, you think about how horrible it would be to have no home to go to and no coat to wear on a cold day and you are thankful that your family lives in a nice place.

That evening at dinner, you tell your mother about the family you saw on the street and ask if she knows what happens to homeless families. She looks at you with serious eyes and says, "I really don't know. I wish we could do something to help them." You think a while about the lonely young girl. You wonder if she might be outside and cold this very minute. You turn to your mother and say that you would like to help them too.

So together, you and your family look around the house and find some clothes, shoes, an extra blanket, canned food, and a coat that no longer fits you to donate to the Center for the Homeless in your city. "I'd like to give something to that little girl I saw today," you tell your mother. "Honey, we're not sure that she will be at the

Homeless Center," she replies. But you don't care, and you are determined to find something for her. You look around your room and in your closet, but it seems too difficult to part with any of your special toys. Then, from across the room, you see your Deluxe Bug-Eye Kaleidoscope sitting on the dresser. Of all the presents you received on your birthday, it is your favorite. You love looking through it, wondering what it would be like to be as small as a fly. You pick it up and put it to your eye. Instead of seeing one bed, you see sixteen! Wouldn't it be great if it could duplicate real objects sixteen times? Suddenly you realize that this is exactly what you wish you could give to the little girl - more of everything she needs. You look carefully at the kaleidoscope in your hands and, with great difficulty, decide that this will be your gift to her.

The next evening, your family packs up all the items in a large box. As you drive down to the center, you silently twirl the magic kaleidoscope between your fingers, having second thoughts. Your mother notices your sad expression and says, "Honey, you don't have to give it away, you know?" You shake your head, look down at the sixteen eyes, and reply hesitantly, "I know. . . but I want to." Once at the shelter, you look everywhere for the little girl and her family, but they are not there. Actually you are a bit relieved because you have decided to keep the kaleidoscope; and just as you slip it into your pocket, you notice a little boy in the corner playing with a puzzle. He smiles and beckons you to come over. "Do you want to play checkers?" he asks. So you sit facing each other over the checker board. As you talk and play, your sad feeling disappears. Too soon, your parents come up from behind and tell you it's time to go. But before you get up, you pull the special gift out of your coat pocket. You look at it for a long time, then hand it to the boy. "Here, I want you to have this." He takes it and turns it over in his hand, then he puts it to his eye. "Wow," he says in wonderment, "It's like magic!" As you and your family turn to walk away, he calls after you, "Say, thanks a lot." And just as he says these words, you feel a happy spark in your heart that spreads and warms your whole body.

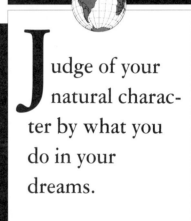

Judge of your natural character by what you do in your dreams.

RALPH WALDO EMERSON

The Story of Ferdinand, by Munro Leaf. Illustrations by Robert Lawson. The Viking Press, NY, 1938.

Ferdinand was an unusual calf. Instead of running, playing, and butting heads with the other calves, he preferred to sit quietly and smell the flowers of the meadow. One day some men came to the pasture to choose a bull to fight in the bull ring in Madrid. By mistake, Ferdinand sat on a bumblebee and the resulting sting made him jump and snort with pain. The men thought he was displaying his fierceness and chose him over all the others. Once in the ring, Ferdinand refused to fight, no matter what the bull fighters did. So he was returned to the pasture and, to this day, can still be found under the cork tree enjoying the flowers. This classic book beautifully illustrates that even though you are put in the ring, you don't have to fight; there is another way. (ages 3 - 7)

Choosing Peace

That Peaceful Feeling

What does "peace" feel like? Because of the abstract nature of the concept, it is necessary for children to relate the feeling of peace within themselves to events in their own lives. To help your children experience peaceful feelings, ask them to close their eyes and listen as you read this short passage. Afterwards, exchange thoughts about what it feels like to be at peace.

Imagine that it has been a very cold and snowy day. As you come in from outside, you are chilled to the bone. Your hands are wet and freezing under your gloves. Goose bumps cover your whole body and your teeth chatter with the cold. You walk into the kitchen and your mother greets you with a pleasant smile that immediately melts your goose bumps away. She helps you remove your wet coat, hat, and gloves, and wraps a warm, soft blanket around your shoulders.

"I knew you would be cold, so I made something special for you," your mother whispers in your ear.

You follow her into the living room where you see a plate of homemade cookies and a mug of steaming hot chocolate. You move to sit near her on the couch, hoping the heat from her body will stop your shivering. She hands you the cocoa and cradles you on her shoulder. The mug is warm and you watch the steam rise and swirl, then evaporate into the room. The heat enters your hands and slowly the numbing cold disappears from your stiff fingers. You bring the mug to your lips and feel the luscious hot chocolate warming your insides. It isn't long before your shivering stops and you can feel your nose again. You sit quietly against your mother, nibbling on a cookie, sipping hot cocoa, and watching the big white flakes float outside your window. The warm glowing feeling stays with you long after the cocoa and cookies are gone.

The Circle of Peace

A peacemaker is someone who feels good about himself, thinks positively about other people, helps others, is forgiving, chooses peace over violence, and has a vision for a peaceful world. To initiate your children into this kind of thinking and living, have them gather into a Peace Circle and share some thoughts. Pass around a globe or picture of the Earth to remind your children, as their thoughts are shared, that the planet is home to everyone. As the globe is passed, each person should tell a story about a time in which they acted as a peacemaker. How did it make them feel? After the stories, ask if anyone would like to make a wish for the Earth. After everyone has had the opportunity to voice their hopes, join hands, and sing a song about peace, such as *It's a Small World* by Walt Disney or *We Are the World* (the song written by Michael Jackson and Lionel Richie, and produced by Quincy Jones).

A Wish for the World

We should all have hope for a better world, one where people live in harmony, not only with themselves, but with all of the inhabitants of the Earth. It is this hope, this vision, that will help to make it a reality. In this activity, you and your children can express your hopes for the Earth by creating a "Wish for the World" cooperative collage. Draw or cut pictures from old magazines, write poems or bits of wisdom, put it all together, and make it come true.

Peace Day Celebration

On August 6, 1945 an atom bomb was dropped on the city of Hiroshima in Japan. Thousands of citizens died instantly and many others suffered radiation which would affect them for years to come. Since then, Japan has set aside August 6 as a day to wish for world peace. Many people across the world join them on this day in hope that the citizens of the Earth will never again use nuclear weapons and will choose peaceful solutions over war. The story *Sadako and the Thousand Paper Cranes* and the following activities will help you and your family or students plan a Peace Day celebration.

"Before we can achieve a peaceful world, we must first imagine one."

Sadako and the Thousand Paper Cranes, by Eleanor Coerr. Illustrations by Ronald Himler. G. P. Putnam's Sons, NY, 1977.

Sadako Sasaki was only two-years old when an atom bomb was dropped on the city of Hiroshima where she lived with her family. Ten years later, she developed leukemia (cancer) as a result of radiation from the bomb. Because of the great courage she displayed during the course of her illness, she is a heroine to the children of Japan today. A memorial has been erected in her honor where children still leave paper cranes in her memory. This is a very sad story, but one full of hope for peace in the future. (read-aloud, ages 7 - 12)

The Earth Has No Boundaries

When you travel across the country on vacation, have you ever really seen any of those state "lines" you supposedly cross? If you look at a globe you will see that our world is full of imaginary, manmade boundaries: property lines, city boundaries, county lines, state borders, country boundaries, continent boundaries, and hemisphere lines. But is the world really chopped up into so many parts? Take this imaginary trip to see that indeed the Earth has no boundaries. Before you begin, ask your participants (a group of mixed ages works well) to sit in a circle, close their eyes, listen to this story and imagine that they depart from the Earth on a fantastic journey.

Ever since you saw the space movie *Star Wars* you've been tinkering in your garage, working on a secret project. You've collected old machine parts and scrap metal from the junk yard and are finally putting the finishing touches on your new invention called the PLeASuRe ship, which is a Personal Land and Space Rover. But before you can tell anyone about it, you have to test it and see if it really works.

So tonight, you drag the PLeASuRe ship into an open field and climb inside. Just for safety's sake, you bring along your brother's old football helmet with the facemask removed, and you slip it over your head. You turn the key and the engines fire up. As you step on the fuel pedal, the spaceship begins to rise and hovers gently over the ground. "Let's give this baby a spin," you say to yourself and off you go. You travel at an incredible speed, covering several miles per second. It isn't long before you reach the border of your country and must stop at the barrier wall. You want to go on, but noticing your strange vehicle, the customs attendant won't let you pass.

Not pleased by the limitations on Earth, you decide it's time to try the rockets. So with a push of a button, you rapidly speed away from the planet at a fantastic rate. It isn't until you are far above the Earth that you turn around and look at it. Suddenly, awed by the beauty of its swirling atmosphere, you release the fuel pedal and gaze lovingly down on your home planet. You watch as the sun rises over the curved edge and slowly comes into full view. Its light gently touches the sleeping world below and you notice for the first time that the Earth is not covered by the lines on a globe, but has no borders or boundaries that you can see. Viewing the Earth in this way reminds you that all people share this one magnificent planet. You realize that although every person on Earth is different from every other, they are all part of one family: the human family. You wish you could spread this vision and message into every home.

You spend the next few minutes circling our unique planet, looking down to see the many beautiful people, plants, and animals who live here.

Allow a moment of peaceful quiet. Then ask everyone to return home and to open their eyes when they have landed. Pass around a picture of the Earth as seen from space, and ask each person to share some special feeling about our planet.

Peaceful Posters

What does peace mean to you and your children? Kids have interesting and insightful ideas about what peace means to them. Pull out your Recycle Craft Box and make some "peaceful" posters, full of people working together or helping one another. Then label each child's poster with a sentence about what peace means to him or her.

Have a Peace Parade

Let your neighborhood or school show its feelings by participating in a parade. Even your youngest children will enjoy decorating their bicycles or tricycles to ride in the event. So get out your streamers and peace posters (see previous activity), and join the march!

Peace Begins With Me

A commitment circle can be an inspirational experience for the participants because voicing a pledge to a group may often help persons to make real changes within themselves. End your Peace Day celebration by bringing everyone together to share their promises for a peaceful future.

1. Ask everyone to form a circle and to hold their neighbors' hands: this act represents the people of the world coming together in peace. While the group's hands are still interlocked, play or sing a song about peace (such as *Imagine* by John Lennon) and sway in time with the music. This will help to unite your group towards this common goal and will set the mood for the commitment circle.

2. After the song, have everyone sit comfortably on the floor facing each other in a circle. Light a large candle and place it in the center of the group and dim the lights. (For young children, place a globe in the center of the circle.) Then begin the pledging by asking a volunteer to come forward and tell the group one way in which he will commit himself to making the world a better and more peaceful place to live.

3. After everyone has had the opportunity to share their promises, pass out a small sheet of paper and writing utensil to each person (for young children provide crayons). Ask all the participants to write their commitments on the pieces of paper. (Young children can draw pictures of themselves engaged in their peacemaking promise.) When this is completed, ask everyone to fold their promises into thirds and to write their names on the outside. If desired, have each person come forward and seal his or her commitment with wax from the candle. *(Note: Hot wax can cause serious burns. This step requires strict adult supervision! Young children may seal their papers with globe stickers or place them in envelopes.)*

4. Place all of the commitments in a special container decorated for the occasion. Tell everyone that at the next Peace Day celebration (or at the end of the school year) they will have the opportunity to open their pledges to see if they were able to fulfill them during that year.

5. End the celebration by reconnecting hands and singing the peace song once again.

Get Involved!

Prejudice Is Learned at Home

A newborn baby does not display prejudice towards any person or race of people; this is something learned from the adults in his life. Just as a biased attitude is learned at home, tolerance and love also start there. To help your children establish good feelings about other races and people of different backgrounds and cultures, here are some strategies that you and your family can pursue every day of your lives.

• It is normal that all people are different, so help to foster a respect for these differences.

• Point out to your children ways in which people are the same.

• Avoid jokes and expressions that stereotype people. Even the slightest indication of a biased attitude will be absorbed by children.

• Try to teach your children as much as you can about the cultures of other groups of people. How are their lifestyles the same as yours and how are they different?

• Know your community and get involved in some project with your neighbors.

• Don't generalize from isolated incidents. Treat each person you meet as an individual, not just as a member of his or her "group."

• Read books and watch programs with your children that are free of racial stereotypes in character, language, or illustrations.

Trick-or-Treat for UNICEF

UNICEF (the United Nations Children's Fund) was created to help the child victims of World War II. When Europe had recovered from the devastation of war and its children were cared for, UNICEF turned its attention to the plight of children in developing nations. It is currently working in 128 countries and strives in all of its programs to bring better health and a hope for the future to the world's poorest children. Every year at Halloween, thousands of children can be seen carrying the familiar UNICEF collection boxes along with their own trick-or-treat bags. This is an excellent project

Group Programs
U.S. Committee for UNICEF
333 East 38th St.
New York, NY 10016

for schools and church groups. To learn more about how to join this yearly appeal or to receive a Collection Kit, write to Group Programs, U.S. Committee for UNICEF.

Kids Meeting Kids

Kids Meeting Kids
c/o Mary Sochet
380 Riverside Drive
New York, NY 10025

What would it be like to live in another country, such as the Soviet Union? To find out, your child can join "Kids Meeting Kids." Your child will receive a Russian recipe book, a book of pictures and letters exchanged between Russian and American children, a yearly newsletter about kids meeting other kids, and information about how to be a pen pal with a child from another country.

Children as the Peacemakers

Children as the Peacemakers
Peace Clubs
950 Battery Street, Second Floor
San Francisco, CA 94111

Since its inception in 1982, the Children as the Peacemakers Foundation has established Pat's Peace Kids International Peace Clubs around the world to help children learn about living peacefully on the planet. Membership entitles you to a newsletter, an adult guidebook, and a series of guidebooks for children. Each is concerned with a different level of club activities, beginning with initiation into the club, continuing with peacemaking skills, and concluding with a peacemaker graduation ceremony. Other club activities include designing your own club constitution, contacting kids from other countries, learning the skills of peacemaking, and writing to world leaders. The cost for club registration is $15.00. Membership in the Children as the Peacemakers Foundation is also available to adults, senior citizens, and groups, and fees are tax-deductible. For more information, write to Children as the Peacemakers.

More Books To Share With Children

Free to Be. . .You and Me, **conceived by Marlo Thomas. Developed and edited by Carole Hart, Letty Cottin Pogrebin, Mary Rodgers and Marlo Thomas.** McGraw-Hill Book Co., NY, 1974. Stories, poems, and songs for children and adults to share that foster individuality and independent thinking. (all ages)

Free to Be. . .a Family, **by Marlo Thomas and friends.** Bantam Books, NY, 1987. Sories, poems, and songs for children and adults to share about different kinds of families and all kinds of belonging. (all ages)

A Country Far Away, **by Nigel Gray and Philippe Dupasquier.** Orchard Books, NY, 1989. Two boys, one in Africa, one in the USA, wake and sleep and play and eat and share their family's life - on opposite sides of the globe. They are unknown to one another, but very much alike in everything they do and feel in spite of the many differences in their societies and surroundings. This is a truly marvelous book to show that we are all brothers. (ages 4 - 8)

People, **by Peter Spier.** Doubleday and Co., NY, 1980. This classic beautifully illustrates the differences, and similarities, among the billions of people on the Earth. (all ages)

All in a Day, **by Mitsumasa Anno plus many others.** Philomel Books, NY, 1986. "Next door to the country you live in, there is another country where children also live. . . In all of the countries throughout the world there are many, many children . . . While you are out playing, some children are fast asleep in a far-off land. While you are building a snowman, some other children somewhere else are swimming in the sea. ." *All in a Day* is the perfect book for illustrating that the Earth is home to us all! (all ages)

The Three Astronauts, **by Umberto Eco.** Illustrations by Eugenio Carmi. Harcourt Brace Jovanovich, NY, 1989. An American, a Russian, and a Chinese take off separately in their rockets. Each wants to be the first man on Mars, but all land at the same time. By nightfall, realizing how much they are alike, they become friends. The next morning, confronted by a green Martian with six arms, they are sure that he is so different from them that they must be enemies. But something happens to make the three realize that even the Martian has the same basic needs and feelings as they do, and that all beings need to support one another. (age 5 and up)

Swimmy, **by Leo Lionni.** Pantheon Books, a division of Random House, NY, 1968. Swimmy is a little black fish who lives in the midst of a school of little red fish, all of whom are his brothers and sisters. One day all of the red fish are gobbled up by a huge, hungry tuna. Swimmy is left alone, sad and frightened. The way that Swimmy solves his problems can be a lesson in cooperation and peacemaking for all young readers. (all ages)

I Hate English! **by Ellen Levine.** Illustrations by Steve Bjorkman. Scholastic, Inc., NY, 1989. When her family moves from Hong Kong to New York's Chinatown, Mei Mei finds it difficult to adjust. This story of one girl's transition will encourage young readers to think about how it feels to be new in a strange place, while also giving them a glimpse of one of the many cultures that make up our nation's immigrant population. (ages 5 - 10)

The Pinkish, Purplish, Bluish Egg, **by Bill Peet.** Houghton Mifflin Co., Boston, 1963. This book is full of surprises and told in rollicking verse with expressive illustrations that will appeal to young readers. (ages 4 - 8)

Old Henry, **by Joan W. Blos.** Illustrations by Stephen Gammell. Mulberry Books of William Morrow Co., NY, 1987. The neighbors are very unhappy about

Henry's beaten-up old house. He doesn't weed his garden or sweep his walk. They harass him so much that he finally moves away. Strangely, his neighbors begin to miss Henry and he misses them. (age 4 and up)

Toddlecreek Post Office, by **Uri Shulevitz.** Farrar, Straus and Giroux, NY, 1990. The post office in Toddlecreek is the hub of the tiny village where animals and people who have no place else to go gather for warmth, conversation, and other kinds of help when it is needed. But one bright, spring morning, something happens that causes everything to change. This book points to the hope that, even in our fast-paced world, we can once again be aware of our neighbors' needs. (all ages)

Let's Be Enemies, by **Janice M. Udry.** Illustrations by Maurice Sendak. Harper & Row, Pub., NY, 1961. This is a simple story about the endurance of friendship. (ages 3 - 5)

A Children's Problem Solving Book Series. Titles include: *I Want It, I Can't Wait, I Want to Play, My Name is Not Dummy,* and *I'm Lost,* all by **Elizabeth Crary.** Illustrations by Marina Megale. Parenting Press, Inc., Seattle, WA, 1982. Each book not only tells a story about conflict and how it can be resolved in different ways, but also poses questions and situations for your children to consider. (ages 4 - 8)

It's Mine, by **Leo Lionni.** Alfred A. Knopf, Pub., NY, 1985. Three selfish frogs quarrel over who owns their pond and island. One day a terrible storm makes them begin to value the benefits of sharing. (ages 4 - 8)

Potatoes, Potatoes, by **Anita Lobel.** Harper and Row, Pub., NY, 1967. There was once an old woman who had a potato farm and two sons. One ran off to join the army of the West; the other, the army of the East. They became enemies and finally met in battle right in front of the potato farm. Their wise mother refused to give

them or their starving comrades one mouthful of potato until all laid down their swords and guns. A timeless parable of the ridiculous nature of war. (all ages)

The Butter Battle Book, by **Dr. Suess.** Random House, NY, 1984. In this story the Yooks, who eat their bread with the butter side up, and the neighboring Zooks, who eat their bread with the butter side down, are engaged in a long-running battle. In an attempt to outdo each other they develop more and more sophisticated weaponry. A satire of the nuclear arms race that children can understand. (age 5 and up)

The Little Brute Family, by **Russell Hoban.** Illustrations by Lillian Hoban. Macmillan Pub. Co., NY, 1966. In the middle of a dark woods lived a family of Brutes. Things seldom went well for them. They ate sand and gravel porridge each morning and stick and stone stew each night. They never smiled. Life might have gone on like this forever, except one day Baby Brute found a wandering, lost "good feeling" in a field of daisies. This simple tale shows how easily happiness can spread. (ages 3 - 6)

Tale of the Vanishing Rainbow, by **Siegfried R. Rupprecht.** Illustrations by Józef Wilkón. North-South Books, NY, 1989. The bears and wolves lived in harmony until one summer day when a rainbow appeared and faded. Each group suspected the other of taking it and prepared to fight for its return. In this eloquent tale, children learn an important lesson about trust and friendship. (ages 4 - 8)

A Children's Chorus: Celebrating the 30th Anniversary of the Universal Declaration of the Rights of the Child, **Introduction by Audrey Hepburn.** E. P. Dutton, NY, 1989. This celebration of the United Nation's unanimously adopted landmark bill of 1959 asserts ten fundamental rights for every child, including the right to adequate food, safe shelter, education, and a loving family. (all ages)

Jack the Bum and the Halloween Handout, by **Janet Schulman.** Illustrations by James Stevenson. Greenwillow Books, NY, 1977. It is Halloween and Jack the Bum is cold and hungry. Thinking it is a good night to ask for a handout, he approaches a man who says "I only give money to UNICEF." What's UNICEF? he wonders. He spends the rest of the night figuring it out and wins a prize for the best Halloween costume. He donates the money to UNICEF. This book, which is endorsed by the U. S. Committee for UNICEF, is a good introduction to a collection project. (ages 4 - 8)

Peace Begins With You, by **Katherine Scholes.** Illustrations by Robert Ingpen. Little Brown and Co., Boston, 1989. This book explains the concept of peace in a way that school age children can understand and suggests the best ways to protect it. (age 8 and up)

The Big Book for Peace, edited by **Ann Durell and Marilyn Sachs.** Dutton Children's Books, NY, 1990. Thirty of the best-loved authors and illustrators for children have combined their talents for *The Big Book for Peace.* The most distinguished figures in the children's book world have crafted poems, stories, and pictures that celebrate harmony and understanding at many different levels - among people of different races and beliefs. (ages 6 - 12)

Children as Teachers of Peace, by **Our Children.** Edited by Gerald G. Jampolsky. Celestial Arts, Berkeley, CA, 1982. This is a book by children about what peace means to them. (all ages)

Resources for Parents and Teachers

The Center for Teaching International Relations (CTIR Publications) offers extra-curricular teaching activity books for K-12. These help teachers promote multicultural awareness and global perspectives. Write c/o the University of Denver, Denver, CO 80208.

For a list of books that most effectively promote the cause of peace, social justice, and world community, write Ruth Chalmers, 777 United Nations Plaza, New York, NY 10017, and ask for the list of Jane Addams Children's Book Award Winners for 1953-1990. Send a self-addressed and stamped envelope.

Educators for Social Responsibility have published "Perspectives: Teaching Guide to the Concepts of Peace" (K-12) and also "A Day of Dialogue," a planning and curriculum guide for dealing with issues concerning the threat of nuclear war (grades 4-12). Write Susan Alexander, 23 Garden Street, Cambridge, MA 02138.

The Lion and the Lamb Peace Arts Center has published a collection of literature for children (K-12), music, and art all with the theme of promoting peace. Also available are videos and teacher's materials that build on the concept of peace and international understanding through the arts and literature for children. Contact Dr. Elizabeth A. Hostetler, Bluffton College, Bluffton, Ohio 45817.

The Parenting for Peace and Justice Network is a network of parents sharing strategies to rear compassionate children in a world of conflict. The organization offers training for parents, teachers, and other groups. It also publishes a newsletter six times a year. Write c/o Kathleen and Jim McGinnis, Institute for Peace and Justice, 4144 Lindell Blvd., St. Louis, MO 63108.

The Peace Child Foundation promotes cultural understanding, conflict resolution, and education in peace and environmental issues through the arts and youth exchange programs. Contact Jerry Champlan, 3977 Chain Bridge Rd., Fairfax, VA 22030.

Peacemaking Associates publishes *Peacemaking for Children* magazine (ages 7-14), and offers videos such as

The U.S. Committee for UNICEF provides lists of educational materials, curriculum guides, hunger kit, slides, and books on peace and intercultural relations. Write to 333 East 28th Street, New York, NY 10016.

Skipping Stones, a "multi-ethnic forum," publishes artwork, poems, stories, and songs by and for kids around the world, in a celebration of cultural and environmental richness. A one-year subscription is $15. Send to *Skipping Stones,* 80574 Hazelton Road, Cottage Grove, OR 97424.

Birthday Friends for Peace matches American and Soviet pen pals by their birthdays. Send 3" x 5" card with name, birthday, and mailing information. Small donations will be appreciated. Write P.O. Box 15514, Pensacola, FL 32514-5514.

The Children's Creative Response to Conflict offers activities, publications, and workshops to promote skills of cooperation, communication, conflict resolution, and mediation. P.O. Box 271, Nyack, NY 10960.

The Global Cooperation for a Better World offers *Cooperation in the Classroom,* a project for teachers. Write P.O. Box 325, Boston, MA 02146.

Little Friend for Peace publishes *Creating a Peace Experience,* a resource guide for setting up a peace day camp, and *Peacemaking for Little Friends,* activities around 12 themes plus a bibliography. Write to 4405 29th Street, Mr. Shasta, CA 96067.

Peace Letter is a quarterly newsletter supporting peace in education. Contact the Children of the Earth Foundation, 231 East La Jolla, Tempe, AZ 85383.

A Wish List for Peace is an eight-page annotated bibliography of books which offer peaceful ways to resolve conflicts. Send a self-addressed 9"x 12" envelope with 45 cents postage to Frances Weinstein, Hammond Public Library, 564 State Street, Hammond, IN 46320.

Learning the Skills of Peacemaking, by Naomi Drew. Jalmar Press, Rolling Hills Estates, CA, 1987. This is an excellent activity guide for elementary-age children on communicating, cooperating, and resolving conflict.

Helping Young Children Understand Peace, War, and the Nuclear Threat, by Nancy Carlsson-Paige and Diane E. Levin. Order from the National Association for the Education of Young Children, 1834 Connecticut Ave., N.W., Washington, D.C. 20009-5786.

Peace Works: Young Peacemakers Project Book II, by Kathleen Fry-Miller, Judith Myers-Walls, and Janet Domer-Shank. Brethren Press, Elgin, IL, 1989.

"He Hit Me Back First!": Creative Visualization Activities for Parenting and Teaching, by Eva D. Fugitt, Jalmar Press, Rolling Hills Estates, CA, 1983.

Peace in the Family: A Workbook of Ideas and Actions, by Lois Dorn. Pantheon, NY, 1983.

The Friendly Classroom for a Small Planet: A Handbook on Creative Approaches to Living and Problem Solving for Children, by Priscilla Prutzman, Children's Creative Response to Conflict, Box 271, Nyack, NY 10960.

We, the Children, published in collaboration with UNICEF. Norton, NY, 1990. This stunning book, which contains over two hundred full-color photographs, offers a glorious celebration of the future of our world - the children.

Partners in Peacemaking is an education and resource organization which provides curricula and projects to develop peace, acceptance, and cooperation. Write to 120 Finderne Avenue, Bridgewater, NY 08807.

Family Council: The Dreikurs Technique for Putting an End to War Between Parents and Children (and Between Children and Children), by Rudolf Dreikurs, Henry Regnery Co., Chicago, 1974.

Earth Educator's Bookshelf

In the past few decades, a new environmental ethic has slowly emerged, one that calls for a radical change in the way people relate to the natural world. It demands that humans shift away from lifestyles and approaches to culture that are destructive to the environment of the planet. Many books dealing with these subjects have been listed and annotated at the conclusion of each chapter in the book. Those listed below, not falling into any particular category dealt with in the preceding chapters, have not yet been called to the reader's attention. They deal with a variety of disciplines including philosophy, history, literature, economics, and wilderness protection. They, too, are essential reading material for parents and educators who wish to be engaged in the crucial task of healing the Earth.

Abbey, Edward. Any reading list of books about the salvation of the Earth should begin with mention of Edward Abbey's works. A good place to begin is with *One Life at a Time, Please* (Henry Holt, NY, 1988), an anthology of pieces including an interview with Joseph Wood Krutch. Also see *Desert Solitaire* (Touchstone Books, NY, 1970), *The Journey Home* (Dutton, NY, 1977), and *The Monkey Wrench Gang* (Dream Garden Press, Salt Lake City, 1985).

Bateson, Gregory. *Mind and Nature: A Necessary Unity.* Dutton, NY, 1979. Bateson, who is an renowned anthropologist as well as a psychologist, discusses the relationship between natural systems and the way humans think about them. Also of note is *Steps to an Ecology of Mind* (Ballantine Books, NY, 1972).

Berry, Thomas. *The Dream of the Earth.* Sierra Club Books, San Francisco, 1988. Father Berry, who calls himself a "geologian," considers our ecological future from a species per-

spective, arguing for an earth-centered cosmology instead of a human-centered one.

Berry, Wendell. *What are People For?* North Point Press, San Francisco, 1990. This is an excellent and representative collection of Berry's essays covering subjects such as diversity, local and regional culture, and the works of Edward Abbey and Wallace Stegner. His other books of essays include *The Unsettling of America: Culture and Agriculture* (Sierra Club Books, San Francisco, 1977), and *Home Economics* (North Point Press, San Francisco, 1987).

Carson, Rachel. *Silent Spring,* Houghton Mifflin, Boston, 1962. This classic, written over twenty-five years ago, still speaks to environmentalists everywhere. It was one of the first works to point out the ecological consequences of the use of pesticides.

Cornell, Joseph. *Listening to Nature: How to Deepen Your Awareness of Nature.* Dawn Publications, Nevada City, CA, 1987. The author of *Sharing Nature with Children* offers adults a sensitive guidebook to a deeper awareness of the natural world. It contains simple, enjoyable activities that give one a direct, personal experience with the wonder and joy of nature.

Devall, Bill. *Simple in Means, Rich in Ends: Practicing Deep Ecology.* Gibbs M. Smith, Layton, UT, 1988. This book provides the guidelines for living in accord with deep ecological principles. It discusses the self, religion, politics, and profession all in terms of ecological impact. Also see *Deep Ecology: Living As If Nature Mattered.* (Written with George Sessions, Peregrine Smith Books, Salt Lake City, UT, 1985).

Fox, Warwick. *Towards a Transpersonal Ecology.* Shambhala Press, Boston, 1990. This work offers an almost encyclopedic overview of the entire field of deep ecology. It presents an important new perspective on the understanding of our relationship to nature.

Fritsch, Albert J. *Renew the Face of the Earth.* Loyola University Press, Chicago, 1987. Father Fritsch, a Jesuit priest, is the author of several books on environmental issues. This book offers a Christian philosophy of the natural world, drawing from scriptural and theological sources.

Halpern, Daniel (Ed.). *On Nature: Nature, Landscape, and Natural History.* North Point Press, San Francisco, 1987. This is an

excellent anthology featuring the works of several prominent nature writers. It also contains an extensive bibliography.

Hubble, Sue. *A Country Year: Living the Questions.* Harper & Row, NY, 1987. This lovely, simple book celebrates the basic everyday elements of living life to the full in the Ozarks of Missouri.

Leopold, Aldo. *Sand County Almanac: And Sketches Here and There.* Oxford University Press, NY, 1987. (Commemorative Edition) This environmental classic, written in 1949, is a must for all Earth educators. It sets out Leopold's concept of what he calls a "land ethic."

McKibben, Bill. *The End of Nature.* Random House, NY, 1989. McKibben makes a convincing and chilling case for the fact that our lifestyles are systematically destroying the Earth.

Muir, John. *Wilderness Essays.* Peregrine Smith Books, Salt Lake City, UT, 1980. This book contains ten of Muir's most famous essays on wilderness.

Naess, Arne. *Ecology, Community, and Life Style.* Cambridge University Press, Cambridge, 1988. Naess, the founder of the deep ecology movement, here discusses the relationship between the evolution of lifestyles and the destruction of the environment.

Nollman, Jim. *Dolphin Dreamtime.* Bantam, NY, 1987. The author, an internationally known pioneer in interspecies communication, vividly describes his experiences of forging new relationships with animals and the environment. Also see *Spiritual Ecology: A Guide for Reconnecting with Nature* (Bantam, NY, 1990).

Snyder, Gary. *The Practice of the Wild.* North Point Press, San Francisco, 1990. These essays deal with the idea of what freedom and wildness really mean. They use the lessons of the Earth to teach man how to live in harmony with nature. Snyder has written several volumes of essays and poetry including the Pulitzer Prize winning *Turtle Island* (New Directions, NY, 1974).

Taylor, Paul W. *Respect for Nature: A Theory of Environmental Ethics.* Princeton University Press, Princeton, 1986. In this study, Taylor points out man's dependent status as only one part of the workings of the biosphere.

Tobias, Michael. *Deep Ecology.* Avant Books, San Diego, 1985. This book presents a collection of essays dealing with the philosophy of deep ecology. It includes writings by Gary Snyder, Arne Naess, Paul Shepard, and Murray Bookchin.

Van Matre, Steve and Bill Weiler. *The Earth Speaks: An Acclimatization Journal.* Institute for Earth Education, Warrenville, IL, l983. In this collection, "the Earth's voice has been captured in the words and images of those who have listened with their hearts." Included are the writings of Henry David Thoreau, John Muir, Aldo Leopold, Hyemeyohsts Storm, Rachel Carson, Gary Snyder, and many others.

Vittachi, Anuradha. *Earth Conference One: Sharing a Vision for Our Planet.* New Science Library, Shambhala, Boston, l989. The Global Survival Conference was held at Oxford in April, l988. Leaders came from around the world, the first time that spiritual and parliamentary leaders had come together with scientific experts to confront today's environmental crisis. This is a record of that compelling event.

Acknowledgments

During the creation of this book, we had help from many special people and would like to acknowledge their support. To Martin, thank you for your continuous encouragement and assistance. To the Florence Park branch of the Tulsa City-County Library system and to the staff of the bookstore Children's Books & Company, we are grateful for help with our research. We also would like to thank the following publishers and organizations for permission to reprint material from their publications. We have made every effort to locate the copyright owners of materials quoted in the text of *Earth Child*. Omissions brought to our attention will be credited in subsequent printings.

The Learning Works, Inc., P.O. Box 6187, Santa Barbara, CA 93160. For permission to reprint the poem "Where the Wild Things Shouldn't Be" by Beverly Armstrong from *Earth Book for Kids,* Linda Schwartz, © 1990.

New Society Publishers, Santa Cruz, CA. For permission to print an adaptiation of the original idea presented in their publication *Thinking Like a Mountain: Towards a Council of All Beings,* John Seed, Joanna Macy, Pat Fleming, and Arne Naess, © 1988.

National Wildlife Federation, Washington, D.C. For permission to reprint the poem "Bouncing Back" from Ranger Rick's *Naturescope, Endangered Species: Wild and Rare,* © 1990.

The Institute for Earth Education, Box 288, Warrenville, IL 60555. For permission to reprint a quotation from their publication *Earth Education . . . A New Beginning,* Steve Van Matre, © 1990.

Columbia University Press, New York, NY. For permission to reprint a quotation from their publication *The Ecology of Imagination in Childhood,* Edith Cobb, © 1977.

North Point Press, Berkeley, CA. For permission to reprint a quotation from their publication *The Unforeseen Wilderness,* Wendell Berry, © 1991.

Kid's FACE, Nashville, TN. For permission to include club information about Kids For a Clean Environment, an organization founded by Melissa Poe.

INDEX

A

acid rain   211
Adopt A Whale   187
air
    awareness of, for children   209
air cycle   117
Air Cycle Relay   117
air pollution   209-212
    awareness of   210
    causes of   210
    testing levels of   210
Ancestor Day   75
ancestors   75
Animal Feelings Charade   266
animal rights   267
animal shelters   273
Animal Welfare Institute   286
animals
    endangered   249-251
    feelings of   265-266
    human relationship to   263
    kindness toward
        activities for children   286
    lost pets   273-275
    needs of   265
    respect for   263-276
        things you can do   285, 286
    similarity to humans   264
Apple Butter   74
Apple Leather   74
apple picking   72
apples   72-74, 89
Applesauce   73
aquarium   170
Arbor Day   154

Arbor Day News   154
Archaeologist's Delight   242
archaeology   242
autumn   72-77
awareness
    exercise to enhance   200

B

backyard wildlife refuge   226
basic needs of life   63, 197, 198, 205, 265
Bat Conservation International   47
bats   36, 38-41
    facts and myths about   46-47
beach cleanup   184
Beach Cleanup Days   186
beans
    exploring as seeds   100
bedtime rituals   39
biodegradability   214
bioregionalism   207
bird boxes   278
bird feeders   277
Bird Sanctuary   279
bird watching   277
birdnests
    how to sprout   100
birds
    feeding   57, 74, 86
birthday   58
    activities to celebrate   58
blue moon   70
bread baking   79
bug cages   123
Build a Plant Game   103
Butterscotch Pennies   84

C

Camera Safari activity   256
camping
    conservation tips   217
campouts   37
candlemaking   85
Candlemas Day   55
candy
    homemade   81-84
Caring Carnival   303
celebrations   55-63, 75, 88, 307-310
cellulose
    as tree product   135
Center for Marine Conservation   186
Chain Story Circle
    related to pet care   274
cheese   81
Children as the Peacemakers   312
Children as the Peacemakers Foundation   312
Children for Old Growth   153
Christmas trees   151
Circle of Peace activity   307
cleaning materials
    environmentally safe   185
clearcutting   152, 219
clock   28
clouds
    experiments to explain to children   166
commercialism   55
Commitment Cakes   254
Community Garden   303
compassion   9

compost   108, 111, 112, 119
compost bin   108
compost bucket   109
compost pile   108
conservation
    as a family project   223, 224
        ways to conserve   223, 224
constellations 43-44
    (see also stars)
constellation cans   44
cooperation and competition   301
cooperative games   301
cork
    as tree product   135
Cosmic Celebration   44
Cottage Cheese   81
Council of All Beings   221-223
Coyote's Song   71

D

daily cycle   19
dandelion   104
    experiments with   104
day and night
    rythm of   17
day diary
    how to create   20
death of a pet   281
deep breathing   13
deep ecology   10, 11
Deluxe Dog Treats   271
diary   57
dinosaurs   236-244
    awareness activity for children   239
    empathy activity   238
    fingerplay   243
    reasons for extinction   240
Dinosaur Dash game   239
Dinosaur Egg game   236
Direct Marketing Association   225
dirt   97, 108
    composting soil   108
Do the Trash Rap   212

Dream Starters   12, 39, 64, 124,
    143, 172, 202, 246,
    276, 304
    definition and techniques for
        using   13
Dried Apple Slices   72
drinking water   160, 177, 185

E

Earth
    as home   197-222
earth awareness   9-13, 199
    enhancing   201
earthworm   122
echolocation   36, 46
ecosystems   235
electricity   22
elephants
    as endangered animals   257
empathy   11, 12
Endangered Animal Musical
        Chairs   250
endangered animals   249-251
    identifying   249
    activities to explain   250-251
    way to help   255-257
Endangered "Pet" Scrap Book   256
endangered species   47, 235-236, 244-
    257
energy conservation   45
    techniques for   45, 46
energy   45, 159
environmental education   12
environmental awareness
    developing in children   9-13
environmental ethics   317
evaporation   26
extinction   47, 235-257
    of dinosaurs   240-244

F

Family Map   76
family pictures   77

family recipes   77
Fancy Cans activity   224
fantasies   12
Feast of the First Flower   59
fertilizer   111
festivals   55-56, 63-70
Fire Ceremony   88
Fire-Baked Apples   89
fireflies   37, 38
First Snowflake Chant   87
flea sachet   271
flea spray   271
flower gardens   118-121
flowers
    coloring wtih food color   118
    drying   121
    preserving   120-122
    pressing   120
    sand drying   121
food
    for wildlife   57
food chain   29-35
    dinosaur's place in   241
    musical activity   32
    nature detective activity   32
    underwater life   170
food chain canopy   34
food chain mobile   32
food chain pyramid   30
food chain story circle   33
food co-ops   127
forests
    old growth   153
fossils   242
fossil fuels   22
Fudge   84
fuel   22
full moon   70

G

Gaia   63
garden   56, 65, 78, 97
    for scent plants   115
    sun and shade gardens   115

sidewalk crack   125
watering   111
windowsill   119
with pizza herbs   115
garden diary   111
garden insects   122-127
garden markers   110
gardens and gardening   97-127
giant panda   244-245
global warming   9
Globe Cake   65
Good Morning Song   19
graffiti   216
Granola Crunch   106
Guacamole   107

H

habitat   198-222, 205-206, 215, 235, 250
    activities for children   208
    backyard habitats   206
    creating a backyard refuge   226
    explaining to young children   205
    game to explain   219
    respect for, increasing awareness of   215
    specificity of   207
Hall of Inheritance   77
Herbal Bug Repellant   116
Herbal Moth Bags   116
Herbal Shampoo   116
herbs   115-116
Hey! Get Off My Train Game   249
homelessness   302, 304-305
Homemade Butter   80
house plants   118
Humane Society of the United States   286
humus   108
Hungry Dinosaurs game   240
hunting
    attitudes toward   282-284
    activities related to issue of   282-284

I

imagination   11
Imagination Journey   70
insecticides   112
insects   122, 142
    habitats   207
    in ponds   169
    perspective of   123
    relation to decaying trees   145
International Whaling Commission   188
It's A Rottin' Home for Me   145

J

Jaguar In the Forest Chant   254
jungle   146-152
Jungle Celebration   146
Jungle Punch   146
Junior Garden Club   127
junk mail   225

K

Keep It Clean!   184
Kids FACE   226
Kids FACE Club   226
Kids Meeting Kids   312
Kind Club   286
Kiss Chocolate Goodbye!   149
kites   61
    how they fly   61

L

leaf rubbings   145
letter writing
    for environmental issues   188
life underwater   168-176
litter   178
    effect on sealife   178
local diet   127

M

Maple Snowcream   87
marine debris
    explanation of effect   179
    puppet show to explain   179
marine shows   188
marsh
    wildlife in   169
massage   13
May baskets   61
    ideas for   62
May Day   62, 126
Maypole   61
    how to make   62
Maypole Dance   62
media
    as related to children's expression   57
mermaid   161
Mock Community Meeting   178
mole   38
moon   41-42, 42, 70
moon phases   41, 57
morning celebrations   19
Mother Earth   63, 66-69, 70, 71
Mother Earth Awareness Walk   71
Mother Earth Celebration   70
Mother Earth, May I?   71
Mother Earth Pageant   66-69
mud   61
    playing with   61
musical instruments   141
    homemade   141
My Lost Dog Song   274

N

National Wildlife Federation   226, 285
Native Americans   74
"natural" cleaners   185
natural world
    awareness of sharing   215
nature walk   199

neighbors
  relationship with   301
night animals   36
night blooming flowers   37
night   35-44
night sky   41-47
"No Bake" Seed Candy   106
No More Room Game   251
nocturnal animals   36, 37
Noises of the Night   38
nursing homes   302
  visiting   302
  "adopting" a grandparent in   302

O

Oatmeal Raisin Cookies   26
oceans   159-162
oil spills   182
organic gardening   111, 126-127
Orphaned and Injured Wildlife,
  Inc.   287
outdoor environments
  increasing respect for   216
owls   36

P

panda *(see giant panda)*
  activities related to   245
Panda Bear Cookies   248
Panda In The Forest   245
Panda Paws   247
paper
  as tree product   135
paper cloud activity   166
peace
  commitment circles   309
  experiencing the feeling   306
  explaining to children   298
  methods of resolving conflict   299
  posters for   309
Peace Day Celebration   307-312
Peace Parade   309
peacemaking practices   297

at home and school   300
pen pals   312
  obtaining for children   312
People for the Ethical Treatment of
  Animals   287
pest control for pets   270
pet care   270
  tips for   269
pets   269-273
pick-your-own produce farm   114
picnicking   112, 137
pizza garden   115
planetarium   43
plant press book   120
plant propagation   107, 126
plants   97-127 *(see also seeds, gardens)*
  Build a Plant Game   103
  parts of   103
  pollination of   104
  relationship with sun   20
  understanding seeds, for children
    100-103
pollutants   9
pollution   22, 65, 78, 160,
    178, 198, 235
  levels of awareness of   211
  of waterways
    efforts to prevent   185
  quiz   211-212
Pollution Pin-up Board   225
ponds   169
Popcorn Balls   83
Potpourri Planting   115
Prehistoric Time Line   244
prejudice   311
prejudice and tolerance
  importance of home attitudes   311
pumpkins   112-114

Q

quilts   83

R

rain   26
  explanation of source to chil-
    dren   165
rain picture   168
Rain, Rain, Don't Go Away   161
rain walk   164
rainbow   21
Raindrop's Relay Game   167
rainforest   146-152, 236
  creatures of   252
  experiments related to   149
  location of
    explaining to children   147-148
  protection of   151-152
  sounds of   252
  stick puppetry   253
Rainforest Jamboree   253
Rainforest Panorama   149
rainforest preservation   152
  ideas for chidren   152
rainforest preservation groups   151-153
Rainforest Smorgasbord   146
recipes
  Apple Butter   74
  Apple Leather   74
  Applesauce   73
  Archaeologist's Delight   242
  Bread Baking   79
  Butterscotch Pennies   84
  Commitment Cakes   254
  Cottage Cheese   81
  Fire-Baked Apples   89
  for herbs   116
  for sprouts   114
  Fudge   84
  Globe Cake   65
  Granola Crunch   106
  Guacamole   107
  Homemade Butter   80
  Jungle Punch   146
  Maple Snowcream   87
  "No Bake" Seed Candy   106
  Oatmeal Raisin Cookies   26

Panda Bear Cookies   248
Panda Paws   247
Popcorn Balls   83
Rainforest Smorgasbord   146
Snowball Cupcakes   82
spice cookies   148
Taffy   82
Toasted Sunflower Seeds   106
recycle craft box
    definition and how to set up   13
recycling   45, 152, 184, 211, 151,
    298
    of Christmas trees   151
    of used toys   303
recycling center
    visit to   215
respect for living creatures
    simple actions to take   268
Reverse Garden   214
rituals   87, 88
rivers   169
    as home for wildlife   169
    as part of water cycle   167
role playing   11
rotation of earth   35

S

sand candles   85
saps
    as tree products   135
Save the Whale Game   175
scale
    awareness activity with   201
scarecrow   111
scavenger hunt   59, 205
sealife   159-160, 168-169, 170-176
    effects of litter on   178-183
seasonal changes   56
seasonal cycles   55-56
seasons   56-57, 98
seed catalog   106
    activities with   106
seed coat   101
seed collector   144

seed companies   110
seed viewer   101
seeds   97, 98-108
    activities with   98-108
    migration of tree seeds   137
    parts of   101
    types of   99
shadow play   21
Shrinking Habitat Game   218
Signs of Spring Scavenger Hunt   59
snow
    activities with   86
Snow Carnival   86
snow ice cream   87
Snowball Cupcakes   82
snowbird man   86
snowflakes   84, 86
Snowflake Mobile   86
snowmen   86, 87
soil   97, 109-111
    creation through composting   108
solar energy   18, 22-34
    experiments and activities with   22-
    26
solar heat
    experiments with   23
solar panels   22
solar snacks   24
solar-dried fruit   26
songs
    Coyote's Song   71
    Do the Trash Rap   212
    Good Morning Song   19
    Hungry Dinosaurs   240
    It's A Rottin' Home for Me   145
    Jaguar In the Forest Chant   254
    Keep It Clean!   184
    Kiss Chocolate Goodbye!   149
    My Lost Dog Song   274
    Noises of the Night   38
    Panda In The Forest   245
    Rain, Rain, Don't Go Away   161
    Take the Trash Out   214
    The Big Good Wolf Song   269
    The Hungry Panda   247
    The Recycle Song   215

The Soup Garden Song   109
The Sun Powers All   32
The Winter Solstice Song   89
Twinkle, Twinkle, Little Star   42
Way Down Yonder in the Pumpkin
    Patch!   112
Who Lives Here?   142
spice cookies   148
spring   59-62
spring bulbs   119
spring equinox   53, 59
sprouts   114
    edible, to make   114
stargazing   43
stars   42-44, 63
    (see also constellations)
Stream Team activity   186
    to reduce water pollution   186
streams   169
    as part of water cycle   167
summer   63-72
sun   17, 18
    awareness of warmth of   19
    place in food chain   29-34
    playing with   21
    relationship with wind   24
Sun and Shade Gardens   115
sun pictures   27
sun reflectors   21
sun tea   24
sun visors   21
sundial   28
sunflowers   104
    how to grow   104
sunrise   18
    experiencing with your children   18
sunset   36
sunset picnic   35

T

Taffy   82
Take the Trash Out   214
The Big Good Wolf Song   269
The Hungry Panda   247

The Izaak Walton League of
America   186
The Jaguar In the Forest Gamet   254
The National Arbor Day Founda-
tion,   154
The Nature Conservancy   257
The Recycle Song   215
The Soup Garden Song   109
The Sun Powers All   32
The Turtle's Mishap: A Puppet Show or
Play   179
The Winter Solstice Song   89
They're Bouncing Back   254
thunderstorm
activity   164
timber cutting   235
time machine   78
Toasted Sunflower Seeds   106
toxic waste   185
traditional holidays   55
trash   212-215
activities to increase awareness
of   213
reducing levels of   212
Trash Treasure Chest   225
Trash Walk   214
tree decomposition   144-145
Tree Diary   137
tree planting   146
Tree Treats   137
trees   133-154
activities to increase understanding
of   136-146
adopting a tree   136
as homes to wildlife and insects   142
as sources of musical instruments   141
awareness of benefits   134
decomposition of 144-145
empathy with   139
how people and trees are alike   138
importance of decomposition   145
products of   135
sprouting   146
tree costume activity   141
uses of   135

Trick-or-Treat for UNICEF   311
Tropical Products Display   146
tropical rainforest–see *rainforest*
Twinkle, Twinkle, Little Star   42

U

underwater life–see *sealife*
underwater viewer   169
UNICEF   311
urbanization   235

V

vegetable gardens   108-117
(see also gardens, gardening)

W

water
awareness of everyday use of   177
as natural resource   159-188
as part of human bodies   183
awareness of   161-163
conservation of   177, 186
sources of   177
states of   163
water conservation
methods of   187
water cycle   26, 27, 149, 160, 162,
164-168
Water for Life   177
water play   161
water pollution
ways to prevent   184
Way Down Yonder in the Pumpkin
Patch!   112
weeds   104, 112
wetland drainage   235
whales   171-176
adoption of   187
empathy with   174
game   175
hunting of   188

how they perceive   171
songs of   174
Whale Adoption Project   187
Where the Wild Things Shouldn't
Be   266
Who Lives Here?   142
wild bird care   280
wilderness
vanishing   215
wildflower plot   119
wildlife   142
feeding   57
in ponds   169
injured
how to help   281
orphaned   280-282
protecting the habitats of   226
wind   24-25
wind chimes   25
windmills   22, 25
Winter   78-89
winter solstice   55, 88
Winter Solstice Celebration   87
Wish for the World cooperative
collage   307
wolves   269
wood
as tree product   135
world trade   208
World Vegetarian Day   287

Z

zoos   256

About the Authors

Kathryn Sheehan taught preschool, kindergarten, and first grade for nine years. She has been a children's librarian and has worked in a children's bookstore. Kathryn was an early kindergarten curriculum coordinator for the Portland, Maine, public school system. Today she lives in Tulsa, Oklahoma, with her husband and preschool daughter.

Mary Waidner, Ph.D. is the mother of eight children. She has been active in environmental issues for many years, was a founder of Earth Concerns of Oklahoma, and is a member of the Institute for Earth Education. She presents programs on environmental awareness to school-age children.

The two are mother and daughter.